# UZUN ALI
SHAME AND SALVATION

*To my beloved mother, Munever*

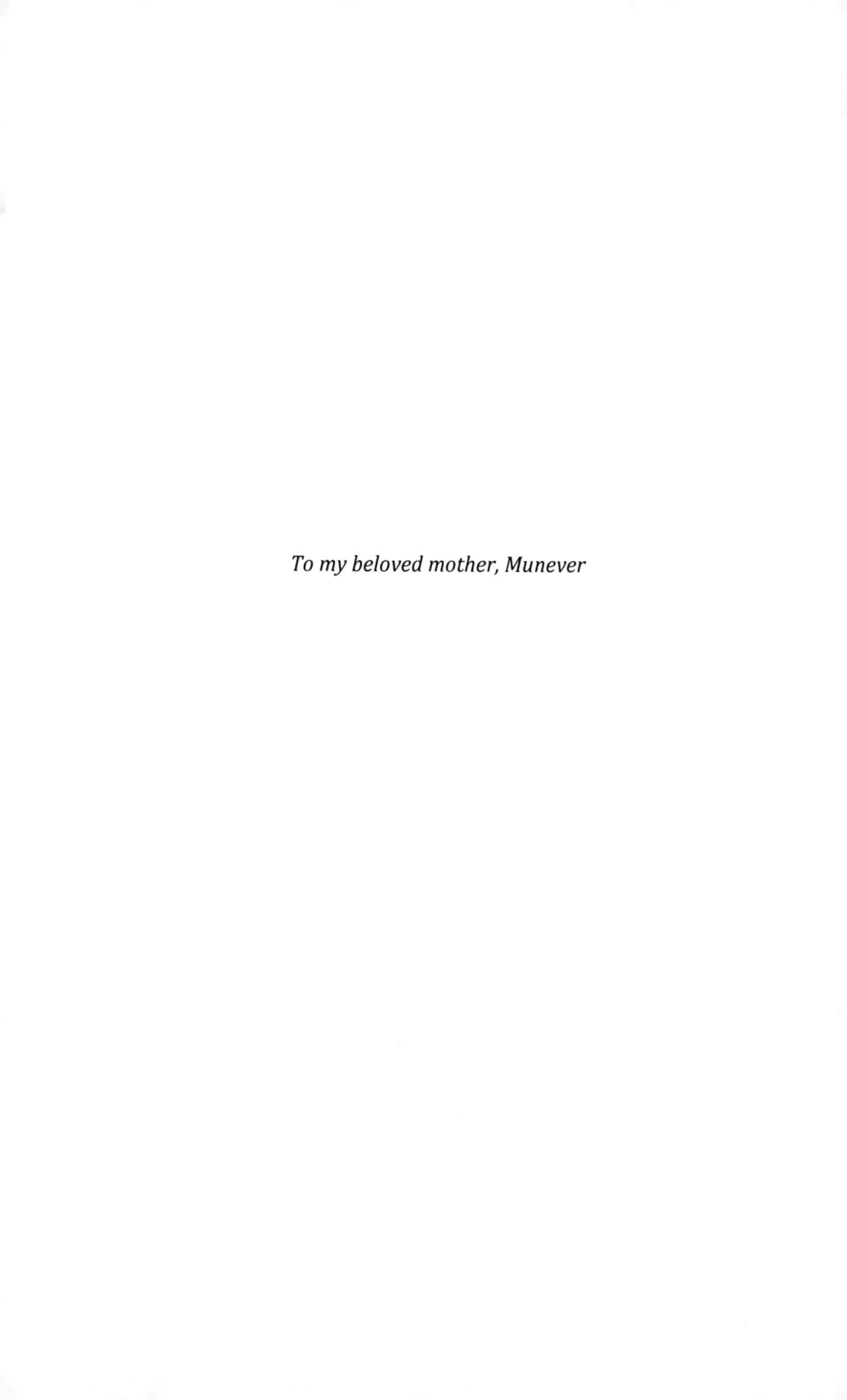

# UZUN ALI
## SHAME AND SALVATION

Ozay Mehmet

Wisdom House

Copyright © 2011 Ozay Mehmet

The right of Ozay Mehmet to be identified as the Author of the Work has been asserted by him in accordance with the Copyright, Designs and Patents Act 1988.

All rights reserved. No part of this publication may be reprinted or reproduced, stored as in a retrieval system, or transmitted in any form or by any means, electronic, mechanical, photocopying, recording or otherwise, now known or hereafter invented, without the prior permission in writing from the publisher.

First published in 2011 by
Wisdom House Publications Ltd.
Unique House, 1 Dolly Lane,
Leeds LS9 7NN, England (UK)
Tel: +44 (0) 113 2420555, Fax: +44 (0) 113 2420963
E-mail: editor@wisdomhousepublications.co.uk
Internet: www.wisdomhousepublications.co.uk

Simultaneously published in India by
Wisdom House Academic Publishers Pvt. Ltd.
126 Housing Board Colony,
Ambala Cantt. – 133 001, Haryana, India
Tel: +91 171 2821237, 2821299, Fax: +91 171 2821282
E-mail: wisdom_hap@yahoo.co.in
Internet: www.wisdomhousepublications.co.uk

Wisdom House is a registered trade mark of Wisdom House Publications Ltd.
Our distribution links across the world

First Edition: 2011
British Library Cataloguing in Publication Data
Ozay Mehmet
*Uzun Ali, Shame and Salvation*

ISBN 978-1-84290-236-3 Paperback,
ISBN 978-1-84290-237-0 Hardbound

Typesetting and cover design by www.wordzworth.com

The sketches are by Mustafa Kansoy especially designed for this novel.

This book is printed on acid free paper in England (United Kingdom).

# CONTENTS

| BOOK I | DISGRACED | 1 |
| BOOK II | ROSES AND TEARS | 135 |
| BOOK III | DISCOVERY | 241 |
| BOOK IV | HYPOCRITES AND ANGELS | 375 |

# BOOK I

## DISGRACED

Asmaalti Inn

# I

I am a history professor at Ankara University, of Turkish Cypriot origin, but I prefer to call myself simply a Turk. I feel, therefore I am a Turk... from Cyprus. My Cypriotness is merely a territorial identification, my place of birth, an expression of physical love for the natural beauty of the island of Aphrodite, of love. Emotionally I belong to the Turkish nation, spread over many lands, not just Turkey. I am also part of a global family with branches in faraway Canada and England, but my roots, our family origins, are in Cyprus.

As you can see I have an identity problem. Who I am? Where do I belong? These questions have long occupied my mind and it was not until very recently that I happened to make a surprising discovery about my roots. My identity was almost lost, along with our family's identity, but, remarkably, miraculously it was regained. This is the story of how it all happened that I now wish to tell you, dear reader. It is an emotional story, but I must restrain myself, and share with you everything, the joys and sadness, all that I remember.

My story must begin with my maternal Grandfather, the womanizer Halil Osman, who best reflects our loss and shame. You see, my dear mother, Aygul Uzun Ali, was a tormented woman and her father, Halil, was responsible for her agony and suffering. From my childhood, I remember with pain in my heart, as she was always ranting and cursing her father and my Grandfather, Halil Osman and the terrible injustice he inflicted on my Grandma. I grew up hating the womanizing policeman Halil, the father and tormentor of my mother, the real killer of the dear mother of my own mother, Emine, the Grandmother I never saw. Come to think of it, neither did my mother. Grandmother died shortly after my mother was born. The depth of my mothers' torment and the hell she must have lived through as a child and as a young woman was a mystery to me, until my discovery about of my family roots.

My shattering discovery happened on the paternal side of our family. My father was a humble man, a product of his traumatic childhood; his origin was anything but humble. My paternal Grandfather, Uzun Ali, was a man of importance. He was the last *Kaimakam* (the provincial governor) of Milltown. He had lost everything when suddenly his Ottoman world came to an end. Overnight, his fortune and status were gone when the British took over Cyprus. But he never gave up his pride or confidence in his family's destiny.

In an age that was all men's, when women's place was behind men's, submitting to fathers and husbands, my Grandparents represented the generation of Ottoman Cypriots. When they died, this generation vanished into oblivion, burdened with loss and disgrace, unable to face the new age of modernity. The British represented the new world, modern technology and knowledge, and modernity belonged to those with the magic wand of education.

***

The British unexpectedly became masters of Cyprus in 1878. They came to the sleepy Ottoman island in eastern Mediterranean, which time seemed to have forgotten, ostensibly to replace the Ottoman misrule with good government. That, however, was merely a political pretext. The locals were too divided for any type of government; the Greek Orthodox, Ottoman Muslims, Maronites and Armenians, all crowded in a small island, yet lived in separate worlds. Proximity meant next to nothing, there was little intermixing of these religious communities who might have lived hundreds or even thousands of miles apart. Besides, the island legally still belonged to the Sultan and the Muslims and Christians were, for all practical purposes, still Ottoman subjects. Banditry was rampant and the peasants paid more heed to native Robin Hoods than to the police, Ottoman or British. Everyone, including the British administrators lived in a state of limbo because who was exactly in charge, and whose law prevailed, was unclear. True, life was, generally speaking, easy, excepting in years of drought and the scourge of locusts in summers of unbearable heat. The native population was extremely conservative, observing time-honored norms and customs. The Ottoman *millet* system allowed Muslims and Christians to look after their own births and deaths, arrange marriages and run schools according to local custom. Each community lived a separate life. The British would not think of touching native culture. For the Muslims, polygamy was the standard; each man entitled to have up to four wives. The Christian *millets*, Greek Orthodox, Maronite or Armenian obeyed their own priests; any transgression meant immediate excommunication and expulsion.

The period following the British occupation constituted a succession of wars and conflict. The Ottoman Empire was dying and the fate of Cyprus, like all other provinces, hanged in balance. Families and nations were unsure of where they stood, what the future held in store. The Ottoman *Millets* were at war against the state; Bulgarians, Albanians, Armenians, Kurds, Arabs, Serbs and others were in a steady state of rebellion fighting for a homeland or some such cause. This was a time also of grand opportunity. The dynasty of the 600-year old House of Osman, the once-fearful *Osmanli*, was, like an old tree, literally and physically collapsing from decay and disease. The imperial seat of power in Istanbul was now a den of corruption, of deceit and intrigue, and utter decadence. During the day, power struggles raged all around for fame and fortune, but at night the rich gambled and feasted while the poor walked aimlessly on empty stomachs. Hungry dogs roamed the streets.

Politics and politicians were discredited. The Young Turks, the party in power, were unsure which way to turn, its leaders plotting against each other and vying for the support of the British or the Germans. The cosmopolitan elite, Greek, Jew, Armenian and Ottoman at the top, aped everything European, imitating the music, dress and half-baked ideas from Europe, believing that these alien fashions could surgically modernize the decaying Ottoman multinational empire. Europe was the magical wand to cure all ills. *A la franca* was considered modern and desirable, *a la turca* backward and in poor taste.

The little, sleepy Ottoman/British Cyprus was then a paradox, uncertain, like someone with no fixed address, of where it belonged, east or west, British or Ottoman, torn between these forces of transition. Within the Ottoman elite, it was fashionable to be a Young Turk outwardly, but inside the Ottoman soul remained oriental and intact, as if frozen in time, as comfortable in the 16$^{th}$ century as now at the outset of the 20$^{th}$. Wearing European dress signaled a taste of the good life in the new age of modernity. The British, in style and outlook, represented the new age of modernity, the new age of trains and automobiles, but above all else, law and order. The Ottoman soul was slowly but surely rotting, but in matters of religion and custom, the Muslim society of British Cyprus was exceedingly traditional: Never more so than in gender relations. Patriarchy was the law. Fathers owned their daughters like chattel; husbands ruled their wives like an absolute monarch and the rich could take up to four of them *at a time*. It was definitely a man's world, British law or not. Externally, the island might have a new master, but *a la turca* ways prevailed within four walls. And, no doubt about it, the Muslim/Ottoman world dominated the inner lives, the private space inside households. The inside-outside boundaries often intersected, as did the Ottoman and British laws and customs, but most did not see the contradiction; the few that did ignored it. My Grandfathers broke all rules, just like rascals and rebels, because at heart they were Ottomans and, for Ottomans, the law was always flexible: you bent it as long as you could and you only accepted it when you had no choice.

My two Grandfathers could not have been more dissimilar. Halil Osman was handsome, blue-eyed, tall and fun-loving youth from Pineview village on the slopes of the Five Fingers Mountains overlooking the blue Mediterranean; he was the ultimate opportunist. He had benefited from the British administration, became a policeman and loved every minute of it because the steady salary he received financed his life of a hedonist, a womanizer. My paternal Grandfather, by contrast, was proud and vane. He never liked or accepted the British. Uzun Ali, was tall, not just physically, but in status: He had been the provincial governor of Milltown, the town eight miles east of Nicosia, famous for its spring and flour mills. He had lost his wealth and status after the British took over the island. After the British took over the island, Uzun Ali declined steadily but surely. He died a broken man. But our family was saved because Uzun Ali never lost his belief in the power of education. Even when he lost everything, and despite all the wars and destruction around him, the old *Kaimakam* never once wavered from his belief that education held the key to a future that he himself never understood.

My own parents, Aygul and Ozkan, grew up in these troubled times, and raised us children under the most difficult circumstances. My identity is buried in these circumstances, within my family history, warts and all, shaped by the violent end of the Ottoman era and the painful transition to British Cyprus.

\*\*\*\*

Suddenly, at the end of June 1908 two far-reaching events took place, in worlds apart, that changed Grandfather Halil Osman's life forever. In far away Istanbul, the Ottoman capital was the scene of yet another revolt. This time it was the rebellious Young Turks. These hotheads staged a palace coup and forced the tyrant Sultan Abdulhamid to restore the constitution and recall parliament, a simple enough decision that marked the short-lived age of liberty and brotherhood of all Ottomans. While the Young Turk hotheads and Armenian nationalists, bitter enemies until yesterday, suddenly jumped with joy and danced in the streets of the capital, in Adana, not 100 miles away from the island of Cyprus in the Mediterranean, horrible things were happening. It started when Armenian gangs celebrated liberty by going on a rampage; massacring the local Muslims and declaring that the Kingdom of Greater Armenia was just round the corner. In the bloody reprisal that followed, Armenians were themselves massacred and not a few ended up as refugees in Cyprus now under British control, ostensibly to bring law and order to the Cypriots, but in fact keeping safe their trade routes to India.

The other event was a purely personal matter. In Nicosia, the capital city of Cyprus, Halil Osman of Pineview village, recently recruited as a *Zaptieh* by the British, but in his heart very much a Young Turk, newly married but unfulfilled at home, felt in the mood for some private celebration. It had been a particularly hot day, but now in the cool evening Halil was ready for fun. As always on occasions like this he decided to walk over to his favorite drinking hole in Asmaalti at Buyuk Han, the Ottoman *kervansaray*, not far from the police headquarters. In the dim-lit bar inside the derelict inn, he would join his nightly drinking buddies, already well advanced in feasting and merrymaking.

## UZUN ALI, SHAME AND SALVATION

Grandfather Halil was at the prime of his life in his early twenties and full of vigor. His wife at home was pregnant and his lover in Kormacit was too far away, so he was cut off from the sensual fulfillment so essential to his nature. In these situations, when sufficiently inebriated, my Grandfather would stumble his way to the Armenian quarter, beyond the central square with its tall Venetian Column, in front of the new colonial administration, past the imposing Moorish style British courts of law and the post office, into the narrow alleys and pathways behind the beautiful Ottoman Arabahmet mosque, to seek pleasure and company with the ladies in the brothels, which recently had been greatly augmented with new arrivals from war-torn Anatolia.

Secretly my Grandfather was an Ottoman patriot, not religious at all, but when expediency required he would invoke religious teachings to suit his needs and requirements. He was first and foremost a social animal with a clear rule on gender relations: "Allah created woman for man's pleasure" was his motto, which endeared him all the more to his drinking buddies, readily nodding their approval in loud bouts of laughter and fun.

Grandfather's patriotism obliged him to dress well. Modern European dress, be believed, projected his *au courant* Young Turk image. That, of course, was external, but no matter. For him, how one looked *outside* was all-important. His dress enhanced his looks, but Grandfather was naturally good looking, with his tall, lean figure and striking blue eyes and a charming smile. Everything he wore made him look handsome. He had presence. In every group, he stood out and was noticed. Whether in dark blue police uniform, or his European pants and shirt or his Ottoman *shalvar* and his red *fez* on his head, he walked around with self-confidence, proud of every bit of his six foot two inches smartly combed fair hair and carefully groomed moustache with its scimitar-looking curves at either end.

Grandfather was a clever and confident man, especially when it came to sex. His confidence sprung from his secret weapon. Beyond his good looks and charm, he would boast to his drinking buddies that Allah made him for lovemaking. "How so?" they would ask. "My big dick is a divine gift... and I can delay ejaculation for as long as any woman desires," he would boast, as his friends stood in awe, feeling envious. These physical attributes, more than the money in his pocket, were his visa to women's hearts. He was a true Ottoman philanderer;

his sex life was governed by certain rules defined in personal mottos. He was egalitarian on the subject of women. He discriminated not a whit, married or single women, for him, were fair game, his motto being: "If a woman, any woman, is ready for lovemaking, it is sin only to reject her." He was a success in the brothels of the Armenian quarter and no less with women in more civilized circles, and his conquests recognized no ethnic boundaries, nor Ottoman orthodoxy. His unquenchable thirst for sex left him constantly unsatisfied. His wife's pregnancy was just the latest excuse. "If a man does not get enough at home, he is free to look for sex elsewhere" was his other motto. And now this appeared truer in the new age of liberty!

"Ahmet" he yelled at his closest buddy, as Halil stepped into the bar, "have you heard the news?"

"Nothing happens to interest me," said Ahmet, the alcoholic. "Get me another jug of wine," he shouted at the bartender.

But, Halil, the man of the world, and the Ottoman patriot now working for the British, persisted: "Our Padisah, has granted every subject liberty." Ahmet, lifted his head toward Halil, looked at him in amazement, unsure of what to make of Halil's muttering.

"All Ottomans now have liberty." Halil announced.

All around the poorly lit inn stared at Halil with astonished looks. Then Ahmet spoke for all present:

"What the hell is liberty anyway?" asked the alcoholic.

"You donkey" replied Halil angrily, "don't you know anything? Liberty is freedom. Now you can do what you want."

All around were puzzled, none more than Ahmet. He had not washed for days and his eyes were bloodied from excessive drinking and lack of sleep. He began to get angry with Halil.

"Halil you are a fool." He said, raising his voice. He emptied his glass, half of it going down his throat, the other half spilling all over his vest and *shalvar*, the baggy Ottoman pants he had been wearing for the last month or so.

He then shouted at Halil:

"Liberty, freedom and whatnot are empty words. Don't you know? We are no longer Ottomans, the British are here. Anyway, stop this nonsense and come and join the party."

Then he went on:

"Those are big words, let them go in from one ear and come out from the other. Come and let's eat, drink and be merry." The hedonist declared triumphantly as all around applauded.

Halil was easily persuaded and he dropped politics and concentrated on his favorite *raki* and *mezze,* those little cups of Turkish delicacies, vegetables, fruits, dairy and meats of all kinds.

"Ahmet" he yelled, "you are the true philosopher. That is what I like about you. You know how to enjoy life, so let's enjoy it."

"Now you are talking, my friend. Let's drink to that." All joined in and pretty soon, there was a terrible chorus of singing and merrymaking, but the cacophony did nothing to dull the joyful cheer.

In the hours that followed, amidst drinking and laughter, sometime broken by shouting and cursing, Halil's mind focused on Elana, his Maronite lover. "Ah! If only she was here" he thought and realized that he must find a permanent solution to his appetite for sex. Armenian girls were fine for the occasional adventure but that was not enough and Emine at home was no longer adequate. And now, late in her pregnancy, Emine was unavailable sexually and Halil was unfulfilled. Now in the age of liberty he was determined to make Elana his second wife. Taking his cue from the Sultan, he must go for an Ottoman solution to a recurrent problem.

And so it was. Halil's abduction plan was put into operation. At midnight Grandfather made up his mind to stage his own *coup*. He put on his red *fez*, buttoned up his vest and tightened the sash around his belly above his *shalvar*, and stumbled out of the bar to implement stage one of his plan. He decided to take matters in his own hand and take a second wife. He knew this would strictly make him a bigamist because Elana was not a Muslim. She was a Maronite from Kormacit, some twenty miles west of Nicosia, nestled amidst pine forests on the northern slopes of the Five Fingers Mountains overlooking the blue Mediterranean. Kormacit was an isolated village, inward and secretive, built, many centuries ago, as a religious community of devout believers escaping persecution in Lebanon and now happy to be left alone. But, no matter Halil was sex-starved. He must act and take matters in his own hand, imitating the Sultan's example.

By 1 am, and now completely under the influence of *raki*, Halil started to reason in Ottoman terms. In those days, an Ottoman gentleman was entitled to a *harem* of women, and the religion permitted one to have up to four wives. Women were raised to obey men, first fathers then husbands. Their wish was the women's command; a newly married woman's first duty was to fulfill her husband's sexual fantasy.

# DISGRACED

To resist was tantamount to instant divorce and social disgrace.

From the drinking hole in Asmaalti, Grandfather stumbled across the main city-square in front of the imposing Courts and Colonial buildings, impressive in their Moorish architecture, brightly shining against the midnight full moon. He walked past the towering Venetian Column in the centre without even noticing it, then down the narrow street leading to the Kyrenia Gate, one of only three ways of getting in and out of the walled city of Nicosia, surrounded by the Venetian Moat. Before the Kyrneia Gate, along the dirt road lined by tall eucalyptus trees, just before the Tekke of the Whirling Dervishes, he turned left past through the newly built housing project at Samanbahce, where three rows of small bungalows were constructed by the Islamic charitable organization, Evkaf, for housing the new cadres of locally recruited colonial employees. Grandfather's house on the flashier Tanzimat Street was just beyond Samanbahce overlooking the Venetian Moat, not far from Kyrenia Gate.

As he approached his house, Grandfather's self-confidence was reaching a new height.

"Am I not entitled to have four wives?" He asked himself, "especially now in the age of liberty" he added.

" What is the point of liberty?" he asked himself, "if a man cannot do what his heart desires?"

Then doubt set in his mind. It took him only minutes to realize that this was utterly futile.

The woman of Halil's choice for a second wife, the beautiful Elana, his willing lover, was a maiden, barely eighteen, living with her parents in Kormacit, only two miles distant from Pineview, some fifteen miles west of Kyrenia. Elana's parents, like all families in Kormacit, were God-fearing Christians. Daughters were raised to marry someone in their own village. That was the golden rule by which the Ayoubs, as everyone else in the village, lived by. They would never consent to their daughter embracing Islam. That was shameful, unthinkable. Halil himself did not even imagine becoming a Christian. The shame of it would kill his family, or more likely, his father would simply kill him to save family honor. The Ottoman society, of mixed races and religions, rested on the unwritten law of separate identities, with invisible, but impenetrable, boundaries behind which each religious community lived side-by-side, but never together. Inter-marriage or assimilation was the ultimate taboo, the most disgraceful act imaginable.

## UZUN ALI, SHAME AND SALVATION

Conversion in Ottoman Cyprus was a grave matter of family dishonor, a disgrace. Life was centered on religion, each community strictly controlled by its own religious leaders. Ethnic communities, in the same village or towns never mixed, beyond minimal social intercourse usually on festival days, each community living in a world apart from others strictly, each minding its own, surviving under the absolute control of the head priest. That was the bedrock of the *millet* system, the unwritten law of peace and tranquility in the Ottoman society. In this system, marriage to one's own group was the most sacred ritual to maintain ethnic purity and peaceful relations between communities. Every religious community, arranged on feudal lines with the priesthood at the top shepherding its respective flock with an iron fist threatening misconduct, as it saw it, with instant excommunication, recognized no law but its own. The Sultan in faraway Istanbul and his local representatives liked it that way as well: peace, order and tranquility were the essential foundations of Ottoman good governance. Any disturbance was an act rebellion, and any rebel was charged with treason and summarily put to death. Fear ruled everywhere; no one dared to break the Sultan's peace.

But for now Halil's mind was made up. He was in a joyous mood. The Sultan announced the age of liberty. Men were now free and he meant to take advantage of the new freedom. As he began walking from Asmaalti home, he had it all figured out. Tomorrow he would go to Kormacit and fetch Elana, install her upstairs, in the empty room, now that his pregnant and, therefore useless wife, Emine, had moved into the basement. Halil required sex, regularly and adequately. Ottomans were now free. So, why could he not have another woman, wife or not?

# II

Meanwhile, that very same night while Halil was celebrating the dawn of liberty, my Grandmother Emine, now in the tenth month of their marriage, was painfully in labor giving birth to a daughter to be named Aygul, my dear mother. In those days, women gave birth in accordance with Mother Nature's rules at home when the baby was ready to come out.

No one was in attendance with poor Grandmother, save the neighborhood *ebe*, the good-hearted Armenian, widow Mariam. This self-taught midwife had migrated with her husband, Aram, to Cyprus from Kayseri in central Anatolia, some twenty years ago, seeking protection under the British. In those days, Anatolia was a multi-ethnic land peopled with Armenians, Kurds, Laz, Circassians and Turkmen all living together. But after the Russian war of 1877, the situation changed suddenly and alarmingly; first the Muslims refugees displaced from the Caucauses in the east, and from the Balkans in the west flooded in and then the Armenian Dashnaks and Hunchaks started shooting and killing people. They terrorized entire districts, no one was sure why; it was all so secret. Peace among ethnic communities ended suddenly and ethnic conflict began. Of course, the Sultan was not happy and he sent in his soldiers and the whole area soon was engulfed in war and killing. Whoever was able to get out did so. Aram was one of the lucky ones. He met Mariam on his travels and finally they managed to escape to Cyprus, now in British hands. Aram died shortly after the move, and Mariam, who, like all Armenians knew very good Turkish, became finally a midwife, mixing and adjusting quite well to the life in the Armenian section near the Arabahmet Mosque, adjoining Mahmut Pasha quarter.

I have to admit, Grandmother was not a particularly attractive woman, but she was strong, healthy and well built. She was 5 feet, 8 inches tall, green eyes, had a rather large nose for her face and walked more like a man. Emine was very much a private person, somewhat unsure of herself, lacking in self-confidence, finding solace in her thoughts, which she revealed to no one, and she showed no particular ambition or expectation in life.

Grandmother had been the only daughter of Mustafa Aga, an important landowner and *Muhtar*, head of the village of Pineview in the heavily wooded hills west of Kyrenia and one of the wealthiest men in the region. The Aga was the patriarch and he ruled his household, especially his wife and daughter with an iron fist. Grandmother did not shine at school, had few friends as a child, and was a withdrawing personality as a young girl. She was a typical Ottoman woman of her day, no originality was expected of her, and she displayed none. In dress and habits she was a conformist, strictly following the rules of the day as defined by her father. Her mother was her closest friend, and indeed the only, source of knowledge when it came to gender relations. "You must obey and please your husband, he knows what is best," her mother would say to her. Emine, the good Ottoman daughter that she was, would accept her mother's advise without question. "Mother knew best" was the golden rule, and to break the rule was *ayib*, shame and dishonor. A good daughter would put loyalty above her own life, if need be, rather than cause *ayib*.

Pineview then was full of gardens and orchards, fed by mountain springs, and the local villagers were relatively prosperous. It was a popular resort town, famed for its cool mountain climate in summer that attracted nobility and rich people from Egypt and Anatolia. The town boasted several mansions, *Konaks,* built and maintained by Pashas and Ottoman dignitaries who came and stayed not only to escape the summer heat in their places of residence, but to admire the beautiful spring for which Pineview was particularly famed. In April and May, the meadows would be full of deep red tulips and white-yellow narcissus, and the pine-covered hills and slopes would be carpeted with lavender and primroses that filled the air with wonderful smells and colors. Holidaymakers fell in love with Pineview and kept coming back, enriching the town and its people.

Mustafa Aga was the patriarch of his family and leader of Pineview. The *Muhtar* was rich and respected. The Aga was an Ottoman autocrat, ruling over his wife, Fatma, as an absolute despot. She was a totally subservient Muslim lady, whose marriage, in Ottoman custom, was arranged as part of a land deal between the fathers. This was the system that had existed for centuries; no one even dared to question it. It was taken for granted; much like the fact that the sun rose every morning in the east and set in the west.

Fatma raised her daughter Emine in her own image to be an obedient woman in a man's world and never question her father or husband. Somehow, it did not seem right, but Emine kept it all a secret. Often she tried not to think about it; instinctively she relied on her mother. Unschooled beyond the barest minimum and ignorant of everything else other than cooking, housekeeping and responding to her husband's sexual needs, she had no particular interests or abilities outside the family. What mattered most was family honor and Fatma was an honorable lady in the community, totally devoted and subservient to her husband. Fatma had raised Emine to be a subservient wife whose only expectation from a future husband was fidelity.

"Emine, you are wonderful," said Mariam, impressed with the self-control and endurance Emine displayed during birthing. There was hardly any of the screaming and shouting which was normally associated with childbirth. She was performing her womanly duty, hoping to have a boy, but was equally happy with her lovely daughter, although she could not help anticipating rejection by Halil who, naturally like all Ottoman men, preferred his first-born to be a boy.

Emine's pregnancy had been difficult. She was always sick with an upset stomach, vomiting and feeling bouts of nausea constantly. At the beginning of her marriage, things were great with Halil and she even enjoyed the first month or so of their marriage. In fact, she was in love right from the start, but her love was mixed with an unusual degree of possessiveness, believing him to be hers and hers only.

"What a handsome husband Halil is?" and "He is mine" she would say to herself in her private moments of reflection in those early days of their marriage with so much sexual activity. She particularly loved Halil in his dark blue *zaptieh* uniform and his red *fez* that gave him the

15

airs of somebody important. For her, he was the center of her world, her solitary existence in the city away from her family in Pineview.

After their marriage, not yet a year ago, Halil had rented a nice, two bedroom stone and mortar house in an alley in the Mahmut Pasa quarter, on Tanzimat (Reform) Street. The house was comfortable and contained two levels, upstairs and downstairs. Upstairs, at the street level the front door opened on to hall with two rooms on either side, one used as a guest-room and the other as bedroom, and down the stairs there was another room, used as a storeroom, bathroom and kitchen facing a small courtyard.

Tanzimat Street was a wide and clean avenue, more like a European boulevard than a tiny Ottoman alley, with stone houses, all well built and prosperous, overlooking the Venetian ramparts, situated between the Paphos and Kyrenia gates, two of the only three points of entry and exit into the walled city. Grandfather was pleased to be a resident on it because it reflected his Ottoman patriotism reinforced now by his elevated status as a salaried policeman in the British administration. The house was a short distance from the new Government Complex, now the centre of all power, formerly the Ottoman Saray, seat of government. To the north was Samanbahce, the section containing the new low-cost houses recently built by the Muslim Trust, *Evkaf,* for civil servants, and the Armenian quarter was on the south, adjoining the red light district, where he had met the British police officer that obliged Halil for favors done by getting him his job.

Then things began to change shortly after Emine became pregnant and sickness set in. There was no doctor and no hospital care to put things right. As her sickness got worse, she began to stay in bed and Halil lost interest in her. Soon no one called and Emine drifted into a solitary world of dreams of angels and demons. Her mind would wonder off to mystical worlds. She longed for Halil, but he was always away in bars and brothels. Rumors began to reach her about his preference for ladies of the night and jealousy possessed her.

But for now, comforted by the midwife Mariam, Emine's private world was pure joy. Her depression and fears suddenly vanished the demons that earlier depressed her were replaced by visions of dancing angels of hope. With the baby in her arms, Emine, with uncommon pride, took a look at her brand new daughter and she liked what see saw.

"Allah! What a lovely baby" she said. "She is mine," she added as if her precious possession was in danger of being lost to some unforeseen force.

What Emine could not imagine was that, at that same moment, she was about to lose something else that would drastically alter her life: Her beloved sex-crazy Halil.

"Yes she is beautiful," agreed the midwife. "May Allah protect her?"

Beaming with the pride of a new mother, Emine said: "My baby is as handsome as my Halil. Isn't she Meryem *ana*?" She asked the Armenian midwife using the affectionate Muslim equivalent of Mariam and calling her "mother", to create a comforting sort of mother-daughter relationship.

Then, she inquired: "Where is Halil?" The midwife said nothing. She, too, had wondered about him, but remained silent.

Grandmother soon fell asleep and the midwife placed the baby next to her and quietly went away. It was a blissful sleep, an innocent and brief happiness, of a new mother experiencing the miracle of giving birth to a newborn. Emine, for the first and last time in her all too brief life, felt a wonderful sense of achievement.

Mariam quietly exited. All behind was dark and quiet.

# III

When Grandfather Halil, his belly full and his head misty from too much *raki*, stumbled in through the front door of his home hours later, all was dark and quiet. He figured that his pregnant wife Emine must have been sleeping downstairs.

"Just as well" he thought and went straight to his own bedroom on the ground floor and instantly fell into a deep slumber. When Emine's pregnancy was advanced, and she was not available for sex, Halil and Emine effectively separated. Actually, it was *his* decision. He moved her downstairs, to the storeroom in front of the kitchen, putting a bed and a chair for her, and leaving the rest of the storeroom intact. The other room upstairs, facing his own, was empty for now.

Two hours later, a baby crying waked him. It came from the bedroom downstairs where Grandmother Emine was living as a virtual prisoner. First he thought he was dreaming and turned over in his bed, but the noise persisted and then Halil realized that he was not dreaming after all.

"Allah, Allah" he exclaimed, "What is this? Am I dreaming?" He rubbed his eyes and tried to gather his strength and concentrate. Then he remembered his wife's pregnancy. "Did Emine give birth?"

Then, Grandfather realized he was now a father. He was not excited or emotional over it. The fact was he was no longer keen about Emine. It started months ago, when his wife was too advanced with her pregnancy to be available for Grandfather's sexual pleasure. That is when Halil turned elsewhere and he only came home to sleep, exhausted from merrymaking with his friends and lovemaking in the Armenian quarter almost every night, with just one thing in mind: to have a good night's sleep, unhindered by Emine's pregnant condition. That is why he had dispatched her downstairs, away from his own bedroom upstairs. His world was far removed from Emine's.

Once certain of the new fact, Grandfather set to thinking. First, he thought of giving up his plans, but then, almost instantly, he decided that he should stick with the plan in his mind. Maybe he had to modify his plans about Elana and bring her into the house as a helper! That is it! "What a good idea" he thought to himself. At least that is how he would explain things to Emine. Within minutes, he was more than ever determined to go ahead with his plan. "What with the baby, and the customary 40 day withholding of sex coming up" he reasoned, he was in for a long dry season. He had to act decisively following the Sultan's example.

As he climbed downstairs, he realized he had a headache. The lamp was lit in Emine's room. He opened the door gingerly and saw Emine sitting up in her bed, holding a baby tightly, breastfeeding. Distracted by his head pain, Halil was, momentarily, lost for words and Emine was the first to notice the husband.

"Halil is that you? You are a father now." She said.

"Is that so?" is all he could say, with an astonished look on his face, his head spinning and feeling unsteady.

"Come and see your daughter. Isn't she beautiful?" Asked Emine as her husband came closer.

Grandfather was anything but happy. With painful eyes and uncertain feeling, he just stood there. He looked long enough to observe that the baby was a girl.

Then he gathered his thoughts as the outlines of his modified plan began to emerge in his mind. Grandfather's mind was not on the baby. He had other plans to worry about.

"Emine, you cannot manage on your own. I must go to Pineview and fetch your mother to look after you and help with the baby."

Grandma was pleased; she smiled gently, looking at the baby. Her husband's lies sounded so reasonable.

Lies or not, Emine was pleased with her husband's words. It was the kindest words she had heard from him for months. "That is wonderful Halil. I want to call our daughter Aygul, because her face is beautiful like the moon and her scent is just like a rose."

"Fine" growled Grandfather, he was hardly interested in the baby. He turned back, climbed the stairs, still bothered by his headache and went into his bedroom.

Once in his room, he fell asleep quickly. His plans were emerging clearly in his head. The next day would be a full day, an eventful day.

# IV

The first thing Grandfather Halil did when he woke up the next day, still dizzy from last night's drinking, and not quiet adjusted to being a father, was to take stock of the new state of affairs in his house on Tanzimat Street. It did not take him long: he decided to go immediately to Lieutenant Joseph Smart, his Indian-looking English boss at the police headquarters behind the Courts of Law in the city center. He was determined to apply in person for a compassionate leave of two days on account of his new status as a father of a new baby daughter. Leaves were executive matters, beyond the control of his immediate boss Sergeant Kazim; besides, Joe Smart owed Halil a favor for services rendered in the brothels of the Armenian quarter.

"I am now a father. My wife gave birth to a baby daughter last night" said Halil and Joe jumped to congratulate him. "I need to go to Pineview village to bring my mother-in-law to look after Emine and the baby."

"Sure Halil, Godspeed" said the affable Joe Smart and Halil immediately started walking briskly toward Deveciler Han, the camel caravan market, then the inter-town transportation center located behind Buyuk Han. His plan was to hire a horse-carriage and go not to Pineview but to Kormacit, not to bring Emine's mother, but to stage an elopement with his lover, the beautiful Elana. She would be waiting for him, of that he was certain.

## UZUN ALI, SHAME AND SALVATION

His plan was simple. With the horse-carriage he would drive straight to Kormacit, go right to Elana's house and fetch her to his house on Tanzimat Street. He would introduce her to Emine as a temporary helper with the excuse that her own mother was sick. It was the best possible plan under the circumstances. Events would unfold according to natural requirements, Emine and Elana would gradually accept one another, and they may even become friends. Given a little bit of female cooperation, Halil's liberty would be guaranteed.

As far as Elana was concerned, Halil was sure his lover would co-operate and go along with his plans. Of her love, he was confident because since their chance encounter in the woods 3 years ago, Halil had become the perfect magician who had cast a spell over the trusting Elana. In the last months, they had talked about elopement, always in surrealistic terms removed from the real Ottoman world they inhabited. Elana, the fragile Ayoub girl was alienated in the suffocating Maronite village of Kormacit. She yearned for Halil's love and protection. Halil knew nothing of her parents, except that Elana did not think highly of them, and would readily give them up for him.

From the police headquarters, Grandfather walked to the central market, passing on the way Asmaalti and Buyuk Han, the grand 16th century Ottoman *kervansaray* dominating Nicosia's marketplace. He went to Deveciler Han, another Ottoman edifice, originally an inn, now used as a terminal for inter-town travel by horse and buggy, the only available means of reasonably rapid transport.

On the way to Deveciler Han, passing the cobblers and *kebab* sellers, hardly noticing the noise and the comings and goings of the multitude of shoppers and sellers amidst the daily ebb and flow of the busy market, he realized he had no money for the hire. Whatever cash he had was all spent on last night's merrymaking. He was then passing in front of the coffee-shop in Buyuk Han where Ahmet the alcoholic, his drinking buddy was working when he was not at some bar getting drunk. Fortunately, Ahmet was sober when Halil noticed him. He yelled:

"Ahmet, come here" he yelled, and his friend rushed toward Halil. He owed Halil many favors and he was glad for an opportunity to repay.

"I need some cash" he began as Ahmet approached. "I need to hire a horse-carriage."

"What on earth for?" said the coffee server.

"Don't ask," he said. "There is someone I will fetch with me."

"I know" Ahmet read his friend's mind. "You are after some woman, again." They both smiled and conspired in silence.

"How much do you need?" Ahmet asked.

"Can you spare a pound?" Halil replied.

"That much eh?"Ahmet was surprised at the large amount required. One pound represented half a month's salary for a civil servant in those days. Ahmet shared everyone's opinion at the time that the policemen, along with all civil servants were extremely well paid. Halil wanted to be sure he had enough for the journey ahead, paying the fare for him and Elana, and leaving him something extra for food and other incidentals expenses on the way.

Dutifully, Ahmet went back into the coffee shop. Fortunately there was enough cash in the till for the advance to Grandfather.

***

Meanwhile, in Kormacit, the day of the elopement had started badly for Elana. She had quarreled with her father, Elias Ayoub, who wanted her to join him and her mother for wage employment in the fields. Actually, the quarrel was the latest episode that had began a few weeks ago when her mother overruled her husband's objection and bought Elana a gold chain with a cross for her 18th birthday. "Why she does not even bother going to church?" he had tried to argue, but Katrina was determined to do something special for the occasion and her husband reluctantly agreed to splurge the meager family savings. Now, as Halil was galloping madly to snatch away their daughter, her father wanted Elana to join him and her mother for work in the fields, but she would hear none of it. " I am reading a beautiful book of romance" she said and walked into her room, shutting her door indifferently at her parents.

At this stage, her lover was coming to rescue her. It was a hot summer day, but Halil made good time, first speeding through the plain west of Nicosia and then through the sparsely treed hilly ground. By noon, he was over the Five Fingers Mountains and thick pine forests, and at the outskirts of Kormacit, just beyond Pineview. As planned, he drove straight to Elana's house, next to the big Church in town centre. She was alone at home, and Halil's plan for elopement went off even more smoothly than he had anticipated. She was glad to see him.

"Elana I have come to take you with me" he said and the love-smitten Maronite girl was pleased. "My prince has come," she thought as she transported herself from the romantic world so beautifully crafted in the book she was reading. She smiled at Halil. Her gentle, innocent beauty too mesmerized him. He lifted her in his arms and they kissed.

It was Grandfather, the schemer, who was in charge. He was the Sultan of the moment, his word was the *firman*, and he called the shots. "Come on" he urged: "We have no time to lose. We must go."

Elana's brain was full of romantic thoughts. "He has come for me, I knew it," she said to herself. "It is going to be so exciting" She reasoned, thinking only of love, pure love in a mystical world peopled only by lovers, no pain and suffering. The naïve girl trusted her lover totally; his love was all the protection she needed. She packed a few things for the journey. Elana, the innocent Maronite maiden, was ready to follow the man she loved to anywhere, in this or next world.

"I'll go with you, my love," she said. It was a well-rehearsed plot, agreed months before. She placed her trust in love and she was confident that Halil's love was all the protection she needed. In Elana's innocent and youthful mind, there was no room for doubt. A romantic at heart shaped more by the romances she had read than by her mother, Elana was a trusting soul. Or, maybe she believed in dreams, she was the angel in a dream world. Before or now, she asked no details of Halil's life, and none was volunteered.

She left no good-bye letter for her parents. Elana, the lonely girl, torn by the fear that her youthful life was melting away in a hostile backwater, had no more than the tiniest regret towards a distant father; she felt just a bit of guilt towards her mother, but merely for a fleeting moment. In the fast-moving lane she was entering, events moved too rapidly. The lovers were gone within minutes. Father, mother and family were all cast away. Elana was rid off the hated prison of Kormacit.

Only a few idle peasants, enjoying their leisure at the village coffee shop facing the big St. George Church, noticed the Ayoub girl make away with her Ottoman lover.

"So it is all true. The rumors about the Ayoub girl and her infidel lover are right, after all" declared one of the idle villagers sitting and sipping Turkish coffee. All heads nodded in approval.

"This is a bad omen. No good will from it." predicted another idler, playing god and sitting in judgment on others.

After a momentary interest, the coffee shop crowd looked the other way. A few yards further down, some worshippers, dressed in black, came out of the Church and were almost run over by the horse-carriage with the lovers rushing out of the village.

"What is the rush?" some one yelled at the driver, but no one paid attention. "It is that Ayoub girl," said one old woman, "running away with her Muslim lover. Mary, Mother of God, have mercy on her" she prayed, asking for forgiveness for past sins, and more still to be committed.

In an instant, the carriage turned the corner and entered the pine forest, the horse galloping toward the pass through the Five Fingers Mountains en route to Nicosia at the center. Then the dust settled along the dirt road and all was quite. The little Maronite village resumed its slumber sinners and all going about their daily chores, good and evil. It was the lull before the storm.

# V

In the evening, Elana moved in to the upstairs bedroom in the house on Tanzimat Street, right above Grandmothers' room downstairs. Grandfather's house on Tanzimat became a *harem* with two kept women over whose lives he ruled like the Sultan, according to his whims and fancies. But Halil's harem was not a happy place and the worst was about to happen. The wheels of misfortune began turning, the hour of doom approaching. The angels of death had laid down their plan well. The tragedy of Grandfather's two women was set in motion, like some Shakespearean play, his Maronite lover upstairs and his Ottoman wife and new mother abandoned downstairs.

I am shocked, writing now about this tragedy, how such an abduction could happen in broad day light in the middle of downtown Nicosia, a stone throw's away from the Police headquarters where Grandfather worked. But in those days, families kept aloof and neighbors minded only their own business; women gossiped but there was little socializing. Men kept their household under tight control, and wives lived submissive, secluded lives. The Ottoman society lived by certain sacred laws, taboos that sheltered men's immorality. They could divorce, remarry, take on a concubine and indulge in all kinds of liberties; it was *ayib*, shameful to expose such immorality. Adultery seemed to apply only against women; men somehow enjoyed exemption. At the superficial surface of society, all was serene, like a calm sea.

But underneath this veneer of serenity, it was different, like undercurrents and turbulence of the ocean. So, from the moment Elana stepped through the front door, Grandfather's house ceased being a home, and evil spirits moved in. Unseen forces began to heat up the volcano. The house on Tanzimat Street ceased to be a place of residence of mortals. It became the scene of an Ottoman tragedy, events unfolding as if according to some devilish plot orchestrated by demigods of ill omen. The actors in this Ottoman plot, Halil, Emine and Elana, of different cultures and religions, were all pitiful figures in their own ways, helpless victims of an oppressive fatalism marching toward self-destruction. But it was not all pre-determined like some divine design, as if the Sick Man was approaching death. The Ottoman world then was in moral decay, men exploiting women and society oppressing all. If I could read Grandfather's mind, I would judge him the plotter, a real scoundrel who misread his Sultan's declaration of liberty. His was the primary responsibility for what happened. My Grandmother was no different than the mistress Elana; they were in his in his harem, in his charge as kept women, put there for his pleasure. My poor mother, the baby Aygul, was too young to observe, but alive enough to be traumatized by the whole episode; she was to carry the scars of the trauma all through her own life.

When Elana willingly eloped with Grandfather and entered his harem on Tanzimat Street in Mahmut Pasa quarter, she left forever her tiny Maronite world and family in Kormacit. Her childhood and youth had been a world of loneliness and rejection. Elana wanted to be loved. Instead she faced bitterness and isolation, unsure and insecure in the oppressive community of Kormacit where she, like her parents, fitted into no extended family.

Until Elana met Halil, she provided her own comfort. She read and walked along the shore or in the meadows, always alone. And, it was during one of these walks, when she was 15 that they met. Their chance meeting was the climax of her life. After Halil everything was different, there was suddenly meaning in her life: "Better a day of love than a life of loneliness" she philosophized. In her idyllic utopia in her dreams and fantasies, love conquered all obstacles. Halil represented love, beauty, and protection, everything she missed in Kormacit.

Kormacit was only a couple of miles from Pineview, situated amidst the pine forests and fields which in spring are filled with poppies and narcissus. Even today I enjoy walking among the pines, breathing the fresh breeze from the blue Mediterranean below, and the imposing mountain tops, with fresh-smelling pines all around. Sixty years ago, the scenery must have been even more idyllic, less unspoilt and more virginal.

For three years Halil and Elana had conducted a secret love affair worthy of *Leyla and Mecnun*, except that this was a love cutting across the Muslim and Christian worlds. It broke all Ottoman rules. Just as the love of *Leyla and Mecnun* had turned the desert into a beautiful oasis of rose gardens and cool springs and waterfalls, so Elana, after meeting Halil, constructed in her mind a magical land, with no one else but her lover, an idyllic never-never land devoid of the boredom and oppression of Kormacit.

Though practically next to each other, proximity and neighborhood meant nothing in the world of Ottoman multiculturalism. An invisible cultural wall cut off Pineview and Kormacit, a wall that was like the Great Wall of China. The Christians and Muslims, as in all parts of Cyprus, even in mixed villages lived separate lives in different worlds. In those days, religion defined identity and honor. Conversion was the ultimate disgrace for family and person and when it happened on rare occasions; those involved were disgraced, becoming social outcasts. Then, death was better than the dishonor that followed.

Elana, as her name indicated, was unusual. The only child of Elias and Katrina Ayoub, she was a free spirit with a passion of the natural beauty around Kormacit, a social misfit, who preferred her own company and filled her time with romantic thoughts from the love stories she enjoyed reading, when at home, closeted in her own room. At the time of her elopement with Halil, she was only a few months over eighteen, exceptionally beautiful with a Mona Lisa smile, black hair and emerald green eyes. She wore a simple golden cross necklace, a gift from her parents on her eighteenth birthday one of the rare gifts she ever received from any one in her life.

Elana was a lonely girl, yearning for pure love, just like the romances she enjoyed reading about valiant knights rescuing maidens in distress. Her abstract world of romance was high in the sky, above clouds, a place of beauty, innocence and everlasting joy. It made her feel warm and pure inside. Kormacit then was the last place on earth to give her the love she desperately needed. Escaping from this closeted community was, in her mind, a necessary step for love and romance.

# DISGRACED

Escaping Kormacit was entering her magical world of romance.

Elana's parents had arrived in Kormacit some twenty years earlier, a refugee family displaced by the latest round of sectarian conflict in Lebanon between the Druze and the Maronites back in 1860s. Elias had supplied the Ottoman authorities with some useful information about the rebellious Druze, and when his life was threatened, he managed to convince his masters in the Ottoman bureaucracy to get him the necessary papers and moved with his wife to the Maronite village of Kormacit joining earlier waves of Maronites. Elana was born in Kormacit barely two years after the family moved there.

The Ayoub family, however, did not find life easy in Kormacit. They did not quite fit in. There were constant rumors that the family had Muslim blood, that Katrina was a Muslim convert, never a Christian in her heart, that Elana was illegitimate, having been fathered by another man in Katrina's life before Elias. To add to these rumors, Elias took little interest in his daughter's welfare and Katrina was a distant and withdrawing woman herself. But the real hardship was lack of an extended family.

Kormacit was a very closely-knit community, an isolated village in a remote region away from the hustle and bustle of the island in the center. Its remoteness had been its attractions for the Maronites escaping persecution from Lebanon. There were two major waves of immigrations from the old country, each creating an inflow of refugees displaced by some Lebanese civil unrest. Families who came as groups stayed together as groups tied together by faith. There were two churches in the town; both Latin but divided on intricate ecclesiastical differences that sustained two sets of politics. The Ayoub family was a newcomer with insufficient roots or connections to belong to one or the other.

There was another invisible divide in Kormacit. The Maronites were apart also from the Greek Cypriots who were Greek Orthodox. One would have thought that at least the more numerous Orthodox Maronites and the Greek Orthodox would be friendly and intermingle. The truth, however, was the exact opposite. Language and custom acted as invisible and insurmountable walls.

Years after the British took control of the island, the Greek Cypriots remained as Ottoman as ever. The Church ruled over all. And for the Greek Cypriots, there was only one legitimate Church and any other gospel outside this Church was just heresy, period. And for the

## UZUN ALI, SHAME AND SALVATION

Greek Cypriot Church, politics as much as dogma, determined allegiance; the Greek Orthodox priests were in the vanguard of ENOSIS, a Hellenic dream to attach Cyprus to Greece. Any one who did not share this sentiment could not belong to the congregation. Accordingly, these Maronites were not really Greek Cypriots; they were even newer guests in Cyprus than those barbaric Ottoman Muslims. Best to keep away from them, have nothing to do with them, and most certainly, forget about such silly notions such as marrying their daughters to boys from Kormacit.

Elana grew up in Kormacit as a free thinker, a girl unrestrained by custom or taboo, one who loved the fields and forests of the area more than the closely-knit community of Kormacit. At the village school, situated next to the Church, overlooking the blue Mediterranean, she had no friends, for no fault of her own. She was always "That Ayoub girl" unwanted and a social outcast.

At first, rejection bothered Elana, who so desperately wanted to be one of the girls; desirable and loved, just like others. Sometimes, when alone in her room, she would cry quietly: "Why are they so mean to me?" she would question herself. Once she had dared to ask her mother, who tied to comfort her, but ended up reinforcing her own insecurity: "They do not like us because we come from a different part of Lebanon."

Gradually she began to accept her condition as an outsider. In time she began to enjoy her freedom to be herself, to read on her own, being alone in her room. She stayed away from socializing with girls of her age and despised them whose sole aim seemed to be to get married and have children just to please their parents. Elana, the outcast, preferred excitement to boredom, and she dreamt about adventure in the world beyond Kormacit.

When she was a teenager, Elana began taking long walks along the coast and often wondered into off the valleys and moors, sometimes going walking along the ocean, sitting on pebbles and listening to the endless waves as they hit the shore. On other occasions, she wondered off into the meadows and pine forest toward the Five Fingers Mountains that stretched east to west blocking the way to Nicosia and center of the island, a world she had never seen. "I wonder what lies beyond. Are people in Nicosia friendlier than in Kormacit?" That is what the Maronite maiden was curious about.

Spring was her favorite season, and she always looked forward to

April. It was sunny and warm, but not hot. She loved the breeze from the ocean whistling in the pine forest, full of migrating birds singing and dancing. The meadows were blanketed in flowers of beauty and color of incredible variety, against endless green of fresh new grass. She would climb over hills and go meandering for miles in the direction of Pineview, the Ottoman village. "I wonder if the Ottomans are as cruel as the Maronites?" She would ask and immediately make up her mind: "No, that would be impossible."

It was on one of these wonderings in the meadows, on a lovely and hot April day, shortly after she had turned fifteen that she stumbled into Grandfather's world. He was hunting in the forest. He was tall and handsome. He was looking for game and she was looking for her Prince Charming. Cynics would laugh; prophets would say: "It was destiny. It was written."

They suddenly came face to face in one of her favorite spots, at a spring and a small pool from which a small stream trickled down in a valley, with grove of pines on both sides, stretching all the way to the sea in the distant horizon. She would stop there for a drink of water and rest before returning back to Kormacit. Suddenly he came to her. He was climbing up, with confident steps, carrying several birds, victims hanging down his side and a shotgun slung over his shoulder. He looked like some Greek demigod, not the least Ottoman, a tall figure with broad shoulders, blond hair and sparkling blue eyes.

Startled by movement and the surprise encounter, he almost shot her with his gun. In the forest, one never knew who was foe or friend. She started running, scared and uncertain of what she could do.

"Wait" he called, but she kept running back toward Kormacit. He gave a chase and in a few minutes, he reached her.

"Please, sir" she implored. "Let me go. I lost my way." She lied. He did not believe her.

"Where do you live?" Halil asked.

"In the village down below. In Kormacit, sir. Please let me go." Said Elana, shy and scared.

"I will accompany you till you reach safety. It is not a good idea for a maiden to be walking in the hills like this. You never know, you might run into bandits and highway robbers. I hear these hills are full of them" he said.

What Halil said about bandits was true. In those days, the hills were full of thieves who made a living from stealing sheep from local shepherds and robbing travelers on roads. In those days only a few of the rich had cars or used horse-carriage and ordinary folk traveled in ox-driven carts that would take two days' journey to reach Nicosia over dirt roads through the passes in the Five Fingers Mountains. The few police that existed were in towns, and rural areas were really at the mercy of bandits.

It was close to noon and the sun shone brightly. The fields were green, and pine forests in the background, the fields around the village in the distance, now clearly visible and covered with young wheat and barley. They walked slowly, side by side and then she began to sense a strange warm feeling, a secret attraction to the man beside her. Elana secretly glanced at Halil and she liked what she saw. "He is quite handsome," she said to herself.

Halil then asked: "Would you like some food?" He was carrying a knapsack and that morning, before leaving Pineview, he had packed a picnic snack of olives, bread and cheese, along with a generous filling of water in his leather water bag.

Elana said "No, thanks" at first, but she felt awfully thirsty. "I just want to go home", but inside her something strange voice guided her otherwise and she secretly wished this strange man, whom she has not seen before, would repeat his kind offer. It was as if a strange mystical force was pulling her toward the stranger.

When Halil repeated with his offer, Elana was glad; she was feeling hungry. She accepted and soon they sat down to a spontaneous lunch at a beautiful picnic spot on a high plateau, with the light blue Mediterranean ahead and the dark blue of Five Fingers Range behind. They were half way between Pineview and Kormacit.

For the first time Halil had a good, close look at the maiden next to him. He was thunderstruck with the beauty before him. Never in his life before, had he come across a more beautiful face, rounded by the loveliest black hair and penetrating emerald green eyes. And her lips were as red as cherries. She was one of these angels about whom poems were written in *One Thousand and One Nights*. He was transported into a world of unspoilt beauty; he felt some strange warmth inside him that pulled him mysteriously toward this beautiful maiden he had run into just a short while ago.

It was a moment made for love. And the two young persons were like pawns in a game of love played by mythical gods in the island of Aphrodite. Race and religion mattered not. Pure love recognized no boundaries. Neither she, nor he, cared for custom or taboo. They communicated in silence; their bodies did the talking. He was gentle and soft, and when their eyes met, Elana felt a spell of magic, pulling her closer toward him. It was nothing else she had experienced. He kissed her red lips and never before had he experienced such a warm, delicious feeling. He was Adonis and she was Aphrodite reborn. It was heaven on earth. They fell on the grass, and let Mother Nature take control.

The picnic was transformed into a furious love scene. The two young persons suddenly pulled by magic, an unimaginable love across the cultural divide when the Ottoman world all around was going up in flames, as nations fought with one another and death and destruction reigned everywhere. For the two lovers in the meadow between Pineview and Kormacit on that beautiful day, nothing mattered at the moment than the pure love they experienced. It was joy that Elana never thought possible.

That day Elana lost her virginity, became a woman and entered Grandfather's world. I feel sorry for her, the poor soul, I believe she utterly trusted Grandfather and her love for him became the high point of her existence. He was too selfish, with Elana just as he had been with mother, and did not realize the sacrifice these women had made for him until it was too late. But, I must also admit in all honesty, Elana was a terribly weak woman and must share much of the blame for the tragedy that followed. From the moment she willingly moved in to the house on Taznimat Street, she was a captive, like a bird in a cage. Grandfather, the perfect hunter, had bagged yet another game. I am sorry to admit, but that is how Grandfather saw women, objects of his desire, ready for the taking, like birds in the forest.

In the weeks and months they met often, but always in secret, in fields and valleys between Kormacit and Pineview. And their love flowered, hopelessly out of their control. In those days, of course, there was no room for a Muslim-Christian marriage. It was disgrace for all the concerned. It would ruin families and destroy innocent lives. Elopement was the only chance and that too typically was a recipe for disaster. But love nurtures on miracles and miracles are what lovers believe, though seldom realize.

***

In his 20th year, Grandfather's marriage was arranged. He was married off to a woman he had never seen or cared for. Grandmother Emine was not a particularly pretty woman. Her principal attraction was being the only daughter of Mustafa Aga, the *Muhtar* of Pineview and a big landowner. It was sad, but true: the marriage was not a love match and it was a singularly uneventful ceremony. That, of course, is what usually happened in those days. Fathers arranged everything, settled the dowry and bride price, neighbors feasted and enjoyed themselves on the wedding day, and the bride and groom were left on their own to make the best of it.

Marriage, when it came, was the last thing on Halil's mind. He was enjoying himself; he had plenty of fun with women of all religions. But, as an Ottoman youth, he could not resist his father's wish. Preserving family honor was above everything else. Family honor, in practical terms, meant the dignity of the father to be able to walk into the coffee shop and hold his head high, to be greeted by all present as a family head able to enforce his decisions in his family.

The mother, though the mistress of the household in domestic matters, played second fiddle to the patriarch who ruled external relations unchallenged and marriage was clearly an inter-family affair, a man's business. At least that is how the Aga saw the world.

And the Ottoman Aga, his would-be father in law, was a man who knew how to get his way, always.

So Grandfather Halil had no say in the subject of his marriage and had to go along with the Aga's plans. In truth, Halil was in a weak bargaining position. Things had reached a limit for Osman, Halil's father, an honest enough villager of simple means. Poor Osman had to put a stop to people gossiping about his good-looking son chasing all those Christian women in the area. Or he would soon have no dignity, no honor left.

"One of these days", neighbors warned Osman on more than one occasion: "That hothead Halil of yours, Allah forbid, will become a Christian and marry an infidel".

As always in matters of sex and women, Grandfather's good looks seemed to come to the rescue. Mustafa Aga, the rich landowner, the *Muhtar* liked him, for no other reason than his looks and wanted him for his daughter, now almost 20 and in danger soon of becoming a stay at home spinster. Consequently, when the Aga took matters into his hands and directly, though somewhat unorthodoxly, approached Osman with his marriage proposal, it was a done deal.

Halil was ordered to marry Emine. She went along with her parents wish. And so, in the custom of the time, an arranged marriage was set. The wedding celebrations lasted five days, starting with musicians hired for the occasion opening in the evening of the first day, entertaining the peasants and villagers. This was followed in the days ensuing until at the end a big wedding feast was organized, the Hodja came and declared Halil and Emine husband and wife. Everyone came to heap respect on the *Muhtar* for arranging such a wonderful match. On the final night, before the consummation of the marriage, Emine's hands were covered in *henna* and bandaged according to custom, "so she would not resist her husband" said the neighbors who waited outside till dawn until the bloodied bed sheet was thrown out of the window testifying her virginity.

And, from then on, they should have lived happily forever. But alas!

# VI

As Grandfather and Elana were galloping away in the horse-carriage through the Five Fingers Mountain passes toward Nicosia, Lieutenant Joseph (Joe) Smart, at the police headquarters was hatching his own shady scheme for the next round of fun and excitement. Working as a law officer during the day, and having fun at night that was the life, he thought, befitting a young, single and dashing Anglo-Asian recently arrived in Cyprus.

Lieutenant Joe was impressed with Grandfather right from the start. The young and good-looking Ottoman, he admitted, had been extremely helpful in unlocking the secrets of this mysterious little island. No doubt, he needed a lot of coaching because he was a stranger in a new world, an Ottoman world that the British were in the process of dismantling. Joe, in the police force, was on the island to bring British law and order to what had been an Ottoman backwater. Feudalism, despite centuries of Ottoman rule, remained little changed from Venetian times, except that now Agas replaced Italian lords and crusading knights, all united with the common aim of exploiting the peasants.

Now it was the turn of the British.

Joe was a half-breed, an Anglo-Asian, the product of British colonialism in far away Malaya, newly added to the expanding Empire for its rich tin mines. Joe was born of an illicit union between a Malay woman and his father, Robert Smart, a lowly British aristocrat who made his fortune in the tin mines of Malaya where he served as a police officer in the Residency in Ipoh, Perak, the tin capital of British Malaya. It was common for British administrators in Malaya then to have temporary wives with local Malay women, and more often than not, no other arrangement was necessary in these liaisons other than simply shacking up with a local woman, ostensibly hired as a cook or housekeeper. That way, the Victorian proper appearances were maintained, and so long as peace was undisturbed no one minded. Everyone pretended not to know. "What else was a young, single man from civilized London placed in the primitive Malayan jungle supposed to do?" was the general sentiment of the genteel society of the British enjoying a life of leisure in their clubs while administering the natives and making fortunes in tin and rubber.

Joseph's birth was an accident, but once born out of wedlock, Robert, his father, did the responsible Victorian thing. He raised the child in proper style. Fortunately, the boy looked like his father and his skin was virtually white, so the locals and British alike accepted him as British. And, with Robert's wealth, thanks to his clever speculation with tin stocks, money was no problem. When old enough, Joe was put on a P&O boat from Singapore and sent to England in the care of his Grandparents and educated in a reputable grammar school. Through family connections, he ended up in the Cyprus police force to spread British justice, but in fact, becoming embroiled in the tragic Ottoman world of Halil, Emine and Elana.

Shortly after his appointment and arrival in Cyprus, Joe chanced to meet Halil in one of the brothels in the Armenian quarter when both young men were looking for easy sex. The night they met had been a particularly hot and sticky all day, but, in Nicosia, in the evenings it cools down and there is a wonderful breeze blowing across the desert-like plain of Mesarya couched between the Five Fingers Mountains to the North and the snowy peaks of Troodos Mountains to the south. The nightlife of Nicosia can be fun, especially for single men with money to spare.

Joe was looking for fun. Dressed in civilian clothes, he looked a dashing young man, with lots of money in his pocket, testing his luck in the market for a night of pleasure in the cool of the evening. He entered the Armenian red-light district that in those days was not out of bounds for the English servicemen. The red-light district of Nicosia was just taking off, fed by new supplies of young Armenian girls from Anatolia thanks to the British who encouraged the influx of refugees and migrants escaping war and massacre.

After looking in a few brothels, he entered the one that looked particularly cheerful. A party seemed to be in progress. There was a young man in the center of festivities. It was, as Joe would soon find out, Halil, my hustler Grandfather.

Joe was impressed with Grandfather right from the start. He had such an ease and carefree outlook about him. Halil, the Ottoman youth looked smashing with a clean and curved beard, striking blue eyes, tall figure and his dark blue baggy pants, white shirt and scarlet sash and red *fez*. He was the darling of the whorehouse. Sure this was a place where money purchased sex, but Halil was a class to himself. He had the look of utter confidence; women literally were all over him. He could have any woman of the house, and for as much as he desired. The ladies were at his disposal, throwing themselves at him, laughing and teasing, and while Joe was sex-starved, begging for female attention, Halil's problem was how to contain the flood of sex invading him from all sides. He definitely had a secret, and it took Joe only a few minutes to determine to find it out Halil's secret ways.

"I am Joe" he introduced himself to the dashing Ottoman.

Grandfather Halil was startled as he turned his head to look at the foreigner. He knew only a few words in English, learnt casually in the Armenian quarter in the past. The ladies themselves learnt English, on the job so to speak, while plying their trade. There seemed to be a parallel expansion of the sex trade and the British administration, as more British arrived on the island, so also was the demand-driven sex trade. The British had the bucks and the Armenians the supply of young ladies. Grandfather provided the critical link.

Halil became Joe's coach in the finer arts of sex. He took Joe's hand and they smiled and exchanged a few words, some which was even understood. It was evident that a warm friendship began to unfold.

The next evening, Joe and Halil were at the same location and this time Halil decided to invite Joe to join him at one of his favorite bars in town. Joe enjoyed the Turkish meze, and kebabs, which reminded him of the Malay *satay*, but he especially like the Cypriot wine, full bodied and aromatic. Halil's favorite was *raki*, but Joe found it too sweet and preferred his Cypriot wine.

"I like job" Halil indicated in one of their early conversations and, after some initial difficulty, Joe got the message that his Ottoman friend was looking for a job.

"Do you want to be a policeman?" asked the Anglo-Asian and with nods and body signs, interspaced with broken English, the deal was struck and within weeks Halil joined the force as a *zaptieh*, the Ottoman equivalent of the police.

In those days, banditry was common in the countryside, and the Cypriot peasants were hard-pressed to choose between bandits and *zaptieh* because both had to be paid. Often one or the other would help themselves to the flock of the shepherds and roasted *kleptico*, the kebab of the stolen sheep, was an island-wide favorite.

On the day that Halil was staging his elopement with Elana from Kormacit back to Nicosia, Joe was in the midst of a delicate assignment. A British group of notables, on tour of the island, in a series of ox-driven carts escorted by the Deputy Resident, had been way-laid in the mountain passes just west of Kyrenia en route to Lefke, the citrus garden of Cyprus, some twenty miles across the bay from Kormacit. A gang of highway robbers had ambushed the British tourists, stole some personal jewellery and it was Joe's assignment to catch the thieves and recover the jewellery. And, it had to be done fast.

"Good God" said his boss, the Superintendent of Police, "what kind of island have we got here? Joe, let's teach the natives a good lesson in British law and order."

And to drive his point home, he added: "Lets do it quickly." He wanted to impress his own boss the Deputy Resident who was personally escorting the touring party. In those days, around the turn of the century, it was fashionable amongst the British upper classes to go on extensive holidays in the exotic and mysterious East, which meant territory beyond Venice and Rome, to the land of Pericles and Plato, in search of Ancient Greek legends. The more adventurous would venture further eastward into Ottoman lands, the Holy Land, sometimes on land on religious or archeological missions. Luxury-seeking travelers preferred cruising on yachts, in ultimate comfort in eastern Mediterranean around Cyprus, the new addition to the British Empire. Land travel was always risky on dangerous roads more in control of robbers and bandits than the police.

That is precisely the fate that befell the Ramsbottom party in Cyprus. The robbery itself was an expert job. The location of the ambush was perfect because the bandits knew the area well and their plan was simple: Wait for the British party at the top of the long and winding uphill road at the crossroad, linking the three highways, one coming from Nicosia and the other uphill from Kyrenia. At the cross road the highway branched sharp to the west toward Pineview and the foothills of Kormacit, and then beyond all the way to Lefke, which, on a clear day, could be seen on the western end across the big blue bay. The British party was traveling by cart, escorted by the Deputy Resident assisted by two *zaptieh*, on horse but lightly armed with two ancient guns barely serviceable, of Crimean vintage.

The bandit chief and his band were old hands at this kind of operation. Besides they had inside knowledge. The chief had been tipped from friendly *zaptieh* in the capital, two days earlier that a rich group of British holidaymakers were due to travel into the area, coming from Kyrenia, almost certainly passing through the crossroad en route to Lefke. They moved into position, encircling the junction, hiding behind the pine groves and bushes on all sides, their horses well fed and rested, ready to make away at an easy pace down the winding road toward the sea and back around the coast toward Kormacit and then onto Gemikonak, the little port town situated just below Lefke on the slopes and in front of the ancient Roman ruin of Soli with its majestic amphitheatre still quite serviceable.

The English party arrived merrily on at the crossroad and bandits attacking from all four sides easily overpowered them.

"Hands up" yelled the chief of the bandits, using all of the English he knew, and everyone in the party, including the two hapless *zaptieh*, complied with no fuss.

The job was done expertly and quickly. Within five minutes the robbers galloped away and disappeared among the pines of the long and winding road down the hill toward Kyrenia. Then the robbers turned westward, heading west, as if they did not wish to be too far away from the British party.

The British travelers were inconvenienced, but no one was hurt or harmed. The men were rudely shaken and the British ladies hardly noticed what had happened. It happened so quickly, everyone told as directed by the bandit chief. The robbers moved in quickly, they knew what to do, and did it with amazing speed. Within minutes they were gone.

The object of the robbery was a diamond broach of Lady Ramsbottom, undoubtedly the most expensive jewellery worn that day in

# DISGRACED

the traveling party. It was a big and brilliant broach, filled with diamonds and rubies. It had a greater value because it was a royal gift, given to the Lady at the Palace by Queen Victoria herself. Lady Ramsbottom was no ordinary female traveler. She had an important lineage. She was the cousin of Lady Nisbet, Countess of Elgin, whose husband, the British envoy to the Ottoman court, had amassed a huge fortune from carting off ancient Greek marbles and antiquities to England. That sort of thing, of course, was exciting, adding spice to the fun of travel, with no custom formalities and too many willing officials in Greece and Turkey to look the other way if the price was right. What was important was the end result: Fortunes, whether from Ottoman lands, India or Malaya, ended up in aristocratic hands in merry England.

Now, at the time of the robbery in Cyprus, the Lady was the wife of a decorated colonel, Robert Ramsbottom, for distinguished service fighting the wild Afghan tribesmen in the Northwest of India in his earlier days. At this moment in retirement, the colonel and his relatives and friends were touring Cyprus, thanks to connections back home through the old boys' network. The decisive factor in the robbery was the personality of the colonel's no-nonsense wife. No one, least of all, the colonel could prevail over her Ladyship who was more attached to her broach than to her husband or anyone else. Her royal gift meant everything to her

The other thing about Lady Ramsbottom was that she was a snob. She loved pomp and circumstance. In that respect she was a true Victorian. "Robert, darling, we must travel in the comfort we are used to, mustn't we?" she declared when the tour was decided. So, to finance their travel of Cyprus and the Greek islands, the prudent colonel had drawn a bankers' draft for a princely sum of 5,000 pounds from his London bank in favor of the Ottoman Bank, Nicosia.

This Bank was Ottoman only in name; it was as British as Queen Victoria herself. It had been set up to pay the British bondholders, owed a mint by the Ottoman Sultan who some years ago had declared bankruptcy. The British government then did some fancy financial accounting channeled the rent for the occupation of Cyprus, which still was nominally an Ottoman possession, to the bondholders that, of course, included the good colonel. That was not all. The British, through extra creative finance, taxed the Cypriots to raise the 92, 000-pound annual rent and when it was discovered that this was inadequate for bondholders' the British administrators placed all the revenue from the Muslim trust agency, *Evkaf*, into the Ottoman Bank at zero interest, in effect taxing the Muslim community of the island for a second time.

Lady Ramsbottom, of course, had no interest in these intricate financial manipulations. Now, taken hostage by some wild Cypriot bandits, all she cared about was her broach. The old lady wanted her broach back and that was all that mattered.

She would hear nothing more on the subject. "You simply must get it back to me. I don't care how," she declared, while turning to the Deputy Resident to ensure he heard her as well.

"Robert, I won't hear another word on the subject. Use your connections," she ordered, looking straight at the Deputy Resident, and her husband had no choice but to comply. The Deputy rose to the occasion and reassured her:

"My dear Lady, rest assured we will catch the thieves in no time. I will personally issue the order to the police. This is a small island." And so it was done.

The problem of organizing a search party ended up on Joe's desk.

That is when Joe Smart desperately needed Halil. His local knowledge of the area and his help in launching a search party to go after the bandits were crucial for success. He sent for Halil, ordering the peon to go straight to Halil's house on Tanzimat Street to fetch the *zaptieh*.

The peon was instructed: "Tell him, his leave is cancelled. Something urgent has come up. I want to see him immediately. Off you go."

That is how Grandfather Halil's well-laid plans for a smooth landing of his lover at his Tanzimat street house were upset.

# VII

It was just after midday and hot in mid-July when Grandfather and his lover arrived at the Tanzimat house, exhausted but well fed thanks to a hearty lunch of *kleptico*, the local delicacy of roasted lamb at a highway restaurant at the village of Gonyeli some five miles northeast of Nicosia. They entered the city through Kyrnia Gate, still guarded by Ali the Cock, the imposing Ottoman official who controlled incoming and outgoing traffic for one reason only: to collect money, ostensibly for the Sultan, but in fact, for himself and his Sheik, the master of the Shrine of Whirling Dervishes not far from Kyrenia Gate. Grandfather was a close friend of Ali the Cock, his drinking buddy, and he showed his customary friendship by allowing the driver to pass through the gate free of charge.

When they arrived. Grandfather's Tanzimat house was transformed into a prison with two kept women, my Grandmother downstairs and Elana, the newcomer, upstairs. The arrival was unnoticed. All was quiet. Grandmother preoccupied with my mother in her arms, did not notice the arrival upstairs. Hardly five minutes had passed after Grandfather and Elana had moved in and were getting ready to settle down. There was a loud knock on the front door when a peon from the police headquarters appeared, looking agitated but glad to see Halil. He delivered the urgent message:

"The Boss wants you at the station immediately" the peon blurted out. "He says your leave is cancelled; something very important has come up. You must come with me."

"Blast" he said annoyed. Grandfather was looking forward to a day of rest and recreation with his new woman. He needed time to explain Elana to Emine as a temporary helper. He was confident he would be able to persuade Emine into active cooperation. "After all, it is temporary until your mother comes" he planned to say to his wife. Now his plan was ruined. He had no time to put it into action. All he was able to do was to take Elana into the upstairs bedroom.

"Damn it" Halil cursed as he realized he had no choice. He began putting on his uniform. He jumped out of his Ottoman garments, throwing off his baggy pants and his muslin shirt, and putting on his dark blue pants and jacket. Finally he put on his English socks and boots and he was ready.

In his rush, Halil did not bother to go downstairs to see his daughter or wife. "I'll speak to Emine, later" he said to himself. He was too much in a rush to worry about such small details.

As he was stepping out of the front door he spoke a few words with Elana.

"I will bring some dinner as soon as I can" is all he said to Elana. The young girl, taken aback by the surprise visit of the peon, nodded her head in approval. She was quite tired from the ride and sunk into the bed to rest. Soon she fell asleep.

*\*\**

It took Lieutenant Joe Smart the whole afternoon to organize a police posse of three, made up of Halil plus Sergeant Kazim, an English-speaking member of the force and himself as the chief of party, for the manhunt in the rugged mountains of Lefke, near the ancient copper mine at Karadag. The time for departure in pursuit of the bandits was fixed at evening the same day. The plan was to move quickly in the cool of the night and catch up with the bandits before they were able to dispose of their loot.

The Leuitenant's plan gave Halil just three hours to get ready. They were to meet at the police headquarters at six and depart at 7.30pm.

Halil made good use of his free time. First he went shopping to buy some *hellim,* local cheese, bread and olives and some fruit for Elana. He did not worry about his wife or baby; that was Emine's business. He had other things on his mind to worry about. When Halil was gone to the headquarters, Elana had a nap, and she was rested when her lover returned with food for her. They barely exchanged words.

"Elana, I have to be away for the next few days, but here is some food." Halil said. Food was the last thing on Elana's mind. She looked at him longingly, said nothing because her eyes said it all and he responded for they could wait no longer.

It began with a warm embrace, kisses and hugs and soon their love for another turned into uncontrollable torment, like a volcano waiting to erupt. Words were neither required nor said on this occasion of lovemaking. The two lovebirds spent the ensuing hours in blissful embrace reaching ecstatic heights fit only for angels in paradise. As their bodies moved in perfect harmony on the big wooden bed, they were both so captivated by the pleasures of their senses that they were totally oblivious to the moans and creaks of the bed.

Grandmother was right below downstairs, my dear mother fast sleep next to her. The moaning and creaking from upstairs was at first mysterious and Emine paid no attention. She had been breastfeeding the baby barely an hour ago, and now both, exhausted, lay next to each other, in a delightful slumber. The creaks persisted, in strange rhythm, as if someone was heaving and sighing, not quite crying but then she noticed voices that belonged to two persons, not one.

Then she was startled and suddenly jumped in her bed. There was a female voice, clear and strong, no mistaking that, a woman with a man, both saying sweet nothings to one another. Emine could not believe her ears.

"My Allah" she exclaimed to herself. "What is going on up there?"

Then, like a thunderbolt, she heard her husband. It was definitely him. "My love, my beautiful pet" he was saying, loud enough for Emine to hear. "I cannot live without you."

It went on for an interminable length of time. This horrible thing, this act of betrayal seemed to last for ever. The bed was about to crush and come falling down over Emine and her baby. She grabbed her baby to protect her, and her embrace woke the baby, and my poor Grandmother was confused, unsure what exactly was happening to her, as her mind was wondering between protective thoughts of her baby and her husband upstairs making love to some unknown female. Of Grandfather's infidelity she was now sure.

But she needed proof. So gingerly and with fear gripping her, trembling and unsteady, she climbed upstairs. The door was closed but unlocked and she took a peep in, barely making out, her husband in the embrace of a naked woman, right here in her own home.

At that moment Grandma's world suddenly was ruined. Her nest, her home was destroyed. An indescribable feeling of shame and humiliation came over Emine. She felt dirty, unloved and rejected. She was frozen for an instant, right where she stood and she rubbed her eyes as if she was seeing a dream she could not bear.

In shock and disbelief, Grandmother tiptoed silently back downstairs to her baby. Tears started to drop from her eyes, she was crying in private. Time passed, for how long she did not remember.

Then suddenly Grandfather, with a false air of authority, stood in front of her bed. He pretended to be in full control. But his secret was out. The schemer was trying to cover up his misdeed. Grandma Emine, holding baby Aygul ever so closely to her chest as if my mother was in some serious danger of being snatched away by an evil person, felt a mixture of shame and jealousy; she did not want to share her husband with another woman. She knew about polygamy and how husbands kept women, but that was not what Grandmother wanted. She wanted her husband all to herself. At that moment, both husband and wife knew they stood at a terrible turning point; Grandma's marriage was in mortal danger. Disgraced, she sank into a distressed silence.

"Emine, I have something to tell you" he began. But she would not acknowledge him. Poor Grandmother, she must have been devastated. She kept her pride and played coy: She wanted to scream out, "I want you to myself, I do not want another woman in the house", but instead she buried her head under the bedcovers, overcome with shame. She was too embarrassed to look at him.

The hedonist knew it. But, masterful at his plundering, he put on a show of cool detachment.

"I have brought a young woman to take care of you until your mother comes." He stood there, waiting for impact. She responded in utter silence.

He looked at her, but she remained motionless, too ashamed to say a word. She buried her head under the cover. He went on: "I will explain everything later. I have to go to the police station on urgent business. " Still no word from Grandma. She was in shock.

And with that he turned back and walked out of Emine's room.

By six pm Halil was back at the police headquarters, confident that his plan was working. "Everything is under control," he said to himself. He was tragically wrong.

When, at the appointed hour, the posse set out for Lefke, Halil's head was full of the pleasurable thoughts from the afternoon's lovemaking. He was on top of the world; all was well in the age of liberty, he reflected, as the posse started their journey to capture the bandits.

It was a cool evening in July, as they set out, the sky full of stars above. Their plan was to travel all night and reach Lefke by midday or afternoon the next day. Traveling in those days was a slow affair, with lots of breaks for tea and food for men and animals. There was no particular rush, all knew that at the end British justice would be done and the bandits caught. It was only a matter of time.

# VIII

The next day, as Lieutenant Joe's posse set out chasing the bandits in Lefke Mountains, Katrina and Elias Ayoub traveled to the office of David Read, the District Officer in Kyrenia. The British had their own system of justice in the island now. The old Ottoman *Millet* system was gone. Where, before each religious community had a *Milletbasi,* headman, who administered justice and settled local disputes, now the British installed a District Officer for dispute settlement. The problem was that the District Officers, DO for short, were inexperienced and the local people were still very Ottoman in their ways and outlook.

Elias and Katrina were social outcasts in Kormacit, without friends, Ottoman or other. Naturally, they turned to the British justice system as soon as they discovered Elana's abduction. Without delay, the father and mother dropped everything the next day, and off they went to Kyrenia in search of British justice.

In truth, Elias was feeling a little guilty over the quarrel with his daughter. "If only I had been a bit gentler with her, maybe she would not run away" he argued, but Katrina would hear none of it. "Don't say those silly things. Elana had been acting strangely for quite some time, and that is why I wanted to give her something special for her birthday." After a moment, she added with uncommon realism that was her mark: "That was yesterday. Today we must do whatever we can to help our Elana."

# DISGRACED

It was a hot and sunny day. Katrina was riding the donkey and Elias walking besides. After three hours of journey through the passes and pine forests of the Five Fingers Mountains, the sharp peaks to their right and the blue Mediterranean to left, they reached the sleepy town of Kyrenia, the district headquarter, climbing the steps into the office of the DO in the impressive stone building overlooking the beautiful Venetian castle and the harbor. At the back rose the imposing Five Fingers Mountains and Nicosia on the other side.

The Ayoubs formally brought charge of abduction against Halil, their daughter's lover who had, the day before, staged a daring but successful raid into Kormacit and got away with their only daughter. The parents were horrified, shocked and dishonored by the whole ugly affair. They were here to demand British justice.

Katrina, the more outgoing parent, put the case to the DO:

"We were harvesting in the fields, and our daughter was at home alone" she began recounting the details of abduction to a perplexed DO. "It happened in broad daylight in front of all neighbors. It was such a shameful thing to do." Read, in his mid-forties, and newly appointed official whose job was to ensure law and order in the district of Kyrenia, in which both Kormacit and Pineview happened to be located, listened in amazement.

The DO looked at the Ayoubs, not quite sure he was hearing correctly, distress written over the parents' innocent faces. He had been in Cyprus barely a year, replacing his retired predecessor who had come shortly after General Wolseley lowered the Ottoman flag in 1878 and raised the Union Jack, delivering Queen's justice to the people of Cyprus. All this time the new rulers had heard no such a thing as abduction.

"We cannot allow abduction under British law" he declared solemnly. He splashed some official papers in front of the distressed parents and comforted them with words he thought appropriate for the occasion:

"Justice, I promise you, will be done." The British officer said. "But, first you have to fill this report and sign it. Then I will ask the police to carry out an investigation." It all sounded highly bureaucratic. The Ayoub family was desperate for urgent action.

"But Halil is a policeman" Katrina blurted out.

"What!" exclaimed the DO. "Good God. That is impossible. How can it be?" He then added excitedly:

49

"These Ottomans, they are no better than animals." It was the voice of exasperation.

The DO recovered in a moment. He regained his official control and realized that the British were in Cyprus, technically an Ottoman territory, on borrowed time. The Queen had rented the island for 92,000 pounds from the Sultan and his law was, for Muslims, the law of the land, like it or not. That meant, Halil was under the Muslim law, *Shari' at*, that governed personal and civil matters, although as a policeman, he would come British law.

"Halil is a Muslim... " Declared the DO with some discomfort... "And I suppose is entitled to four wives", his words confirming the worst fears of the parents.

"You mean our dear Elana will become a second wife?" Katrina asked alarmed, as Elias added, "or maybe third or fourth?"

"I do not know," replied the DO. "But I daresay it is not impossible. We have to find out."

"What if Halil claims Elana is a second wife?" inquired Elias.

"Then, I'm afraid, things can get messy," said the DO. "We have to consult the *Kadi*, the Muslim religious judge and find out what is the legal situation. Of course, we can take disciplinary action against Halil for his misconduct, but kicking him out of the police would not return your daughter. It appears she went off with the scoundrel willingly." The parents looked puzzled, their faces blank.

"You sign the affidavit and I'll check things around with authorities in Nicosia." But he played safe, warning the couple not to expect miracles: "It will take some time, and it may not amount to much."

After leaving the DO in Kyrenia, the Ayoubs sank into a dreadful state of helplessness. Their mood matched the weather which suddenly turned stormy, dark clouds appeared from nowhere, surrounding the tips of the high mountains around Lapta as the dejected couple journeyed back, convinced the God-fearing Christians of Kormacit would show no mercy on the poor Ayoubs. A sinking feeling came over them. They paid no need to the storm that was brewing over the dark green Mediterranean on their right. They were lost deep in bitter thoughts and uncertain future that lay ahead. One thought dominated both parents as they silently walked over the moors and valleys toward their empty abode in Kormacit: Their daughter was gone; there was no one who could help them to get her back.

As a social historian of the Ottoman period, I have a good sense of the humiliation the Ayoubs must have felt in the small society of Kormacit. Outwardly serene and well-ordered, families in Ottoman villages were expected to keep their daughters, especially marriageable teenagers, under strict control to preserve family honor. Daughters represented family honor and it was the parents' responsibility to keep them pure and virginal until a marriage could be arranged. Anything less was disgraceful and now the Ayoubs were a family disgraced.

I was particularly sympathetic toward Katrina. I felt she was far smarter than her husband and it was initially her idea to seek British justice to get Elana back. Now her confidence in British justice was shaken by their interview with the DO. But Katrina had a deeper, darker fear, beyond the bitter fact of a lost daughter. She now began to realize that they were a family in deep trouble in Kormacit: Katrina's mind was a jungle of conflicting emotions and pain. She could not decide which the greater pain was: The loss of her daughter was something she could not accept, but she also knew that the social shame and stigma they would face in Kormacit would be enormous. The simple, but highly conservative Maronite community did not approve scandals of this kind besmirching their public honor. The Ayoubs, marginalized as it was, would now be held responsible for their daughters' misadventure. The parents would be blamed for the elopement of their daughter. She was, in law and custom, their charge and they, as parents, had failed to protect her – and most important of all, to safeguard the community honor. The Ayoubs had proved by their misdeed that they did not fit in. It was that simple.

# IX

Meanwhile, another drama was unfolding at Grandfather's harem in Nicosia. While Elana was fast asleep upstairs, and barely minutes after Halil returned to the police headquarters, Grandmother, with my mother in her arms downstairs had a visitor. Her Armenian neighbor and midwife, Mariam (or Meryem as Emine used to call her), came back visiting and checking up on her. The kind Armenian midwife sensed that things at the Tanzimat street house were not as they ought to be.

Mariam found Emine crying. "Heaven forbid! May Allah protect you, my dear child. And you have just given birth to such a lovely baby. You should be happy. What is the matter?" Mariam was chatting away excitedly.

"I want to die," said Emine quietly, sobbing, unsure and shaking.

"My dear, what is the matter? Are you not going to tell me?" Mariam sat on the only chair in the room, pulling it next to the bed.

Grandmother looked straight at Mariam's old face, excitement written over it, and slowly she let it out:

"Meryem Ana, my mother, Halil has betrayed me. He brought a woman upstairs last night. I am so ashamed I want to die." It was a devastating admission, a terrible confession by a woman rejected by her husband. In those days, with polygamy as the rule, it was by no means unusual for a man to bring a second wife, but still for poor Grandmother, the only daughter of an Aga, it was a humiliating admission.

# DISGRACED

The Armenian mid-wife had seen enough dreadful things in her own days. Nothing, anymore, shocked her. All she could do was offer sympathy, some words of comfort.

"Men are scoundrels," the old woman said. "May Allah give you patience and wisdom, my child. Don't do anything rush. Men are beasts; they do awful things to women." She sighed and continued, "Look at me, my child. This old woman you see, she has gone through so much hurt and suffering." She then recounted her life story, hoping in the process to lighten up Grandmother's burden of shame.

"When I was young and beautiful we had a comfortable life in Kayseri, my father owned a sausage factory and he was a good provider; we were respected by all, Armenians and Turks. Then our youth started secret societies to fight the Sultan. I was foolish and young and madly in love with one these fighters and I followed him to the forest. It was a life of banditry, living off the land. Some of the Armenian bands were Hunchaks, like Russian revolutionaries set to create a communist order, others were nationalist Dashanks, but all were oppressing the ordinary folk, seeking money, food and clothing and other things all in short supply. Our band robbed peasants and travelers, and in some cases, we killed innocent people. It was kill or die."

Emine looked on in amazement. She knew nothing about Mariam's past. She listened as the old lady carried on:

"You know what the worst part was?" Mariam asked and Emine, with a worried look on her face asked: "What?"

"It was in the evenings, usually after drinking. Men would take turn to have their fun with me. They were animals, supposedly patriots. It was awful, but I could do nothing about it. I was a prisoner." There was silence. Emine looked on at Mariam's face and she could identify with Mariam's pain.

"Then one day I met Aram, my husband. He was not like the others. He was kind and took pity on me, I guess. In time, we became close friends and slowly we decided to get married, settle down and return back to normal life."

"What did you do then?" asked Emine, temporarily absorbed in Mariam's story.

"Aram and I decided to abandon the group and stop our fight against the Sultan. Of course, we could not go back to Kayseri; the gang would come after and kill us. So we decided to push on to Izmir and we finally got a boat and came to Cyprus to live under the British.

That was twenty years ago. Aram died soon after we landed in Famagusta, killed on the job. He was working for the British, something having to do with the Suez Canal. He was dismantling stones from the old Venetian ruins and the moat to take them to the Suez Canal when he fell from the scaffolding. You know, the British came to Cyprus in order to trade with their colonies in India. They were not really interested in Cyprus. So poor Aram was gone and I was left alone at 35, and men showed interest in me and paid me for my company and charm."

She paused and pondered, Emine listening in silence. Mariam resumed her story,

"Emine you have a roof over your head. I know how you feel, but don't do anything stupid. May be it is a temporary flame; it may go away tomorrow. Men do stupid and mean things to women. But we have to be tough and endure."

"What are you saying?" said Emine. "Shall I sit and watch my husband make love to some prostitute upstairs while I sit here with our baby? Is it not enough he is always womanizing outside my home?"

"What a disgusting thing to do" she thought to herself, but said nothing to Emine, not to inflame her even more.

Emine went on in agony: "I can't stand it. I will go mad" She spoke so harshly, the baby woke up.

"No my dear child" said Mariam as Emine picked up her baby and cuddled her in her bosom. "Show a little patience. Wait a day or two. Allah always plans for tomorrow."

# X

It is offensive and painful for me to write about it now, about skeletons in our family cupboard. But a social historian is no less a scientist than a physicist. There are rules of ethics that guide professional research, including family history such as ours. I feel duty bound to tell it all, to let the ugly truth come out. That seems to be to be the only way to understand my mother's tormented life.

In trying to understand our family secrets, I came across many shocking events and mysteries. One of the most bizarre involved a Jewish conspiracy centered on Davud Kahin, Grandfather's merchant neighbor. Davud was a secret Jew, a *donme,* a convert to Islam whose real name was David Cohen. He had come from Salonika, about ten years earlier. Davud was a small man on a big mission, physically undistinguished but a man with an idea committed to a grand mission. He was the youngest son of an Saphardic Jew who managed to escape from the Spanish Inquisition some three hundred years before and settle and prosper in Ottoman Salonika. There the Cohens went into some trade and made a success of it quickly thanks, in a large measure, to the *Sabetayist* movement, the secretive organization of converted Jews, outwardly Muslims but devotees of Sabetay Sevi who claimed to be the new Messiah sent for the salvation of the Jewish nation. In the late 19th century, in the aftermath of the Dryfus scandal in Paris, Herzog specified Ottoman Palestine as the future national

55

homeland of the Jews suffering from oppression in Russia and elsewhere in Europe.

The example of Sevi showed the way for the Ottoman Jews of cities such as Salonika. When the young and fiery Rabi proclaimed that he was the Messiah to create at last the New Jerusalem, he was brought before the all-powerful government of the Sultan and given a terrible choice: convert or die. He chose life, preaching his followers to do likewise, "Obey the Sultan... But never give up your heritage." The Cohen's became Muslim, changed their family name to Kahen, but otherwise carried on in trade and society as before. The *Sebatayist* Jews liked to join secret societies, such as the Muslim mystic *terikats* that sheltered them in their real pursuits.

Single and approaching mid-life, Davud Kahin joined the Zionist movement and became an active agent for the exodus of oppressed Jews trekking to Palestine. For this mission, beyond absolute secrecy, two things worked in his favor: Profits from a successful trade, and Arab nationalism. Not long after the British takeover Davud traveled to Cyprus, installing himself there, thanks to his business network, as a wholesale importer of Egyptian wheat to the island. But his real mission was to facilitate and finance the Jewish exodus. His timing was perfect. Davud received help from a most unusual source: viz. the Arab nationalists who, unwittingly of course, facilitated his cause. They all clamored and worked for the dismemberment of the Ottoman Empire. But, at the same time, these same Palestinians, especially rich and landowning elites willingly sold out to the Zionists, preferring the security of cash to the Sultan's protection.

Then, all of a sudden, in July 1908, Davud's peace was disturbed, his concentration diverted by Grandfather's womanizing. You see, after Elana's intrusion into my grandmother's life, the Ottoman neighborhood of Tanzimat Street was humming with gossip concerning Elana. Neighbors were shamed by news of two women in Grandfather's harem. Respectable families in the neighborhood were suddenly at risk: honor, that most precious public commodity was in danger of being soiled by the actions of none other than Halil Osman, the new policeman who should have known better.

"What shame! What is going on? What is going to happen to public morality?" The pious, good people of the neighborhood might soon demand to know. And, what then would happen to the good name of respectable tradesmen and businessmen?

# DISGRACED

\*\*\*

No one, it seemed, was concerned about Grandmother's wellbeing. She had become virtually a helpless bird captive in an Ottoman cage. Elana was no different. The two women would meet, face to face, infrequently and accidentally. Poor Grandmother, she was humiliated and terribly hurt, she knew she was losing her husband, her beloved Halil. She still loved him secretly, but, just at the moment of her glory when she gave birth to mother, she was virtually an abandoned woman. She knew of the woman upstairs, supposedly to be her temporary helper until her own mother would show up. But she knew better and realized that her husband was lying to her. She was betrayed, and the betrayal was eating her, like cancer slowly spreading inside her body, her torment and shame growing all the time.

"She is a prostitute" Emine thought, "She has no business being here." She was determined on that point. Her anger grew by the hour.

The encounter was brief and casual. It happened as Elana, the unwanted guest, slipped out of her voluntary imprisonment upstairs, to go to the only bathroom in the house, at the bottom of the stairs. Emine was coming out of the kitchen at that same moment. The two women exchanged momentary looks, like two lionesses in the same den. But the moment was long enough for Emine to notice Elana's cross necklace, testifying her Christian faith.

The encounter was finished almost as soon as it started. Emine's mind was confused in a mix of sharp anger and bittersweet kindness. She was angry that some other woman, unwanted and unwelcome, had intruded her nest, especially at the moment of her childbearing. At the same time, she experienced a strange feeling of jealousy for the beauty that stood before her momentarily. The woman she encountered surprised Elana, for her part and she rushed before Emine could collect herself. The brief encounter settled things in Emine's mind.

"She cannot stay here," Emine repeated to herself. She was resolved to confront her husband as soon as he came home. "How dare he bring in another woman into the house?" Emine reasoned.

She had no idea where Halil was at that point in time. He said he was on some urgent assignment. But, she hoped he would show up sometime in the evening. "I have so many questions to ask him," she told herself. As always, she was disappointed.

The evening came and went, and there was no sign of Halil. Emine kept waiting, her anger building up by the minute. She fed the baby and waited. It was ten o'clock and still no sign of Halil. She fed the baby at midnight, but her ears were upstairs listening in vain to the front door, hoping her Halil would at last appear, come down to visit her and explain everything to her satisfaction. No sight of Halil, only the pain of waiting. She looked at the tiny baby next to her and cried, warm tears coming down her cheeks slowly. Then early in the morning, she finally fell asleep.

***

When Mariam left Emine, she did not go home. Instead, she crossed the road and called on a mutual neighbor, Ayse, in her thirties, the second wife of Davud, the wheat merchant, one of the wealthiest in the neighborhood.

When his first wife died ten years ago, while he was barely 40, Davud married Ayse, the youngest daughter of a fellow merchant, and despite the twenty odd year's difference, it had been a happy marriage. Davud was physically rather petite, and not much was known about him, but he was wealthy. He dressed like a devout Muslim, and was an influential person in the community. Meryem had one thought: Perhaps Ayse might be persuaded to ask her husband to get Grandfather to mend his womanizing habits now that he was a father. Ayse's marriage had been a success; Davud was a respectable man, of considerable influence in the neighborhood.

As soon as Mariam entered Ayse's parlor, she began excitedly: "I fear bad things will happen in poor Emine's house. That husband of hers is up to no good, Ayse" the Armenian midwife began. Ayse was all ears, like all Ottoman women, she loved gossip. But she had to perform her duty as a hostess. She served Mariam coffee, followed by sour cherry in honey syrup, a local delicacy, all the while eager to hear more of the juicy details of Grandfather's harem.

"You don't say?" she interjected, encouraging Mariam to go on. "What happened?"

""Poor Emine, she gave birth to a lovely girl, and what does he do?" Mariam asked and proceeded to answer: "He brings in a young woman, likely an Armenian, and installs her upstairs, right above his wife and baby. Day and night they make love and poor Emine has to close her ears not to hear the moans and creeks above. "

DISGRACED

"Allah. This is serious" Ayse declared. "It is a bad sign. Did you say Armenian? That is awful."

"Halil is always in the Armenian quarter." Said the mid-wife.

"What about her parents?" Ayse inquired, thinking of Grandma's folks at the village.

She was thinking of the normal thing to do in these sorts of difficulties that often happened in those days in dysfunctional arranged marriages. The bride went back to her parents' home. But disgrace followed, as always the blame was placed on the wife. While the husband walked away and was free to remarry with no social rebuke or disapproval, the young woman was damaged goods, condemned to remain a spinster or, if marriage did happen, it would be socially inferior, like marrying to an elderly person, or a blind or lame man, more to provide physical care. Loving remarriages rarely occurred.

"Emine told me that her mother is sick and will come as soon as she is better. I do not know when that may be," said Mariam. Neither she nor Ayse knew of Halil's lies.

Ayse then said: "I know that rich Agas" and then she stopped. She had heard of wealthy landlords in Konaks with a harem full of kept women, *cariyes* and *odaliks*, and that sometimes they took several wives. But that did not apply to his neighbor, the lowly paid policeman.

"Halil is not a wealthy man. He is only a *zaptieh*." She added.

Mariam concurred: "Yes, of course. Something is very strange in Halil's house."

Then, the midwife came to the point:

"Perhaps your husband, Davud, could have a word with Halil." She said. "He is a man of influence in the neighborhood and Halil may mend his bad ways. Can you speak to him?"

There was silence, Ayse reflected on Emine's predicament. With her post-natal abstinence for 40 days, as custom required, she knew it would be difficult to restrain Halil's plundering. It was a man's world and Ottoman women accepted the facts readily. It was common knowledge that a man, healthy and with means, could obtain any number of women. There was a steady market in maidens of all colors and ages, Circassians, Abyssinians and Christians to satisfy this demand. The social disease at the time afflicted in particular the wealthy Agas; everyone knew but none dared to speak about it. Of course, Grandfather was no Aga, but he was handsome and at the top of his vigor, and, thanks to his monthly salary from the British, he had money in his pocket, at least some of the time. So, there was little check on his philandering life-style.

"I do not know what we can do," Ayse blurted out, with a pained look on her face. The poor woman was afraid to get mixed up with messy affairs, although, as a woman, she could identify with Grandmother's predicament.

Mariam got up to leave. "I must be off" she said. "I hope you do not mind me coming like this, but I feel a certain affinity for that poor child Emine. She is so strong and courageous." Said the Armenian woman.

"Oh no! I am glad you came," replied the hostess, in a gentle and sympathetic voice. And, almost, effortlessly, the words came out of her mouth: "I will talk to Davud."

Later on that evening when her husband came home, Ayse kept her word and recounted Mariam's story to her husband Davud the wheat merchant.

The trader happened to be in an unusually good mood that evening. It had been an unusually profitable day in the market. There was talk of war in Crete, where Greek nationalists were rioting for ENOSIS to join Greece and that never ending trouble with Armenians in the east, the price of corn was on the rise again, and Davud was confident that his recent acquisition of large quantities of wheat would pay handsomely in capital gains.

He listened patiently to his wife, and, as a gesture of civility, promised her that he would think about the matter. That was more than a quick dismissal and disapproval Ayse expected, like "Woman, don't get involved in others' affairs; it is none of your business."

# XI

The more he thought about his neighbor the policeman Halil, the more Davud was intrigued by Grandfather's hedonistic ways. He made some inquiries in the market, and discovered who Halil's drinking buddies were, where he enjoyed himself, and then, being, for all appearances, a religious person, he made up his mind that maybe there was something he might do to reform the philanderer and set him on the straight path. Davud's interest in Grandfather developed slowly in a curious manner.

The wheat merchant was, first and foremost, a careful man measuring everything according to his secret mission; he did not want to rush into a problem he could not handle or upset his carefully set plans. Moreover, he knew several wealthy men who had kept women in private harems. In those days, harems and wealth went hand in hand, and husbands always had female problems. But Halil was not wealthy. When he thought about Halil, it was not the fact of a second female in his house that troubled Davud; it was rather the possibility of a scandal in the neighborhood. The last thing Davud wanted was that his neighborhood would become a hotbed of immorality. That might upset the secrecy so essential to his work as an undercover Jewish agent. He had to do something about Halil before something regrettable happened.

Within the hour he made up his mind and informed his wife: "We have to do something to preserve the good name of our neighborhood. I will see what I can do." Ayse was pleased.

That very evening Davud acted on the matter. The wheat trader during the day happened to be a mystic at night. He was a devotee of the Sheik Ali at the Mevlevi *Tekke*, the Shrine of Whirling Dervishes near the Kyrenia Gate, not far from Tanzimat Street. This was a small secretive group of worshippers who believed in the power of meditation, of reaching divine grace and salvation of the soul through dance and music. It required great spiritual commitment and Davud found that speculation in wheat trading he was involved in during the daytime was best moderated by his nightly search of inner peace and tranquility through mysticism. It was an escape that made his profits in wheeling and dealing acceptable in his own mind and in the wider society. Davud, the successful wheat trader was at the same time a man of outwardly Islamic piety and that provided him with a wide spectrum of respectability along with secrecy demanded by his mission.

The *Tekke* then was run by two Ali's, the Sheik and the gatekeeper, both sharing the same name. Sheik Ali was a mystic, a devotee of Cellaledin Rumi, a man who preferred a contemplative life, isolated in his monastery during the day, and praying and whirling the nights to achieve divine ecstasy following the footsteps of the great Mevlena. He left the day-to-day running of the *Tekke* to the gatekeeper Horoz Ali, (Ali the Cock), a big lanky man, a ladies-man like Halil, always in a colorful Ottoman *shalvar* and *sash. B*ut what made people take notice of Horoz Ali was his imposing Ottoman beard and moustache that gave him a much more elevated standing than the mere door keeper that was his official title. Every night when Davud came for prayers Ali the Cock was there for the customary *selam*, bowing his head humbly half way down his big body and saying: "Davud Effendi. You bring honor with your presence." He was duly rewarded for his deference.

Afterwards Davud the wheat merchant would distribute the customary farthings to the beggars assembled near the gate. He would then go through the courtyard, enclosed with walls full of tombstones in beautiful Ottoman scripture, containing verses from the Holy Koran, and enter the room of worshippers, a specious floor covered with oriental carpets. Every worshipper entered the sanctuary after performing the obligatory ablutions, washing of the hands, feet and hands in the fountain in the courtyard, a spiritual cleansing before taking one's presence in the holy enclave inside. The chanting and

## DISGRACED

dancing, the *sema*, would follow, the novices performing the rituals of whirling, under the guidance of the headman, in harmony with the flute as the dancers circled endlessly until with dizziness they would enter a mystical world in search of divine unity. Davud and the rest of the assembled congregation would feel themselves liberated joined with angels and other souls seeking inner salvation.

After the ritual, there was always opportunity for conversation and exchange of news. Tonight Davud had a mission and he waited for the end of the ceremony to act. He sent word to the Sheik that he was donating a handsome amount of charity at the upcoming Festival and would appreciate a word with His Highness.

"Good evening, Your Highness" he began, as he was shown into the presence of the Sheik.

The holy man knew Davud well. He had a good name as a kind, gentle man at the shrine. He was known as a devout member, one who was not shy with his alms especially at the Festival of the Sacrifice. On other occasions, too, the wheat merchant would give generously. The crafty trader courted the Sheik's friendship with a carefully planned scheme; it was good for his trade and social standing. Halil's affair provided an opportunity to enhance his standing in the market as well as in the Tekke.

The Sheik, in his white beard and elaborate religious garment, most visibly his green turban, greeted Davud with a slight bow of his head.

"I seek your advice Your Holiness," he said.

"Only Allah can show the way" the Holy Man declared, "we can only listen to what He instructs through the heart."

Then, after a moment of silence, the Sheik continued:

"What is it you seek Davud Effendi?" He asked.

"It is a woman problem, Your Holiness," said Davud, unsure of the subject he wished to discuss.

"Come with me" said the Sheik with a surprising urgency, and the two went inside a private little office behind the courtyard. When the two were comfortably seated on Turkish divans neatly placed against the wall, the conversation began.

"Now, tell me the facts" the Sheik invited Davud.

"My wife tells me that our new neighbor, the *Zaptieh* Halil has brought a woman into his house" he said.

"Well what is wrong with that?" asked the Sheik.

"I am told she is a common woman. Halil is already married to a

## UZUN ALI, SHAME AND SALVATION

good wife, daughter of the *Muhtar* of Pineview. She has just given birth to a baby," answered Davud, the wheat merchant.

"Why do you say the woman is common? It is sin to make a false accusation. And, of course, every man can have up to four wives. That is the way of our Prophet, peace be upon him," declared the Sheik.

"I cannot be certain, but my wife informs me that Halil's woman is not a Muslim," said Davud.

"Then, she must convert to the true faith," ruled the Sheik with unusual certainty. Even in those days, conversions were uncommon. "Halil can keep this woman, but our Muslim law must be upheld."

"What do you suggest I do?" He asked.

"Tell Halil to come with you. I will explain the law to him," said the Sheik.

Davud was pleased to have the support of the religious man. He went home that night pretty satisfied that he had accomplished an important mission. His wife was already asleep, and he did not wish to disturb her. The news could wait.

What Davud did not know was Grandfather Halil's views on religion. Had he known anything at all about his policeman neighbor, he would have known that Halil had more in common with Horoz Ali than with the Sheik or Davud, the wheat merchant. There was no possibility that these two womanizers could be reformed or saved by religious persuasion.

# XII

In the real world beyond the *Tekke* and the Sheik, events unfolded fast, taking their own course. The British justice channeled through the Kyrenia District Office, unable to rescue Elana, worked remarkably fast in the hands of Joe Smart. It did achieve an amazing success in the case of Lady Ramsbottom's jewels. They were recovered when least expected, in the most surprising manner.

Joe Smart and his posse had traveled on horseback till midnight, over-nighted in the open in an orchard of oranges beyond the Greek Cypriot town of Morphou, and traveled again all day the next day. In late afternoon, they reached the harbor town of Gemikonak, a few miles north of Lefke on the coast overlooking the beautiful, crescent shaped bay, with Kormacit barely visible in the east, on the slopes of the Five Fingers Mountains. It had been a long and dusty ride through the rugged terrain, past the town famous for its orange groves, and now the posse was looking forward to an evening of rest and recreation.

They were to be hosted at dinner by Ahmet Bey, the custom officer at Gemikonak, not far from the abandoned Roman amphitheatre at Soli and under the mountaintop of Vuni, which, in antiquity, housed a Roman palace. When Cyprus was a province of Rome, it was renown for its copper mines, and the region then was prosperous. Now, it was all barren, overgrown with shrubs and thorns. The posse made slow progress. Their destination was the small Ottoman customhouse, and an inn for the occasional visitors was available nearby. There was also a famous fish restaurant serving local delicacies.

The police posse called on Ahmet Bey as planned. "Welcome, welcome" began the former Ottoman official, whose salary was now taken over by the British administration payroll. The friendly Ahmet was especially appreciative of the regular pay, in British pounds, enabling him and his family to live like royalty in the small community of Gemikonak. Ahmet had a reasonable command of English, thanks to his education in the English school, recently opened in the island by Anglican missionaries. For a beaurocrat, Ahmet was unusually astute observer of current affairs.

Not much happened in the community or at the port, which in earlier Ottoman period had served as a minor port. But in recent years this suddenly had changed because of rumors of American mining interests who, it was reported, would soon start exploiting the rich copper mines of Karadag near Lefke. The region had not only copper, but gold as well. Ancient sites and palaces, now in ruin, testified to past days of glory. At the moment, with a British-American investment project in the works, a new town was being built. Almost daily vessels were arriving from Greece, bringing in boatloads of people intended for employment in the mines.

Ahmet Bey, who saw the world from Ottoman lenses, was not happy about this development at all. In fact, he felt it was a British plot to change the demographic composition of the island and make it more Christian and less Muslim.

After the official ceremony of meeting and introduction, Ahmet Bey behaved as the perfect host and invited the party to dinner at Lame Yorgo's fish restaurant. "It is the best fish," he boasted. "You will enjoy it very good."

So, when the posse gathered around the dinner table at Lame Yorgo's later on that evening, there was no surprise about the quality and variety of fish. Everything was as good as the host had advertised, even better. What was indeed surprising was the subject of conversation. It was not, as might have been expected, about bandits and Lady Ramsbottom's jewels, but rather it was immigration.

"I do not like it" began Ahmet. "Everyday boats come in, bringing in hundreds of Greeks. They say the Americans are going to build a new town near us to house all these Greeks they are now shipping in."

"Why are they bringing these Greeks? Aren't there workers here on the island?" asked Sergeant Kazim who was a more recent graduate of the same English school and whose ability in English was the reason for his promotion in the police force.

"They say that local people are too lazy. They do not want to work in mines, deep in the ground. It is dangerous and dirty work," replied Ahmet Bey.

In fact, the local people were well off. The area was famous for its oranges and mandarins and everyone owned gardens and orchards from which adequate income was derived. So, much to the astonishment of the Americans and the British, the locals had no interest in becoming miners, however attractive the wages might be.

Joe, the Anglo-Asian knew something about mining, the tin mines in Malaya where he was born and spent his childhood. He got interested in the topic and said: "The British are experts in large-scale immigration. That is what they did in Malaya, where I was born."

"How so?" asked the curious custom official.

"Well," said Joe, "when the British developed the tin mines in Malaya, they went to China and brought in large number of coolies to do the dirty work. Later on, when they started planting rubber all over Malaya, they did it again, this time importing hundreds of thousands of indentured Tamils from India. All this development left the local Malay people isolated in poverty, cultivating rice and fishing."

While all this talk about mining and Greek immigrants was going on, Grandfather was getting bored. His interests were limited and his politics were local and Ottoman. These other topics, now under discussion around the table, were of little interest to him, and his eyes were focused on more exciting things like women, one in particular. Lame Yorgo and his wife were going back and forth, fetching food and drink from the kitchen for the party. Joe was already on his second bottle of wine, and Halil and the Sergeant were sipping *raki*. Ahmet Bey, teetotaler, was drinking freshly squeezed orange juice, boasting to anyone who would listen that Lefke produced the best oranges in the world.

"In ten years' time, this area will be rich," predicted Joe, and Ahmet Bey's ears opened wide. "How so?" he asked and declared: "May Allah be praised, we are not too badly off now, but more prosperity is always better".

"Well" began Joe, "once the mine starts operations and the town is built, new businesses will open, the company will build schools, a hospital and maybe even a golf course."

"What is a golf course?" asked the Ottoman.

"It is a game rich people play chasing a small white ball hitting it into a small hole quite a distant way away." said Joe. The party around the dinner table looked puzzled.

By this time, Halil's focus began to drift away from the table and got fixed on Lame Yorgo's wife, Eleni. No doubt, she was a good-looking woman, in her mid-twenties, wearing a skirt and a blouse around her slim body that made her look very attractive. She had a way of walking that, for Grandfather conveyed a message of seduction. He, as always in the cool evening with plenty of food and drinking, was at his best. That night it was Eleni who took the lead, and Grandfather was ready for her. It began with the strong and determined steps she took while serving them, then suddenly throwing a stare at him, then seductively shaking her well-formed bosom in the process, letting her breasts swing like two oranges on a branch. Her black hair was nicely done in a careful ring at the back of her dainty head.

Grandfather began to pay her closer attention, as she was bringing *kalamari*, red mullet and sea bass, and all kinds of other fish which Lame Yorgo had harvested himself that very day. Fishing was Yorgo's passion. He was gone fishing most of the day and at night he cooked and served the customers. He had nearly lost his left leg in an accident in a stormy sea while fishing some five years ago, in the second year of his marriage to Eleni. The accident had also damaged Yorgo's sex drive and poor Eleni was deprived, at her prime of the pleasure of the marriage bed.

It began at first quite innocently when Grandfather gave a friendly smile, but to his surprise she showed unusual warmth in her response. Eleni looked straight in Halil's eyes, suggestively. "She is a flirt" thought Grandfather at first, and as the conversation at the table drifted into esoteric places and topics, my sexy Grandfather developed more romantic notions in his head: "I believe she is available" he concluded.

Grandfather was a master when it came to women. As the rest around the feasting table talked politics, the old pro concentrated on enjoying himself, seducing and being seduced. In the following hour or two an emotional relationship blossomed between Grandfather and Eleni, quite unnoticed by others. By the time the dinner was nearing its end, some three hours later, Halil, the ladies man, smelt success. "Hey, when a woman is ready, it is sin to refuse" he said to himself quietly as he got up and went toward the washroom, next to the kitchen, signaling, ever so privately, to Eleni, who responded and followed.

"Meet you at midnight?" he inquired of the woman, and she nodded. "Come to the gate at *Solis*" she said quickly and precisely.

*Solis*, the Roman amphitheatre was right behind the restaurant, five minutes away. By eleven o'clock every one was fast asleep, tired from daylong traveling. Not Halil who was getting ready for the romance to follow. In the inn he washed and lay down on his bed for a short rest, and at fifteen minutes to midnight, as agreed, he walked to the entrance of the old Roman site.

Sharp at midnight, he spotted Eleni coming toward him and his heart leaped with excitement and anticipation. "I hope I am not late," she said as she got close to Halil.

It was a lovely summer night; the sky full of stars above and there was a gentle breeze from the ocean not far. One month later it would have been uncomfortable to be out in the open, mosquitoes and bugs making it impossible, but now in mid-July, it was a perfect night made for love.

"No you are just on time," he said as he grabbed Eleni's slim body in his strong arms and they started kissing with hot passion. It was obvious that Eleni had not had sex for months, and she was ready. Halil's charm had won her over and she was hungry for love.

They dropped on the old stage, where in ancient times Roman actors performed to standing ovation, but now Halil and Eleni had the entire stage to themselves for love that would have pleased every Roman god. It was a performance Aphrodite herself would have been proud. The lovers undressed in a desperate, urgent rush. It was as if this was their last chance and they had to use the moment to the fullest before their time was up. The demigods of romance were cooperating fully. There was a gentle breeze from the waves of the blue Mediterranean, the noise sounding more like an enchanting melody, and the full moon above with stars above scattered like pearls on the dark blue sky giving just enough light so the demigods could marvel at the beautiful bodies in the love act. Here was an Ottoman and a Greek woman, supposedly separated by religion and culture, united temporarily in passion, oblivious to the concerns of the entire world. In the land of Aphrodite, Halil and Eleni, two lost souls, in perfect harmony and understanding with one another, while Lady

Ramsbottom nearby, and the Sultan in faraway Istanbul, were obsessed about recovering lost possessions.

By dawn the two lovers were exhausted. Eleni had never before experienced such pleasure. She fell asleep, but only for a short time. The sound of roosters in farmhouses not far suddenly awoke her, and with fear and anxiety she put her clothes on, and rushed back to the inn on the beach. When she reached the inn she took a sigh of relief: All looked normal and quiet, everyone still fast sleep. Everyone, except Yorgo!

He was waiting at the door. "Where were you?" he demand to know. "I saw what you did, you whore" He was cursing and screaming.

"Be silent, you will wake up the neighbors" said Eleni.

"I do not care. You are a whore," he kept on shouting.

"You bastard, what do you expect me to do?" roared back Eleni. "You don't care for me. When was the last time you showed the slightest bit of interest in me? All you care is work, work and work. I am sick and tired of it." She went, passing poor Yorgo, right back into the house.

She went into the bedroom, locked the door and poor Yorgo was left all alone, standing in the garden.

Slowly Yorgo's anger subsided. "Poor girl" he admitted, "it must be difficult for her. No children, no sex." But his pride was hurt and he decided to do something about it. "I am not going to let that scoundrel get away with it," he said to himself.

The next morning, Lame Yorgo went early calling on Inspector Joe Smart and lodged a complaint. "Your *zaptieh*" he said, "took advantage of my wife and my handicap. It is a shame. I demand satisfaction," he stated.

The Inspector looked serious, but he did recollect catching a glimpse of romantic liaison between Halil and Eleni the night before. He was not sure there was much he could do other than feel jealous of Halil's conquest, and sorry for poor Lame Yorgo.

"Leave it to me and I'll speak to Halil" And, to pacify Lame Yorgo further, he added. "I am sorry for your predicament." Yorgo seemed satisfied with this apology as he walked away, his ego hurt, but helpless.

# XIII

I love the region around Gemikonak and Lefke, rugged and steep hills and mountains, rising out of the blue Mediterranean and stretching all the way back to the horizon inland as far as the eye can see. The area is full of mountains and valleys, not pine-covered like the Five Fingers Range around Pineview and Kormacit. These are the foothills of Troodos Mountains, rising to over 6000 feet at the snowy zenith, far away in the south. In those days, the only roads in the region were earthen paths passable by carts pulled by hardy oxen. Donkeys were for individual transport. Or, more often than not, people simply walked, to get from one village to the next, going through hidden pathways and mountain passes that only the locals knew.

The distance between Gemikonak and Lefke is merely two miles, as the crow flies, but it is difficult terrain. At first, as you leave Gemikonak, one has to negotiate a wide riverbed, full of brush and stones and rocks, brought down by flush floods coming from high mountains at the back. Then, there is a long slope, getting steeper and steeper, as one approaches Lefke, impossible to see as the whole town is sheltered inside a deep valley, covered on all sides with sweet smelling orchards of oranges, mandarins, almonds and pomegranates, with springs and water canals everywhere. It is a beautiful setting.

This is the area in which the hunt for Lady Ramsbottom's jewels was unfolding. The Midas robbers had the upper hand in the hunt

## UZUN ALI, SHAME AND SALVATION

because they had local knowledge.

Actually, the bandits who Joe Smart and his posse were looking for were close by all the time. The pursued was actually in pursuit. That was the trademark of Midas, the bandit leader. With the advantage of local knowledge and with speed as his asset, Midas, from a safe distance and always under the cover of trees and terrain, was constantly keeping an eye on Joe Smart's posse, while also checking on the party of the English tourists.

The other advantage that Midas possessed was his connections with the local peasants and villagers. In fact, he was well liked by the local communities because, in return for small payments often in kind, he gave the people the rudiments of law and order. He was a fair-minded bandit, had a peculiar pride in banditry, and had a well-earned reputation in the area as a straight man. Often he would show up at key weddings and festivals, joining in the fun and celebrating with the people. In turn, people felt closer to the bandit chief than to central authority, especially the distant British who were now replacing the Ottoman officials.

"I want to keep an eye on the British tourists" Midas would confide to his trusted lieutenants, "because they have more money than brains. They think they own this island now, and can come and go as they wish."

"Why do you say so Boss?" asked his lieutenant.

"Why because I can hold them again any time I chose." He said and then revealed his game plan, "But I want to stay near because when the right time comes, we will demand a hefty payment for the jewels in our possession. I am sure they will pay up." The other looked stupefied.

"These jewels are no good to us," explained the chief bandit. Midas had it all figured out. "You try and dispose them in the market, and you are dead as a duck. The police will get you. That is stupid."

The thieves looked at their Boss with surprise and respect.

"So what do we do Boss?" asked one of the bandits.

"You will see," said the chief. He had a sinister smile on his dirty face.

He was not going to reveal his game plan, not yet. He had a mysterious air of confidence. His men loved him for it.

They looked on as he declared with complete certainty: "At the right time we will get these filthy rich British to pay a King's ransom."

The bandits all cheered, as Midas relished his coming victory. It did not take too long in time.

# XIV

After his inconclusive interview with Joe Smart, Lame Yorgo returned to his kitchen. He was feeling dejected, and was in a sour mood. Soon, however, he was over it because within the hour, he had a visitor who demanded all his attention. Midas, the chief of the bandits, dropped in at Yorgo's unexpectedly. It was not the first time. In fact, Yorgo's business depended more on the goodwill of Midas than on official authority, Ottoman or British.

"Yorgo, look here" shouted the Bandit Chief with considerable authority, his big fat belly bursting out of baggy pants and Ottoman beard dominating his sun-dried face. "I am here on business," he declared. Lame Yorgo dropped everything and waited for instructions from the big man.

"Yes, sir, Boss." He uttered in obedience.

Midas was a classic, no-nonsense bandit whose word was the law around these parts. He was feared and revered all at once. Banditry was a kind of Robin-Hood culture and Midas was one of the most well known. He would kill at the drop of a hat for an offense he judged inappropriate, but at the same he had a rugged sense of fairness in his dealings with the ordinary people. Local poets wrote songs of praise for him, and his legend lived on; when the man died another bandit took on his name so the legend lived on.

"Look at this." He said to Lame Yorgo.

He placed on the kitchen table Mrs. Ramsbottom's diamond broach. It was a thing of beauty; brilliant and sparkling like a big, bright star on a dark night. Lame Yorgo had never seen such a big and impressive work of art before. He was dazzled by what he saw.

"Where did you get it?" He inquired gingerly, unthinkingly.

"Never you mind," said the bandit.

"Here is what I want you to do. Go back to that bastard British inspector and tell him I want one thousand pounds for it." Midas knew the movements of the police posse very well; they had been tracking it all the time.

Lame Yorgo's eyes almost popped out with the shock of such a princely sum. He had never heard of such a high ransom demand. A man could work all his life, and never dream of making so much.

In the next moment, Yorgo collected himself: "OK, Midas" he said. "I'll do as you say." Actually he was already beginning to feel good about evening the scores with the stupid British policeman.

"Tell me what to do and I will do it." He finally had a chance for revenge.

"We have to be fast" began the bandit chief. "Tell the inspector, he has two days to deliver the money. He gives it to you, you bring it to me and he gets back the broach at midnight following."

He had it all planned out in his mind. One day to notify higher authority in Nicosia, and one more to fetch it to Yorgo's restaurant. They had to be fast, or it was no deal.

"You will get 10 pounds for your services" Midas said, "and I appreciate your cooperation" as he disappeared out of the door.

# XV

Meanwhile, in the colonial capital Nicosia, it was stiflingly hot, still two hours before lunch and the siesta time to follow. No further upsetting events occurred for the top echelons of the bureaucracy since the departure of Joe Smart's posse to deliver British justice. Police Superintendent James was trying to keep cool, enjoying a brief moment of solitude in his office overlooking the central square, in the old Ottoman *Saray*, now converted into British central administration complex, with arches and verandahs that represented the standard colonial architecture.

At mid-morning the Superintendent's quiet was suddenly disturbed. The messenger came in and handed James a brown, sealed envelope. It was a file from the Kyrenia District Officer Read. "Good chap" he thought, recalling the chance meeting of the Superintendent and the District Officer a few weeks ago.

Superintendent James opened and started reading what was an official transcript of a private meeting the day earlier between the Ayoub family and the District Officer Read. James was immediately shocked by what he was reading.

"Good God" he yelled to himself, "an abduction case? What will happen next in this miserable place?" His shock was replaced by disbelief when he read on and discovered that the key person was a policeman in his own force.

At its critical passage, the report stated:

"A certain Halil Osman, apparently one of the new recruits to the police force, reportedly made a daring raid a couple of days ago into the girl's home and made away with her. The parents, who were absent at the time, came and personally complained to me, requesting my intervention to rescue their daughter."

The Superintendent stopped in disbelief. "How could a policeman do such a thing?" It was incredible. He read on:

"I informed the parents, upon discovering that the policeman is a Muslim, that the matter comes under Muslim law, but it occurs to me, and the parents have so stated, that since the accused is a policeman, then something should be done by his superiors before the matter goes any further."

Then the District Officer reported that the parents were decent looking Maronites from the village of Kormacit and the girl, a certain Elana, was barely 18, most likely a willing accomplice in the whole, nasty affair. He also warned some potential complications with the Muslim law, but James Read wanted a decision as soon as possible.

"Damn it" he shouted. His peace was disturbed, as the police chief was not happy about it. After a few minutes of reflection, the Superintendent decided to act.

"Who is this Halil fellow?" He called in his deputy and demanded that the fellow be brought to his presence without delay. The deputy ran out, and came back within minutes:

"Sir, he is away in Joe Smart's posse in pursuit of bandits who made away with Lady Ramsbottom jewels." He reported. "If we send for him, it will be late tomorrow at the earliest that he can be here. What shall I do?"

"Yes, yes," James said, "send for him immediately, post haste. I want to have a talk with him right away. Bring him in to my office as soon as you get hold of him."

When again alone in his office, James recalled his own women problems in Madras in India years ago when the Resident was dishonored and disowned for having secretly taken a Muslim princess for a wife. James had done the same thing himself; after all, it was common practice, every Tom, Dick and Harry did it, so long as, for appearance sake, one never officially admitted to it. That had been the difference between the Resident and James. Now in Cyprus, following his promotion in Her Majesty's Service, James was determined to run a clean police.

## DISGRACED

So a messenger was readied, post haste and dispatched to locate Inspector Smart's posse in Lefke and bring back Halil for an interrogation by Superintendent James.

# XVI

Earlier in the day, after a hearty breakfast, Joe Smart's posse had set out from Gemikonak. During the two-mile trip to Lefke, Joe had a talk with Grandfather as he had promised to Lame Yorgo. One thing I know very well about my Grandfather. When in trouble, he would first play cool, listen and keep quite, but when he was sure of his ground, he would get on the offensive. His self-confidence was supreme and, whenever he was sure of himself, his position was "attack is the best form of defense."

On that particular day, after a night of pleasure with Eleni, he was on top of the world. He was up, bright and cheerful, and he was ready to display his sense of duty to the Crown, and play his part in the chase under Joe's capable leadership.

"Halil I have something to say" he began, speaking very slowly and using body language to make sure he was understood "where were you last night after dinner?"

Halil realized that Joe, somehow, had come into possession of the details of his romance with Lame Yorgo's wife. He also knew that Joe was a sympathetic friend, secretly feeling jealous himself.

"I take Eleni, Lame Yorgo's wife walking," he admitted.

"I have to warn you Halil. Lame Yorgo came to complain that you seduced his wife. I just barely managed to stop him from making an official complaint against you. "

Halil objected, putting his hands crosswise. Joe knew that when it came to seduction, it was not Halil's doing, more the other way round. Somehow, Halil conveyed to Joe the fact that in Ottoman custom, it is sin to reject the advances of a woman.

Joe chuckled, and went on lecturing Halil: "You are a police officer and we the British; we have a funny sense of official duty. What you do in your private life is your business, but when you are on duty, you must behave like an officer. We represent the King" Joe ended his lecture, and Halil said nothing because there was nothing to be said. He was, however, pleased to be linked to the King. It gave him a sort of self-importance he had not realized before.

But one thing in Joe's words remained stuck in Halil's mind: His private life was his own business. It sort of tied in with his own philosophy in the new age of liberty he had now decided to make his own.

Later on the posse reached the Lefke police station in time for lunch.

In the afternoon, the posse finally began work at the local police station to plan chase of the bandits to recover stolen jewelry. They were given intelligence that the notorious bandit ring led by Midas was operating in the mountains in the area, and it was quickly concluded that Lady Ramsbottom's jewellery robbery was definitely his work. The problem for the police was logistical: The villagers were friendly to Midas and it might be useful to talk to them, but the villages were several miles apart and could be reached only on horseback. Finding the bandits was not going to be easy.

Then unexpectedly Lame Yorgo showed up. He went to Joe and said "I have a message for you" and without wasting any time, he added: "Midas wants one thousand pounds to return the jewels." As usual, his body odor was terrible. He was wearing the same old clothes. It was obvious he had not recently bathed or changed his clothes for a long time, nor had he bothered to wash his face before coming to see Joe Smart.

"What are you talking about?" Joe asked in amazement. And Lame Yorgo explained Midas' visit earlier that day.

"Do you accept? I have to report back," said Yorgo.

Joe had to do some quick thinking. He could lay an ambush around Yorgo's restaurant and try to kill or catch Midas. But he immediately dismissed the idea as too risky with just two untested Ottoman *zaptiehs*. He would be glad to close the stupid case and avoid trekking in difficult terrain, so he said:

"OK, I have to refer the demand to my boss in Nicosia. It will take time. How much time do we have?"

"Tomorrow midnight" said Lame Yorgo. "Midas wants the money tomorrow midnight at the restaurant. First the money and then he will hand back the jewel. Agree?"

Joe was, once again, in a dilemma. He had to decide fast. To get word to Nicosia would require sending a messenger traveling all night to get approval and bring the money in time for the rendezvous at midnight tomorrow.

At that moment, there was commotion outside and Superintendent's messenger was shown in. He came in exhausted, having ridden non-stop from the capital.

"Superintendent James wants Halil in his office without delay." All eyes turned on Halil. It was evident he was in deep trouble, whatever the matter it looked serious and urgent.

Joe Smart guessed it was some woman trouble again. And he wanted to return with Halil, but this matter of Lady Ramsbottom's jewels was proving to be a nuisance. "Damn the stupid royalty, they are always causing problems." He cursed at himself, not knowing where to turn next.

Then lady luck smiled on the English tourists. By noon, the Ramsbottom touring party rambled into Lefke, tired and filthy from all the dust and sweat. The last two miles from Gemikonak, up the steep hill to Lefke had been especially difficult, first passing through a stony riverbed, full of brush and scrub. All around there were steep hills, home of famous copper mines in ancient times and still containing rich deposit of the valuable ore. The riverbed was dry, but extremely wide. It would flood annually during winter when snow fell on the Troodos Mountains at the back and then flooding would render travel between Gemikonak and Lefke impossible. The entire region was ideal for banditry. It was Mida's favorite hideout. In fact at that very moment, as Joe Smart's party was negotiating their way through the difficult valleys and rocky riverbed, they had no knowledge of the fact that Midas and the bandits were hot on their heels, hiding and watching their every step.

The bandits kept a close distance, always discreetly hiding behind the trees and hills. In the last two days, the whole group, the bandits and tourists, as separate entities, had been gallivanting around all the ancient sites in the area such as *Solis* and the ruins of the palace of

# DISGRACED

*Vuni*. The tourists were looking forward to a restful night in the orchard town of Lefke, enjoying the famous oranges and mandarins of the gardens, and they planned to go on to the mountain heights in Troodos the next day.

But a surprise waited the party on arrival. Lieutenant Smart was one happy man when he saw the tourists pull in to Lefke.

"What a stroke of luck" he said and he immediately rushed to colonel Ramsbottom:

"Sir, we found your wife's jewels.... at least we know how to get them back."

"Capital, capital" yelled the colonel. "Well, where are they?" he demanded.

"There is a small problem of ransom, Sir," said Joe.

"Ransom, what?" blurted the colonel. The Deputy Resident looked on.

"Well, you see, Sir, the bandits who made away with your wife's jewels want one thousand pounds in exchange." The colonel looked at Joe's face, which was now pale and blank, with distressed look of disgust at the whole sordid affair.

"I am afraid we have no choice in the matter, Sir" he began. "These are dangerous bandits, and we do not have the men and time to go after them. I suggest your group discuss the matter and pay the ransom."

The colonel wanted to resist and argue, but at that moment his wife came over. "What is the matter John? You look distressed." She said.

"It is those infernal jewels of yours" he began, and realized he had said the wrong thing.

She was visibly upset, and was about to speak up her mind, but he was quick.

"It is your jewels, dear, the bandits have them, but they demand a ransom of one thousand pounds to return them."

That was it. Lady Ramsbottom would hear no more.

"Well, where are they? If they are recovered, let me have them" she declared. She added almost child-like: "I want my broach back. The Queen herself gave it to me. It is worth the whole world for me."

So Midas, the bandit chief got his ransom and the Lady her broach. The obliging Deputy Resident made the necessary financial arrangements.

# XVII

The storm, the final deluge was approaching, the end was near. In the Ottoman capital as well as in Grandfather's harem on Tanzimat Street things were out of control. The doomsday was near. Evil spirits were in charge.

In parliament, during the short-lived age of liberty, pandemonium was the order of the day. Armenian deputies demanded nothing less than their own country in the east; they were already terrorizing the local Muslim population. The Young Turk opportunists, whose secret societies had been formed on the Armenian model, were offering them autonomy, but that was not enough. The Arab deputies from Beirut, Damascus and Arabia, bought over by the sweet promises of support by the French and British agents, had their own demands for home rule. In the Balkans, Macedonia was in revolt, and the Serbs, Bulgarians, Albanians and the Greeks were all scheming for some version of greater homeland. The Ottoman elite in the capital was split into two groups, those aping the modern European ways, called *ala franca,* and the conservative pious households who stuck to time-honored traditions and customs, *ala turca.* While the traditionalists carried on in their harems, exchanging social visits in *selamliks,* strictly practicing female seclusion in their harems, all in outward demonstration of piety and to preserve family honor, the *ala franca* households indulged in gambling, drinking and other forms of decadence. As the motherland burnt all around, the Sultan cared solely for his throne, and the enemies from within and without schemed and competed with one another for a piece of territory.

My Grandfather mirrored this abnormal duality; he was a living paradox, combining decadence with an absurd sense of patriotism. Outwardly he was a modern Young Turk, so dashing in European dress, but privately he lived a life of a party animal, a perfect oriental despot seeking pleasure as if there would be no tomorrow. He was so preoccupied with his own sensual desires; he had no idea of the coming disaster his immorality had engineered. His unbounded self-confidence provided him with an artificial sense of security, an overwhelming sense of personal capacity to overcome all adversity. He was so wrong, it makes me want to cry as write now, so many years after the tragedy.

Grandfather's house on Tanzimat Street, with its stone façade, looked impressive from outside, but inside it was more like an oppressive prison. When Elana moved in it ceased being a home, and became an Ottoman harem. He shared his bedroom upstairs with Elana, so that his two kept women were literally one on top of the other.

Grandfather's two women stayed apart, like birds in separate cages, one kept upstairs and the other downstairs. An uneasy truce, a temporary peace prevailed, each female using the common bathroom and kitchen in turns while the other was in her own room. But sometimes encounters happened and the females were forced to share the same space. Then, bitter looks were exchanged, each rushing away like wild animals in the forest. It was a dangerous climate, an explosion waiting to happen. Elana did not behave like a servant girl, and Emine made her unwelcome.

Poor Grandmother was driven by jealousy and betrayal at her moment of triumph when, right after her first childbirth, she expected warmth and affection from her Halil. Her love was shaken; her husband was drifting away from her. "How could he do it?" Emine loved him dearly and wanted Halil all to herself: "Didn't he know?" These doubts and questions she could not answer. Of one thing she felt sure: This young woman was a seducer, and she had no right to claim what was hers and hers alone.

Maybe the wise words of Meryem, the midwife, spoken earlier, had had some soothing effects on Grandmother. Yet, she could not help it. Her heart was full of anger and revenge. Gradually the love in Emine's

## UZUN ALI, SHAME AND SALVATION

heart toward Halil began to turn into hate, but at the same time she realized her helplessness. Like an innocent victim wrongly imprisoned, she sat quietly in her room, feeding and looking after her precious Aygul, at least for now accepting her fate. She lived on dry foods like beans, stored in the kitchen and her health began to sink as her spirits.

Elana, after a blissful afternoon of lovemaking, finally woke up at around 10 o'clock, feeling hungry. She lit the lamp besides her bed and helped herself to some of the snacks Halil had brought her. She had not eaten all day. Then she stepped out of her room, to go to the bathroom, it was dark. She tiptoed ever so quietly walking down the stairs feeling unsteady.

Then, a baby crying in a room downstairs startled her. The door opened and Emine stepped out. For a moment, the two females looked at each other like two tigresses facing each other. Not a word was exchanged, simply stares. Immediately, Emine closed the door, but not before noticing once again the cross necklace around Elana's neck. The necklace, for some reason, seemed to swell the fury inside Emine.

Elana was confused, unsure of her ground and surroundings. She did not know what to make of Emine. She must be a stranger or a relative visiting with her baby. Halil had said nothing about others or a baby in the house. "He must have forgotten in the rush to get back to work" she reasoned her naiveté.

And, so Elana's predicament in the stone house on Tanzimat Street began to unfold toward a tragic end. She was unaware that she had walked, willingly and unknowingly, into a trap, a world of deceit that her youthful mind, full of love, did not comprehend. Poor Elana did not know that her lover, the man she trusted fully was an incurable philanderer. In the meadows of Kormacit she had seen only one side of him, the perfect prince charming, loving and caring.

When she went back to her room upstairs, she suddenly felt homesick. "I wonder what my mother is doing. Did my parents notice that I eloped?" she reflected. She had not had this feeling of loss before because she had never been away from them: True, she often stayed in her room for long periods in solitude, and she had never been very warm and loving with them, but she had her freedom to go and come whenever she felt like it. And, she enjoyed her walks in the meadows and valleys around Kormacit some times breathing in the smell of the pine forests, and sometimes sitting over the cliffs and watching the blue Mediterranean.

Suddenly, it dawned on her. It came like a thunder, shaking her inner soul with unaccustomed force: Elana was a prisoner; she could not go out. She was in a strange place; she knew no one. Dark thoughts entered her mind. For the first time in her life, she began to doubt herself and her feelings. All along, after her accidental encounter with Halil in the pine forest, the helpless Maronite girl had lived in a dream world peopled only by two lovers. Halil was the perfect Adonis, a worthy recipient of her virginity. And Elana pictured herself an angel of purity and innocence, entering the seventh heaven, where no evil spirits resided.

Then she heard footsteps outside. She got up and peeped out of her door. It was an elderly couple, an Ottoman gentleman and his woman, walking behind him, heading downstairs.

# XVIII

The visitors were Grandmother's parents. I do not know much about them and have not been able to discover much from family records. What I do know is that they were ordinary, simple decent folk, carrying on in the traditional Ottoman ways. Family life was all they knew, and their norm was that the wife should be submissive, dutiful to her husband, while all that was expected of him was that he should be a good provider. Occasionally, on religious festivals, the young would come paying the elders their respect, but at other times husband and wife kept pretty much to themselves, raising their children according to time-honored custom.

Now that poor Grandmother had given birth, it was expected that her parents would be dutifully informed. But no such news had arrived, and their visit was in reality a visit of concern. They came to check on her pregnancy for they were in the dark. Emine herself was taken by surprise as she had believed Halil's report that her mother was sick and would be unable to visit her for some time.

"Mother" she almost screamed delighted to see her parents "Are you well?" Without waiting for an answer, she went to her father, took his hand and kissed it, putting it on her forehead in dutiful Ottoman style of respect. "Look at my lovely little baby?" Her mother took the baby in her arms with pride, as Mustafa Aga looked on.

"My dear daughter" said the mother, rushing to kiss Emine lying in bed next to the baby. "No one told us you had a baby."

"Halil came to see you. He told me you were sick" she said to her mother, as her parents sat down in the two chairs in the austere room, near the window overlooking the courtyard.

"What?" exclaimed her father, "We never saw Halil. He did not call or send word." Emine was astonished. "We decided to come just to see how you are doing."

All three were in shock. Each kept staring at the other two. Her mother spoke first.

"My dear child" her mother said. "We were worried because we had no news from you for a long time."

Then, Emine began to cry. Tears began falling down her cheeks, and soon she was sobbing uncontrollably. Fatma got up and embraced her daughter and asked with great anxiety.

"What is the matter with my daughter? You should be happy. You have given us such a lovely grandchild. Why are you crying?"

Emine had trouble controlling her sobbing. She suddenly stopped and said:

"There is a woman upstairs. Halil brought her in the day after my baby was born." She let it out.

"What?" demanded Mustafa Aga in a rather loud voice "Explain yourself child" he ordered his daughter.

Then Emine gave her parents the sordid details, broken by sobbing she could not resist, torn by her feelings of betrayal and abandonment.

At the end of it, she looked at her mother as if begging. "I want to come home with you with my baby." She was desperate. Her parents were her last hope.

"My dear little girl" began her mother. "This is terrible. Halil is a liar and a cheat." She looked at her own husband for sympathy and, above all, for a judgment. This is serious matter and in proper Ottoman etiquette it demanded a man's decision.

Mustafa Aga knew it. His wife and daughter's eyes were turned on him. There he stood, the old patriarch, in total silence.

He took a deep breath. He was about to make an important ruling. As always in these moments, the Aga put family honor first. For him Cyprus was Ottoman, regardless of what the British did or thought. Mustafa Aga was an Ottoman autocrat; he saw the world as an Ottoman world.

"Pregnancy" began the patriarch "is difficult for a man as well. Halil is a young man at his prime." He did not talk for long.

Fatma, with alarm showing on her face, interjected.

"Mustafa," she said lovingly in uncharacteristically bold tone, "there is no excuse. No respectable man will bring in a woman into his house." She stopped to make sure her point was understood. There was silence.

Fatma continued. "This is disgraceful. We must take our daughter and child with us to Pineview. " She had never spoken to her husband like this. She surprised herself with her decisiveness.

The Aga was taken aback. But he was equally adamant.

"That is impossible," he ruled. "The shame of it will ruin us."

Then, more to the point, he said: "I shall be disgraced. What will the whole village say?"

It was true. In those days, a married woman, returning back to her parents' home was a woman disgraced. And, the disgrace ruined the family honor, too. There was virtually no chance of re-marriage, especially with a baby. She was damaged goods, bound to stay a widower, looking after the baby without a father. But, Mustafa Aga's reputation would disappear. He would become a dishonorable man in the village. He would never again be proud, able to walk with his head up. He would have to stop being *Muhtar* and accept his daughter's shame as his own. It was too much.

There was silence. Fatma frightened and bewildered, looked at her husband. Poor Grandmother was terrified and ashamed. Her duty was to be respectful to her parents, and persevere; yet the torment inside her was unbearable. With eyes full of tears, suckling her baby, she looked helplessly at her parents, shocked by her father's words, but unable to counter, holding herself against any sign of disrespect to her father.

Mustafa Aga went on, lecturing his daughter: "My dear girl. You have to show courage" he began. "You must understand that Halil has a government job now, a salary. He is entitled to take a second wife. This is our law."

Then the patriarch changed his tone and said:

"It must be a passing thing" trying to comfort his distressed daughter. "It is infatuation. You are young and do not know men. They have needs. Women get pregnant, but men have urges," he went on his daughter and his wife getting worried all the while.

## DISGRACED

There was a visible discomfort, a dangerous chasm between father and daughter and between husband and wife. The women were driven by fear, the Ottoman autocrat by vanity.

Finally, he decided. "Listen, here is my decision" ruled the Ottoman patriarch, turning to his daughter. "I want you to be patient. I promise you within week the matter will be resolved. Halil will come back to you. Just believe me."

The women looked terrified, beaten. Grandma Emine knew better. She was disappointed in her father. The Aga's pride was large enough to sacrifice his daughter to a life of misery. She had to face her fate alone, in her own way. "My poor, helpless mother" reflected my desperate Grandma.

As the parents got up to leave, Mustafa Aga went to the washroom. Then, Emine, in desperation, said: "Mother, that woman upstairs is a Christian."

"How do you know?" her mother asked.

"I saw a cross around her neck." Her mother exclaimed: "Allah, please forgive us."

Mother and daughter shed tears, helpless in the face of the overarching Ottoman male pride.

Soon the parents were gone. Grandmother was left all alone. She, one solitary soul and a brand new baby, against the entire hostile planet, no one cared. She felt totally abandoned.

Emine was sacrificed for her father's ego. The visit had crushed Emine further, sinking her to the depths of loneliness; a terrible fear took hold of her, and her last ounce of hope vanished. She did not know what to do, where to turn.

But the visit's greatest impact was on the baby Aygul, my dear mother. Since birth she had been a model baby, sleeping innocently and gracefully almost all the time save when she needed feeding. Her mother was always there, smiling and comforting. But now with all the screaming and anger around her, little Aygul kept waking up in torments of crying as if she was suddenly becoming witness of the tragedy unfolding all around her. It was a pattern that was to become routine in the rest of her life.

For herself, Emine was comforted in one thought alone. She was glad to break with the Ottoman tradition of naming the newborn after Grandparents. Aygul was a modern name, unlike Fatma and Emine, and she was glad she had chosen it for her beautiful girl. It meant moon rose, combination of romantic hope and natural beauty.

At last she fell asleep next to little Aygul. She had no idea how long she was able to sleep. It was a sleep of torment; completely unaware she was sweating and agonizing in pain.

Suddenly, some hours later she was woken by, once again, love-making sounds coming from the bedroom upstairs. Halil was back and he was in bed with the stranger woman. Emine lay quietly in her bed, clasping to her baby ever so more closely and gently." Where is my baby's father?" she asked and broke into sobs, and tears steamed down her cheeks, once again. She sat there, frozen, listening to her lost love, wondering why fate had chosen to heap all this unhappiness on such a helpless mother and her child.

# XIX

The next day, after they returned from Lefke, Grandfather was busy with official duty. He was expected to go to the police headquarters and report to Superintendent James's office. He was still tired from the overnight journey back from Lefke, but all tiredness was forgotten by Elena's warm welcome and embrace. She was glad to see him back so soon, and they celebrated the happy reunion with passion and love, oblivious to Emine's discomfort and mounting jealousy from downstairs. Her earlier fears of entrapment were gone, at least for now.

Halil's day began well. He got up early, put on his uniform, polished his shoes and, looking his best, he went straight to Superintendent James's office. He had never been in such exalted company before, and with his poor English and even less appreciation of English custom, he looked very uncomfortable and unsure of what he should do. He decided that the occasion demand the utmost formality, and so he marched in and stood to attention right in front of the Superintendentent's large desk, his right hand pointing at his ear, as if he were on a parading ground.

The Superintendent, taken aback by this sudden show of discipline, accepted Halil's salute with a show of his right hand, ordering, "stand at ease," and went straight to the core of the abduction business at hand.

"Look here, young man" he began, "you are a police officer, in His Majesty's Service, you have to behave yourself. Do you know what a police officer represents? Law and order. You have to uphold the law, when on duty as well as when you are off."

The Superintendent paused for a moment, and then continued, "There has been a serious charge against you. I have here a report from the DO in Kyrenia. The parents of a young girl, 18 years of age, are laying a charge of abduction against you. That is a serious charge that can get you dismissed, you understand?"

Halil looked on with a blank face. He stood to attention and saluted the Superintendent once again. James felt obliged to take the salute and, after a pause, the continued, "What do you say? You realize that you are in deep trouble, don't you?" Again, Halil was unresponsive.

That is when James realized that he had been talking in futility because the man in front of him knew virtually no English. "Do you understand me? Do you?" he yelled and Halil looked on with the same blank, stupid face that finally convinced the Superintendent he had been wasting his breath lecturing to a man that did not understand English.

Then he screamed out of his office in search of the peon. "Go get me a man who can act as an interpreter. I have been talking to a donkey all morning."

Within five minutes. Sergeant Kazim stood behind the big boss who had to repeat the charge against Halil. And at long last, the Superintendent began to get down to the ugly facts of the case.

"Sir" began Kazim, translating, "Halil claims there is no abduction. The girl came to him willingly. No force was used and she is happy with Halil, who is a Muslim entitled to have up to four wives. He believes he is doing a competent job as a police officer and he demonstrated his loyalty to the King with his help in recovering Lady Ramsbottom's jewels in Lefke so expeditiously. " That was all true and the Superintendent knew.

He took in a deep breath, partly in desperation and partly as a sign of frustration from realization that officially and strictly speaking, the Superintendent of Police could do virtually nothing. He must write back to the DO Kyrenia and regretfully refer him to the Muslim judge, the *Kadi*, knowing full well this would in all probability end up in a useless chase. The scoundrel in front of him was technically safe, at least for now. There was no criminal offense. Yet, Superintendent James felt a stern warning was in order, so before letting Halil off, he went on:

"Now, look here, young man." His tone and words indicated that he was about to make a serious statement. "I warn you. You are heading toward big trouble, unless you mend your ways. I am suspending my judgment in this abduction case pending an investigation by the *Kadi* of Kyrenia. Dismissed." The wheels of British justice turned slowly.

Grandfather was, once again, off the hook, at least for now. His pride was a little shaken, but his self-confidence had won another round.

# XX

Meanwhile, in neighboring Kormacit, another wheel was turning in the tragic cycle of events. The following day, the Ayoub family had received word from the District Officer that their complaint had produced no satisfactory result, except a recommendation that since the abduction charge involved a Muslim man, it was a civil matter falling outside the King's jurisdiction. Accordingly, Elana's parents might be advised to take their complaint to the *Kadi*, the Muslim judge competent in these cases. Earlier, Mr. Read sent word to the *Kadi* of Kyrenia about the Elana case.

So Elana's parents, in a desperate move to save their daughter, were back in Kyrenia, this time seeking Muslim justice. Now they were going to the office, or more correctly house of the *Kadi* to plead their case. It was a typical Ottoman building, with beautiful lattice veneer outside, next to the pretty Mosque and Minaret, about half a mile up the steep pebbled road overlooking the Venetian harbor. Inside, the entrance lead into a huge *Selamlik*, guest room, covered with oriental carpets and settees all around the four walls. About seven feet high on the walls were delicately carved wooden shelves with antique Iznik and China plates, giving the room a museum like appearance. Clearly, this is where the *Kadi* held court.

Hafiz Effendi, the *Kadi* of Kyrenia, was an Ottoman gentleman, well in his sixties, very serious looking in his official long gown and

# DISGRACED

white turban but with no special training in Muslim law, except that he had, long ago, learnt the Qur'an by heart. The rest of his qualification was on the job training, common sense and influence derived from his family honor as a man of means in Kyrenia. In those days, the town was primarily Muslim and the family of Hafiz, literally meaning, a learned cleric, had a reputation of dynastic hold on the office of *Kadi*.

He received the Ayoub family with courtesy and civility. He looked distinguished; his gentle smile suggested a cordial welcome to his Maronite visitors. He sat in his big throne-like chair and invited Katrina and Elias to seat in chairs in front of him. He knew why they had come.

"I heard from the District Officer about your daughter eloping with a *Zaptieh*" he began. Katrina looked at her husband, and Elias spoke first.

"Your Honor, it was abduction." He said.

"Well, that is what we need to decide, don't we?" inquired the *Kadi*, looking very serious and official.

"Please tell me what happened?" He asked. Elias gave a summary. The *Kadi* reflected for a moment or two and then delivered his judgment in a long and winded lecture:

"A good Muslim who does his duty toward Allah and is full of virtue, can have up to four wives. That is Allah's wish and the edict of our Prophet, peace be upon him." He wanted to make sure his words were understood. The Ayoub couple listened in silence, their anxiety growing. Hafiz Effendi went on: "Our religion is against *zulm*, cruelty, and a man who marries more than once must show respect to his wives. He should not beat them or mistreat them. Women are Allah's gift to men. Wives are the custodians of the family honor; they must support and follow their husbands' commands. The husband is the family head and she must follow his instructions."

He then lectured on women's proper code of dress and conduct. "So long as they cover their adornments and do not speak to strangers, women are honorable." The Ayoub family listened patiently and politely as the learned *Kadi* concluded with further injunctions provided by Islam:

"Of course, there are limits and conditions that must be observed," added the *Kadi*. "A devout Muslim who takes additional wives must provide equally for each wife's wellbeing. If he buys a dress for one, he must do the same for the others. He must spend equal time with each wife and give equal attention to all the children."

The Ayoub couple had no knowledge of Elana's life in Tanzimat Street. They could not contest the words of the *Kadi*.

Katrina interjected: "How does the law apply in the case of our daughter?" she asked, showing considerable boldness. The Kadi responded with bitter clarity:

"I assume your daughter has converted to the faith," replied the judge. In shocked silence from the parents, he continued: "I understand from the District Officer's report, your daughter was not forcibly removed from your house. She went off willingly."

The Ayoub couple unhappily had to agree. "That, I am afraid, establishes one thing: there is no abduction." He waited for his message to sink in. Elana"s parents were stupefied; they stood there in front of the holy man in silence. Neither could find words to reply. The *Kadi* continued:

"If your daughter consented to go with this man," he continued, "there is nothing to be done. And I can only intervene if she accepted the faith and became a Muslim. Then I can investigate further to determine whether her husband is treating her fairly in accordance with the rules of our Prophet, peace be upon him."

The *Kadi* had spoken and the parents were at the end of their rope. They had exhausted all avenues with official channels. They had to accept the bitter fact of official impasse. Now, they were faced with the stigma of social disgrace in Kormacit. Their daughter's fate was sealed; she was in a trap, one that she had walked into innocently.

"If only I knew which house our Elana has been taken to," wondered Elias as they headed back to Kormacit. Exasperated, he was at his wits end.

He had had enough of British or Ottoman justice. He was inclined to take matters into his own hand. But he knew not where to go.

I must say, there was a strange parallel between the Ayoub' and my Grandmother's predicament. They, as much as her, were as helpless, trapped in an Ottoman tragedy, in which they were all actors, inexorably unfolding beyond anyone's control. Fate, it seemed, was in others' hands.

# XXI

My Grandfather's behavior, his false sense of self-confidence and his utter selfishness, in the coming tragedy, leaves me cold, as write these lines. I am torn by anger and pity. I pity not only my dear Grandmother, I also feel for the naïve and young Elana. Her parents, too, good people that they were, I ask myself, how is it possible that they could not get justice? It is all so frustrating.

Anyway, I must press on with the story. After his meeting with the Ayoub couple the *Kadi* had another visitor. It was Mr. David Read, the English District Officer, whose *kavaz*, the Ottoman messenger who was retained in service primarily for purposes of helping guide the new officials of His Majesty's Service in Cyprus meander and find their way through maze of Ottoman administration, called on the *Kadi* to request an interview on behalf of his superior. The *Kadi* obliged. So, exactly at three pm the DO was shown into the *Selamlik* vacated by the Ayoub parents just a few hours earlier. The *kavaz* was also useful as an official interpreter on account of his broken English.

"Thank you for seeing me at such short notice" began the English DO politely. His host, equally graciously bowed his head, as a close substitute for his lack of English. He waved Mr. Read to a chair next to his own throne-like ornamental chair.

"I am here to discuss the abduction of the Ayoub girl. I previously advised you of the case and have referred her parents to come and see you," he said.

The *Kadi* replied, and the *kavaz* (interpreter) translated.

"Yes, they visited me this morning" said the *Kadi*.

Mr. Read was troubled as he felt in a moral no-man's land in the case. He said:

"I am here because the British justice system may be inadequate in the case. It involves a gray area in law, but I fear if we do not act quickly, the poor girl may find herself in deeper trouble. I want to find out what the Muslim law provides." He waited for the translation, and continued because he felt he must explain himself better:

"You see, Your Honor, Cyprus is not a Crown Colony; strictly it is not a British territory. We are obliged under the Convention to protect and respect Muslim law and custom of the land. But, quite frankly, the case of the Ayoub girl is a boundary case, and clearly we cannot deal with it strictly under the British law. That is why the parents were advised to seek your guidance and help."

The *Kadi* looked on with considerable puzzlement evident on his face, only some of which was eliminated after the translation. He was aware of David Read's moral dilemma. Read, in reality, was visiting his host, beyond the call of duty, in order to clear his own conscience.

"I want your help so we can rescue the girl" said the Englishman and waited for the *Kadi* to pronounce on the matter.

After looking somber and serious, the *Kadi* started to talk and the translator did his best to convey his message to the DO.

"You British are masters of the island now" he began. "Our Sultan and Caliph has entrusted you with the welfare of our people. You must deliver good government, and you are required to respect Muslim religion and custom."

David Read listened and nodded his head to indicate approval. What he heard so far was fine, but he wished the learned Muslim judge would come to the point. He continued:

"When there is a dispute between a Muslim man and woman, the law is clear. Two respectable witnesses are required to attest to the truth of the charges. The word of the woman counts half as much as man's." He stopped to allow translation and catch his breath and then he pressed forward:

"In the case of a dispute between a Muslim man and a Christian woman, the matter is complicated. Each community is responsible for its own peace and order. Our Prophet, peace be upon him, has ruled that Christians are people of the book, so they must be treated with respect; there can be no *zulm,* torture, applied on them."

By this time, the DO was getting a sinking feeling. He began to wonder if he were on a fishing expedition. Trying not to show his growing impatience, he intervened and said to the *kavaz:*

"Please ask his Honor whether Muslim law provides any guidelines in the case of an abduction of a non-Muslim girl?"

After translation, the *Kadi* turned to David Read:

"Abduction? I am told the Ayoub girl consented to go with the man."

The DO had to make a retreat. The *Kadi* was strictly speaking correct.

"Yes, yes" he said with his excitement this time showing. "I know, but surely there must be something we can do to help? We just cannot sit and do nothing." He was using his last moral ace in the pack.

"I am afraid" the learned cleric began, "there is no moral guide here. The case involves two consenting adults and unless there is violation of our moral code, until there is some sort of dispute, I fear there is nothing to be done." He stopped and looked at David.

He suddenly found something in what he heard that encouraged him. He said:

"What would be a violation of the Muslim code in this case?"

Then the *Kadi* said:

"You say there is a second woman, a Muslim woman, involved." He looked at the DO.

"Yes" he concurred. "There is Halil's Muslim wife."

"Then, go see her. Find out if she is happy about the whole affair." The *Kadi* stopped.

David Read's eyes brightened and he had a flash going through his brain:

"Yes, of course" he said. "We must talk to Halil's wife. I am sure she is not happy having a lover in her house."

David got up, and almost ran out of the *Kadi*'s house, barely saying good-bye and thank you. He made up his mind to travel to Nicosia to see the police chief, the very next morning. The delay was a fatal mistake.

# XXII

Meanwhile, in Pineview my great Grandparents were troubled and unhappy, as they ought to be. They had left Grandmother in a terrible state that much they realized. In fact, their world of peace and tranquility was rapidly coming to an end.

The visit to their daughter had been a completely sad and unhappy event. But husband and wife saw the events differently, at least at that moment of time. Back at Pineview, a seed of discord was sown between the old Aga and his obedient wife who now started a revolt of her own, never before seen in their long married life. Fatma, for the first time in her life made a decision by herself: Her sense of justice conflicted with her husband's perception of honor. Fatma could not stomach abandoning her daughter for the sake of her husband's honor.

"After all, she is only a child; Mustafa Aga is a mature old man" she reasoned in her own mind. "My dear girl, I wonder how she is now? How she is coping?"

Things got worse in the days following. Fatma became moody and she started sulking. She could not help it. It was as if she lost interest in life itself. She lost interest in cooking and housekeeping. Most visibly, she stopped talking to her husband, answering in monosyllables whenever she felt obliged to say anything, which was less and less the rule. The old cordial home atmosphere was gone, replaced by mistrust approaching hostility.

# DISGRACED

At first, the patriarch thought nothing of it. "Women are strange creatures" he declared in selfish arrogance and thought no more of it. "She will recover in a few days, just as Emine will learn to cope with a man having two wives. Our religion permits it. It happens all the time."

He began to spend more time at the coffee shop and he started, for the first time in his life, gambling at the cards. Villagers were startled and began to wonder what happened to their *Muhtar*? He also started another first for Mustafa Aga, to drink wine at Dimitri's bar in the nearby Greek Cypriot village. He stopped coming home to escape the sour looks and bitterness, which, like dark clouds before the storm, had descended over his household.

The neighbors noticed that a sad change had come about in their *Muhtar's* home. But here too a conflict emerged between honor and duty. Fatma Hanim was enough of an Ottoman lady to maintain, for outward appearance of order for duty's sake, befitting a respectable Ottoman wife, a show of respectability with neighbors. When neighbors anxiously visited, but actually looking for bits of gossip, Fatma would say, "Oh, there is really nothing." But they persisted, and rumors began to circulate.

"Fatma Hanim, I heard your daughter, Emine, gave birth," her closest neighbor, Huriye said. "Yes, she gave us a wonderful little girl, thanks be to Allah" Fatma acknowledged.

"I heard that you and your husband went visiting her?" Huriye inquisitively pressed to know more. Unwillingly, Fatma, said: "Yes, poor Emine is alone" she began and then, uncontrollably, she burst crying, "I pray that Allah will forgive me I fear my daughter is in danger, but I feel helpless." She surprised herself.

Huriye was taken aback. She could hardly believe her ears. Fatma was revealing a family secret, a no-no; she was breaking a well-established Ottoman taboo of never sharing family shame with strangers. Most importantly, she was disgracing her husband's honor, challenging his authority. This was war, but she could not help it. Words just came out of her mouth against her own wish. She did not want to do it. Some invisible voice inside her was doing the talking.

"What on earth are you talking about?" asked the neighbor. Fatma looked at her with fear written all over her face. "I do not know" she blurted out and kept crying, silently, privately, tears coming down on her face.

"I must do something for my dear Emine. Something is wrong with her husband. He brought a common woman into the house."

"Oh my God, what a disgraceful thing" said the neighbor. She had heard of cases of multiple wives before, womanizing men taking on new wives. That was not unheard of. It was not even unlawful. But it always ended up breaking families, in tragic consequences, ruining and disgracing otherwise honorable families, more accurately men with big egos.

"Emine wants to come home with her baby, but Mustafa Aga will hear nothing of it. I do not know what to do. I cannot sleep. I cannot eat. I worry all the time. I am constantly thinking about my girl and her baby." There she said it all.

The news spread around the village like fire. Within a couple of hours, the shame of it all hit Mustafa Aga. He was sitting in the coffee shop, playing cards with his friends. It began when he noticed that he was suddenly the object of strange looks from other customers in the coffee shop. He immediately knew he was the target of unfriendly gossip. Men whispered words to each other, while others showered strange looks at him. He became self-conscious. The disgrace was too much. He got up, walked out of the coffee shop and went to Dimitri's bar to get drunk, something he had not done in years.

The next morning, as the Ayoub parents were trekking to see David Read, the Aga's dutiful wife finally rebelled. As he was dressing, Fatma spoke to him in anger and frustration: "How could you sit and do nothing when Halil brings in an infidel prostitute? How can you expect our Emine to tolerate that, eh?" She asked.

Then, the Aga's eyes popped out. "Woman, explain yourself" he demanded. "What do you mean, 'infidel prostitute'?"

"Just what I said" Fatma insisted. "Halil's woman upstairs wore a cross around her neck."

The word "infidel" was too much. It hit the Aga like a bombshell. He dropped the pants he was trying to put on and turned virtually naked to his wife: "Who told you that?" He demanded.

"Emine told me herself when we visited her." Fatma said.

Then, Mustafa Aga crashed on the bed, a sense of humiliation overcoming the old patriarch. "My God" he began, "That low-down Halil broke the promise he gave me at the time of the marriage contract. I knew about his affairs with Christian women and I made him promise that he would put a stop to it."

He waited for a minute, his wife watching. Then he reached his decision: "We must go back and fetch Emine and the baby." The Aga had realized his mistake.

It was too late, much too late.

# XXIII

The tragedy unfolded quickly on the third day after Grandfather's return from Lefke. Like the lull before the deluge, his return home had begun so well. The police posse came back, with a great sense of success having recovered Lady Ramsbottom's royal jewels, thus redeeming in some manner, the British justice. It was close to midnight when the party was back in the capital. Elana was sleeping upstairs, and all was quite downstairs when Halil returned to his Tanzimat street house. "All is peaceful," he said to himself.

Elana woke up, welcoming her lover with a tempting smile and those emerald green eyes and red lips were irresistible. Several times during the following hours, the stone house on Tanzimat Street was the scene of exquisite lovemaking upstairs. But downstairs my poor Grandmother heard it all in utter shame. My dear poor mother, little baby Aygul, if at all aware, could only sense the great infidelity and the cruelty of my Grandfather upstairs. How could a man hurt a woman so much?

Early the following morning Grandfather went for his interview with the Superintendent and was tied up at the police headquarters all day. Halil was given the next two days off for his special duty over the Lefke pursuit. He also collected his pay now in arrears on account of his absence from the capital.

When, in the cool evening his day was done at the police station, the selfish man did not return to his Tanzimat harem. He wanted first to have a little celebration with his drinking buddies at *Asmaalti*. He had missed their company; it had been several days since their last feasting. Ahmet lived in Yeni Cami area so he started walking, passing by the Tekke Monastery.

Horoz Ali, as usual on guard at the gate was the first to notice him.

"Halil, you devil, where have you been? It has been ages since I saw you" said the lanky gatekeeper.

"Don't ask Ali" he replied. "I have been busy chasing Midas and his bandits," he said.

Then he added: "Ali come and have a few drinks at *Asmaalti*. Life is too short my friend. What do you say?"

"Too true, Halil. OK, as soon as the *sema* service is over tonight, I'll come and join you."

Ahmet the drunk was sleeping at home when Halil suddenly called. The place was empty and the door open, his wife gossiping with neighbors next door. He walked in, as on previous occasions unannounced, went into Ahmet's room and started yelling, standing over the bed as his friend snored loudly.

"Get up, you lazy man. You are good for nothing. It is time to celebrate." Halil went on.

"Who is there?" screamed the drunk without opening his eyes. He turned over and said: "Go away. I want to sleep."

Then Halil went to the kitchen and got a bucket full of water and poured it over the huge fellow in bed. That woke him up.

"Halil" he yelled, opening his eyes, "Why didn't you say so in the first place" he taunted his friend. "I have been sick with worry, wondering what happened to you?"

"Don't ask" Halil said impatiently. "Just get up and let's go. I want to drink *raki* and sing. I have not had a celebration for days."

They were at their favorite drinking hole within the hour. Tonight was also special because the musicians were on deck, all gypsy band and singers, entertaining the merrymakers with love songs and ballads of gallantry. Halil loved it all.

"Do you know Midas?" began Halil finally, when there was sufficient food and drink in his stomach, and he felt that the time had come for conversation. Ahmet, now rested and quite alert, replied: "He is the chief of the bandits. I have heard about him from my friends."

Halil cut him short. "Yes. That is who we were chasing in Lefke," he said. Then he added for special effect: "What a guy?"

105

Others stopped eating and drinking. Even the gypsy singer, who casually heard the conversation, came to hear Halil, as Ahmet asked: "What did Midas do?"

"He collected a huge sum of one thousand British pounds from those stupid British tourists. That is what he did," he announced.

Everyone was amazed. "Wow" said several around the table. Many could not comprehend the amount Halil mentioned and asked for confirmation: "How much did you say?"

"One-thousand-pounds that is what I said" repeated Halil and summarized with relish the details of the ransom deal in Lefke."The British tourists are crazy. Midas played with them like cat and mouse."

"Midas is a hero," yelled someone. "What will he do with all that money?" asked another.

"I bet he will distribute the money to the peasants around the region. That is what I heard he does and people love him – more than the police I'll say," said Halil.

Then someone proposed: "I'll drink to Midas" and as there was a general cheer, there was commotion at the front door. Horoz Ali walked in. All eyes were turned on him.

"Halil what is going on here? What lies are you telling everyone?" Horoz Ali asked provokingly.

"You scoundrel" replied Halil, looking at Horoz Ali, "Come and join the party."

They all moved to make space for the big fellow around the table. Where three would sit, Horoz Ali could barely fit, but he had to squeeze in because the inn at *Asmaalti* was small. But once accommodated, the party resumed and Horoz Ali asked:

"What is the occasion? Are you married again Halil or what?"

Amidst laughter, Halil replied: "Hell no. What is the point of marrying? We are now living in the age of liberty," he expounded.

Then turning to his friend Ahmet, he said: "Ahmet is treating us tonight."

Then he took a pound note from his pocket and said: "You see this pound Ahmet. It was the one you gave me the other day."

Ahmet had forgotten the event and looked on with surprise evident on his face.

Halil said: "You have no idea how much love it has provided me."

# XXIV

As Grandfather was celebrating with his drinking buddies in the *kervansaray* in *Asmaalti*, his two women in the Tanzimat street harem descended into Demonland, each entering its Gate, separately, one following the other but none aware of the other's presence. Elana upstairs, and Emine downstairs next to baby Aygul below in the basement, had, in different moments of real time, vanished into a mysterious land peopled by non-humans and strange creatures never seen before.

Demonland was a place beyond all hope, across River Acheron. In this land, there was no time, no sunrise and no sunset. Darkness ruled everywhere and everything stood still. Only forms and shapes prevailed, truth and reality did not exist. Fear and terror were everywhere, manifested by horrifying objects, fire and anguish in everlasting abundance. There were strange beings, partly human partly beast, in different proportions, yet all spoke like humans. The landscape was desolate and dreadful; mountains on fire, rivers and pools burning, swamps full of fish-like creatures with heads of dragons going in circles, swearing and cursing to all around. The whole place stung as one huge open sewer, with unbearable filth and odor everywhere. At the edge of this swamp there were groups of fearsome creatures of fantastic diversity and form, some two legged bulls with horns, others four legged birds of prey looking like dinosaurs, yet others other forms half lion, half deer.

There was jeering, cussing and screaming, all in a deafening cacophony coming from all quarters. In the far distant there was constant thunder and lightening, fires ablaze, and steam spewing out from geysers, potholes and boiling pools. It was unbearably hot. Darkness prevailed except for the occasional flush of a fire or lightening in the distant. Terrifying creatures were everywhere, some breathing flames, others gorging on other creatures, blood oozing from their jaws and mouths, searching for more victims, ready to jump on the weak and unsuspecting.

"What in *Seytan's* (Lucifer's) name are you doing here?" yelled a female voice from behind. Emine turned back to see where the voice came. She saw no one. Scared and defenseless, she turned and looked behind, and then she turned the other way, shaking all over with fear.

"I am standing in front of you," said the voice. Emine looked below, near her feet, and finally noticed a snake-like fish, stuck in the sewer, a couple of feet away from her. She was puzzled and unsure, so she asked: "Who are you? Where are you?"

"Look at me, right here just in front of you" the creature replied. To make sure, it wiggled in the foul semi-liquid, revealing all of its three feet length at the end of which was a human head in skeleton.

"How can you talk? What are you?" Asked Emine amazed.

"I used to be an *odalik* in the harem," said the creature, "until jealousy made me poison the Aga's favorite concubine, Gulbahar, that bitch who took my place. I came here to this I do not know when. There is no measure of time. No days, no weeks and months, everything is the same. Here we are what we are, at the pleasure of Great Demon. All we do is chatter and tell on each other, living out our jealousy to our hearts' content. That is why the noise all around. Our form is what matters here. The Great Demon determines your form. Please him and he can reconstruct you into some other form. For me, my Revenge is so sweet: All I do is kill perpetually in word and in deed that tormentor of mine, Gulbahar. I hit her this way, and that way, heaping scorn on her, and that is all I want to do."

"But it is so foul smelling here, how you can speak of sweet?" said Emine unsteadily.

"It is good," replied the creature. "You get to enjoy it. I am thankful to the Great Demon. He knows everything in my heart."

"How is it that you can talk? You are no human." Emine could not hold back her curiosity.

# DISGRACED

"We are all driven here by Passion. It is what attracts us to the Great Demon."

"Who is the Great Demon?" inquired Emine, trembling with fear.

"He is the Lord of Demonland. He gives each a soul, each according to one's Passion, endowed with a new form. Mine is Revenge, yours might be Greed, and someone else can have Deceit. The Great Demon gives us speech to revel in our Passion to the utmost. He hears everything, and decides to reward or punish you. He can reconstruct you in a higher or lower form."

Emine looked into the darkness but could see nothing. Puzzled and shaken by fear, she wanted to ask a myriad of questions, but the creature disappeared with a human-like apology:" I must go to my shift." And it swam away into the swamp and was gone in a flash.

Emine in her sleep smiled, "Revenge is sweet," she repeated, and then she started to transpose Infidelity into Revenge. Abandoned in this life, jealousy and infidelity tore the poor Ottoman woman apart. Her descent toward demonic possession made sense. The Gate beyond hope across Acheron looked enticing.

\*\*\*

Beyond the high mountains over River Acheron, Elana was observing a strange ceremony presided over by the Great Demon. All around strange forms and creatures were in assembly, a roar of chanting filling the space, yet not a soul was to be seen. At the far end, perched on a rock surrounded by burning fires amidst moving mountains molten lava was oozing all around, and in an island in the middle of it all was situated a throne-like settee with pythons on one side and lions on the other, all looking fearsome and threatening. On the settee sat a massive animal in the shape of unicorn atop a human body, with a golden horn, wearing a huge robe, shining brightly and flowing in the wind.

"Oh! Great Demon" shouted all around. "Grant us your favors. Protect us and save our speech. Reconstruct us in higher form." They prayed.

The Great Demon had two hands, almost like a human, and his face was more like a cow's, and in his right hand he held a high stuff with a cobra at its top ready to strike. In his left hand he held a torch of fire with which he would burn, just for the pleasure of it seemed, things within reach. Fire oozed out of his eyes, and his tongue extended out like a snake, sometimes coiling sometimes ready to strike. He was officiating what looked like a strange ceremony. In front of the Great Demon there was a huge block of rock, and next to it stood a creature, its elephant head standing on a human body and only two legs. Elana could distinguish the figure of a beautiful young woman, and she could make out her own features as if in a mirror.

She began to feel excruciatingly hot and felt sweat all over, her body aching in torment, as she began to identify with the body on the sacrifice block, with vulture-like birds and hyenas feasting on her, fighting for scraps of flesh and bone, while some other creatures, half vulture and half hyena, stealing big chunks and as blood oozed in every direction. Elana did not like what she saw; there was pandemonium, screams and voices of agony piercing her ears. She started turning and twisting in bed, tormented by what she was seeing in Demonland.

Then someone unseen spoke to Elana. "You must be the little Ayoub girl from Kormacit?" Elana turned to look at the direction of the voice. It was a female voice, coming from a dog-faced creature with wings and a human body on top of two legs. Elana was in shock and awe at this strange creature speaking just like her. And what is more, the creature was not alone. There was a multitude around the dog-like creatures. They were all steering at her, whispering to each other, taunting her, some laughing and jeering. "Pity on her" said one, "she believed his lover." Another added in agreement: "Stupid girl….is what I say."

"How do you know who I am?" Asked Elana, shaking with fear, still unable to see anyone and unsure of her condition.

"We know," said the dog faced, looking deadly serious, "just as we know that you are one of us here. You poor thing, you left your parents in Kormacit, run away with that Halil the womanizer. He too belongs here."

"What is this place? Why are you talking to me like that?" She inquired rather courageously.

"This is abode of all the adulterers and sex workers," said the creature. "But don't worry. It is not a bad place, really, everyone lives in the big cesspool, trying to improve the place. But it is an impossible task; with more newcomers, the cesspool grows bigger. So we have to do more. If you work hard, you are rewarded. You may even be selected for Reconstruction into a higher form."

# DISGRACED

"What is Reconstruction?" she asked.

"What we are now witnessing," said the voice. "It is liberation and you become a new form. Reconstruction is a reward by the Great Demon. Here we are all possessed by Him. He is the Source. Praise Him, and you may even be recast into to the lion-figure. Then you can terrorize to your hearts' content."

The screams were reaching a break point. Terror struck all around for no apparent reason. All around the Great Demon was fire, fires burning. He rose above it all, towering everyone and everything, gesticulating with his hands in all directions and a rain of toxic gases was blanketing all around, while in front of the Great Demon a lion-faced dragon was taking form. Then terror struck everywhere. Creatures of all fantastic shapes and forms stampeded, all running for cover from some unseen enemy, some jumping into burning waters, some flying, yet others seeking cover in holes in the marshes.

Elana was bewildered and confused. She just stood there and wanted to ask so many more questions. But she never got the chance. The voice disappeared. Elana was alone, terrified and shaking with fear. Her body was sweating all over.

"Halil, where are you?" she screamed. "Protect me, please. Come to me" she yelled. She then opened her eyes, tentatively. For a moment she was transfixed, unsure of her surroundings, trying to recover.

As if a miracle was unfolding, right then her lover stepped in, entering through the front door. She was sweating heavily, fear dominated her, and with sleepy eyes, in the dark room, she could barely make out her lover walk in.

# XXV

It was after midnight when Halil finally came home, quite intoxicated but full of energy. Outwardly his harem was peaceful, but the two women it housed, one upstairs and one down, were in Demonland, each turning in bed, agonizing and tormenting themselves with demons, possessed by the devil.

Elana was awakened as Grandfather stumbled into the bedroom. It took her several minutes to transport herself from the terrible nightmare she had been having to the reality of Halil next to her. No words were exchanged, but she was comforted by her lover's presence. He crawled into bed with uncommon gentleness, embraced her with his strong arms where she felt secure and protected. The last shred of fear of demons quickly vanished from her memory.

Their lovemaking resumed with fury and passion, reserved for demigods rarely attained by mortals. Emine, clasping dear mother in her bosom, downstairs sank into unimaginable depths of agony and humiliation. The next days, Halil was on holiday, and they took full advantage of it. There was one thing in their mind: lovemaking. It went on for day and night, never once occurring to Halil that he was a father and husband.

On the third night, the lovemaking in the house on Tanzimat Street was the most intense and furious yet. Halil and Elana reached new heights of bliss in the bed now losing whatever suspension hold it might have had. The creaks of their bed and their moans went on for hours. Emine curled up in her bed, fear and shame overtaking her. Baby Aygul, in her arms, began to cry.

The limit was reached. The volcano was getting ready to erupt.

Then suddenly it all subsided. Morning came. It was a day off for Grandfather, a beautiful sunny day, in mid-July and he was now completely satiated, having filled his appetite for sex the night before upstairs in Elana's room, suddenly at last he felt in a fatherly mood and went downstairs to see his newly born baby.

Emine was in no mood for games. The visit erupted into a terrible fight. A fight was the last thing on Halil's mind. His life was perfect without Emine and baby Aygul.

Grandmother was pushed over the edge. She was back in Demon-land surrounded by demons. She had had enough and could take it no more. Abandoned and humiliated, she consoled herself only with the warmth of her baby. She held her tightly and would not put her down. The more the noise from the bed upstairs, heaving and creaking with repeated acts of passionate sex between an immoral husband and some cheap kept woman usurping her rightful place, the more Emine revolted. She could control her mind or feelings no more. Her reason was gone; anger, humiliation, jealousy, revenge, and several other emotions all combined to drive her over the limit. When she saw him, it was like the bursting of the dam with flood rushing over destroying everything in its path.

"You bastard, shameless pimp" began Grandmother, shouting and cursing at the man, in theory her husband, the moment he stepped in her room. She knew not where the vocabulary or her anger was coming from. She was transposed into a wild, female animal of the jungle, completely consumed by destructive vengeance.

Boiling with fury Grandma burst out: "You whoring, womanizer, how dare you treat me like this? Shame on you, don't come near me. Don't touch the baby. Go away." But he would not listen.

Dearest little Aygul, disturbed by the noise, began to cry, but no one paid the slightest attention to her, not even her mother this time.

"Be quiet woman." Halil said trying to show restraint. But, by then he had no more restraining influence on Emine. She was now a wild animal in fury, seeking revenge, tearing and destroying everything around.

Emine was pushed beyond endurance, past the break point. She had gone too far, gone down the path of self-destruction. Her world, her life was finished and she cared no more. The love she once had for Halil, just days before, had now been completely replaced by revenge bordering on madness. Emine, after days of agony and abandonment, finally took justice into her own hands, British or Ottoman justice she cared not, she wanted her revenge NOW.

"You bastard" she screamed at him, "Allah will burn you in Hell." She was beyond all reason. A woman terrorized, she had lost all reasoning.

"You are a devil. You have no decency, no shame. I gave birth to your baby and you are going around whorehouses. And, now you brought a whore into my house, one wearing a cross."

Halil wanted to hear no more. He stepped forward toward Emine, but then he changed his mind.

"Hold your tongue, woman" he shouted. "Better to exercise self control" he thought to himself. After all, he knew what he had done.

He turned his back and tried to walk to the door, to escape. Emine followed him and rushed into the kitchen, opposite her own room, wild with anger. She was a woman in rage, looking fierce as if she was possessed by the devil. Halil had never seen her like this and was, momentarily, confused. For the first time in his life, he was unsure and doubts emerged in his mind. "Dear Allah" confessed the philanderer, in a desperate appeal to his Creator, "shall I go for help?" he wondered, then dismissing the idea as impractical.

But, at that instant, Halil ran into Elana, trying to enter Emine's room. The noise from the fighting downstairs had woken her up and first she listened in anxiety mixed with fear. A woman, likely Emine, was screaming and yelling at Halil. Her voice was different and almost unrecognizable.

Sadly, curiosity took hold of Elana and she quietly climbed downstairs while still in her nightgown. It was the wrong move. Events happened, fast and furious, far too quickly for any one to control. I have never experienced human behavior beyond the point when reason stops to function. I can only imagine and conjecture what happens when human mind suddenly stops to work. Some strange, in- or sub-human motives or forces must take over and I am not even sure where the boundaries of responsible acts end and animal instincts take over.

All that I know is what I have been able to determine, many years afterwards from bits of pieces of information from close family members. These, of course, are family secrets, not generally pleasing to talk or share with anyone. I am not sure I have the full picture, or even what is fact and what is imagination. At the exact point in time when life ends, things happen too quickly.

Grandfather finally realized what was happening. He rushed after Elana while she was stepping in through the small door of the kitchen. He grabbed her and tried to push her out Emine's reach, but it was too late. In the commotion, he slipped and fell behind Elana who stood there, like a sacrificial lamb. In the next minute, as if traveling at lightening speed, Emine darted at her nemesis. Like a tigress at the moment of a kill, she raised the kitchen knife and before Halil's own eyes, lunged at Elana, thrusting the deadly instrument into her chest and shoulders, repeatedly and violently. Grandfather was awe-struck, frozen in time, right there but quite helpless, and poor Elana fell into his arms, her precious life gone out of her.

Grandfather screamed, "Stop woman" unconsciously and uncharacteristically appealing to God, "In Allah's name, STOP!" None heard his screams and prayers.

Then he turned on himself, the dreadful burden of his terrible deed at long last coming home, terrorizing him in all its horror. He wept, utterly a broken man.

"What I have done? My God, what have I done?"

It was the afternoon siesta time and all around an eerie silence prevailed. No one heard, no one witnessed the dastardly deed. A stifling heat, as if straight from Hell, engulfed the kitchen, but otherwise the house on Taznimat Street looked as peaceful as ever.

In shock, Grandfather lifted Elana, holding her in his arms. Helplessly he looked straight at her beautiful emerald green eyes as if in sleep as precious life went out of his lover.

As Grandfather realized what was happening, Grandma, now like an exploded volcano after eruption, subsided and fell herself, almost lifeless, on the ground. Terror and destruction spewed out like magma flowing out of the volcano. Halil, in shock and awe, torn between the two women, his lover and his wife, barely noticed the screams of baby Aygul witnessing the horrible deed, too young and innocent to understand but old enough to feel the torment. Some unseen spirit, an angel maybe, gave little mother Aygul a lesson, a lifelong instruction, in man's inhumanity to a woman, a lesson the little baby was to bear witness in her own troubled life.

Grandfather then lost his control. Terrified he started kicking and hitting his desperate wife on the floor with the bloodied instrument of murder still in her hand.

Then he rushed out of the door and out of the house. It was now late afternoon. He starting walking aimlessly, feeling like fish out of water, with no address or destination in mind. Momentarily, Grandfather felt anger against women for he saw them for the first time not as sex objects, but as persons with emotions that could erupt into horrible suffering.

After an hour or two, he found himself in the park near Paphos Gate, past the Armenian Church. He walked along the Venetian moat toward the park. It was getting dark and he sat on a bench and stayed there for hours, lost to the world. The fog covered everything. He was unsure where he was and whether he was sleeping or awake. Hours passed unnoticed. Grandfather was lost in time. Hours later, as the cocks announced the arrival of a new day, the fog in his head began to lift, and the full impact of the tragedy just completed began to sink in.

Perhaps for the second time in that day, the Ottoman patriot and hedonist, invoked his God, "My Allah" he screamed, "What have I done? I have ruined it all."

I believe Grandfather then, probably for the first time ever in his life, felt a deep remorse. In agony he realized that he had been living a lie. His Young Turk veneer was a thin external shield; in his true heart Halil was a tyrannical and selfish autocrat. His self-confidence and his good looks were merely his tools to exploit women, to treat them like chattel. But Emine would not stand for it. Her courage, her sacrifice was stronger than his superficial ego.

He then changed course and started walking back, slowly and unsteadily towards to the Police headquarters. The sun was just beginning to rise. Early in the morning, he turned himself in. The sleepy policeman on duty, who had been dozing off and on idling for hours, was taken aback when Grandfather appeared before him, looking like a dead man walking.

# XXVI

While Grandfather was walking aimlessly heading to the Police Headquarters to turn himself in, the District Officer from Kyrenia was entering the same address through a different door. David Read went straight upstairs to the police chief, jumping up the steps two at a time, as if he were in a race.

The earliest the DO could see the Police Superintendent was the following morning after his interview with the *Kadi*. He was off to Nicosia in the crack of dawn the next day. The journey from Kyrenia to Nicosia over the Five Finger Mountain pass would normally take two hours by a horse-carriage. In those days, only the Resident and one or two of the most senior officers had cars. Even traveling by car would have taken an hour.

By the time David Read was at the Police Headquarters it was ten am. And, then he had to wait for Mr. James, the Superintendent to arrive at his office. James was a man of habit, and every morning he enjoyed spending an hour doing mediation and yoga, habits he had acquired in his Indian days. "Helps clear the mind, and it is damn good for the soul." He would say to his friends who regarded the habit too Oriental.

By the time David Read was able to see James, the police chief it was eleven.

"To what do I owe this unexpected pleasure?" The police chief began when his unexpected visitor was shown in.

"Something important, Sir" he said, "about the Ayoub girl. You know, the abduction case involving one of your *zaptiehs?* I believe his name is Halil Osman."

"Oh! That one. I know, I had the chap in the other day, before I wrote to you about it." He began. "I'm afraid, little we can do. Purely civil matter, as you know. I gave the fellow a tongue-lashing." His mind drifted momentarily back to his own Madras days and his own Muslim women troubles. There, he recalled, some years back the Resident himself, had lost his job in disgrace for having secretly married the daughter of the Muslim maharaja. "These bloody entanglements with local women are always messy," he thought to himself, wondering if he should have been tougher with Halil, perhaps suspending him for a few weeks or a month for his indiscretion.

"But, Sir" said the DO respectfully, "I think I found a solution for the case." He stopped for impact.

"You did. How so?" said the Superintendent of Police.

"Yes, Sir. I went to see the *Kadi* of Kyrenia, as you suggested." The chief of police looked on, and waited in silence for David Read to finish his story:

"The old man says if we can talk to Halil's wife, she may lodge a complaint against him. Then the Muslim law can kick in."

"Is that so?" asked James. He was more skeptical than David: "And how do you suppose we talk to the lady?"

"We ask Halil to take us to see her, Sir," said David. The Superintendent thought for a minute and then he made up his mind. His eyes sparkled and a gentle smile appeared on his face.

"You are right David. It is worth a try." David was delighted. He was already beginning to feel a huge moral weight off his back. The police chief went on: "What have we got to lose?"

He then yelled out to the peon outside his office. The man rushed in and stood to attention.

"Go get me Halil" He said. "I want him to come right here, on the double. You hear?"

The peon went out.

He was back in the Superintendent's office in ten minutes, looking grim and frightened.

He was too late.

"Halil is downstairs, Sir" said the peon. Read and James stared at him, surprise written on both their faces.

"Sir" began the peon. "Something terrible has happened. Halil confessed it. There has been a murder. He is in custody below."

# XXVII

When Grandmother's parents rushed to the Tanzimat Street house the next day, they were one day late. They arrived just as the police were rushing to the same address. They found their daughter, fear written all over her face, sitting in the corner of her downstairs room, not far from the dead body of Elana covered in blood, drying and ejecting an awful odor, the kitchen knife all covered in blood next to the slain body. Little Aygul was asleep, exhausted finally after crying for hours through the long night while Grandma was stupefied and oblivious to it all. But somehow she fed the baby with her milk, more out of habit than design. It was a terrible sight, frightened Grandma sitting in the corner, Elana's body lifeless on the floor, too horrific for human eyes.

"My Allah" screamed Fatma, first rushing toward Emine, then picking up baby Aygul, while the patriarch, Mustafa Aga stood there frozen by shock, overcome by emotion to say anything. The depth of his terrible mistake was sinking in.

In the next moment, the police came and arrested Emine. "We have to take her to the police headquarters" said Sergeant Kazim, who turned to the parents and added:

"Halil confessed everything."

The parents stood motionless, helpless, and unsure this was happening to them.

Then baby Aygul and her Grandparents made their way to Pineview.

# DISGRACED

\*\*\*

Emine's trial for manslaughter was set in three months hence in order to give time for the new British justice in the island to prepare the case for the prosecution in the case of *Emine vs. The King*.

Grandma was arrested and put in jail pending trail for manslaughter. She was taken to the central prisoner behind the police headquarters and put in solitary confinement with a guard outside her cell. No visitors were allowed and no one called. She refused food and went into total silence.

"Poor woman" pitied the prison guard, "she must be remorseful. Why would a Muslim woman kill the second wife of her husband? Her disgrace is her ultimate humiliation" He judged.

No doubt, Grandmother was misunderstood by the gentle Ottoman society of Nicosia that accepted male domination as normal. She became a disgraced female murderer, a woman who rebelled against her husband's abuse. She was judged and condemned before her trial. That was the public moral code of the times, the harsh and sexist Ottoman double standard. The Young Turks who believed in liberty and freedom – but only for men, especially men in politics and public life. Women belonged in the harem, kept there for men's pleasure.

None of these signs of social disapproval had any effect on Grandmother. She had ceased to register external happenings around her; the moment she rebelled against injustice is the moment she stopped to care. The pain of rejection by her husband and by her parents was unbearable enough. Now she had to endure the loss of her little Aygul. I have no idea of how dear little mother felt at the time, but judging from her behavior in later years, I am convinced the trauma left lifelong scars.

Suddenly Grandmother remembered her baby. "Where is my dear little Aygul?" she asked. But she remembered her only for a moment because her mind began to drift away into a world of demons and ghosts. She was being carried through dark corridors into mysterious worlds peopled by horrible figures, half human and half animal with horns and tails. She was oblivious to the reality of abandonment and confinement, and sank into a deep void, uttering strange words to non-human figures that seemed to come from all direction overcrowding and tormenting her for her sin.

The pain became more intense. In the days following, Emine's mental condition got worse and the wheels of the British justice started turning, ever so slowly. Finally, the officials, with all due pomp and circumstance, determined that the proper charge was that of unpremeditated manslaughter. It would have been a first-degree murder, punishable by hanging, had it not been for the fact that the Maronite girl was judged, in British law, to be a trespasser, brought into Emine's home and kept there against the wife's will. And the act of killing with a kitchen knife was clearly not a case of premeditated murder. Emine had not planned it. She was provoked by her husband's behavior, which amounted to unusual and cruel punishment. In her hour of need, her family, victim to her own fathers' vain ego, abandoned dear Grandmother Emine. She had nowhere to turn; she was trapped by an oppressive culture.

I cannot help but draw a tragic parallel between Grandmother's condition and another pathetic contemporary of her's, Franz Kafka's circumstances in far away Prague whose writings helped me greatly in coming to terms with my own self. Of course, Kafka and Grandmother Emine were in totally different circumstances, each tormented by fears and phantoms of their own making, unaware of the wider world beyond. But the two were amazingly similar in some spiritual or psychological way. Like Grandma, Kafka, was a fragile figure dominated by a father patriarch situated in a cultural environment in Prague no less oppressive than Grandma's Ottoman world on Tanzimat Street in Nicosia. They were complex personalities, far from fulfillment with inner needs that outer society, not even close family members, neither acknowledged nor cared. They were cast away, abandoned, unnourished in love, condemned to perish for, and wither away, to pay for the sins of others.

Grandfather Halil's sins were the heaviest in Emine's tragic end. He was too selfish. In the end, he confessed his wrongdoing. He admitted the planning of Elana's abduction and abandoning his wife and baby Aygul. He was immediately dismissed from the police force for misconduct and as the principal accomplice in the tragic murder of the Maronite girl. He had also acted with unusual and unreasonable cruelty toward his wife. He was put in jail, pending trial. In the end, he was sentenced to twenty years term. It was not enough. When released as a free man, in mid-forties, there appeared to be no serious damage done to Halil's capacity to win women's heart. He resumed his old womanizing ways, going at full speed often as if he was in a hurry to make up lost time.

## DISGRACED

Grandmother Emine's case was unprecedented, an Ottoman woman being charged for the murder of a young Maronite girl. The British law in an Ottoman society was rough justice. The colonial authorities were puzzled on how to proceed in these uncharted waters, except that every precaution was taken to make sure proper decorum was observed and due process strictly followed.

The trial never took place. What happened was something else.

When the police came to the house on Tanzimat Street, right after the parents, Emine was calm and waiting. They arrested her and handcuffed her. She cooperated fully. In fact, she seemed almost glad to be out of this house of misery. She clasped at little Aygul, in silence, and would not let her go. But they would not let her keep her baby. Emine started to cry, in quiet, for she sensed what was coming. Her intuition whispered silent words to her mind that there was no room for little Aygul where she was about to be taken. The police passed her to the Grandparents.

Grandmother Emine gave a last, loving look at the baby, and quietly, privately she started crying. No one noticed. None cared. She had lost everything. Like a wary traveler, she had reached the end of her journey. The end of hope, love was extinguished, what remained of life seemed an eternity, an unbearable burden. She was ushered into her solitary prison cell. With her exit out of the front door of the stone house on Tanzimat Street, she left one world, a world in which she realized brief love that had produced her beloved Aygul, now torn away from her forever. She was entering a new world, of demons and ghosts, like the Demonland she had visited in her nightmare just days before.

At the police station, officers gathered around, mostly in curiosity, trying to catch a glimpse of a female murderer.

"What on earth drove her to it?" Some wondered.

"Jealousy" whispered some one else.

Another more philosophical ventured: "Who knows? You see smoke come out a chimney, but what exactly is cooking inside, nobody knows."

By the time they transported her to the cell in the police station, Emine was already incoherent and reality mattered less and less. She did not care what answers she gave the police who kept on demanding answers at the station. She uttered words that made little sense, and soon that little semblance of rationality evaporated into nothing. The police report remained incomplete, lacking essential detail and her signature.

Then sergeant Kazim had the notion that the trauma Emine had suffered had damaged her brain and he convinced his superiors to call in the psychiatrist from the mental hospital. It was a wise move.

The doctor came to examine Emine within a few days, and when he examined her she was effectively insane. It took the doctor a few hours to declare Emine mentally unfit for trial on account of the trauma she had gone through and the mental dislocation she had suffered.

She was taken to the mental hospital. But poor Emine's suffering did not end quickly. Her behavior worsened and no care or medicine seemed to help her. She refused to eat, talk or respond to repeated attempts by doctors to help her. She had lost her interest in living and within a short time her health declined.

Emine died, oblivious to people and events around her within the month following Elana's murder. She died from self-inflicted causes of lack of nourishment. Abandoned by people from whom she expected love, Emine, the poor Ottoman woman had suffered the ultimate disgrace of being forced to part from her child, the one joy still unrealized in her short life.

Only the Armenian midwife, Mariam, staged a show of sympathy for Emine. She was not new to human suffering. The day she heard of Emine's death, she walked to Ayse, the wife of Davud the mysterious wheat merchant.

"Ayse, have you heard the news about poor Emine?" she inquired. The neighbor looked at Mariam with surprise. "No" she said, "I have not heard a thing."

"The worst I feared has happened" began Mariam and updated Ayse.

"Oh my Allah" she suddenly exclaimed remembering their conversation not two weeks ago. "I mentioned it to Davud, and he promised me to look into the matter."

Davud had never had a chance to catch up with Halil and nothing came of talk with the Sheik. Davud, or rather the real David Cohen, concentrated on organizing the exodus of the terror-stricken Jews of Europe en route to their homeland, while the Sheik slept during the day and whirled away by night seeking divine salvation through mysteries beyond most mortals. The two ladies, Ayse and Mariam, exchanged their sympathies and agreed that Emine was dealt an unfair fate. "Poor girl, she had such a lovely baby. May she rest in peace, Amin?" they said.

At the Tekke of the Whirling Dervishes only Horoz Ali remembered Halil. The Sheik passed his judgment: "Life is full of surprises. Allah knows best", while the gatekeeper, with more realism, said to himself: "Poor Halil, he knew how to enjoy life."

Within a decade of Grandma's death, the Ottoman world ceased to exist as well. It was as if her sacrifice was an early sign. The Empire's death was just as violent as my dear Grandmother's, except that it took place on a much larger scale. The human suffering it generated was colossal. The innocent were all victims of immorality in a world in which human liberty was misunderstood, women were still chattel, and dignity had no room.

# XXVIII

Now I must account for my dear mother's terrible start in life. I long wondered why she went through life as if she lived in Hell. Her torment seemed to have no end; it was like she had come to life to experience nothing but misery. Yet, in moments of calm and serenity, she was some times pure joy to be with; full of kindness of heart, generous of her everything earthly she owned, and always understanding of human suffering. She walked about and talked with one and all with a mysterious and deep concern, as if to inquire: "Do you know the meaning of torment? Can you imagine how someone closest to you can also be your tormentor?"

Her Grandparents took little Aygul, my dear mother, to Pineview. Barely two weeks old, she was raised by a wet nurse, in fact her aunt, Pembe who had recently given birth to a baby girl herself.

Mustafa Aga died not long after the murder. He died from the pain of social disgrace that he could bear no more. His own external image was what mattered most, now his honor destroyed. In the days following the murder, he passed a cruel judgment on his own reprehensible behavior: "How I can face my neighbors? How can I look at them and expect them to talk to me like old times? It is humiliating, Fatma. " He confided to his wife; for her, what mattered was the wrong he had committed against their daughter. Fatma's torment was internal; she cared not for what people thought.

## DISGRACED

For the once proud Aga, self-pity turned his remaining days into a private Hell. He lost his appetite, he stopped going out to the coffee shop, and he became a recluse. Just sitting at home, lost in his thoughts, unaware and uninterested in human affairs.

Fatma, heavy of heart herself for having failed her own daughter, was in no mood to comfort her husband. She gave him a bittersweet look. Sure, she felt pity for him, but her anger towards her husband was no less.

Most of all Fatma felt a dreadful sense of guilt. "Why did I not tell him about the necklace before it was too late?" There was no answer.

"If only I knew of Halil's word at the wedding." More and more she began to feel responsible for the tragedy.

Then, at a moment of high self-pity and emotional give and take between husband and wife, Fatma admonished her husband in unaccustomed candor:

"Don't you go around with foolish notions of honor in your head" she chided him.

"We killed our daughter. We turned our back and walked away, leaving her alone in her misery. May Allah have pity on us?"

Her prayers had no impact on the Aga. He started sulking, stopped going out and socializing, and at home he bothered his wife no more.

In the days that followed he grew solitary and lost his energy. Life had become tedious, meaningless. "Too much guilt, too much disgrace for one's shoulders to carry" the gossipers whispered at the village coffee shop. The once proud Aga was a broken man. "How quickly he has fallen" said another villager. Remorse and sadness were visible on everyone's face. Privately, deep inside the soul, however, it was different. Some, remembering old feuds in days when the Agha was mighty and powerful, said: "Allah works in mysterious ways: in the end justice is done." Neighbors, torn between ignorance and disbelief, stayed away, as if totally indifferent to these tragic events.

At home there was no longer peace and serenity. In silence, the suffering escalated. Husband and wife drifted away and in the *Muhtar's* mansion disorder and decline set in where once order had ruled and strict Ottoman custom prevailed. Nothing seemed to cheer them, and food stopped being tasty, and even talking was tiresome.

Mustafa Aga died within a few months. His wife did not weep. She was herself declining rapidly. And she too was gone within three months.

"An evil eye has cast a bad spell on this family" said some neighbors.

Yet others, with less knowledge and more arrogance, had a different judgment. "They died from disgrace. May Allah save us from the disgrace of a daughter who ends up like Emine."

# XXIX

Dear Reader, let me now revisit to another family in torment, also Ottoman, a family as much a victim of moral decay as our own. All paid dearly for the oppressive culture different Ottoman communities then willingly or unwillingly upheld.

In the nearby Kormacit, the Ayoub family was experiencing their own disgrace. Elana's death heaped on the Maronite family unbearable private pain and public scorn. Villagers who had been cold and unwelcoming before, at last had found an excuse for vindication.

The funeral was a lonely affair. Only the parents grieved, the villagers stayed away. It was their ultimate revenge for the scandal the Ayoub family had caused on their good name.

"I told you, that family will come to no good," gossiped their neighbors.

"It is the fault of the mother, she never taught that girl of theirs any manners" declared a churchgoer, feeling temporarily uplifted after her own confession at the church earlier that very morning.

Another would extemporize: "When you allow your daughters so much liberty, this is the terrible end you will meet. You reap what you sow."

The thing, which upset the people of Kormacit, was the perceived attack on public morality. Somehow, it appeared that the entire Maronite community felt a collective shame of Elana's murder. It was as if she was punishing them.

How could she do this to them? Suddenly the villagers became the victim and it was all Ayoubs' fault. The girls' parents could have prevented it, saving the community all this disgrace, but they did not. They wanted to punish the good people of Kormacit, to take a crazy sort of revenge. The whole thing was so mean and nasty.

There were so many questions. "How could a good Maronite girl end up with an immoral infidel like Halil? Why, he was already a married man, wasn't he?" The villagers had all kinds of questions, and wanted to know, except there was no one to provide the answers. That made things worse.

After the funeral hardly anyone came visiting the Ayoub family, and no one expressed condolences. Their house might have been hit by the plague.

There was one exception. The priest did come over to offer his condolences and to pray for the soul of departed Elana. "We are all sinners," he pronounced: "We have a lot to answer for our misdeeds. Come soon and confess it all." This intensified the heavy sense of guilt that Elias and Katrina Ayoub were already carrying. It did nothing to reduce their pain or disgrace.

At one point, Katrina was moved to say something in her and her husband's defense, explaining their futile efforts with both the British and Muslim authorities to get them to do something about their daughter's abduction. She looked at her husband and saw the blank face of a man as if asking her: "What is the point? It is done. Elana is gone and there is nothing to bring her back."

In the days following, the Ayoub's' worst fears and predictions came true: The couple became social outcasts. Their life in Kormacit became a boring, lonely, meaningless endurance. The feeling of disgrace was overpowering. Elias and Katrina walked in the village like condemned criminals.

There was one thing to do. Elias and his wife quietly decided to pull up stakes once again and migrate. That is what they did; this time, with the help of David Read they migrated to London, England to make a new start. They left the little community of Kormacit forever. Life in the little Maronite village then settled down to its peaceful pattern, and no scandals followed for years to come. Soon Elana and her unfortunate parents were forgotten.

# XXX

In the Ottoman capital the age of liberty was as short lived as in Grandfather Halil's world in Nicosia. It had produced tragic results in both cases with death and destruction. The Young Turks took power and the tired and decadent Ottoman Sultanate began its last decade of bleeding to its final death.

When Grandfather ended up in jail for his terrible misdeeds, the sun was finally setting on the Ottomans. Morally bankrupt and financially ruined, the Sultan kept losing countries and people. The Sick Man of Europe was dying. As the Empire shrunk, moral decay and corruption set in. The Young Turk's tyranny and misrule dominated the Ottoman capital and war engulfed the Empire from within and without. The Armenians revolted in the east, and the British and the other European powers moved in from the west, occupying Egypt, Arabia, Libya and the Balkans.

In the island of Cyprus, the Ottoman era was finally over and the British occupation took hold. British law and order gradually replaced Ottoman. Lady Ramsbottom, wearing all her jewellery and accompanied by her husband, only slightly less poor and her touring party, left the island in a joyful mood, confident with the knowledge that British law and order was gaining ground. Midas, the bandit chief, had a different idea on the matter.

The Ottoman ruling elite of the island, top to bottom, was dispossessed; fortunes were lost and families torn. One of those who lost was my other Grandfather, Uzun Ali, the Kaimakam of Milltown, another lovely Ottoman village eight miles to the east of Nicosia right under the fingers of the Five Fingers Mountains. As the Ottoman era ended, this peaceful multi-ethnic village, like the whole island, faced an uncertain future.

In 1908, my paternal Grandfather Uzun Ali was approaching middle age; the former Kaimakam sat alone in his *Selamlik* in the Konak, making plans for the future. He too, had been a man of Tanzimat, the Ottoman patriot and reformer, but now he was disillusioned and betrayed by the Sultan. Reluctantly, he had to adjust himself for the age of the British. In the end, he failed to do so, and died a broken man. But not before he secured his greatest legacy, his two sons, my father and uncle, who later on, in their own diametrically differing ways, were able to redeem the family fortunes.

Baby Aygul, my dear mother, initially traumatized by the violence during her first week of existence, gradually adjusted to carefree life in Pineview in the gentle care of her aunt Pembe, who became first the milk-mother and subsequently her actual mother. But the loss of her real mother remained with Aygul throughout her life. The pain of growing up motherless, without real maternal love was Aygul's unbearable burden she would carry throughout her life.

Even at an early age, she behaved as if she had been a witness to it all. It was, of course, impossible. There was simply no way a baby, barely out of her mother's womb, could witness the cruel punishment to which her mother was subjected by a ruthless father whose morality was Ottoman through and through. He felt entitled to his own harem and the Sultan's declaration of liberty was, for Halil, as invitation to libertine living.

When mother was old enough to know, she developed a passion to learn more about her mother. Every bit of new information she collected reinforced her conviction that her father was the real murderer. Her mother was innocent before her Creator. She was a woman, denied love, abandoned and at the end driven to madness. The more she learnt about her father's cruelty and her mother's revolt against injustice, the bitterer Aygul became.

Vindication of her mother became her lifelong passion, the intensity of her passion only matched by the hatred of her father. Grandmother Emine's premature death precluded a mother's love that mother could never experience. Her brief life was a struggle for a triumph of fidelity of a wife over the immorality of a womanizing father. The father she came to hate had cared neither for wife nor child. Her mother, by contrast, represented purity of commitment. She had died for mother Aygul.

Grandmother's tomb in the public graveyard of Nicosia, beyond the new railway line, became mother's Mecca for silent, private prayers. She would go there often, sometimes daily, to pray for forgiveness and to cry her heart out for an innocent life lost, a human sacrifice in the Ottoman altar of family honor in a brief period of false liberty totally abused by a father she wished she had never had.

Mother got married at the young age 15 at the end of October 1923. She was then a beautiful young lady, brilliant at school, and the man she married was, like her own father, a policeman. Father Ozkan was dashing and handsome, the youngest son of Uzun Ali, the old Kaimakam of Milltown.

How this marriage came about is another story, a story of transition, of death and rebirth, struggles and suffering symbolizing the violent end of the Ottoman world and the birth of the Turkish Republic. Cyprus then became a British colony and new conspiracies were hatched and tried out, usually ending up with new rounds of conflict, misery and bitterness.

On the day my parents, Aygul and Ozkan married modern Turkey was born, so the union of mother and father was wrapped up in the emergence of Modern Turkish Republic. A new day began. Moral decay was arrested, an awakening and a rebirth launched. It was not easy. Ottoman identity was rejected, sometimes forcibly, and a new Turkish one forged top down. Modern names became fashionable, signaling new identity and hope, but change, as always, was painful. In British Cyprus, Ottoman Muslims became Turks of Cyprus. It took several years of struggle before polygamy was ended and new civil laws were introduced establishing legal equality of women.

# THE END

# BOOK II

## ROSES AND TEARS

Buyuk Han

# I

Dear Reader, I must start with a confession. I was not fond of my maternal grandfather, Halil Osman. I disapproved of his values and womanizing ways. For me, he bore the prime responsibility for my grandmother's death and my dear mother Aygul's tormented life. Mother became an adult at the early age of 15, when she was married off thanks to the efforts of the neighborhood matchmaker, but her torment began right at her birth and the tragic murder scene she experienced. Her torment was revived with the disillusionment at her wedding night on 29th October 1923. Grandfather Halil had to miss the wedding, of course; he was in jail for causing the sudden and premature death of my grandmother, the beloved mother whom Aygul had lost right after birth. He was responsible for this unbearable loss.

My paternal grandfather was a different sort of man. Sure he had gambled away the family fortune, and he died a broken man in debt. What he lost was material things; grandpa Uzun Ali never lost his inner soul, his identity. He had an abiding confidence in the power of education as a means of overcoming all obstacles. Even when he was down, he never wavered from his belief that learning was the key to the modern world. He was confident that, through modern knowledge, one day his family would rise again to reclaim its greatness. His two sons, my father and uncle, are his lasting legacy, for through them he left his imprint on all of us: His life and time were like roses and tears, beautiful and sad, bitter and sweet, all at once. We are all Uzun Ali's and I am truly grateful for the vision of my paternal grandfather.

This is his story, our story.

Like all families, we have our secrets and closets with skeletons inside. It has taken me long and tedious work to unearth all the mysteries and intrigues, piece it all together, the good and the bad. I must record them all with all the sincerity at my command. I have used many family documents, letters and papers. I have talked with many, first and foremost my dear mother, father and my uncle. Grandpa was dead many years before I was born. Relations between father and grandpa had been cool, because his favorite son was uncle Munir, ten years senior to father who was second fiddle. Many years later, and especially after father's death, mother and uncle Munir developed a close, emotional relationship and I learnt a great of family history from him. Mother, and me, we always had a special feeling and naturally she has been my main confidant, my guide, and my informer. This is no less her story than grandpa's.

*** 

Uzun Ali was the Kaimakam of Milltown, the provincial governor, until the British took over Cyprus in 1878, with two sons from different mothers. Munir, ten years senior, and Ozkan were half brothers, but then in those days mothers mattered less, so they were brothers for all practical purposes and they were known as such. When the British became masters of the island, the comfortable Ottoman life in the Kaimakam's mansion, the Konak, ended. Where luxury and leisure ruled, now decline set in. The decline was both material and moral.

Milltown was a mixed town, half Muslim half Christian, situated right underneath the Five Fingers of the same Mountain Range, overlooking Nicosia at the center of Mesarya plain. Milltown was like an oasis in the desert, green and beautiful with olive groves and orchards, vegetable gardens and prosperous. The town was fed by a spring that issued in the mountains and provided the best quality drinking water on the island, or so at least the locals believed, and there was water aplenty for farming. "This water is Allah's gift; it is so plentiful, it provides life to seven villages." Peasants and princes would boast.

Kaimakam was the district governor, the all-powerful Ottoman administrator of Milltown, and an unusually high office for a mid-size town. The importance derived from the fact that Milltown had 16 flourmills that provided bread for the capital, Nicosia, only 10 miles to the south. In earlier times it was the scene of countless rebellions by greedy mill owners who had an interesting way of obtaining better prices for their flour. They would shut down the mills and Nicosia would starve, the Ottoman government finally giving the mill owners what they wanted. To settle the matter for once and for all, after the reform period of Tanzimat that commenced in 1839, Milltown was elevated to a *nahiye,* a sub-district with a Kaimakam installed to keep things under control. With the office came ownership of several mills and extensive land holdings. Most of these lands were leased out to tenants, primarily Greek Cypriots who paid rent, which made possible the luxury of the Konak. Kaimakam's official salary was next to nothing.

I never met grandpa. He died several years before I was born. But I do remember the Konak, his mansion, with its extensive female quarter, the *harem,* and the stately *selamlik,* the Ottoman official chamber where grandfather conducted his meetings and held court. It was partly a library, holding valuable tracts and *Korans* all stored in magnificent bookcases built of rare oak, all nicely placed under a row of carved shelving on all four walls, interspaced by precious Ottoman plates and glasses, handcrafted by Iznik masters of centuries before. On the floor were myriad of Persian carpets and prayer rugs, each one more beautiful than the next, all together projecting an air of tranquility and magnificent order.

Most of all, I remember the grounds surrounding the Konak, the orchards of oranges and mandarins, and the endless groves of olive trees. I am told there was once a beautiful rose garden, the pride of Konak, situated right under the latticed windows of the *harem*. To me the roses symbolized the Rose Revolution in Ottoman history, the great reform movement, the Royal *Tanzimat* Proclamation of 1839, the daring, but ill-fated idea of progress that was meant to modernize and Europeanize the Ottoman state. Instead it created confusion as few understood such alien terms as liberty and freedom, and ended hastening the Empire's end and destruction, causing tears for so many people. Grandpa was amongst those who had lost just about everything, most important, his status.

The Kaimakam, Uzun Ali, so named for his imposing 6 foot 4 inches, owned no less than 6 of these mills. That was only for openers. Grandpa Uzun Ali was also the biggest landowner in the area, with *ciftliks*, estates, houses, water rights, olive groves, fields of wheat and barley, and property of all sizes and description in every part of the town. His extensive land holdings were largely due to his ability to marry rich women, in the usual custom of the day. Uzun Ali had four wives and two sons, uncle Munir and my own father Ozkan. The sons were born from two different wives ten years apart, the eldest in 1890, the other two wives dying infertile, enriching him only in land.

No doubt about it, uncle Munir was grandpa's favorite. Everything about Munir had entirely his father's temperament and looks, slightly dark complexion with piercing brown eyes. Born in 1890 of the Kaimakam's second wife, he liked being modern, a habit he inherited from the Kaimakam who prided himself as a man of Tanzimat, an outwardly progressive Ottoman. The Kaimakam had the same hopes for his youngest, my father, born of his 3rd wife, but fate spoiled it all. Father was a shy boy; not very good at school and so he ended up as second fiddle, although just being second had a lot to do with it as well. Grandpa alone had picked father's name, a brand new non-Arabic name, meaning pure blood, commemorating modernity and new hope, born as he was on 1st January 1900, and it was again grandpa who determined that father was to remain second fiddle to his brother Munir. That is how Ozkan's life was mapped and lived: always in the shadow of his elder brother, Munir, chosen very early to be grandpa's heir.

Uncle Munir became a lawyer, in fact, one of the first English-trained lawyers in the capital. Father was fortunate to become a lowly policeman, and that was only thanks to his brother's influence peddling. While his brother enjoyed wealth and luxury, father always struggled to make ends meet from month to month on a meager salary. The story of the two brothers is buried in the secrets of Uzun Ali's Konak, secrets I discovered by chance only recently. Once I made this discovery, I felt I had to write down our family history.

The date of 29th October 1923 is a turning point in our family history. It is, actually, a date of double celebration. Not just the wedding day of father and mother, in itself an insignificant event in the sleepy capital of colonial Cyprus, except that for us it signaled the rebirth of the new generation of the Uzun Ali clan. The date is also a major national holiday. On that day, in the new Turkish capital in Ankara, the Republic was officially born and Modern Turkey replaced the Ottoman Empire.

On that day, in the neighborhood of Samanbahce in Nicosia, a modest wedding ceremony was taking place in a low-cost housing neighborhood, recently completed by the Evkaf, the religious endowment fund, right behind the Police Headquarters. Aygul and Ozkan were tying the knot, amidst a joyous crowd of revelers and neighbors. There was music and food and everyone was celebrating.

The wedding was finally here. It took no less than five years in the making, thanks to the expertise of the neighborhood matchmaker, Hatice Hanim. At long last today, my father Ozkan Uzun Ali, the policeman, was marrying my mother Aygul Halil Osman, a stunningly beautiful girl, just turned 15, raised by an aunt who became her surrogate mother after her mother, Emine, my maternal grandmother died in the mental hospital. Her tragic death came before she could be tried for the murder of grandfather Halil's kept woman, Elana from the Maronite village of Kormacit.

My mother Aygul belonged to the modern generation, too, having discarded the Ottoman veil and *carsaf* in favor of European dress. But her generation was only half modern. The Ottoman custom of marrying females early was still very much in practice, and polygamy was still the rule. Modernity was more symbolic than real: it was relatively easy to discard Arabic names and give the newborn brand new Turkish names. Thus boys were no longer Mehmet, Ali, Huseyin; they became Ergun, Erdil and Caner; the female names Ayse, Fatma and Emine were replaced by the likes of Gulay, Gonul and Sevil. This was the time of a fresh new historical epoch with new forms of dress, a brand new alphabet and pure Turkish names instead of Arabic ones. The new generation was to be modern, at least externally, top down.

The triumphant Gazi, Mustafa Kemal, had crashed into the sea the invading imperialists and their Greek proxy armies and a Modern Turkish Republic was resurrected from the dead Ottomans. Ottoman Muslims were reborn now as Turks, the *fez* was gone, wearing European clothes, learning Latin alphabet and resting on Sundays suddenly became the modern ways. Everyone was expected to fall in. In Turkey it was the law; in British Cyprus it was by popular choice. The British only resisted reform in polygamy and religious matters considered too sensitive. Otherwise, the future looked bright and promising. Modernized Turks, until yesterday Muslims or Ottomans, believed they could overcome any obstacle, conquer all science and knowledge, and master every form of nation building.

No parents or blood relations were present at my parents' wedding. Uzun Ali was in his grave, Halil, Aygul's father in name was in jail as was father's elder brother Munir, both for their misdeeds in the murder of two innocent females. This crazy situation coincided with the end of the Great War and the demise of the Ottomans. Grandpa Uzun Ali had been the Ottoman notable in Milltown, but he died at the end of 1918 an impecunious and downhearted man. He was a patriot whose dreams were dashed. Tanzimat, declared with so much enthusiasm, had failed completely to modernize the Ottoman Empire, to unite its various *millets* in peace and harmony, and to transform the Sultanate into constitutional monarchy more like the British.

***

But let me go back to the year 1875. It was a good year. In Milltown, life was easy and luxury ruled for the landed gentry. It was a time of promise, of reform. The dreaded locust epidemic was finally behind. Years of drought were now replaced with plenty. Grandpa had been very much part of the reform movement because, unlike my maternal grandfather, Uzun Ali was a man of action. He wanted to implement the Tanzimat reforms; indeed in some respects he was a man ahead of his time. He unilaterally declared polygamy backward, though, as it turned out, he nevertheless ended up having four wives, but not simultaneously. The fact was that it was not grandpa's fault. It was due to a combination of misfortune and bad health on the part of women arranged to be his wives.

The four wives produced just two sons for grandpa, but again, that was Allah's will, not his choice. Actually his first wife was barren and after 15 years of waiting in vain for a son and heir, Ali had to quit, divorce the poor woman and get himself a new wife, expecting her to be more fertile. Thus finally Uzun Ali got his wish for a son when his beloved Munir was born when he was 35 in 1890. His second son, my father Ozkan was born on New Years' Day, from another mother, Uzun Ali's third wife, at the start of the new century. In a mood of double celebration, grandpa named his new offspring, Ozkan, new blood, signifying a new beginning. After all, such an event happened only once in a century. Father's birth sadly also marked the death of his mother, and so the old Kaimakam married for a fourth time in 1905, his last wife Neslihan.

Besides his wives, the other distinction of grandpa was his nickname. Uzun, meaning tall, was a natural label for a man standing 6 feet 4 inches, enabling him to be noticed in any society. When Uzun Ali died, at the ripe old age of sixty five in late 1918, he had left behind an incredibly rich life, a life of ups and downs through war and peace, during which a succession of four wives merely represented but a little spice. His two sons, uncle Munir and father Ozkan, so totally different, were the man's chief legacy. To his last day, Uzun Ali remained a man of Tanzimat, an idea of reform and progress that never materialized; when he passed away so did the Ottoman age, reform and all.

# II

At the beginning, back in 1870s, at the age of 25, grandpa became the Kaimakam of Milltown. That was high honor and made him a member of the Ottoman elite. He was the district governor, lord of several villages. His word was the law; he represented the all-powerful Sultan, away in the glorious capital of the Ottomans, the magical Istanbul, center of the world known to all islanders, Christians and Muslim alike.

Young and resourceful, grandpa was awarded this high office plus huge land holdings and a Mansion, the *Konak,* his official residence with 20 servants, for his valuable service to the Governor Said Pasha who had achieved great success in eliminating the dreaded locust, long the scourge of the island. In just one year, 50,000 *okka* of locust eggs were collected and destroyed thanks to the hard work of Uzun Ali and other unknown officials aided by Italian technicians specifically invited for the job. The Pasha got as his reward from the Sultan, the Star of *Mecidiye*, 2nd class. Grandpa got his office and all the rewards that came with it. Years of comfort ensued. Milltown prospered.

The prize estate in Uzun Ali's possession was the Beyler *Ciftlik,* 100 donums of prime land, irrigated from the waters of the Milltown spring. It produced the best vegetables in summer and winter and provided steady income for the Kaimakam of over 100 pounds annually, enough to pay for his entire household of servants. In addition, no less than two dozen peasant families earned their living from the *Ciftlik* as cultivators and tenant farmers; they looked up to the Kaimakam as their lord. The Beyler *Ciftlik* was the jewel in the Kaimakam's crown.

Suddenly the Kaimakam lost his crown. The year 1878 started badly for grandpa, just at the same time as the Ottomans went bankrupt and suffered big losses at the hands of the Tsar. In quick succession he lost his father and mother. Then he found out that his wife was infertile and that was sufficient ground in those days for divorce. But the defining event was a ceremony in the Konak Square in Nicosia on 11th July, which he did not attend. Indeed, he knew nothing of it. Actually, it was a humiliating event. An English emissary, Walter Baring, came all the way from Istanbul with the sultan's *ferman* (a royal letter) and, lo and behold, it was announced that the island was now a British possession. People were shocked and surprised. The Union Jack was hoisted in the Konak Square and Admiral John Jay became the acting governor. Uzun Ali was shamed and abandoned. The axe fell in one sudden swoop. The man of Tanzimat felt like a sacrificial lamb, sold out.

"What?" he shouted aloud. "What is going on?" He decided to travel to Nicosia and called on the *Muftu*, the religious head in the capital. If anyone knew what was going on, it would be the *Muftu*. Grandpa dressed in his official best garments and traveled to the capital, going straight to the *Muftu*'s house behind the Saray square. He was ushered into the *Muftu*'s *selamlik* decorated with expensive carpets and Ottoman furniture.

"Our *Padisah* has given the island to his new friends the British," said the *Muftu* in a bitter tone. The *Muftu* was the head of the religious establishment, and like Grandpa, he knew full well what the transfer of power meant. The British now were the masters, and all the Ottoman notables were about to lose their privileged status on the island. He was unhappy, but he was a devout Muslim and fatalistic about things political, well beyond his control.

"What on earth for?" asked grandpa. He knew it was not the *Muftu*'s fault. But he was hurt and angry, feeling betrayed, yet his civility prevailed as he managed to keep his temper within respectable limits toward his venerable old host.

"We do not always comprehend Allah's will," said the holy man, appealing to God when, as mortal, he felt helpless. Uzun Ali recognized *Muftu*'s helplessness; he sat there in silence, staring at his host.

After a minute, the old man continued:

"I do not know for sure, but I gather it is in return for help the British provided in securing peace after the recent disastrous war with the Tsar" said the *Muftu*.

"Well? What happens now?" asked Uzun Ali anxiously. His comfortable world was crumbling. He felt completely helpless in the face of an approaching disaster.

The *Muftu* tried to calm down the younger man. "May be there is no need to worry. They say it is temporary. When the soldiers of the Tsar leave Kars and Ardahan in eastern Anatolia, then the British will leave Cyprus."

Grandpa was not much comforted. He left his meeting with a heavy heart, in sadness.

Grandpa had every reason to feel unhappy. The *Muftu* had been no comfort, he knew no more than he did. The fact was that the Sultan's government was bankrupt and he was obliged to sell off his possessions, like Egypt and Cyprus, in order to pay interest on the huge Ottoman debt. "We are being sold like sheep." He reflected on his pitiful condition.

It was late in the afternoon when he returned to the Konak. He walked upstairs, not saying a word to the servants downstairs, avoided the *Harem*, went straight to his favorite window seat in the *Selamlik* overlooking the courtyard and just sat there alone in his study, staring at the plants and flowers in the garden, full of gloom and doom. The Kaimakam was visibly in a foul mood, refused to dine with his wife and when she persisted with questions about his visit to the *Muftu* in the capital he got angry. "Woman, just leave me alone." He commanded when she politely inquired what the matter was.

A little later Uzun Ali's mind was made. He declared abruptly: "I will go visiting my miller friends uptown."

His wife knew what he meant. It was a code word for gambling with his Greek Cypriot cronies. Grandpa walked the short distance of less than a mile through the olive orchards, along a stream, to his usual gambling hall, the upstairs of a mill house upstream. A Greek Cypriot, Hajicosta, owned it. He was Haji because he was a lay official in the local Church, but religion was no barrier to good social relations between the Ottoman *millets*, so he was always cordial to the old Kaimakam, smiling and making him welcome with every sign of respect as a representative of the Sultan.

"Ah, Your Honor," Hajicosta said by way of greeting, as soon as he saw Uzun Ali, "our respected Kaimakam is gracing us with his presence. This is a great honor. We will celebrate, eat and drink and have great fun."

"Well, Hajicosta, you are always so hospitable. You know how to make a sad person happy" said Uzun Ali.

"Heaven forbid, what seems to be the trouble, your Honor?" asked Hajicosta.

"Don't ask," he said, and then a moment later he explained: "Hajicosta, I do not understand what is going on anymore. Our world is changing too fast." The mill owner looked surprised and no wiser.

"What has happened, Ali Effendi? I trust no one in your esteemed family has passed away." He inquired more intimately.

"I am told our emerald island is being transferred to the British," said the Kaimakam. It was a bombshell and Hajicosta almost bit his tongue. The mill owner could barely control his emotion.

"Your Honor" he said, "you are joking, of course. Our Padisah, may Allah give him a long life; will not do such a thing. Why everyone here is so satisfied with the glorious rule our sovereign is providing to us through wise administrators like your good self."

"Yes, yes," said Uzun Ali, "but that may not prevent foolish decisions, nevertheless" he said, bitterness obvious in his tone.

"Very true, Your Honor" said Hajicosta and stood in silence. He could think of nothing more to say. Uzun Ali continued:

"Allah will let us know what he has in store for us tomorrow. Tonight we eat and play and have some fun. Life is too short. Is it not?"

"Spoken so wisely" approved Hajicosta.

Then he yelled to his wife and his young daughter. "Prepare dinner for our honored guest. We will have roast lamb, *kleptico* with potatoes, lots of salad with tomatoes, lettuce and cucumber, all accompanied by a great variety of *meze.*" He turned to his teenage son, and ordered: " Dimitri, off you go quickly, go ask the neighbors Andreas, Savvas and Hristo to come over. We will first eat and drink and then we play cards." He took a breath and then added: "Tell them, the Kaimakam of Milltown is our guest tonight."

After the feasting, the five sat around the table to start gambling. Already, the Kaimakam was a little drunk, but he was feeling extremely light and cheerful. The host placed two decks of cards on the table.

"Your Honor" he asked politely, "what shall we play?" He knew that draw poker was Uzun Ali's favorite, but he wanted to act as the good host.

"The usual" said Uzun Ali, as everyone around the table nodded. "Yes, yes" they agreed.

At first, luck was with Uzun Ali and he piled his winnings in front of him in piles of British pounds. The Kaimakam was finally relaxing from what had been a difficult day. At this rate, the day would end up with a handsome profit.

It was getting close to midnight. Then Uzun Ali's luck suddenly ran out. First his straight ace high was beaten by a full house and he lost almost a third of his entire winnings. Then, right after he was dealt a full house and he felt he could not lose, so he gambled the entire amount in front of him. But he was beaten by four 10s. The Kaimakam kept his cool and the atmosphere in the room became more electrified.

In the following half hour, Uzun Ali's cash was all gone.

He got up to go. Hajicosta knew it well. It was not the first time.

"Your Honor" he said. "We are having so much fun. Why are you in a hurry?"

"Well, Hajicosta" he said, "the truth is I have run out of cash and it is getting late."

"What is cash among friends?" said his host. "Your word is our law. We trust each other, you know that."

It was a script that was familiar among the group; everyone nodded their heads in endorsement of what Hajicosta was saying.

Then they discussed a land-for-cash deal.

"I can exchange the 20 donum field near the mosque by the stream," offered the Kaimakam. "In today's value, it is worth hundred pounds easily," said Uzun Ali, doubling the going price.

"Your Honor, that is a fair price" agreed Hajicosta, "but I have a better suggestion."

What is that Hajicosta?" asked the Kaimakam.

"I will give 500 pounds for the Beyler *chiftlik* in the east end of the town" he said referring to the 100 donum prime property, all irrigated land yielding two crops of vegetables and crops a year and that sustained two dozen peasant families.

The Kaimakam was taken aback. That was a large sum of money. The Beyler *ciftlik* provided him an annual income of 100 pounds that covered the Konak's expenses. But, then, he was in a fix and he realized he had to make a sacrifice. The offer was quite generous. The 500 pounds represented a great deal of money, enough to keep a family in luxury for several years. He remained silent and Hajicosta spoke:

"Of course, I do not have such an amount of ready cash with me right now" he said. The total amount that changed hands at the table amounted to 100 pounds, a princely sum indeed.

He continued: "I will give half of it to you tonight, the other half tomorrow night if you are willing" he said. The Kaimakam agreed.

In the following hour, he had lost what was advanced.

Grandpa took his loss philosophically. "Don't worry" said Hajicosta, "this is poker. One time you lose the next one you win. Better luck next time."

"Yes" agreed grandpa. "Today has been a bad day, so bad, I am sure next game can only be better."

The next day Hajicosta went to his priest and got the other half of the money. The Church had a special fund for such land transfers from Muslims: it was part of a long-term strategy of increasing land ownership of Greek Cypriots at the expense of Muslims.

The gambling continued the following night, Grandpa playing one against four. Predictably, he lost it all. So in return for two nights' dinner and gambling, Uzun Ali's pride possession was gone. That was how grandpa had tried in vain to take his revenge on his Sultan for the royal betrayal. They both gambled and lost.

# III

As a historian, I must say the terms of the secret Cyprus convention between the Sultan and the British were nothing less than a clever drafting of ambiguity. In reality it reflected the balance of power, the weakness of the Sultan on the one hand, and the rising power of the British on the other. In one clause, the agreement made it clear that Cyprus was rented to the British, as a temporary measure, to be returned back to the Sultan, but when that would happen was a matter of conjecture. In the meantime, Muslim religion and institutions were safeguarded, and the Sultan remained in theory the owner of the island. It was all so iffy, linked to if and when the Russian army evacuated the eastern vilayets of Kars, Batum and Ardahan. Legal ambiguity or not, on the island, the British were the real masters, happy possessing an outpost which now secured the trade route to India through the new Suez canal, next to Egypt and just east of the island of Cyprus.

At the end of 1878 Uzun Ali lost his job as Kaimakam. The event was expected, but when it happened the loss was heavy and it got worse as time went by. There was no ceremony, no word of thanks from the Sultan or regret, and no provision for retirement. The days of power and luxury were suddenly over at the Konak. The slow and painful decline set in.

He did not know it then, but grandpa was a victim of high level secret plans cooked in London linked to India. More precisely his fate was tied to the profits from the India trade that was making lots of rich people in London richer and more powerful, including Disraeli the Prime Minister and Queen Victoria's favorite politician. Disraeli was a foxy, crafty Jewish upstart who wanted to outsmart his rival Gladstone who was famous for his hatred of everything Ottoman. Just a year earlier he had made an inflammatory speech denouncing the Sultan over Bulgarian atrocities and announcing a policy of kicking Ottoman army out of the Balkans, "bag and baggage." Disraeli took full advantage of the opportunity. Through cunning and intrigue he wrested the control of the Suez Canal from the French and the Sultan, and he made his Queen the Empress of India. Now he wanted a place of arms, a military base in the Eastern Mediterranean to protect British trade routes to India. So the British came, unannounced claiming Cyprus. Famous generals like Kitchener and Wolseley started their empire-building careers in Cyprus and in the Middle East.

Within a short time after the British takeover, the office of Kaimakam was abolished and a new system of District Administration was created. Uzun Ali then became an idle landlord, with little to do, a man of leisure. The Konak suddenly ceased to be a beehive of activity, a court to which Christians and Muslims in the district all rushed for justice and dispute settlement. At the beginning, grandpa still had lots of land. But with lots of time at hand, he quickly got bored, and started visiting bars and gambling places with increasing frequency. Soon Uzun Ali became an addict, an incurable gambler. He gambled away all his mills and then his land. It was a slow death.

The gambling and drinking ways of grandpa mirrored his deep disappointment with the Ottoman decline. The once mighty Empire, its invincible armies, the terror of Europe, looked like an old man, in declining health, terminally sick. It was not merely enemies from outside, plotting and coveting large territories of the "Sick Man of Europe." Even more dangerous was internal disunity, created from ethnic division and conflict within the Empire itself. The old harmony and tolerance between Muslims and non-Muslims had disappeared, to be replaced by animosity and mistrust. Three hundred years ago, expelled Jews had taken refuge in Ottoman lands, escaping death and destruction from the Grand Inquisition. The Greeks and Armenians had amassed great fortunes handling the finances and trade of the Ottomans in times of war and peace. Now everyone was fighting with everyone else, it seemed. Greeks, Bulgarians, Serbs, Armenians were all up in revolt, no longer loyal subjects of the Empire, clamoring for a national homeland of their own. Grandpa, at heart a progressive man, never wavered from his own sense of identity, his own sense of someone special. He was Muslim with an abiding belief in the One, All-powerful Allah and the Prophet, Allah's true and final Messenger, but he was different from and superior to the Arabs. He was an Ottoman, a gentleman, a man of tolerance and equity. His language was Turkish and his outlook on life was Turkish. He was proud to be part of the ruling class of the Empire. His sense of identity was strong and definite, like some stone building that stood the test of time, multi-layered and well ordered. His faith in Allah gave him serenity, his official status a keen sense of justice for all the *millets* ['we are all Allah's children, His creation' he believed], and he believed in the intrinsic goodness of his fellow human beings.

Now it seemed this world, his world, was suddenly coming to an end. He knew nothing about the English, the new masters of the island. All he knew was that they were masters of new technology, and their power derived from mastery of new knowledge. "Knowledge is Power" became Uzun Ali's motto, his abiding vision.

\*\*\*

Milltown then was a large and mixed town of some 5,000 souls half Muslim, half Greek Orthodox. It was a prosperous town, the Muslims were the upper class, owning most of the mills and the olive gardens, and the Greeks were mostly the artisans, farmers and workers. But Milltown was changing fast. The change agent was the Church. From mid-nineteenth century on there were new churches being built in Milltown as well as elsewhere in Cyprus. The church construction was supervised by a group of missionary clergy from Greece. The clergy came like a crusading army building congregations everywhere converting and forcing every peasant to attend the Church and follow the dogma. The local priest was also a financier with a special mission to extend ready cash to any member of the congregation for land purchase from the Ottomans. That was the way to acquire possession of the island in the long struggle as part of the *Megali Idea* on the way toward a new Hellenic Byzantium.

Without a job and a chronic gambling habit, Uzun Ali needed new supply of land to sustain his lifestyle. So, he decided to dump his barren wife. After fifteen years his patience ran out with a wife who gave him no sons and he went for divorce. In the presence of four male witnesses, he uttered the words: "I divorce thee" three times, and it was done. Uzun Ali soon remarried, this time getting the second daughter of the *Muhtar* in the next village. The decision to re-marry significantly replenished Uzun Ali's land holdings, and at the age of 35, he finally had a son. His beloved Munir was born in 1890.

But the arrival of an heir did not arrest and reverse grandpa's decline. He steadily lost land; his decline paralleled the Empire's. As the Ottoman Empire became a sick man of Europe, so the former Kaimakam, continued, like other Ottoman notables in Cyprus, selling land and the Greek Church took the lead in providing members of its new congregation with easy credit for these land purchases. This was a period of transition. Land was changing hands all the time, as a result of gambling and womanizing habits, which spread amongst the Ottoman elite like the plague.

Within a decade, Uzun Ali was, once again, in the marriage market. It was all a mystery, his second wife was suddenly found dead in her bed one morning in the summer of 1898, and Uzun Ali quickly took on a new wife. His third wife was carefully chosen. She was another daughter from a landed family able to replenish Uzun Ali's holdings, at least for a time. Moreover, this lady performed a miracle: she produced Uzun Ali's second son on the first day of the new Millenium creating in the former Kaimakam a rare mood of celebration. The newborn, my father was named Ozkan, the new blood, signifying a fresh start for the dynasty's dwindling fortunes. Father Ozkan was expected to be a harbinger of good luck, rescuer of family fortune, an injection of dynamic new blood. However, he was a failure from the start. He was the cause of his mother's death. The poor woman became victim to hemorrhaging.

Now in his mid forties, this time Uzun Ali decided to take a different course of action. Instead of remarrying in a hurry, he started recruiting concubines, *odaliks*, maids and *halayiks*, wet-nurses and servants for the children and his own needs, all the time nourishing his gambling ways. There was a steady supply of young Circassians, Abyssians, and other young girls from diverse races all over the Empire in the slave market in Famagusta. This was a market, left over from Venetians and earlier times, which the Ottoman traders developed further with links to the Sudan and other African sources of supply.

## ROSES AND TEARS

Then finally in 1905, on reaching half century, grandpa felt romantic briefly and married for the fourth and last time, Neslihan. This marriage, like his earlier ones, was one of convenience. Uzun Ali agreed to marry Neslihan when her first husband, the Egyptian cotton baron on the island at the time, Dervish Aga, died suddenly from an unknown illness, with no offspring. His wealth passed to Neslihan and that, rather than her looks was more attractive to the Kaimakam. In fact, his last wife, in her mid fifties, was a few years older than Uzun Ali. But that was a trivial matter compared with the lady's immovable assets.

Neslihan knew her limits in the Konak, as grandpa was well aware of her origin and background. By birth, she was the daughter of a Russian noble displaced and dispossessed at the time of the Crimean War in Moldovia. Originally named Natasha, her family somehow managed to find its way to Istanbul, impoverished but lucky to be alive. Her beauty, her blue eyes, red lips and fair hair, is what saved the family; Natasha was sold in the slave market at the tender age of sixteen, repurchased by Dervish Aga some years later, then on holiday in the Ottoman seat of power in Beyoglu, from a Greek Madame for a King's ransom.

"I want a virgin," insisted Dervish Aga. "Of course, you can be sure of that," confirmed the Madame, well experienced in such secretive matters requiring unusual mix of tact and creativity.

So, Natasha's virginity was re-engineered with simple solutions under the Madam's supervision. As part of the transaction, Natasha became Neslihan, and subsequently Dervish Aga settled in Cyprus getting wealthy in cotton trading with Egypt thanks to his extensive network of connections in commerce and politics in Cairo and Istanbul. Lady Neslihan gave Dervish Aga much pleasure, but no children, during their years of marriage, but he was not a man that would be satisfied with one woman. His interest in concubines remained as alive as his trade in cotton to his last days. When he died, there were rumors of death by poisoning, but whatever the reason Dervish Aga took it with him to his grave. Neslihan entered the Kaimakam's harem, her Russian identity long since forgotten.

In October 1905 a technological revolution occurred in British Cyprus. A brand new railway line started service, linking the port town of Famagusta in the east with the capital city Nicosia in central Mesaoria plain. Later on the line was extended all the way west to the copper mines just north of Lefke. There was a station not far from

## UZUN ALI, SHAME AND SALVATION

Milltown and Grandpa was one of the local notables that included the Greek Orthodox priest and the Hodja, all seated at the head of the honor line welcoming the age of the "iron horse" as it was popularly known amongst the local people. When the train duly reached the station, whistle blowing and white and dark clouds bellowing from its chimney, it was quite a sight, something no one had ever seen before. The event rocketed the prestige of the British sky high, certifying for all skeptics the power of modern knowledge. It testified, once more to grandpa's satisfaction, not that proof was required, of the superiority of British technical know-how.

Right after the ceremony, a group of Greek Cypriots approached Grandpa. It looked like a delegation on a business deal headed by the *Muhtar*, the headman of the Greek Cypriot community in Milltown.

"Selam and greeting, Your Honor" the leader announced, displaying all of the old formality and respect as if Uzun Ali was still the old Kaimakam and the Ottomans, not the British were masters of Cyprus.

"We have come to request your advice," said the leader of the group. He then stated their problem. It was yet another case of water dispute, a case of stolen water. The water from the Milltown spring fed farms and orchards for miles around, and water rights were still regulated according to age-old Ottoman system of titles and rotation by the hour. Upstream in Milltown there was an Ottoman weir that regulated the water flows and apportioned it amongst a number of villages downstream. Every village had a time-honored share and the system worked well since time immemorial. In the past, disputes were always settled by appeal to the Kaimakam. Within a given village, the farmers had access to the water flowing in channels for specific number of portion of twenty-four hours per day. Water was a very precious commodity, determining land values, the most prized farms being those with irrigation rights. Having water right was a matter of wealth. If you had water to irrigate, you could grow two, sometimes three crops a year. In short, water meant prosperity. So, water disputes were by no means uncommon, especially in periods of drought.

Grandpa asked briefly what the nature of the dispute was. "Your Honor" began the leader of the delegation. "Last night, it seems some children diverted the water flow at the weir to increase their father's flow. We discovered who they were." Grandpa had heard it so many times before.

"Come to the Konak this afternoon." He declared to the obvious pleasure of the delegation. That was the old Ottoman way of handling and settling disputes like this one. It required listening to both sides and then, when all had had their say, grandpa would render a decision. It was a sign of his high standing in the community that his judgments were valued and respected. This case would be no different. In the *selamlik* in the Konak that afternoon, a court was held, the guilt was voluntarily accepted, and a fair sentence delivered that satisfied all parties. The judgment was all simplicity: Ten shillings cash imposed on the guilty man, payable immediately in equal shares to two farmers whose water had been stolen. Case closed, everyone went home satisfied. That was how grandpa, even in British times well after the end of Ottoman rule in Cyprus, was perceived in Milltown, amongst Greek and Turkish Cypriots alike: a respected notable, a fair-minded person, a man of justice.

***

At the Konak, however, things were different. By the time uncle Munir was ready for university education, the old Kaimakam was running out of money and with his advancing age, the marriage market was no longer an option. What he did for his eldest, he could not deliver for his youngest son. The proud former Kaimakam of Milltown was humbled by financial difficulties and hard times loomed in the horizon. Uzun Ali's demise was not all the fault of the British; it was more the result of his passion for gambling. First he gambled away his mills, and then he began to sell his extensive landholdings, *ciftliks* and water rights in order to settle his debts. It was a losing battle. "Thanks be to Allah", the Kaimakam would express gratification in the face of impending personal disaster, "I am educating my eldest son", fully expecting that Munir would be his heir, rebuilding family fame and fortune once his eldest and heir became a lawyer. Munir was his investment, his future hope. Father remained in the background, as if he were not his son.

"Sure it was a long time," he would concede acknowledging that it took Munir seven years, instead of the original four to become a lawyer, but there were good reasons, not the least was that this was a period of war and conflict. Grandpa never lost hope in his eldest son. "He will succeed, you will see" he would say and prevail over skeptics, inside or outside the Konak.

Uncle Munir started university in Istanbul, finished it seven years later in London. In the decadent and decaying Ottoman capital Munir made an incredibly significant discovery: A new world was emerging and it belonged to the British. From then on, Munir realized that the way to riches was to become an Anglophone and Anglophile. He had no trouble convincing his father of the changed plan. Oblivious to risks and heavy costs, Uzun Ali stood by his eldest son to the bitter end. The gambling Kaimakam bet not only with his son, but also with the British. The whole world was going British, and Munir was among the first to realize it. "So who I am to refuse the obvious? That boy is smart; he can see the future" Uzun Ali was convinced, and he backed his son all the way until he ran out of money and none was left for father Ozkan.

Father, Munir's 10 years' junior, was of a different sort. Same father, but different mother, and what difference chemistry seemed to make in the brothers? The elder boy was extravert, adventurous and daring, my father was so different it was as if he had been fathered by someone else rather than Uzun Ali. The half-brothers were worlds apart, and not just because of their names, one traditional the other modern. From separate mothers they inherited different looks and temperaments; their aspirations and goals were so contrary, strangers never considered them brothers. Munir was short and stocky; dark skinned and had big brown eyes and dark hair, in contrast to the tall, slim and blond Ozkan. Material ends and pecuniary goals were what mattered for the self-centered Munir, always looking out for his own self, the no-nonsense go-getter, whereas Ozkan was modest and withdrawn, thinking of others first, often at his own peril. Ozkan would not hurt a bird. Munir always got his way, if others stood in his way, he would steam ahead and proceed no matter what the consequences. Father's modesty was such that he never once complained about Uzun Ali's preference for his eldest; that was just the way it was. He accepted the fact as normal. When old enough to realize what was happening, the half-brothers had their own unique solution. Uncle Munir sought the help of the British, flying high, while father was self-reliant, biting small amounts that he was sure he could chew, taking his time and working things out slowly in manageable steps.

These differences between my father and his elder brother might have been patched if the two grew up under normal circumstances. In the Konak nothing was normal after Grandpa's loss of his status. Nevertheless, when the relations between the two half-brothers exploded, it all happened in the most unexpected way.

# IV

The person, who distanced the two half brothers was Nilufer, an *odalik*, a maid, now 16, one of some 20 household staff of servants, maids, cooks, horsemen and gardeners who provided the luxury of the Konak. It was a self-contained mansion, befitting a rich and wealthy Ottoman notable. But now under the British, this lifestyle actually belonged to history long gone. Uzun Ali's way of life was now in rapid decline, and he was no longer the Kaimakam. Yet, oblivious to the transition, Uzun Ali maintained his exorbitant life style, living well beyond his means.

The Nilufer affair, the rape in the rose garden, occurred in the summer of 1908, shortly after the day of Liberation was announced in Istanbul. Liberation sparked all sorts of crazy celebrations in honor of freedom and brotherhood of all Ottomans. But in the Milltown Konak life was untouched, except Nilufer who lost her virginity in a fury of violence. The Nilufer affair, which was to have such a painful and sordid impact in Munir's life and our family history, was a legacy of the odious slave trading in Cyprus that extended all the way back to Byzantium times. In those medieval times, slaves belonged to rich landlords who worked them on sugar plantations and farms on the island. When the Venetians came they expanded slavery. The port city of Famagusta became a center of slave trade, as merchant families got rich on olives, carobs and other agricultural produce of the island.

When the Ottomans replaced the Venetians as owners of Cyprus, the slave trade in Famagusta continued. Even the church and consular staff were engaged in it, so were the rich Ottoman families. Indeed, these families could not afford the luxury they enjoyed without domestics purchased in the slave market.

Nilufer was a Circassian girl, bought some ten years ago in the Famagusta slave market. She joined the former Kaimakam's mansion in which there were African slaves, *halayiks, dadis* and all kinds of servants, male and female, doing the menial chores in the *harem*, serving in the *selamlik*, growing vegetables in the garden, and all sorts of menial tasks including laundry, cooking and house cleaning. Nilufer, meaning water lily, was like her name, beautiful and virginal, every bit Circassian, and clever with the intrigues of the Ottoman harem. When she was approaching her teen years, she was assigned to be the chief lady in waiting for the Mistress of the household, the fourth wife of Uzun Ali, Neslihan Hanim, who was now well passed her prime. Nowadays she had a passion for flowers, in particular roses. Neslihan's pride was her rose garden. It was a garden like no other in the entire Milltown, roses of every possible color and description. Every morning, Nilufer's duty was to go into the rose garden and collect fresh roses of different colors for her mistress who would carefully arrange them in vases, place each one meticulously in her spacious room and then sit on the cushions next to one of the several windows overlooking the rose garden, enjoying the medley of colors, and quietly admiring her creation, often in the company of other ladies in her circle. Neslihan also enjoyed her own company, thinking about her past and present. Roses, their colors and smell, had a magic effect on her. She would sit for hours on a settee in front of one of the several-latticed windows, contemplating serenely as if she was sucking in the beauty rising from the roses in bloom below.

Then suddenly Neslihan's rose garden became an ugly scene. It happened in the secluded part of the garden, on a hot and humid midmorning in August, a month famed for its excessive heat. Munir, 18 and on holidays from his residential high school in Nicosia, was taking a walk in the orchard, enjoying a snack of fresh oranges and mandarins. For the last several years, he had developed a taste for young females, often visiting the brothels in the Armenian quarter of Nicosia with his schoolmates. Munir found these forays pleasurable, a test of his manliness, and that is how he came to view women as sex objects.

# ROSES AND TEARS

That day in the rose garden uncle Munir was at his terrible worst. I only know him as a good man, generous and kind, someone who would not hurt a fly. But the uncle I knew did not exist until the dreadful event at Buyuk Han years later. On this day in 1908, he was a selfish brute, I guess having been brought up by *odaliks*, never experienced a mother's love and affection, a father who was by then a pathological gambler, one who dished out affection even to his favorite son in small doses, most of the time staying aloof from family matters.

Munir suddenly noticed the beautiful maid Nilufer as she was daintily going around in the garden. She was young and lovely maid, moving ever so seductively, her blond hair contrasting her blue eyes that sparkled in the morning sun, brilliant red lips and round breasts, taller, slimmer than other maids, and overall gorgeous, but a shy and withdrawing figure. It was her looks and what she was wearing that made her so seductive for Uzun Ali's eldest son. Munir had a weakness for slim, blond ladies. Nilufer was wearing a light blue head-scarf, a beautiful floral blouse which, in the mid morning sun made her youthful breasts look like pomegranates; she had a red silk baggy pants and soft leather moccasins in which she walked ever so daintily, like an angel dancing in the sky. Her blond hair matched her blue eyes and her red lips in a striking mix that captivated Munir instantly. Waking around the red, white and blue roses, she looked stunning.

"What have we here?" He exclaimed privately when suddenly he saw her.

He immediately decided to have Nilufer. He had not had sex for weeks and, like some hungry wolf, he was ready for the game suddenly placed in front of him.

"Why not?" he reasoned, and immediately justified the plan in his selfish mind. "The maids are our property. I am on holiday and am I to be denied a little fun?"

Munir walked closer to Nilufer, picking roses, with a mischievous smile on his cunning face.

"Good morning" he said as politely as he could, which startled the young maid. She stopped picking roses and looked up.

"Oh! Good morning, sir" replied the shy maid, recognizing the elder son of Uzun Ali. They had never before talked.

"Beautiful roses" he said, putting on a suggestive look on his face, looking straight at Nilufer's lovely face, noticing, at close range, her soft, brilliant skin, blue eyes, blonde hair under the scarf and her daintily crafted blouse and vest hiding her well rounded breasts.

"Yes, they are lovely." She said.

"I am picking them for your mother." She said respectfully. She knew Neslihan Hanim was not Munir's real mother, but custom dictated that she be addressed as if she were.

"It is quite hot, come and sit here in the shade," Munir said, pointing to the bench under the fig tree nearby.

"Come and sit here." He ordered. Nilufer's status demanded that she comply. Nervously she did.

Munir liked her smell. It was like jasmine in the evening.

That is when she started to get worried. Men did not suddenly show an interest in maids like her without wanting something, and what men usually wanted was serious stuff that could get a young maid like Nilufer into trouble. If she resisted, she could be dismissed, and end up in the brothels of Nicosia. If she let him have his way, she had no idea how she might cope, but Nilufer was anything but stupid. She knew that many famous Ottoman ladies of the Harem had risen to positions of prominence and power going down this same path, giving birth to sons who became powerful and influential.

"Just for a minute" She said uncommittingly, "My Mistress will be wondering, if I am late." She sat down and placed her basket of roses on the ground.

"What beautiful eyes you have? What is your name?"

"I am Nilufer, sir," she said.

"How long have you been in our Konak?" He asked and she replied: "Six years, now."

"Do you like it here?" He inquired. "Your mother is very kind." She replied diplomatically. It was actually true. Neslihan Hanim, the latest Mistress of the Konak, was the passive ruler of the mansion. Uzun Ali was away just about every night, and sometimes for days, gambling and feasting with his mysterious friends, usually Greek mill owners.

Munir crept closer to her and she did not move. "Maybe she likes me," he reflected vainly.

He leaned over and kissed her, first on her cheeks, and, meeting no resistance still, on her well formed lips. They were red hot and Munir had a powerful, irresistible urge. He leaned over, grabbed her waist and pulled her down on the ground, amidst the rose bushes. Furiously he pulled her garments off and still she did not resist.

"She is enjoying it as much as me," thought the selfish young man.

The discovery sent him into a frantic excitement he had never experienced before. He had had women before, in whorehouses, but none had been like Nilufer. She was pure and virginal, and what drove Munir mad, she was responsive. It made him feel like a man, a conqueror. He kept on the pace; his heart was throbbing faster, his body heaving, rising and falling like waves in a storm.

When he was reaching climax, lying on top of Nilufer, suddenly my father Ozkan, barely eight year old appeared on the scene.

Father then was a kid, did not know much about sex, but when he saw his brother on top of the maid, in furious embrace and jerking up and down on her, he felt a sensation he had never experienced before. He was curiously excited and some invisible voice inside him wanted him to stay there and watch it all. At that very moment, his eyes met Nilufer's and he noticed agony in her looks. Father felt shame.

Without thinking, "Munir *abi*, my brother" he yelled. "What are you doing?"

But no one answered. He saw the two naked bodies, too entangled to stop, too close to climax to turn back, and there stood the child, watching it all.

Then in the next moment, Ozkan ran off, without saying anything else. He went upstairs and closeted himself in his father's study, sulking and wishing to see no one. In the days and weeks ahead, he kept his secret private. Munir and Nilufer met in private again, several times, but no more witnesses, each occasion creating a feeling of conquest in Munir's mind. Then the summer was gone and Munir went back to his studies. The matter seemed forgotten, buried in history.

The event, however, was to have a lasting impact on all three. Nilufer's life was changed forever. The two half-brothers drifted further apart, an icy cold and wide distance emerged between them. For now, it seemed, no one else knew the secret; shame or conquest, neither dared to speak about it, yet both knew an invisible, moral line was crossed. The moral impact of the rape in the rose garden in the shorter run was greatest on my father. This short-term impact was to be nothing compared to the longer effect on our family.

# V

Afterwards, as soon as Munir was gone, Nilufer got up, put on her garments and walked to her room, cleaned herself and went to deliver the roses to Neslihan Hanim. She was already late, so she sensed she would be in some difficulty with the Mistress.

"Where have you been, girl? You have been away for so long." She spoke rather briskly, not aware of the dire experience Nilufer had gone through.

Before Nilufer could reply, she took a good, hard look at her face. She noticed some twigs still in her hair.

"I went to the rose garden, madam. I collected the roses." She put the basket full of roses on the table.

But the old Mistress was not so easily fooled. Years of experience in delicate female matters must count for something. She had had years of education from her first husband Dervish Aga on concubines and maidens of the harem. Long ago, she had herself been in situations similar to Nilufer's.

"Have you been seeing a man?" She asked directly, looking straight at her face.

Nilufer knew she was in a predicament. Either she had to tell the truth or she could be in serious trouble.

"Madam" she began, almost in tears, "something awful happened. I do not know where to begin." She said, afraid and unsteady.

"Start at the beginning. Tell me everything" Neslihan demanded.

"I have been attacked in the rose garden by Munir." She said. The old Mistress got closer to her, her interest much heightened.

"He forced me down and pulled off my clothes," said the maid. She started crying from shame and fear.

"My dear, come here." Neslihan said in a soft and motherly voice this time. Becoming more serious, the Lady instructed and maid dutifully obeyed.

"Now, sit down and tell me exactly what happened." Neslihan Hanim said.

Nilufer did exactly as instructed. She recounted all the details of the rape. Silence followed. Both sat there, motionless. Minutes passed. Nilufer looked on.

Neslihan was thinking and scheming.

Nilufer waited for the Mistress to speak. She waited for several minutes, until the Lady was ready. Clearly she was deep in thought, reflecting and planning. This was an unexpected turn of events, potentially a significant turning point.

Then at last the Lady spoke:

"Now listen to me, and listen carefully." She had never seen the Lady of the mansion so serious before. "You and I will keep this as a secret. You must do exactly as I say, OK?"

"Yes, Madam" Nilufer complied fully.

"First, Munir will almost certainly come visiting you again in the days ahead. Do not refuse him. Let him have his way. Men are no better than beasts." He was not her son and she wanted to have something, some sort of ammunition against Uzun Ali's favorite son to be used later, at some future moment at her own choosing.

"Second" the old Lady said like some military commander instructing a subordinate, "you will probably end up getting pregnant. You will know in about three or four weeks when you will stop menstruating. You will immediately come and tell me about it, OK?"

"Yes, Madam" the maid said.

"Afterward, will decide what to do… together, you understand?"

"Yes" said Nilufer, and stood there.

She was partly comforted by the knowledge that she had an ally now, a partner as in some secret crime. At the same, Nilufer was quite sure that her life was now forever changed. She was afraid and knew not how to face the consequences, whatever they might be. Her destiny was now in Neslihan's hands. The old Lady tasted now, for the first time, power in the Konak.

# VI

Nine months later, Nilufer had a baby son. It was nothing unusual in the *harem*, and no one minded. There were lots of wet-nurses around, no one worried about who belonged to whom. Only one other person came to know the boy's father. It was Neslihan Hanim who suddenly became an accomplice in the cover-up. Nilufer's son was named Ayfer. It was a name she picked from a romance story she had once read. No one had the slightest notion of the decisive influence Ayfer would have on our family.

Poor Ayfer! The gods were against him from the outset. He knew his mother, of course, unlike my father and uncle. Ayfer's problem was lack of a father. He paid for this loss dearly, obliged, as he was to live in man's world deprived of a loving male figure. But Ayfer's loss did not end with him; it was passed on to all of us, we paid for Ayfer's misdeed.

All three, my father, uncle and Ayfer shared the deep emotional scars of a missing parent. Munir and Ozkan were half brothers and never experienced mother's love. Ayfer never knew his father. All three were raised by wet-nurses, or surrogate mothers assigned by the former Kaimakam for the specific task of feeding the babies. Ayfer had something that my uncle and father did not: mothers' love and affection. But the Ottoman world was then a man's world, and poor Ayfer's deficiency was far more serious than that of Munir and

Ozkan's lack of a real mother. Each brother was like half a person, possessing a sort of warped personality; each tried to overcome the deficiency through diametrically opposed perceptions of human relations. In Ayfer's case, the deficiency was to be fatal.

After the Nilufer affair, the summer ended and Munir was gone, life in the Konak returned back to its normal routine. The maid was left to care for her pregnancy in the Konak, and no one noticed anything unusual for months. She was not alone to face her new condition. Nilufer had a secret ally in Neslihan Hanim, the mistress of Konak. She masterminded the conspiracy and made sure the secret remained intact for years to come.

Munir completed his high school and in 1910, at the age of 20, Uzun Ali dispatched his first-born to the University in Istanbul to become a lawyer. "There will be a bright future for a man of law" he predicted. It was true enough, but then sex and politics got in the way and upset Uzun Ali's well-laid plans. Munir was enamored with the free and cosmopolitan life of Istanbul, especially the Greek sections of Pera and Beyoglu. He enjoyed himself in the top hotels of the area, Pera Palas and the Grand London Hotel, and so long as Uzun Ali kept funds flowing, Munir was learning more about the decadent life in the decaying Ottoman capital, than about the intricacies of the *Mecelle* and the *Seri' at*, the Muslim law. There was a fervent debate in the newspapers of the day about the fate of the Ottoman Empire, and about Ottomanism, Islamism and Turkism, but these were idle theories and ideas for Munir. His interest was immediate and his days were occupied with having fun. So the first year was wasted, but no matter, now at last Munir was finally getting started with his legal studies, actually showing up in some of his classes at the university.

Then, all hell broke loose. The Balkan Wars broke out and the Ottomans lost practically all their European territories. The Ottoman capital was full of refugees and displaced people streaming in from the Balkans. Millions of desperate people, hungry and in great pain, somehow made their way into Anatolia, only to face the terror of Armenians now in open revolt defying the Sultan and massacring all Muslims, whether refugees or old timers. In the cosmopolitan Istanbul, easy life was suddenly replaced by gloom and doom. A fog of pessimism set in and everyday the news got worse still. Soon after the Italians grabbed Libya, and before the dust settled on the desert, the world was set aflame with war and conflict everywhere. Intrigue and plots were everywhere and the dictatorship of the Young Turks took control. The Ottoman government was then in the hands of a triumvirate backed by a highly secretive Committee of Union and Progress party, created in secrecy in Salonica and Macedonia with strong Jewish and Masonic roots and funding. The strongman of the triumvirate was Enver, the Minister of War. Of gypsy origins, he was ambitious and ruthless, known to have strong German sympathies. The other two in the all-powerful dictatorship was Talat and Cemal, responsible for internal security.

Life in the Ottoman capital was stressful and uncomfortable. Every day the newspapers were full of yet another defeat of the once mighty Ottoman army, and another distant territory breaking away and declaring its independence of the Empire. The Ottoman society was hopelessly divided, some arguing for Pan-Islamism, others for Ottomanism and still some others for a brand new Turkish nationalism. "Turkey for Turks" declared Ziya Gokalp, one of the rising intellectuals of the day. All the while, the Greeks and other Christian subjects of the Sultan, now jubilant after the recent success of Balkan states, were dreaming and scheming for Greater Greece or Greater Bulgaria or some such project. The Armenians, originally partners with the Young Turks, parted company and went forward to launch a bloody revolt in Anatolia for independent Armenia.

Amidst of all this chaos, Munir first tried to keep calm and stay the course. It soon became impossible. There was simply too much excitement and revolutionary change in the air for any studying or enjoyment. The more he reflected on daily events and all that was happening around him, the more he realized he had to make a decision. But what? That is where his mind was all confused and every day he felt like he was living in a collapsing world like a lost soul with mist all around him.

The mood of pessimism extended all the way to Cyprus. Grandpa's decline paralleled the Empire's. Uzun Ali's gambling in Milltown got worse, too, but it was nothing in comparison to the gambling by the Young Turks in control of the Ottoman government in Istanbul. Still, Grandpa never lost his head amidst all of this gloom and doom. The Ottoman armies might be defeated on the battlefield, or incompetent and corrupt officials might misgovern the Empire. Surely, these were temporary mishaps that could be fixed with modern knowledge. The key lay in progress and knowledge. Education was the answer to fix all ills for Uzun Ali as well as the Empire. He must be ready for better times ahead. In his belief in the power of education, Grandpa stood steadfast. He never once wavered in his confidence that in his eldest son's education lay the future of his own family. He stood by him and believed that his education was the most important thing in his life. He was already selling land to feed his gambling, so an additional holding here and there for Munir's education seemed perfectly natural.

Then suddenly some shocking news came. Uncle Munir then decided to drop out of University in Istanbul and wanted to go to London, England, I suspect, as much to study common law as to have fun with English girls, preferably blond. You see, deep down, uncle Munir was an Anglophile, the product of his schooling. He was not only disillusioned with life in Istanbul and the incompetent politicians in charge; he was slowly making up his mind that the future belonged to the mighty British. "The sun never sets on their Empire," he would remark to the few friends he had. "It is foolish for Enver and his cronies to side with the Germans" he would argue. Privately he made up his mind that he would bet on the British.

Then he acted. Uncle Munir was clever, even in his youth; he knew how to get his way around his dad. He explained it all in a crafty letter to Grandpa: "A new dawn is on the horizon. A new world is rising fast. The British will dominate the new world. Britannia will rule the waves. I want to be part of this new world." Munir went on. It was persuasive and it appealed to the risk-taking mind of the gambling old Kaimakam of Milltown.

What he did not say in his letter was that Uncle Munir had seen the decay of the morally bankrupt Ottomans and the Young Turks leadership from within. He said to himself astutely and privately, not daring to share with his father: "The Ottoman Empire is sinking fast. I do not like the government of Enver, Talat and Cemal. They are young and inexperienced, not like Kamil Pasha," he argued. He was referring to the old *Sadrazam* (Ottoman Prime Minister) from Cyprus, who, like him, was pro-British. Uncle knew that Uzun Ali knew and admired Kamil Pasha. But as a young man, uncle stayed away from Kamil and other politicians.

The most important part of Uncle Munir's letter to his father was the cleverest. It argued with amazing foresight and clarity: "European powers are racing amongst themselves for colonies. Don't be surprised if a terrible war erupts. If that happened, I am sure the British will win in the end. They have a powerful navy and colonies all over. The future belongs to the British. I want to study in England."

When the letter arrived, Uzun Ali was, in truth, quite impressed with his son's reasoning. "That boy is smart, he will go places." He said with pride.

Uzun Ali sold off more land and sent Munir the required money who, with difficulty going through Athens and Paris, eventually found his way to London where he spent the next five years, for studies that should have taken half as much time.

Uncle Munir arrived in London in fall 1913, enrolled in Grays Inn to become a Barrister at law, normally taking two to three years to complete. His arrival was auspicious. He read in the newspapers, shortly after his arrival, that the Ottoman government signed a treaty with the British government giving Britain the sole right to oil exploration in Arabia, Mesopotamia and Syria. With automobiles everywhere, the world needed oil and a bright future was just around the corner. If, only, peace could be sustained, the future would be secure. But, on that score, Munir had serious doubts.

Gay London was so much more fun than the decaying Ottoman capital. Everywhere there were lights and restaurants and evidence of riches, people dressed fashionably. In Piccadilly, in Trafalgar square and the Strand, there were crowds enjoying themselves. Cinematography was a new passion, and theatergoers were excited over Bernard Shaw's new play *Pygmalion* making its triumphant debut. Munir was for the first time hearing about world affairs. He marveled at the news of the opening of the Panama Canal in faraway Central America, a world he had little knowledge of before. London was the center of a new world, an exciting world, and full of opportunities, unlike the sinking ship of the Ottomans. He also noticed that London was the scene of constant demonstrations by the Irish, the *Sein Fein* and home rule, and suffragettes demanding votes for women, but these were, for Munir, minor issues, compared to the chaos and confusion that reigned in Istanbul at the time. He was glad to be in London.

It took Munir five years because he was in no particular hurry. It was, after all, a time of war and crisis. No matter, he had his own life to run, and for now he wanted to have fun. Munir took full advantage of the opportunities in the British capital, and he believed, as did most Londoners, that it would be a short war. In the meantime, there was no shortage of English blonds, especially after the general mobilization and Kitchener's "Your Country Needs YOU" signs went up all over sucking up all the eligible young men. And, thanks to his dad's generosity, Munir was never short of cash.

He rented a small flat in Kingsway, not far from his college, and he began spending a lot of time in Soho, full of bright lights and cheerful ladies ready to show a good time on demand for any man with ready cash. The first year was a wasted year: the Great War broke out, Munir found it extremely difficult to concentrate on his studies, with all the able-bodied men off to the front, and all those fun-loving girls left behind. There was so much demand on his free time, Munir acquired a new life-style: He would sleep all day and party all night, learning as much about the London nightlife as about British law. He paid little attention to politics or the World War that exploded only months after his arrival in London. He naturally took interest in the Gallipoli landings, but he would dismiss the whole bloody affair with sarcasm: "It is not worth half a million lives just to be able to force the Turkish Straits and rescue Russia."

His father, the former Kaimakam of Milltown was more patriotic and followed war news with interest and concern. He celebrated the short-lived victory of the Ottoman navy and armies at Gallipoli. Then his mood sunk with every Ottoman defeat. Undaunted, however, he sent his beloved Munir in London the required funds for his studies. It was no easy task, money transfers from Cyprus to London was no mean accomplishment. But, thanks to the Ottoman Bank, it was done with relative ease and Munir financed his days in London reasonably comfortably while all around everyone seemed sucked into the inferno of the war.

# VII

Some memories do not fade with time they grow and magnify. The passage of time strengthens them, and they become bigger. Uncle Munir's rape of Nilufer in the rose garden in the summer of 1908 was one such event. Its consequences expanded over time, just as Ayfer the unwanted child from the rape, grew from childhood to adulthood. The affair of the rose garden engulfed more and more people in its tentacles, spreading death and destruction in its path. When I first visited the rose garden, years later after ruin had already set in, it was abandoned and I knew nothing of what I know now. It was now a place of tears, no longer of roses, its beauty and splendor long since gone.

On this very spot, knowing what I now know, I shed tears for Nilufer, the poor Circassian maid, who was another female victim of the male Ottoman world. Little did she know that here the agony she endured was to have such a decisive impact on all our lives.

In the beginning, right after her rape, it was all quiet in Grandpa's *Konak*. Right after she confided to her mistress what had happened, Neslihan took control of her life. During the last three months of her pregnancy, Nilufer was virtually a prisoner in Neslihan's quarters. The old lady wanted to make sure that Nilufer's pregnancy went unnoticed, especially by the old Kaimakam. She had her own plans, which, for the time being, must remain secret. The old lady looked after every detail and aspect of pregnancy, taking good care of Nilufer as if she was carrying valuable cargo. Outwardly, Neslihan saw to it that Nilufer's life changed as little as possible, although as her pregnancy advanced her movements beyond the *harem* virtually ceased. Of course, such pregnancies as Nilufer's were not uncommon in mansions like Grandpa's. No one noticed anything unusual. Even after the birth of her son, Nilufer's life changed little and her son Ayfer became just another member of the Konak establishment. The boy grew into an infant and young child pretty well unnoticed.

Years went by and Grandpa kept selling land to support Munir in London and finance his gambling at home. By the time Ozkan reached his teens the old Kaimakam began to experience money problems. Decline accelerated in the Konak, Uzun Ali, like all Ottomans nervously listening to the gloomy news of war and conflict outside Cyprus. Munir continued his studies in London, in his slow and pleasurable way, and Uzun Ali managed to finance his son's academic and extracurricular activities.

Milltown jogged along as a sleepy town, except in one respect. Ozkan and Ayfer became friends. Although nine years separated the two boys, once Ayfer started school, the two spent more and more time playing and keeping company, two soul mates that fate had cast together, like discards from a shipwreck washed on a lonely shore by storms past.

***

Meanwhile, in wartime London, events were far more hectic. The British armies were victorious in Palestine and the Ottoman armies were withdrawing on every front. But the war in Europe persisted. In London, Uncle Munir's interests were focused on lesser, more personal matters of the moment.

He decided to move from Kingsway, close to Soho, towards the more genteel district of Hampstead on Heath. He reckoned this was an area more conducive to his academic pursuit, although in his heart he really enjoyed the Bohemian atmosphere of his new neighborhood more than the bars and brothels of Soho and Piccadilly. His academics were OK, he was literally eating his way to the Bar, but the pace was slow. He did not mind that actually, except that it was so exhausting for Munir always to choose amongst girl friends. These English girls were classier, not like those obliging Istanbul women he had known, ready to satisfy a man with ready cash They were demanding and they insisted on eating out at expensive restaurants and go to theater. Their favors did not come cheap. Lately, there were signs of grumblings from Uzun Ali about funds, but still cash flowed in regularly from Nicosia, and Munir kept up with his libertine life in London. He divided his time equally between girls and books, sometimes tilting his time allocation in favor of the former. As a result, he pace of academic progress was, at best, half of what it should have been. Munir had one full year yet to complete his Bar requirements, but was assuming full time academic workload.

One of the girl friends he was especially fond of was Mary Edward, a typist working in a law firm in Golders Green, the youngest daughter of a poor Irish family from Dublin. With too many brothers and sisters and not enough income for the family, Mary was obliged to come to London for work and was able to find a job as a secretary-typist. The Irish girl enjoyed the good life Munir was able to provide. He was a pleasant, funny fellow, a bit short and overweight, but otherwise a charming enough man.

They usually met Friday evenings, first dining at some fancy restaurant near the Heath or Golders Green, then going to the theater and finally to Munir's apartment for a night of amorous pleasure. That is what she enjoyed the most about Munir: in bed. The Mediterranean's hot blood, his passion and strength were captivating. Munir made Mary feel like a whole woman; she experienced ecstasy she never knew she could attain. Munir took her to new heights of sensual love and she gradually developed an emotional yearning for their weekly encounters on Friday nights.

"Munir" she began as they were completing dinner with desert one night, "I missed my period this month." She said, "I need to have some pregnancy test done."

This was bad news. Munir wanted carefree sex, no entanglements. "Are you sure?" he asked in a casual sort of way. She was rather puzzled at his lukewarm response, but said nothing.

"When will you know for sure?" He asked.

"Not for a couple of weeks" said Mary. There the matter stood, an uneasy truce prevailed.

The rest of the evening was a little depressing. Munir's cheerfulness was somehow subdued which Mary noticed but said nothing. Their sex act later on was more mechanical and Mary began to worry.

## UZUN ALI, SHAME AND SALVATION

Abortion was always a possibility, but, as a good Catholic girl, that would be sinful. Making love was okay, but having children out of wedlock was unforgivable.

Mary's values were Irish. She was raised in a poor Catholic neighborhood of Dublin, families who still remembered the terrible days of the "Great Famine". There were always troubles between the English and the Irish. Her father had died in some Irish demonstration when the English soldiers shot at the crowd. Her mother became a cleaning lady to put bread on the table and Mary was sent off to London to earn her living the best way she could. But Mary was lucky; she had learnt rudimentary typing and reached London at the right moment. With all the young men off to fight the war, there was a general shortage of secretaries, and she had no trouble finding a position, rent a flat and take care of things. She was even able to send a quid or two to her mother once in a while. That was always welcome.

On Saturday nights, Mary and her Irish friends would go to a local dancing hall to have some fun. That is where she met Munir, the rather dark, but strong young man who looked like he came from Italy or the Balkans. Mary had a streak of adventure in her veins and she was attracted to Munir more for what she imagined him to be than what he actually was. They danced and soon became friends. He was gentle and seemed to have plenty of money, taking Mary to expensive restaurants in Soho and Piccadilly square she had never been before.

The thing Mary liked the most about Munir was his passion in lovemaking. He was strong and could make repeated love, and Mary for the first time felt utterly fulfilled, sensing gratification she never experienced from the many Irish boys before in Dublin or London. Munir was gentle and passionate in bed; his kisses were hot, and he knew how to use his hands. He was crafty and could turn her on like some expert rider on a horse. Her body responded, and the two lovers produced something beautiful, a romantic air from a fine violin played by a master.

But, there was another side to Munir. While great in bed, sometimes he would turn moody and get angry unpredictably, turn explosive even at trivial things. They had several fights, because Mary's Irish temperament matched Munir's unpredictability. But, no matter, that was OK. They always seemed to patch up their differences, usually with highly gratifying lovemaking. It always ended like that: bouts of anger, followed by ecstasy of passionate sex. So, angry words were exchanged, strong opinions stated. But always it was all quickly forgotten.

That was the pattern, which governed Munir's relationship with Mary. The two seemed to have developed a bittersweet, love-hate relationship. It was as if their fighting was a deliberate scheme, a weird foreplay, getting their emotions and bodies ready for the passion to follow. When, after an interlude, the two lovers would meet, there would be no recriminations, no angry words exchanged, just warm embraces and tenderness, always climaxing in satisfying lovemaking in his or her flat.

Mary and Munir, two colonial souls whom fate had united in the Empire's capital, made the most of what London offered, as war raged on all around. The more I learnt about Mary the more I realized as if a mysterious, dreadful force of tragic destiny attracting these colonial souls toward a sad end, both victims of British rule. Mary, to me, represented a pathetic young girl, a child of the Great Famine for which the British must bear a great moral responsibility, and Uncle Munir, himself a creation of the dying Ottoman world, who gambled his all on the British and lost!

# VIII

Meanwhile, the clock ticked away in little Milltown, Cyprus, an insignificant dot on the map far away from the bloody fighting in Europe and the Middle East. The news of war was terrible for Grandpa, his mood sank as the Ottomans were defeated everywhere and everyday more and more bad news arrived. The British in Cyprus cut off the Ottoman links. The British and Ottoman armies were locked in a terrible war on several fronts.

Uzun Ali was now on the enemy side in British Cyprus. Life in the Konak got more and more difficult to manage. Grandpa's decline in wealth and status continued. His land holdings were diminishing by the month. Yet, his pride in his first-born never wavered. He would always boast to his friends about Munir soon to return as an English-trained lawyer. Privately, Munir's return became Uzun Ali's salvation, his last hope. His youngest, my father Ozkan was left to his own devices. Lately, Grandpa's health began to give cause for worry. He was now past sixty, and started to feel periodic chest pains, but he was determined to keep it a secret. He chose to ignore it, partly out of pride, and worse still, he persisted in his bad habits, spending more and more nights at the gambling tables with his Greek friends. Before too long he was facing money problems and he had to borrow from banks against the security of the Konak.

It was a beautiful April morning in 1917, the sun shining and the spring flowers in full bloom, right after breakfast. Neslihan Hanim was sitting in the living room drinking her morning cup of sweet Turkish coffee. She was surprised to see Uzun Ali enter her quarters. He had a sad, somber look; the news that morning had been particularly unhappy: the Ottoman army had been forced out of Baghdad and the British were marching onwards and forward on every front. Neslihan Hanim had not seen her husband for months. They lived separate lives, he with his gambling cronies, and Neslihan in her own quarters. It was rumored he had been gambling quite heavily losing continuously and sinking further into debt.

"He must be facing some financial difficulty," she thought to herself, trying to think of a possible motive for this sudden visit. "May be he will demand some of my jewels. He already got rid of my land holdings," she reflected.

But, Grandpa had come to discuss a far more delicate matter, something not entirely unrelated.

"Neslihan Hanim, it is about my eldest son, Munir" he began slowly. She remained silent.

"I know you are not his mother," he said, meaning he understood that Munir was not her favorite.

"Munir is a fine young man. I hear he is doing well with his studies in London" she replied in a neutral tone, realizing how much his eldest son, and in particular his education, meant to Uzun Ali.

"Yes, yes, but I hear he is having some women problems in London." Grandpa stopped to see her reaction. This was news to Neslihan. She had no knowledge of Munir's life in far away London.

"How do you know? What sort of problems?" She inquired.

Uzun Ali with clear discomfort visibly evident on his face, said: "I have my sources," he said, not wishing to disclose them.

In the last year, Munir's requirement for cash had exploded and the old Kaimakam had to secure a substantial bank loan to provide the funds, but as a precaution, he had asked a friend with connections in London to keep an eye on his son and report anything odd. The loan was secret, and he had no wish for disclosing it. Now, he had received solid proof that Munir was partying as much as studying.

"My source informs me that your son is especially close to an Irish girl called Mary," the informant told the old Kaimakam. "They spend several days and almost all weekends together. Maybe they are even married, but I cannot be certain," reported the private eye.

177

Grandpa was clearly a worried man. After this news, he could not sleep. He had bet on Munir's education. With his land holdings all gone, his eldest son's education was all he had. All his investment in Munir could evaporate over night should Munir decide to take on an English wife, quit his law education and settle down in London. His hefty debt at the bank in Nicosia was something beyond his means of repayment. It meant certain ruin. His hope for revival of family fortune, including his own comfort and old age security would vanish.

"I came over to seek female advice on this delicate situation," said Uzun Ali to his wife. In truth, despite his years of experience, Grandpa was familiar only with a world dominated by men only. When it came to female matters, he was exceedingly limited and vulnerable.

He asked his fourth wife: "What do you think can be done?"

That is when Neslihan decided to act decisively. It took her little time to decide that her moment had finally arrived. This is what she had been waiting all this time.

Old Neslihan now must share the long-kept secret of the rose garden nine years ago. All those years of waiting, planning and conspiracy: She had patiently waited, right after Nilufer's pregnancy and birth of Ayfer. Now her moment had arrived and Neslihan wanted to act with determination and authority.

"Uzun Ali" she began, and waited for a brief moment, just enough for him to notice that she was about to deliver something unusually important.

Nesilhan, when sure that she had the old Kaimakam's undivided attention, went on:

"I am afraid, this is not the first female problem Munir has had," she said. "There is a secret I must now share with you."

Grandpa was frozen where he stood. His eyes were fixed on her. He was clearly excited and he immediately felt like an accused to hear a terrible judgment. Uzun Ali was about to hear something extra-ordinary.

Neslihan took a good look at her husband, aware of the pain on his face. She then said slowly and deliberately: "Remember the summer Munir spent with us here before going to Istanbul?"

After a moment of reflection, Grandpa answered with an unsteady voice.

"Yes, I do." Grandpa said:" What about it?"

"Well, Munir did something naughty at that time. He raped Nilufer, my maid. He abused her all summer."

He listened in silence. Then she added:

"Nilufer got pregnant, and gave birth to his son." She stopped waiting for Grandpa's response.

"Allah, Allah" Said Grandpa in shame. He was in shock.

He sat in silence, quite unsure how to respond, as his fourth wife looked on triumphantly.

Neslihan savored her victory over Munir, the son she always secretly disliked. Moreover, she felt a warm sense of revenge for all the selfishness and agony over Grandpa's gambling, especially squandering her own land and jewels.

But Neslihan knew her limit. Enough was enough.

She realized Grandpa was an old man, probably in declining health. She was not privy to his private life, how well he was or what ailed him. All she knew was that he was still far more valuable to her alive than dead.

What Neslihan was reporting was bad news for Uzun Ali. It was bad for his health. The fact was that he himself did not know what was wrong with his health, but the old Kaimakam, after years of drinking and smoking, had weakened his heart, his arteries were dangerously blocked and his blood circulation had become erratic. What is worse, he refused to have it diagnosed and even if he did, it is unlikely he could have followed the strict regime his doctor would have prescribed. Grandpa was not one to obey strict orders, health or otherwise.

"My Munir fathered a child. What shame?" admitted the old Kaimakam. He sat there in shocked silence. Husband and wife were, for once, united in spirit.

Minutes passed. Neslihan watched him. Half an hour later, he continued in self-pity. His worst fears were being realized; the old Kaimakam's investment in the eldest son was in serious danger. For the first time, Grandpa was alarmed.

"This is very bad news. I am ruined. What can I do? Why is Allah punishing me so?" He was almost in tears, crying his heart out in front of his wife. Uncharacteristically, Grandpa was vulnerable, indulging in self-pity.

Neslihan sat in front of Grandpa, hardly concealing some secret satisfaction in his agony. She heard herself thinking: "It is too late, dear husband. I wish you had treated me more like a real wife, a partner in your life." She knew these were private thoughts, never to be shared with anyone, including Uzun Ali. Now it was too late.

But wisdom prevailed. She pushed her thoughts of vengeance out of her mind, and chose pity.

"Come now" the old Mistress of the Konak said, in a female comforting tone. She was putting on a magnanimous face: "He is a young man, a hot head, Uzun Ali," She added: "Don't be too hard on your eldest. What do you expect?"

Miraculously, her words had a calming effect; he appreciated his wife's kindness.

"What can we do about Munir?" asked Grandpa, clearly asking for Neslihan's help.

She was glad to become a partner in the solution of her husband's problem.

"Nothing" she said, "except do not send him any more money, other than his fees and school expenses. Tell him to complete his studies and come home as soon as possible."

Grandpa was relieved. He was in a desperate situation. His wife's counsel made sense in his predicament.

He liked Neslihan's advice. He got up to leave her, feeling considerably relaxed and better than when he had walked in.

"Dear wife" he addressed her at the door, in an affectionate tone she had not heard from him for years, "you have given me a sound idea. You are truly my life partner and I am grateful to you."

Old Neslihan smiled. Her conspiracy had paid off!

***

In the days following everyone began to notice a change in Uzun Ali. Grandpa became more compassionate; he started taking more interest in his family.

Father Ozkan's life then took a turn for the better. Uzun Ali began to show an interest in his youngest son, but what was even more astonishing was his awareness of Ayfer. This led to a remarkable, but slow transformation in the Konak. Everyone in the household, but especially the servants and maids, noticed a marked improvement in Ayfer's status in the Konak. Ayfer, now eight, was no longer an orphan to be ignored and excluded, but someone to be treated as part of the Uzun Ali family.

One of the last to notice Grandpa's change was father Ozkan. He was now approaching his 17th birthday, not many days after Grandpa's meeting with Neslihan Hanim. He noticed, for the first time, that the old Kaimakam was more approachable, talking to him more, asking questions, however trivial. Father began to feel like a real son. His father was human after all, and the feeling boosted his self-image. Soon, Grandpa took more interest not only in Ozkan's schoolwork, but also in what he might do for a living. That was amazing, something that never happened before.

The new relationship between father and son reached a climax on a clear summer day.

It was about a month after the eventful meeting with Neslihan. Father Ozkan and Grandpa were walking together in the garden. Uzun Ali asked his younger son:

"Son, what would you like to be?" Father was taken aback.

Ozkan was not ready for such a question. He remained silent, lost in his thoughts. In truth, he was simply elated. Father felt exhilarated. For the first time ever, Ozkan felt he had a father, till now he had been adrift in the Konak, not much different than Nilufer's mysterious son Ayfer.

"I want to be a farmer," said father in his usual modesty, and Grandpa was surprised at the quick decision of his youngest. He was also secretly pleased because deep down in his heart Uzun Ali had an abiding love of land and an emotional respect for farming.

"Is that so?" he said, partly in jest, partly out of curiosity.

After his youngest expressed an interest in farming, Uzun Ali began to purchase a few cows and placed them in his son's care supervised by farm hands in the Konak. This happened at a fortunate moment. Grandpa's luck, for once, had turned around and in the last gambling session with his Greek Cypriot cronies he had won a sizeable amount of cash. Of course, it was no more than an aberration, but it was one of those rare moments in his life when Lady Luck smiled on father and son.

The most noticeable development in the Konak was Ozkan and Ayfer's growing stature, again thanks to Grandpa's initiative. It was a three-way relationship, a sort of mysterious bond between the old man, his youngest son and Nilufer's kid. Ozkan was busy with his cows, which brought father and son closer, and the kid, now eight years old, was doing well at school, his mother Nilufer and her mistress, Neslihan hanim, catering to his every need, helping him with school work and his hobbies. Uzun Ali, for all his faults and shortcoming, was always interested in books and learning, so when Ayfer showed some academic aptitude, Grandpa was interested.

Then the mysterious loss of Grandpa's silver antique watch happened.

It was truly a sad story. Ayfer had an unusual interest for watches, wristwatches, silver and gold, big and small. He seemed to love them all. Their intricacies were well beyond the comprehension of the youth, but he was captivated by the sound of the antique clock in the corner of Neslihan's room and he would spend hours fascinated by its movements, as seconds and minutes slowly moved forward.

Grandpa had an antique silver watch, a thing of beauty, with Ottoman numbers on it, a treasured gift of his father, attached at the end of his golden chain, which he wore in a special pocket on his vest made for the beautiful object d'art. It was his pride and joy. As the relationship blossomed between Nilufer's boy and Uzun Ali, Ayfer took a liking toward the old Kaimakam's watch. Ayfer would take it into his hands, open its silver cap, and watch it endlessly. The look of utter fascination was pure pleasure for Uzun Ali to observe. The kid would ask questions, and he old man would answer. It was a nice, warm relationship that both cherished.

Suddenly the watch disappeared, quite mysteriously. Uzun Ali's treasured watch was gone. They searched for it everywhere, in every room. They combed the entire Konak, top to bottom. Everyone was questioned and interrogated. All pleaded not guilty. Everyone was amazed and shocked at this theft, a first in the Konak.

It was found two days later when the missing watch was brought back to the Konak and restored to its rightful owner by one of the neighbors. He had a simple enough explanation:

"Nilufer's Ayfer brought it over to us," said the neighbor, embarrassed, but glad to do a favor for the old Kaimakam.

Everyone was happy, especially father who took a good look at the antique and was amazed with its brilliant beauty, its Ottoman numbers and wonderful inlaid craftsmanship. Impressed with Ozkan's obvious pleasure with the watch, Grandpa said: "Maybe I will give it to you, one day" and father was delighted. It was the kindest words his dad had ever said to him.

Still shocked at the theft, Neslihan Hanim wanted to know. "But why? Why would Ayfer do such a silly thing? What made him do it?"

There was no answer. No one, including Nilufer, could give an answer. Little Ayfer shrugged his shoulders and all he could say, "I don't know."

But a big change did happen. Grandpa's confidence in his illegitimate grandson was shaken. He was beginning to get comfortable about having a grandson, but the stolen watch incident put a stop to the idea.

Uzun Ali dropped Ayfer from his mind. He simply lost interest in the child.

Ayfer, of course, continued to develop, like some thorn in the wild, on his own.

# IX

In London, Uncle Munir's studies were at last coming to an end; he had just completed his last "dinner" before admission to the Bar. His relationship with Mary Edwards was also reaching its climax, literally and emotionally. It was about a month after their nervous discussion about her pregnancy alarm. With his law studies just about completed and his mind made for a triumphal return to his father in Cyprus, he was in an especially good mood. He was ready for fun. For one thing, peace, at last was in the air, November 11, 1918 joyously celebrated as the Armistice Day.

On this occasion, so was Mary. She had good reason to be exceptionally cheerful: She had some good news to share with Munir. It was a beautiful, sunny day in June. She was wearing a polka dot dress with red and white dots and a matching red sweater.

They went to their favorite restaurant on the Strand, not far from Trafalgar Square. Toward the end, she said: "I have good news." Uncle Munir looked on excitedly. They had plans to catch a play at Haymarket, just below Piccadilly, and she wanted to add a bit more to their enjoyment. Munir looked at her with great anticipation

"What is it?" he asked, smiling, for he knew when Mary was in a pleasing mode or not.

"I am not pregnant," announced Mary, smiling, clearly a huge weight off her back. The Catholic girl had been a nervous wreck all past month.

In truth, Munir had forgotten about Mary's situation, his studies and exams, temporarily, taking priority in his life in the course of the past several weeks.

"That is wonderful" he replied trying to be seem as cheerful as he could.

Mary went on: "I had my period a week ago. That was a big relief," she said.

In reality Munir was not interested in such female details; for him the great news was the fact that a potential complication was avoided. "Yes dear" he said smiling at Mary and thinking to himself of the good times in store for post-show in his flat.

"It is great news," he repeated. Then they discussed plans for the evening, in cheerful mood and great anticipation. After an enjoyable dinner, they went to the theater and watched a comedy in Haymarket that made them laugh like they had never done before.

Later on that night, in Uncle Munir's flat, they made love, unusually gentle and caring. It had been almost a month since their last get together; physically and emotionally, they had missed each other. Their lovemaking turned out to be a truly memorable event. On this occasion, their last get-together in London, the two lovers were like thirsty travelers in the desert suddenly coming across a spring in the oasis. It was a fitting climax to a relationship that had been bittersweet, now suddenly in its last phase.

This time Mary really got pregnant. And it was really the worst time for such a responsibility: By the time she was sure, a month later, her lover, uncle Munir was gone. He had already left for Cyprus a week earlier. Poor Mary, the God-fearing Irish girl, felt lonely and abandoned. She had no one in London to turn to.

But Mary was nothing if not brave and determined. At first, she panicked: "Oh my God, what am I going to do?" she asked, as a feeling of Catholic guilt came over her: "Dear Father, I have sinned. Forgive me," she prayed as fear of the unknown took control of her. It did not last long. She regained her composure and made up her mind. She was resolved to save her baby. Instinctively her act symbolized Mary's giving and nurturing character.

She continued working for the next few months as her pregnancy progressed, and then Mary decided to return home to her mother in Dublin for delivery. She confessed everything to her mother. "You can have the baby here," she said, but you cannot stay at home, dear. I cannot support you and your baby," She said. "We have to give the baby for adoption."

Mary would not hear of it. But she also understood that there was no chance of staying at home, looking after her baby. Times were tough. There was political unrest, with nationalists and republicans at loggerheads and a general election coming. Jobs were hard to find, so Mary was forced to remain, for the time being at least, as an unemployed, expecting mother. Her mother's income was hardly sufficient to cover expenses.

In the end Mary, the God-fearing Catholic girl, ended up entering the convent. She gave birth to a son, lightly dark skin, but Irish blond, healthy and strong like Uncle Munir. The Sisters were glad to look after her the baby while she herself went into self-imposed period of prayers in silence and solitude for the remission of sins committed. It did not last long. Mary's adventurous nature boiled over and she ran away from the convent.

Within a year Mary was back in London, resuming her life as a secretary, her little boy left behind in the convent in Dublin. Munir was gone, but Mary could not forget him. She could not help it; back in London she felt lonely, and missed him terribly. She would remember their passionate lovemaking and constantly ask: "Where is he? How I miss him."

Uncle Munir, in colonial Nicosia, was the right man and the right place. His timing was perfect. Recently the British had annexed Cyprus and at the end of the war they were determined to build the island into a thriving economy and a strong military base to watch developments in the Middle East. They needed English-speaking, professionals like Uncle Munir. From the start, Uncle had the Midas touch: Prosperity was guaranteed for the brand new British-trained lawyer in town.

# X

After a tiring, but otherwise uneventful trip by boat, Uncle Munir returned home by New Year 1919. Considering the recent war, his travel was fine, in the sense that no interruptions or major delays were encountered. Of course, everywhere there were plenty of terrible scars of war: damaged buildings, food shortages and destitute crowds going about looking miserable and in desperate straits. Munir concentrated on his own achievement and his thoughts about the bright future waiting him kept his spirits up. In the last leg of the trip, the boat from Athens to the port of Famagusta carried not only the British trained lawyer, the heir apparent to Grandpa's throne in decline, it was also full of Cypriot muleteers, hundreds of troops with Cypriot mules who had fought with the Allies in the Great War. He made a triumphant disembarkation, almost lost in the multitude of demobilized motley crowd, happy to be back in Cyprus.

Uncle Munir's return home should have been for Grandpa the fulfillment of his dream, the day when, literally his ship reached port. It should have been occasion for celebration and rejoicing. But that is not the way it happened.

By then Grandpa was a sick man, terminally sick. He had kept his true state of health a secret, hidden from all in his family. He was too proud a man to share his declining health. It was the same with his wealth, now long since exhausted. Actually, Munir's arrival was days

## UZUN ALI, SHAME AND SALVATION

after Uzun Ali had suffered a stroke, a relatively mild one, but it was a sign of Grandpa's precarious and failing health. It was, maybe in part, due to his vanity or carelessness; he simply chose to hide his true health behind his large pride. Moreover, uncle Munir's return was overshadowed with a truly landmark event: Uzun Ali was now officially bankrupt. The notice from the bank arrived on the same day as his eldest son. Again, he kept it secret, too embarrassed to let anyone else know his true financial situation. Even in this financial difficulty, Grandpa maintained his external dignity. Outwardly he was still the old Kaimakam, and everyone still deferred to him as such. He was an Ottoman gentleman, a proud man to the bitter end. Inwardly he believed that his financial troubles were transitory, like clouds in the sky, they would disappear once his eldest was finally home as a British-trained lawyer. Munir would restore the family fortune; in the meantime, there was nothing to worry. Now, all he needed for the family wheel of fortune to turn was time.

Unfortunately, what Grandpa did not know was that time he did not have.

No doubt, though, the day Uncle Munir arrived was Grandpa's triumph, his vindication. The long years of patience were over and his costly investment was about to pay big dividends. He believed his money problems would soon be over. His declining health would recover. And his family would regain its status and power. At this moment in time, with his dear Munir back as a lawyer, he was, once again, the proud Kaimakam, just like the old Ottoman times. Now he could really boast, at least for a brief moment: "I told you so. My son, my Munir, would not let me down. I knew it all along. The age of the British is finally here. And my son, a London-trained lawyer, will quickly restore my wealth and status" He felt a great sense of relief.

Grandpa's moment of glory was, alas, all too brief, too late.

In the larger scale of events, no doubt, the return of Grandpa's eldest son and heir could not have been more perfectly timed. The Great War had ended, exactly as Munir had predicted. The British were triumphant in the Holy Land, in Africa and Europe. They were the new masters of the entire world. Like all Ottoman patriots, Grandpa was sorry that the Ottoman Empire was in ruins, but he was comforted by his son's foresight in predicting years ago that a new age, British supremacy, was dawning.

"Our Padisah is in trouble again," he reflected privately, but he did not particularly worry. "Thanks to Munir I will now regain my wealth." He expected that his son would fix things up at the bank and restore the wealth and status of the Uzun Ali dynasty. "That son of mine is smart. The world now belongs to the British and my son is ready for it."

That, however, is not how the nationalist leader, Mustafa Kemal, the hero of Gallipoli saw it in the Turkish mainland. The British were now firmly in control of Cyprus under High Commissioner Stevenson. Soon, the island would become formally a colony. A new Governor named Storrs, of recent fame in British Palestine, arrived to make the island into a strong military base, cut its links to Turkey and to bring British justice and good government to the inhabitants. The colonial masters needed trained staff, willing to work with the British, exactly like Uncle Munir.

But when Uncle Munir came back, the war was not over yet, not for the Turks and Greeks. Across the short Mediterranean Sea separating Cyprus from Asia Minor, a new Kemalist Turkey was rising, like some phoenix rising out of the ashes of the dead Ottomans. If the British got in his way, the Gazi was determined to take them on. It was a dangerous moment.

The war in Europe was finished, but not in Turkey. A new round of war began there, lasting another four years, the National War of Independence to liberate the Turkish motherland. Terrible things were happening in Anatolia. The Greeks invaded the Turkish heartland and started burning villages and killings and massacres ensued on all fronts. Turks were fighting Greeks; Armenians were fighting Kurds; the French, the English and the Italians were in Syria, Lebanon and the Holy Land. Jews, escaping the holocaust in Russia, were streaming through Cyprus. Thousands of refugees began arriving in Cyprus. Armenians, Greeks and Jews were everywhere. It was madness and there was chaos and misery.

But amidst all, Uncle Munir pressed full steam ahead. No sooner than he returned to the island, than he began making friends with the British. He became friends with the new master of the island. He was rewarded handsomely, for they could use a pro-English attorney who knew not only their language, but also some elements of the British law.

But Grandpa never recovered the wealth he anticipated. Munir did become rich and powerful, but it was for no one, but himself. That included his father. Sure enough he had intervened at the bank on behalf of Uzun Ali, but Munir was a city man and in Nicosia he lived more like he belonged to the British colonial set. Munir worked and spent all his time with his British friends; he had little time for his old father at the Konak in Milltown. He did the barest minimum required at the bank to keep the Konak with his father so long as he lived.

Uncle Munir was always respectful of his father, and his respect was greater now befitting his advanced age and fragile health. Uncle worked and lived in Nicosia and he was immediately immersed in ever-increasing deals and transactions. But, he always found time for frequent visits to his father. Uzun Ali was too proud to ask financial help from his son; the prodigal son offered none. In truth, Uncle Munir was not aware of the true state of finances in the Konak. Besides, by nature he was inclined to put himself first. So, Uncle Munir figured, his father was too old now, best left undisturbed as much as possible. He assumed that his father had little use for money.

Then, unexpectedly, Uzun Ali did solicit Munir's help. It was not for money; it was on account of father Ozkan.

"Munir, my dear son" said Grandpa, one day when uncle Munir called on his aging father at one of his visits to the Milltown Konak, "lately I have realized that I may have been unfair as a father."

"Father what are you saying," protested Munir. "You have treated me extremely well. No one can match your generosity," he said.

"I am not sure," said the old Kaimakam. Uncle Munir looked puzzled, and Grandpa waited for a few moments, and then went on.

"It is your brother, I am talking about" he said.

Munir, so busy with his practice and busy life in Nicosia, had only a superficial knowledge of his younger brother. The two had had no contact and lived totally separate lives. With frozen relations since the affair of the rose garden, the two half-brothers were in suspended truce.

His father continued as uncle Munir waited for his father's speech.

"Munir, my son, I always believed in you. I knew you would be a success. I am now truly proud of you." Then he stopped for a deep breath and resumed. "But lately I have been worried about your brother Ozkan" he said. "He is working in the fields like a farm hand. I feel I should have been fairer with him. Now, I want you to help him. Get him a government job so he can enjoy security and steady income."

Respectfully, uncle Munir said: "OK, father. Of course I will help. I will talk to my English friends."

That is how father became a policeman and moved to Nicosia. It was amazing how quickly Uncle Munir could get results. His connections were, no doubt, critical. But, the new colonial masters were in desperate need of personnel to keep law and order in this strange island.

Father rented a room in a house in Samanbahce, near the police headquarters. In truth, father Ozkan was glad to end his farming days and truly he was grateful for his big brother's help. While the frostiness in their relations remained, both father and uncle now opened a new chapter.

But uncle Munir did nothing for his aging and dying father, in part because he did not know how precarious his father's situation was. The following months were painful. Uzun Ali suffered another stroke, more serious than the first, and to the end he was too proud or vain to ask his son for financial help. The son was too selfish, and began to stay away from his father; his visits to the Konak became less frequent. He was too busy with his law practice and cultivating his English friends in Nicosia. Not long after the peace was announced, Uzun Ali had crossed the limit. He was given three months to move out of the Konak, previously and secretly pledged as security for Uzun Ali's last line of credit. When the eviction notice arrived, he suffered a huge stroke and died the following week, at the ripe of age of 65.

At his death, Grandpa, the former Kaimakam of Milltown, was, a heart-broken man. He never adjusted to a life under the British. Munir's success in becoming a lawyer turned out to be no more than a fleeting relief. Uzun Ali never recovered his wealth and status; he died penniless and, although he had lived in grand-style in the old Ottoman Konak in Milltown, the Ottoman world was gone with the wind.

The funeral itself was dignified, but low-key. The old Kaimakam was buried in the Milltown cemetery the day after his death, at midday immediately following the noon prayers as the custom required. All the Konak's servants came to pay their last respects, and after the burial, officiated by the Milltown imam, Munir and Ozkan along with their stepmother Neslihan received condolences from friends and villagers. Notables and peasants, Greeks and Turks, from surrounding villages and districts, all came to show respect to a man who towered amongst his peers, one who symbolized old customs and traditions when justice to all was the rule and a man's word passed as his honor.

## UZUN ALI, SHAME AND SALVATION

Uzun Ali lived and died a proud Ottoman. His hopes and dreams from Tanzimat remained a fanciful history. Grandpa, the Ottoman patriot, died before seeing the progress he had yearned and worked for in his native land which, to him, was an integral part of the Sultan's dominion. He took with him to his grave a number of secrets, not just the unfulfilled hopes of a patriot too humiliated to stomach the reality of a British Cyprus, but also many family secrets. When Uzun Ali died, my father and uncle lost their father, as everyone knew. What was unknown was that Ayfer lost his only Grandfather, his only hope for a normal life. Now, only Nilufer and Neslihan were privy to the fact that Ayfer was Munir's son. The father and the son were like two strangers in the street.

\*\*\*

In the aftermath of Grandpa's death, uncle Munir at last learnt the bitter and full story of his father's finances. He had no choice but go through Uzun Ali's papers. The shocking truth was laid out before his eyes, in all its ugly and painful details. He immediately made the necessary arrangements to settle Uzun Ali's huge debts at the bank that meant that he would remain a bachelor for the foreseeable future. Of course, it suited him quite well because he was now spending most of his leisure at the Nicosia Club, virtually as a member of the British elite, cut off from the Ottoman/Turkish community.

Within weeks after the funeral, uncle Munir took several drastic measures. He came to the Konak alone and with no previous discussion with my father. His decision was as ruthless as sudden. He dismissed the entire household at the Konak. "There is no money for repairs and restoration," he declared. It made no sense in view of his urban lifestyle in Nicosia. No one now stayed at the Konak, except Neslihan and one servant to look after her. That was the limit of uncle Munir's generosity. That much he felt he owed to his dad's memory.

He had one last encounter with Nilufer. The young girl he had raped a decade ago in the rose garden now had come to see him in Uzun Ali's *Selamlik*. She had come with high hopes; certain he would remember how he had taken advantage of her in the rose garden.

"What will I do?" She asked. "Where shall I go?" she looked at Munir. He was unmoved. There was no hint of memories gone by.

"I cannot afford to keep you here. You have to go," He said.

The beautiful *odalik* was almost in tears. In her late twenties and still very attractive, Nilufer was downcast. With a son not quite ten yet, she had nowhere to go.

Uncle Munir was unmoved. He offered her a five-pound note that she refused. She surveyed him tip to toe.

Then Nilufer spoke again. "I will go" she said and took a few steps toward the door. She then stopped and turned back to Munir and said: "We will meet again" and she walked out. He did not know what to make of Nilufer's remark.

Uncle Munir, still the old heartless man, looked on. Poor Nilufer was dejected, but sustained her dignity to the bitter end.

I am heartbroken to say, but Nilufer became a prostitute. That was the harsh reality of those days. Hard times began for Nilufer and her fatherless son. Mother and son moved to Nicosia, she into the red light district in the Armenian quarter because, for a kept woman in an Ottoman Konak, in those days, there was no other choice. Nilufer, now passed her prime, had enough charm yet to earn an adequate income servicing a steady stream of fun-seeking young men in Nicosia. It was a well trodden road for many Circassian ladies of the harem, once they could no longer be cared for by their old masters, on account of death or destitution. In time, the likes of Nilufer would become Madams of public houses, in charge of new supplies of younger and less experienced girls, keeping a delicate balance between supply and demand in the Nicosia sex market.

Nilufer's son, Ayfer aged ten, was put in the orphanage in the city. The boy had no chance. His budding friendship with father Ozkan, at the old Konak in Milltown, was gone. He moved out with his mother, abandoned and discarded like some useless furniture, sold to used goods dealers purely for material gain.

Life in the orphanage was nasty, brutish and short. It lasted barely two years. During this time, Ayfer suffered abuse at the hands of uncaring people who were supposed to be paid by some Islamic charity to look after the less fortunate in the memory of the wealthy deceased. The salaries were always in arrears and the staff provided food and care according to personal contributions of relatives and relations of the inmates. Since Ayfer had none, his portions were minimal and whenever he asked for more food, he was beaten.

So, as soon as Ayfer reached his teens he was gone. But he had nowhere to go. The streets and alleys became his home. He slept in the corners of Buyuk Han, the Grand Hamam, sometimes in the open under the Venetian Moat, and during the day he lived off scraps of food he managed to obtain from food stalls near the grand bazaar. The Great War was well behind, but law and order was a major headache for the colonial masters of Cyprus. The police was expanding rapidly to cope with bandits in the mountains, and urban gangs. The streets of Nicosia that Ayfer now inhabited were dangerous as Ayfer quickly found out. He moved into a contested space, a valuable zone in which competing gangsters fought one another for extortion and control while the colonial police looked the other way. Ayfer soon became a pawn in the hands of these gangsters who controlled the Nicosia underworld far more effectively than the colonial police regulated the daily life.

The urban gangs were well organized and operated like guilds with their own rules and procedures. The gang leader chose his men very carefully and trust within the gang was a matter of strict discipline, any infringement of the leader's orders was punishable by execution. The critical element in gang operations was the collection. This happened at the end of every month, and it worked according to time-honored system similar to tax collection. Members of the gang would call on specific groups of merchants and traders in the area and collect agreed amounts of revenue, to be taken and handed to the leader. Everyone knew how much money changed hands, and how much was delivered to the leader. Out of the collection, the leader distributed payments to gang members, strictly in accordance with seniority and discretion of the leader. The discretionary component was a special reward for jobs done in exemplary manner to the satisfaction of the leader.

The streets in the area from Asmaalti covering the Buyuk Han, and to the Grand Hamam were the prize territory in town because it included the Grand Bazaar. It raised the maximum collection. It was the envy of all gangsters in town. When Ayfer joined the gang, its leader was Blind Ahmet, the most prestigious leader of the Nicosia underworld at the time. He was big and powerful, in midlife, dressed in the traditional Ottoman garb of an *efe*, a mountain warrior, with colorful baggy pants and headwear atop a rugged face dominated by a shapely moustache and blue eyes. Despite his name, both his eyes were fine, although there was a big scar around his left eye. Blind Ahmet always carried a scimitar-like sword hidden in his dress and he never wavered from his determination to use it to settle disputes or fights.

## ROSES AND TEARS

Young Ayfer was at the turning point of his life. He was lonely and desperately in need of protection. After he ran away from the orphanage, he called at Nilufer in the whorehouse in the Armenian quarter.

"Mother" he said, "I do not like the orphanage. They are mean to me." Nilufer was half expecting that something like this would happen.

"My dear son" she said with sadness "What did they do to you?"

"They made me work from dawn to dusk; they never gave me enough food; and when I asked for more, they beat me." He said and looked at Nilufer for comfort.

There was no point in insisting on the impossible. She knew Ayfer would not go back; just as well as she knew he could not stay with her. A whorehouse was no place for an 11 year old.

"My dear," she began, "here is a pound, take it, but I want to ask you a favor. Will you do it?" She looked at him almost in tears as Ayfer took the money from his mother and put it in his pocket.

"What do you want me to do, mother?" He asked.

"I want you to go visit a lawyer in town. Mr. Munir Uzun Ali" then Ayfer interjected,

"Why mother? I have done nothing wrong."

"I know my dear. Just go see him and tell him I sent you. That is all." She kept the rest of her story a secret from the boy.

Ayfer then got up and left. He was not persuaded by his mother's plea. Maybe if she had told him about the rape in the rose garden, things might have been different. As it was, he was in no mood to get mixed up with lawyers and high society, and with his dirty baggy pants and torn vest, he was not sure that he would be admitted into a lawyer's office.

As he left, Nilufer stood by the window, watching her son go into the streets of Nicosia. It was as if she knew that he was walking into a trap. There she stood by helplessly watching the fatherless son disappear into the darkness of the town around the Grand Bazaar, Asmaalti and the Buyuk Han.

That is how Ayfer joined the Blind Ahmet's gang. He became the latest addition to Nicosia's underworld. The King's justice meant to him as much as the Sultan's.

# XI

When Ayfer joined the Blind Ahmet gang, my father Ozkan had been in the police force for three years. Becoming a policeman was a huge step-up for father. It gave him status and put money in his pocket. For the first time in his life, father was sensing and enjoying independence. It all happened thanks to the new Superintendent of Police Joseph Smart, a good friend of Uncle Munir. He fixed it all, behind the scenes.

Superintendent Smart had been in Cyprus for over 10 years when he confirmed the appointment of father Ozkan Uzun Ali to the police force. Father's brother Munir was a good friend. Anglo-Asian by background, born out of wedlock in Malaya, he had come to the island in 1908, starting as a Lieutenant thanks to his father's London connections. Two years ago, when his former boss, Superintendent James had retired, he took over the top police job. It was fully deserved, both on experience and skill he had displayed.

Superintendent Smart had a rare skill in picking good local men to join the force. In truth, Ozkan was one recent example. Of good family background, father joined the force at a young age of 18, right at the end of the Great War. His father used to be an Ottoman notable in Milltown, not far from the capital. But what made the difference in his appointment was his English-trained lawyer brother, uncle Munir, newly returned from his legal studies in London, a person of great promise, a friend of the British.

"I would like my younger brother to be considered for an appointment" he had proposed to Smart, when Munir had performed a valuable service to the King. He drew up the legal papers for a huge land transfer, out of the hands of Evkaf, the Muslim endowment trust, right into the hands of the British administration for a military barracks, just outside the moat, beyond the Paphos Gate.

"Bring your brother to see me tomorrow morning" Smart said. "I am sure the police force can use young and loyal recruits." He said, emphasizing loyalty to the King as a crucial requirement, not because the Superintendent had any doubts about Munir's Anglophile position, but rather because lately the Ottoman Muslims of Cyprus were showing unusual excitement in expressing solidarity with Kemalist Turkey.

It was a few weeks after father Ozkan had joined the police force. He sat in his living room in a reflective, self-satisfying mode. He liked his new job as a policeman. Now he could sit back and relax, drawing a steady salary of three pounds at the beginning of each month, regardless of how much he exerted himself. Being a policeman was not like the farming he had been doing in Milltown for the last five years. He congratulated himself for winning a steady government job so easily and at such a young age. A man of modest ambition, Ozkan could already look to carefree retirement some forty years later.

Life as a policeman suited father's temperament. Day in, day out he was doing the same routine, and he liked it. There were no surprises and he enjoyed the feeling of calling his own shots, first time ever away from the crippling influence of the Konak. He rented rooms in a house in Samanbahce, not far from the police headquarters and began to learn the requirements of urban living. In his third year as a police recruit father Ozkan was given more responsibility and assigned to patrol duty. His beat included the Asmaalti area extending from the Grand Bazaar to the Grand Hamam. That is how he briefly met Ayfer, his half cousin at the Konak, the latest addition to the Nicosia underworld. But, in the three years that had lapsed, both had changed so much, especially Ayfer, that at the time of the unexpected encounter Ayfer and Ozkan were beyond recognition.

Father Ozkan was on patrol duty at midnight in Asmaalti when suddenly he heard screaming coming from a bakery nearby. He rushed to look and he noticed that the baker was struggling with a youth, maybe twelve or thirteen, who apparently was trying to break into his bakery.

"Police, police" shouted the baker "get the thief." When father Ozkan appeared on the scene, the baker said excitedly: "He is a troublemaker. Arrest him."

Ozkan grabbed the frightened youth. He smelt awful in dirty clothes, long hair and unwashed face.

"What are you doing? Is it true you are stealing?" asked Ozkan. He took a good look at the young criminal. Somehow he seemed familiar:

The boy stood there in silence.

"Don't I know you from somewhere?" father asked.

Ayfer did not answer. In the three years since he had left the Konak at Milltown, his rough life had changed him beyond recognition. He clothes were torn; his hair was long and unwashed. He looked tough and dirty.

"I was hungry" began Ayfer.

The baker shouted: "He was trying to steal money from my safe."

"No I was not," yelled Ayfer.

Then father recognized the youth who had also stolen Grandpa's silver watch at the Konak. He then made up his mind.

"Come" he said, "I'll take you in" and as the baker looked on, he walked out of the shop with Ayfer.

As soon as they turned the corner, he stopped, looked straight at his eyes and said to the youth: "Are you not Ayfer?"

"No" he said, lying. "I do not know you."

Father was not convinced. "Who is your boss?" He asked.

My father knew there were criminal gangs operating in the area and he was hoping to get some useful intelligence to pass on to his superiors. That way, he thought, he might be able to get Ayfer off the hook.

But Ayfer was not cooperating and he just stood in silence. Father felt pity for him.

"How old are you?" Asked father.

"Twelve" said Ayfer, in a moment of rare cooperation with authority, exaggerating his age.

"You should be at home" said father, but immediately recalled the circumstances of Nilufer's dismissal from the Konak by his elder brother. At that moment, it all came back to him. Father felt a touch of guilt that his childhood friend was now a street kid, and then decided to set free the boy with a warning, concealing his identity. "Now, go but be careful. You are a kid. Next time, you way not be so lucky." And

Ayfer was gone.

I must admit I admire British justice based on common law. What I like about it is that it is based on reasonable limits. The Ottoman law was arbitrary; British law and order was applied humanely. There were clear limits for wrongdoing and Ayfer was well below legal age of eighteen for a criminal charge. Father Ozkan decided that the boy, his childhood friend who mysteriously wished to keep his identity hidden, now an abandoned street kid, needed mercy. And, in some small measure, he applied common law in accordance with customary humane way. Yet, had he decided to apply the law strictly and taken the boy into custody, maybe all our lives could have been different. He might have avoided a great deal of misfortune and agony. I just cannot say.

The chance encounter with father taught Ayfer a lesson. He decided that for his survival on the street he needed protection. He went towards the Grand Hamam and the next morning he became a member of the notorious Blind Ahmet gang. Actually, it happened by pure chance. Ayfer was very hungry when the sun rose the next day. He had not been able to steal at the bakery and now he was desperate. That is when he noticed a group of men, laughing and noisy, about to enter the Grand Hamam.

"Hey kid," shouted one of the groups, noticing Ayfer standing pitifully next to the entrance. "Want to make some quick cash?" asked the obese fellow and Ayfer nodded.

"Come along then" he said and Ayfer went inside the Hamam and from that moment on he was the junior member of Blind Ahmet's gang.

For the next three years, Ayfer learnt all about the underworld, the survival skills of street fighting and the ways of extortion from merchants in the market place. Above all, he learnt the necessity of unquestioned loyalty to his boss, Blind Ahmet.

He never for once thought about visiting Munir the lawyer like his mother had asked him.

The father and son passed the chance to meet.

# XII

It was the third year of peace and life in London was difficult. Mary, uncle Munir's Irish girl friend, was bored in London without Munir. It wasn't that she had difficulty finding boyfriends. Rather it was the fact that none came even close to his standard. She needed him desperately. That is how she started making plans to come for a surprise visit to Cyprus. It was an astonishing idea!

The remarkable thing about Mary was her iron determination; once she was resolved on something, nothing could make her change her mind. It was her Irish spirit; it was in her genes, so she accepted it as part of nature. "No point in fighting uphill" she would reason to herself, "life is too short for that. Better to go with the flow and enjoy life to the fullest" resolved the Irish girl.

Shortly after returning to London, and safely back in her secretarial job fetching a handsome two pounds, ten shillings a week, quite a decent wage in postwar London with food shortages and demobilized soldiers all hungry for jobs, she realized that there was one big hole in her life without Munir. Her social life was empty. "Work, work and all work", no fun, no excitement, she reflected on the sad state of her solitary life. She tried several boy friends. None gave her the excitement and fulfillment that Munir did, the short and slightly dark Mediterranean. Mary missed him, the exciting times with him. "May be it is love, I don't know," she would say to herself. Sure they would sometime have arguments, but always their moments of difference would end up in blissful lovemaking and all would be forgiven and forgotten.

Love mixed with adventure made up Mary's mind. "I am young and fun-loving," she declared one day suddenly: "I must go to Cyprus, to join Munir." That was it. From that day on, Mary had a definite purpose and a clear plan. She must save and then travel east and find her man. No one had loved her like Munir. She missed him.

The next day, at her lunch break, she went to visit the Thomas Cooks' Travel Agency, near Trafalgar Square. "How much will it cost to travel to Cyprus?" She asked the clerk at the counter, who looked straight at the feisty Irish secretary, thought for a few moments choosing his words carefully, and then said: "Miss, did you say Cyprus?" He put on the face of a Grammar School teacher admonishing a student for asking a stupid question.

"Yes I did," said Mary emphatically. "You are the Thomas Cooks' Travel Agency? Are you not? Famous for organizing tours to Africa and exotic places?" Mary had done some homework on the subject.

"Yes, Miss, we are indeed." He realized immediately that he was talking to a young woman with uncommon determination. So he changed both his tone and tactic, and merely asked: "What would you like to know?"

"The fare, please" said Mary. "How much is the cheapest ticket to Cyprus?"

"Well" said the travel clerk, "If you travel by boat, which is what I'd recommend given unreliable train service in central Europe and the Balkans" he said in a business-like manner, "you may travel from London to Piraeus, that is the port of Athens. That would cost 200 pounds, round figures, and you may be able to get a boat from there to Cyprus for another 50 pounds I'd say."

He looked straight at Mary's eyes. They looked like they were about to pop out their sockets. Mary was completely taken aback by the huge amount the clerk was mentioning. She thought of her meager wages of 2 pounds 10 shillings a week and her zero savings.

"Thank you very much" is all she could think of saying. She went out of the Thomas Cooks' Travel Agency and was gone in an instant. "There is no way for me to go" was her first reaction. "It would take me years to save up just the fare, if I tried my best to save. And then there are all those other expenses." It looked like an impossible dream.

But, once determined, it was unlike Mary to give up. Before not too long, her mind was working on new and daring schemes. "I could take in typing," she said. "And I could work on weekends in part-time positions."

That is exactly what she did.

Within two years, Mary was on the boat to Piraeus. It was August 1923. During the preceding year, Mary developed a second hobby: she started reading the dailies. She began to read stories, and followed news of the Greek-Turkish War in Anatolia, mainly to map out her route for her travel to the region, but also to satisfy her curiosity about the mysterious East where Munir lived. Lately she had taken a special interest in the articles written by Arnold Toynbee in the *Manchester Guardian*. He was a war correspondent in Asia Minor writing all those horrible stories about Greek atrocities, burning villages and massacring people as the Kemalist armies were pushing the invaders out of the Turkish homeland. It reminded her a little of Ireland, but deep down, she felt some sort of affinity for Munir's people. Then she read something about a political crisis in the government of Lloyd George, who wanted to fight the Kemalist forces, and it had made no sense to her at all. "The Turks are fighting for their homeland, what is wrong with that?" She would ask herself. So, she was not unhappy when the newspapers reported that Lloyd George was forced to resign in disgrace and the Turks had won a major victory. "Now that the war is over, it must be safe to go to Cyprus" judged Mary.

When she landed in Piraeus, she had a first taste of her miscalculation. Refugees were everywhere, shouting and screaming, it was a human flood, misery everywhere, people coming and going aimlessly, searching food and shelter. Chaos ruled. There was suffering on a scale she had not seen or imagined before. On 9 May 1919 the Greek Army had landed in Izmir to establish Greater Greece; three years later, the Ottoman Greeks were dispossessed of their homeland. Boatloads of refugees were crowding little Greece, and new waves of them arrived daily. Once proud and prosperous merchants were now begging in the streets of Piraeus and Athens. Mary had never seen so many desperate people, speaking strange languages, Greek and Turkish, screaming at each other as if they were engaged in a perpetual fight. "Greeks were leaving their homeland in Asia Minor," she remembered; but it made no sense to her. Neither did the human pain she witnessed dent Mary's determination to go on. She never wavered from her plan to go to Cyprus, to find Munir.

Finally, after a stormy boat trip in an empty Greek boat going to Cyprus to bring more food to Greece, Mary at last realized her ambition. She landed in the port of Famagusta and cleared British customs late in October 1923. Her first decision on the island was a smart one: She rejected travel by ox-driven carts or taxi on dusty and dangerous roads through malaria-infected plains of Mesarya. Instead, she traveled on the new train service to Nicosia and arrived late afternoon on the terminal building not quite a mile north of Kyrenia Gate.

"What is the nearest hotel?" she inquired at the ticket office at the terminal

The official with an Ottoman beard in British khaki shorts and shirt, looked puzzled at the lone British woman, but managed to answer,

"Buyuk Han."

That was the direction Mary gave to the driver of the horse-driven buggy she hired. She then traveled through the dusty and dirty highway, lined with huge eucalyptus trees past the Kyrenia Gate and the monastery of the Whirling Dervishes on the left, bravely traveling toward the town-center with its imposing Venetian Column. Exhausted but undaunted, in the evening of 27 October Mary checked in at Buyuk Han, in Asmaalti, a medieval *Kervansaray*, the only inn in the old Ottoman capital.

# XIII

Mary checked in at the *Kervansaray*, the Buyuk Han, just two days before my parents' wedding. It was a remarkable timing, full of puzzles and contradictions.

At the check-in, the innkeeper, who had been the wrestling champion of Cyprus, was totally floored by the lone foreign lady traveler, all the way from England, standing in front of him. He was in traditional Ottoman garments, a shaggy pants, shirt and vest covering a huge potbelly, and a round shiny face dominated by a huge moustache with the standard scimitar-like curls at either end. He did not know English, except "room", "welcome" and maybe half a dozen more which he had picked up from the more learned of his drinking buddies. "You never know, when these strange words, might come in handy," he would say with a sense of humor. On the day Mary checked it, they sure were handy.

It was May 27, 1923. Mary might have been a guest for my parent's wedding set for the 29th, except of course, the fact that Mary knew nothing of the wedding.

As soon as she was accommodated in the best suite upstairs in the otherwise empty inn, the innkeeper, yelled at his assistant: "Ahmet, come here right now" he said, in a tone of desperation. The assistant rushed to his boss, whom the poor fellow thought had had an accident and was in great pain.

"What is the matter boss?" he complied. "I am right here."

"Did you see that?" He was still in the shock of the English woman who came alone, unannounced, looking for accommodation. "Do you have a room?" She had asked. Never before, had a lone English female asked the innkeeper such a question. Only men were the customers, typically men of the camel caravans, bringing in dates and henna from Syria and Arabia via the port of Famagusta. While the caravan men slept in the sixty-odd rooms, counting upstairs and downstairs, the camels rested in the large courtyard and drank water from the fountain in the middle. Since the British arrived in Cyprus, the increasing flow of tourists from Europe was staying in the luxury hotels of Limassol and Larnaca on the coast rather than in such places as the Buyuk Han.

"Did you see that English lady?" said the innkeeper to his assistant. All blond Europeans were English, so far as the innkeeper was concerned. Ethnicity was a matter of trivial detail.

"No, boss" replied the assistant. "I was cleaning the dung from the camels last night" he said. The innkeeper by then had lost interest in the subject, so dismissed his assistant: "OK, then, go back to work." And he ran off and disappeared, back to his cleaning chore in the courtyard.

Upstairs, in her room, Mary was too tired to notice the surroundings; the room was poorly lit, and everything was dingy. She was, however, more than a little discomforted by strange smells and odors she had not encountered before. There was one advantage: the room was amazingly cool from the breeze that came through her window. Outside it was dark. Mary, exhausted, went straight to bed and was soon fast asleep.

She slept soundly that night, the cool breeze of Nicosia providing natural protection against bugs and the camel smell of the courtyard below. There was the occasional noise from boisterous merrymakers in the bars of Asmaalti, just beyond her window, but Mary was blissfully asleep to notice them. She slept till it was hot the next morning, waking up around 10 o'clock.

She could hardly believe her eyes. "What is this place?" She asked herself as she surveyed her room, rented the night before for a grand sum of a shilling. There was hardly any furniture, except the bed she had slept on and a chair on which he had placed her garments, rather haphazardly the night before. The train ride from Famagusta, through the entire length of Mesarya semi-desert, had been exhausting, but by now, after the misery of Piraeus, Mary had become used to facing and overcoming discomfort and human suffering around.

She went downstairs, and there was the same innkeeper, this time trying to be friendly with a big smile on his face. He muttered something, which sounded like 'Good morning', Mary smiled at the man.

"Good morning" she began. "I am looking for a lawyer called Munir Uzun Ali"

The former wrestling champion's eyes beamed, just like he had won a major trophy.

"Munir Uzun Ali?" He repeated. "Him lawyer." Rather pleased with himself, the innkeeper kept on smiling.

The innkeeper and the foreign guest were now communicating. Mary, feeling successful in this strange place, said: "My friend from London. I need to see him."

The innkeeper did not reply to Mary. He immediately yelled at his assistant: "Ahmet, go fetch Munir Bey, right away." Ahmet knew where to go looking; Munir was the successful English-trained lawyer. His law firm at Sarayonu, the central square, was not more than five minutes away.

That is how Mary was re-united with my uncle Munir. He was shocked at the news. He dropped everything and rushed to Buyuk Han. He was standing in front of Mary, his London girlfriend, in minutes, still unbelieving it all.

It took him a minute or two to get used to the reality of the woman standing before him. They had not seen each other for five years. Mary was instantly satisfied; he was more distinguished looking now wearing a new suit, and heavier around his waist. Surprise was written all over his face. He smiled and surveyed his Irish lover, in truth pleased to see her. Mary now looked prettier, though evidently tired from the harrowing journey from London.

Uncle Munir was still in shock. "Mary, what are you doing here?" were his first words. Never in his wildest dreams could he imagine a visit by his ex-girl friend. They had not communicated since his return. "You should have written to me."

"I wanted to surprise you" she began. Then they embraced and kissed on both cheeks. Of course, in public, a more passionate kiss would be inappropriate.

"Come let's go. You must be hungry. There is a restaurant across" he said. She was; she had not eaten since the boat.

As they finished breakfast, she said: "Can we visit the Konak at Milltown?" She had an idyllic picture of the town in which Munir had grown up from his accounts in London when he had been homesick and gave Mary a rather a romantic and now clearly an outdated image of opulence at the old Konak mansion.

But now uncle held back. Mary's request seemed to discomfort Munir. It was as if he did not wish to go to Milltown. Almost a minute passed. Finally, "yes, of course" he said rather unenthusiastically.

Then he added, almost casually: "My father died shortly after my return, you know." and almost added, "and heartbroken with heavy debt." But he decided to keep this vital information till later. He was not entirely sure why, but maybe Munir felt embarrassed to reveal so soon the actual state of his father's death as a bankrupt old man.

Of course, uncle Munir himself was doing fine in Nicosia, cultivating his British connections and building up his practice. In Milltown, things had gone from bad to worse ever since his return. He had spent much of the past five years settling his father's debts, but with no more land to be sold, and my father Ozkan, formerly an impecunious farmer now a lowly paid policeman, it was an uphill battle to resist the inevitable. That is why he had not been able to marry some rich landowners' daughter right after his return. As a consequence uncle Munir was spending more time with his English friends than in the high circles of the local Turkish/Ottoman elite.

The old Konak was now in a pitiful state. It was just a few months before the bank proposed to auction it off. But, at the last minute, uncle Munir decided against it, for Grandpa's sake and as a favor to old Neslihan who was still living there, and made the necessary arrangements at the bank. On the day of their visit, the place was in a desperate state of disrepair.

There was one luxury that uncle Munir definitely enjoyed. He was the proud owner of the only automobile in town, a Ford Model T, a second hand, but highly serviceable car he had purchased from a departing British officer a year earlier. Mary was duly impressed; after all the discomfort of the boat trip, now she could enjoy a little luxury. She had come out seeking Munir for love and it was comforting for her, after all the miseries of her long journey through war-torn Europe, to see evidence of wealth in her ex-boy friend. "I am sick of being a poor typist in London. I want a life of luxury and comfort." She would say to herself every time she was down, which was quite often during the difficult journey to Cyprus.

She recalled the happy times with Munir in Soho and Hampstead Heath when he would boast to her of her father's wealth, the Konak and the estates and servants, reminding him of the easy life of Irish nobility back home. That was a good deal of what had attracted her to Cyprus. But, beyond money and wealth, Mary was a woman in love when she set foot on the island. Munir's absence from London made her realize that the love affair in London had been more meaningful than either had originally realized. She hoped, and sometimes even believed, Munir shared her feelings. That, indeed, was the truth, but some mysterious distance still separated the two lovers.

Uncle and Mary drove past the central square with its tall Venetian pillar in front of the Government Complex, through a narrow avenue, past the Tekke of the Whirling Dervishes, leading to the Kyrenia Gate, a dark and small tunnel dug out of the moat though which, Mary remembered passing through the day before, and they were passing a huge Muslim cemetery going in the direction of the train station.

Then, she asked: "Tell me about your father. How did he die?"

Uncle Munir had never written to her. "When I came back my father had aged, his health was poor. I had not seen him for years. He was sad and did not say much. I was actually kept in dark. " Munir became serious and awkward.

He was about to say something important and painful, but he held off. They hit on the dusty road toward the hills of the Five Fingers Mountains, some 10 miles away. It was a winding road, and although late in October, the temperature in the midday sun was already above 30 degrees. Mary kept her composure. Uncle Munir went on:

"He passed away within a few months of my return. He had a massive stroke." He stopped as if he did not wish to volunteer any more details.

"I am so sorry," said Mary. "I didn't know".

He then went on: "It was so sudden. I was away in Nicosia. There was nothing to do to save him." Munir's matter-of-fact tone came as cold and uncaring to Mary. She felt it was an uncomfortable subject, best left alone. She kept her silence.

He then changed the subject.

"Don't be surprised if you are disappointed in the Konak" he warned Mary as they entered Milltown. "It is not the place it used to be."

"It is a pretty town," she said as they approached Milltown. Mary had long thought about it, and she was now determined to put everything in the most positive light possible. She definitely did not wish to upset Munir, for she knew from London how quick-tempered and explosive he could be. Fortunately, she enjoyed the scenery around and, as they entered Milltown, she was truly impressed with everything she saw. They drove along a lovely stream, amidst scented orchards of olives, citrus and vegetable gardens. The Five Fingers Mountains in the background, covered in their most appealing dark blue colors, provided a most wondrous background.

"Yes" he agreed, "Milltown is a lovely town. Most of what you see used to belong to my dad when I was a little boy. This stream powers sixteen mills, many of which used to belong to my father. That was before the British took over the island. The good old days, as my father used to say" he said with a little touch of melancholy, a sad remembrance of family fortune now gone.

Mary knew it all. He had told her many times in London about Uzun Ali, the Ottoman governor of the district, an Aga and the most powerful and wealthy man in the area. Yet, now somehow Mary had visions of great expectations; she longed to see evidence of the old grandeur and luxury of the Uzun Ali Konak.

I, too, have often wondered myself, like Mary, sometimes sitting amidst ruins, and reflecting of the old times when this Ottoman mansion was a bee-hive of activity, centered on Uzun Ali, his wealth and power in abundance all around. It must have been grand, with so many servants and spacious rooms, all beautifully decorated. That is how I, too, idealized Grandpa's life-style.

Instead a big surprise awaited Mary as they entered through the front gate of the old Konak. It was not at all what she had pictured it in her mind. Gone were the splendor and glory in Munir's accounts. The gate was torn down, and dirt and cow dung was piled just inside the gate on the right as the car pulled in. He parked the car next to a huge hill of dung and it stunk badly. A few cows made some noise from a barn on the left. There were, scattered in the yard, various agricultural implements, no longer in use, and there was no sign of life anywhere. The mansion was in ruins.

Mary and uncle Munir got out of the Ford. "I am sorry the place is run down a bit," he said apologetically. That was an understatement. No one seemed to be around and nobody came to welcome him or her.

"Where is everyone?" asked Mary, bewildered. "This place looks abandoned."

"No one else lives here except my step mother Neslihan." Munir said.

Uncle led her upstairs to where his old father used to hold court. The old mansion was in a shadow of its past, and Munir felt guilty about it. Neslihan, his step mother now in her sixties, was living alone upstairs, with just one elderly servant looking after her, but her rose garden was no more. After his return from London, Munir was more respectful of her, mostly due to his father's memory, and the step-mother never revealed her true feelings of him: In Neslihan's view he, the apple of his father's eyes, was as much to blame for his father's bankruptcy as his own gambling habit. Uzun Ali had squandered her property and jewels. Neslihan also kept another, more vital secret from Munir: That he had a son in Nicosia, a son born to Nilufer, called Ayfer, then a member of the Nicosia underworld. The unfortunate Nilufer joined the sex trade in the Armenian quarter.

Mary followed uncle and they went upstairs, entered a big room, comfortable but full of bric-a-brac. Around the walls, on all four sides, were Ottoman divans, on the walls above, rafters still full of china. The floor was covered in Persian and Turkish rugs, most in poor state. The room was clearly in use, but it had seen much, much better days.

"This is where Uzun Ali used to live," said uncle. Then they noticed Neslihan Hanim, seating in a sofa, next to a window overlooking the ground where once the rose garden and the orchards below existed.

"Mother this is Mary, my friend from London" he said out of courtesy as she noticed Munir and the blond young lady. She smiled at her visitors graciously, got up and greeted them.

Mary was captivated by the graceful and mature presence of Neslihan. Her look disclosed just a tiny sense of the glamour that once belonged to the Mistress of the Kaimakam's Konak. Mary felt a sense of history gone by.

Neslihan, of course, knew no English and Munir had to act as temporary translator. She immediately took a liking to Mary; maybe it was a mysterious feeling of female vulnerability she experienced between the guest and the hostess. Uncle Munir broke the silence.

"Mother" said uncle Munir respectfully. "Mary has come all the way from London, to see the Konak and visit us." The old Mistress was visibly impressed.

"Welcome" she said, with a charming smile and bow of her head, as if she was welcoming some Ottoman dignitary long ago. "Please sit down." As they did, she called the servant and asked for coffee and sweets. Then she continued:

"Ah! The Konak, it is not what it used to be" she said mournfully.

They made small talk while sipping Turkish coffee. It was Mary's first homemade Turkish coffee and she liked it.

There was an eerie feeling of unease in the air that Mary felt, but could not understand. The fact was that Munir had never spoken to Mary of the latent hostility that existed between him and Neslihan. Mary knew nothing about the maiden Nilufer and the rape in the rose garden. That was uncle's personal secret, long buried in his subconscious.

Then Neslihan got up, went to a desk and pulled out an antique box containing a watch. She came and gave Mary a gift, Uzun Ali's silver watch. She turned to Munir: "It used to belong to your father. It was special to him; once it was lost and recovered."

Mary looked on in amazement. She was speechless, clearly touched by the Mistress's unexpected generosity.

"I would like you to have it, in memory of Uzun Ali. It is good of you to travel all this way to come here," said Neslihan. Then she added: "I believe Uzun Ali would have liked you. Once we talked about you, but that was without the advantage of seeing you in person."

Mary was touched, and rather embarrassed by this surprise gift. "Thank you" she said awkwardly.

"It is an old Ottoman custom" uncle explained. "A gift is presented in honor of an important visit, a symbol to remember the occasion," he said.

They left shortly afterwards, Neslihan and Munir agreeing to meet tomorrow at Ozkan's wedding. "Make sure you bring Mary along to the wedding," said Neslihan as if somehow Munir would be remiss in his hospitality.

***

Their big fight occurred during the drive back to Nicosia. It began with a rather innocent remark, almost casually when Mary said. "She is such a gracious lady, why is she living in such a ruin?" She waited for a response. Munir remained silent, embarrassed.

Then Mary, almost unthinkingly, persisted. "You should have restored the Konak for her."

That did it.

"Mary, look here" he said, rather abruptly. "I have been paying my fathers' debts ever since I came back. He died a poor man; he gambled away all the family fortune. Neslihan was his fourth wife and she just stood there watching the family fortune disappear. She did not lift a finger."

There was anger in his tone. But she failed to grasp the mounting anger in him. She had touched a raw nerve, but carelessly she took sides in a deep family feud.

"Poor lady, maybe she was helpless," said Mary, coming to Neslihan's defense. "I heard about the *harem* life in a book once. How women like Neslihan were mistreated." The remark hurt and upset uncle Munir.

"You don't know" he jumped showing his anger. "She was not a good wife. And, she was not a good mother. She was the former wife of a rich Egyptian merchant. Why are you defending her?" He asked without looking at Mary.

"It must have been difficult for women in the Konak." She said indifferently.

"It was difficult for everyone. She drove him away and into bad habits." He hit back, anger boiling inside him.

"What about your expensive life in London?" she suddenly asked. And she hit the soft spot in uncle Munir's psyche.

"In that case you are to blame just like Neslihan," he said in an accusing tone.

Mary's Irish temper then took hold and things were suddenly electrified. Angry words followed one another, pointlessly but nevertheless poisoning their relationship before it was restarted.

"I had nothing to do with it, Munir and you know it. You took advantage of me. You left me pregnant and ran. Your son is abandoned in the convent in Dublin."

She was letting it out. She told him the difficult trip back home to her mother and how heartbreaking it was for her to abandon her son to the care of the nuns in the convent.

"Maybe that is exactly how your old man behaved to poor Neslihan too." That was unnecessary and too much.

She was sorry almost as she was saying it, but it was said. It was too late; the damage was done.

"I do not know why you are here?" He was now boiling in anger, words coming out of his mouth unthinkingly: "You came all this way to tell me that?" He demanded to know.

Mary did not answer. The Irish girl had said too much already. It was not their first fight; but it was to be the last. What really hurt was that she meant none of it. She came seeking his love, but was foolish enough not to express it, and now she was just being stupid and stubborn.

She sat there in silence as they entered the city through Kyrenia Gate. Then uncle Munir changed plans. Their fight had ruined everything. He had earlier decided to check her out of the Buyuk Han and move her into his own house in Kosklu Ciftlik, the upscale part of the town. But he was angry and wanted to punish her. So he drove and left her at the Han. He walked her upstairs to her room, some angry words were exchanged, but no good-byes said.

The two lovers of London were too proud or vain to admit that they were still in love. They parted as enemies; it was to be their last meeting.

# XIV

My father in Samanbahce was a happy, busy man. His wedding plans were moving ahead in high gear. The wedding had been a long time in planning, and father was excited, running here and there, making sure every small detail was fine. He could hardly believe that it was finally taking place. No one had worked harder at this wedding than the neighborhood matchmaker Hatice Hanim, the crafty neighbor who, several years ago, had determined that mother and father were ideally suited to each other. I do not exactly know why, but that was how matchmakers in those days arranged marriages of love. I guess, she took it as a personal challenge, once she discovered that neither father nor mother had parents to arrange their marriage.

Hatice went to work back in 1918 when father, the newly police recruit, had rented rooms in Samanbahce. Well experienced in matters of the heart, the matchmaker rose to the challenge. She guessed it perfectly that Ozkan was or soon would be in the marriage market. She liked Ozkan's looks, especially in his smart dark blue police uniform, showing all of his eighteen years to maximum advantage. The eligible bachelor became the secret target of the clever matchmaker. First, Hatice checked out father's pedigree and she was highly pleased with what she discovered; "Oh! Dear me, Ozkan comes from a good family," she said to herself with great satisfaction. Then, she thought of Pembe Hanim, her niece in Pineview, and the young girl she was raising with loving care as if she was her own daughter. Mother, little Aygul, at that time was not quite ten yet, but serious matchmaking was a carefully planned action sometimes taking several years in the making. So, the crafty matchmaker sent word to Pembe inviting her to come for a visit, and to be sure to bring along young Aygul.

It was during one of these visits to Samanhace that Hatice put her scheme into action. Unseen, from the window in her house, she pointed Ozkan to Aygul:

"See" she said to mother, "that is him. Do you like him?"

Father was wearing his uniform, about to go out of the front door where Aygul saw him, quite handsome against the bright sun. He looked dashing, smartly dressed, lean and tall. His blond hair was neatly combed, his brown eyes sharp and his face newly shaved. He was clean, youthful and vigorous.

Mother simply nodded her head. That was enough for matchmaker. The rest was detail to be managed skillfully by her expert hands.

On subsequent occasions, as Hatice and her guests from Pineview were coming and going, Aygul would catch a glimpse of an unsuspecting Ozkan from closer range. So, as if in slow motion, a one-way romance began to unfold, deftly managed by the matchmaker, cultivating a relationship in which Aygul's love secretly blossomed while father went off in his own merry way, unaware of the romantic plot of which he was the target.

Not long after something unexpected happened in the police prison. As a gesture of celebrating the end of the Great War, the day after Armistice Day, the colonial government announced a three-day special leave for all well-behaved prisoners. That gave Grandfather Halil a brief spell of freedom; he still had almost ten more years of his jail sentence. Hatice, the matchmaker, had no trouble tracking down Halil on parole on an important mission.

"Do that girl of yours a favor for a change. She will soon be marriageable." She said.

Grandfather Halil, who knew the matchmaker from the neighborhood, was taken aback by Hatice's forwardness. But, then in an instant, he realized his own inadequacy when it came to his daughter. As a father, he had done next to nothing for Aygul, and, so with a mixture of guilt and curiosity, he asked:

## UZUN ALI, SHAME AND SALVATION

"Well! What do you want me to do?" And Hatice was ready with the answer.

"Go see the old Kaimakam in Milltown, the father of the new policeman in Samanbahce. That is what you should do. I am sure his son the policeman likes your daughter" she said.

"What about Aygul?" He asked.

"She likes him. Leave the rest to me and Pembe Hanim." Said Hatice.

"But she is so young." He said.

"These things take time," said the matchmaker "Trust me. I'll take care of the rest, I tell you." She could have added: "When you are in jail" but she said nothing more.

Grandfather promised to follow Hatice's instructions. "No need to upset the matchmaker," he thought.

It wasn't too long afterwards that news reached her of the sudden death of Uzun Ali, becoming a victim of a massive stroke. Pembe came with mother visiting again shortly after the funeral of the old Kaimakam of Milltown, but a funeral was no time for matchmaking, so Hatice postponed any action to a later date. Grandfather Halil was back in jail and Hatice Hanim never knew that in fact her advice was acted upon. It was soon forgotten and lost in more pressing events in everyone's life.

In the days after Grandpa's funeral, father Ozkan and uncle Munir observed mourning for several weeks and months. Neighbors came and paid their respects, and father began to get used to the life of a lonely policeman. Without a father and mother, it was not easy to find a good, respectable girl. But father's real handicap was that he had no land or wealth Grandpa having died in bankruptcy.

As time went by father's loneliness intensified. One year passed after his father's death, and then another; and still no prospects. A sinking feeling got hold of him; should he panic about his advancing age? But every time he looked at himself in the mirror, he was impressed. "Well now" he said, "I am not a bad looking fellow." True enough with his brown eyes and blond clean-cut hair, well combed and neat, he was highly eligible. Not quite as tall as his father, but still tall enough so that his height had always given him an edge over his elder brother.

Then he said: "Maybe I will take matters in my own hand" he said. "I will be my own matchmaker and talk to Hatice Hanim; see what is available in the market. After all, this is the modern era."

Father felt uplifted when he thought of himself as a modern man. He was now fully Turkish, no longer Ottoman. Gazi Mustafa Kemal was winning victories against the invading Greeks in Asia Minor and there was a new wave of optimism amongst the Turks of Cyprus. A bright, new era was about to start.

"Yes" he said, "that is exactly what I will do. I will follow in the footsteps of the victorious Gazi. The world is mine to conquer. I must take the initiative."

It was his off-duty day. Feeling confident and cheerful, he decided to go for a walk along the moat up toward the Kyrenia Gate, within an easy walking distance of Samanbahce. Coincidentally Hatice was hosting Pembe and mother Aygul from Pineview, on one of their frequent visits to Hatice Hanim. As soon as father came out to go for a walk, the women came out as well, ostensibly for shopping. Father was approaching the junction at the Venetian moat, and that is the spot they first met. He came face to face with the stunningly beautiful Aygul, my dear mother, who was then approaching puberty and soon to be marriageable, walking in between Pembe and Hatice.

"She is so beautiful." Father whispered so quietly to himself. "She smiled back; she must like me." He was right. It was his first look of her, but not vice versa. Mother had been secretly watching him, and she had picked him long ago as her life partner.

At the road junction at Kyrenia Gate on that day, it was love, magical love, at first sight. The matchmaker's plan had worked perfectly. Two years' of hard work had paid off. Father Ozkan was thunderstruck by Aygul's stunning beauty. "She has such lovely skin, and those blue eyes, my Allah."

He was so happy he wanted to jump as he walked away and the women walked toward Samanbahce. Father could not take the girl she saw out of his mind. What he liked was that young Aygul was not covered like other girls; she wore no veil, no *hejab*. In fact, she looked divine in the blue dress and her blue eyes matched her dress. She walked in confident strides and as they were passing she gave father a seductive look. He was captivated.

So, two hours later, when he returned to his room, father's mind was made up. He decided to take a chance and walk to Hatice Hanim's house, knock at the door with a lame excuse that he wanted to borrow some cooking utensils, but, in fact, hoping to catch a glimpse, once more if he could, of the beautiful young lady.

But this time he was out of luck. The guests he was really expecting to see had already gone. Only the matchmaker Hatice Hanim was home. She welcomed father at the door with businesslike hospitality, otherwise no apparent or outward sign of special interest. "Yes? Neighbor" she asked, "What may I do for you?" Father was taken aback, but after a moment, he lamely said:

"I came to borrow a pot." It was true enough. But he tried to conceal that he had come hoping to steal a look at his heart's desire, my dear mother. She had left some half hour ago with Pembe Hanim. Father went on, as his eyes were searching Hatice Hanim's house: "Mine is damaged and I need to cook." He said. The neighbor was too clever to fall for it; he had never before called on such an errand.

"Yes of course" she said. "Come in for a second." He was glad to be invited inside.

As she went into the kitchen to fetch the pot, father looked around and satisfied himself that the house was indeed empty.

Then Hatice Hanim returned with the pot. Father then said: "I see your guests have gone."

"Yes, my niece and her step-daughter" she said. "They are from Pineview. They came to visit me and do some shopping."

The matchmaker surveyed father even more carefully than on previous occasions. No doubt, she thought, he was secretly, but surely, in love with Aygul. That realization made her happy. She realized that she was at the verge of clinching the deal.

"Ozkan bey" she said, "you should not be doing any cooking. Young, handsome man like yourself, you should start getting yourself a good-looking wife." She looked at father with smile and barely hiding her sarcasm. She almost blinked her eyes at him. He got the message and he felt warm and encouraged in his heart.

Father was pleased with what he heard. He was sure Hatice Hanim was encouraging him. He took the cue.

"Hatice Hanim" he said, "may I inquire about the young lady's name?"

"It is Aygul. Do you like it?" she asked. Father nodded his head in approval.

Then, Hatice said, "She is still a young girl."

"I do not mind waiting for her. She is so beautiful." He said. "She is worth waiting for, don't you think?" Hatice Hanim smiled and nodded in return.

In the days following, Hatice Hanim evolved into a sort of mentor for father, coaching and guiding him in the finer aspects of love. Father began to save and get ready for the next phase of his life. For his part, father was a willing, indeed happy, learner. He listened to the matchmaker as she micromanaged the romance between father and mother. I do not know whether, in those days, Hatice Hanim ever confided her secrets with mother, but there was no doubt about the old lady's timing and expertise in these affairs of the heart.

"Allah's reward is enough," she would repeat every time father would express his thanks for gems of advice or instruction she gave father. At the top of her list of what father should do was exercise patience. "Ozkan bey" she would beg, "please try and be patient. Your wife-to-be is till quite young and inexperienced. You must learn to treat her with kindness and love. But for now, do not worry too much. Leave things to me. I will take care of everything."

"But how can I repay you?" father would ask.

Hatice Hanim would simply reply: "Allah's reward for the work of matchmaker is sufficient."

***

In 1921, shortly after her puberty, Ozkan and Aygul were engaged in a traditional *Nishan* ceremony, a formal exchange of promise to marry. The marriage itself, to be concluded at a formal wedding ceremony, the *Nikah,* performed before a religious authority, had to wait a further two years so Uzun Ali's younger son could save for his wedding. Never once did father think of approaching his elder brother, the successful lawyer in town, for a loan. It suited the two half brothers to remain cool toward one another. Although father appreciated uncle Munir's help in becoming a policeman, they chose to live separate lives, operating in different worlds, each with sharply different memories of the rape in the rose garden.

From his grave in Milltown Grandpa's spirit must have smiled with satisfaction: Ozkan's marriage represented the rebirth of the Uzun Ali dynasty. This was a miracle, like the dead rising to walk again.

# XV

Dear Reader, I must now take a pause in order to go away from Cyprus to the Turkish mainland. I feel obliged to leave the island of Aphrodite and love, and travel across the narrow channel to the Turkish heartland to inform you of a new national identity, another miracle unfolding at the time of my parents' wedding. Beyond the blue Five Fingers Mountain and the turquoise Mediterranean to the North, in Turkey a truly miraculous resurrection was taking place. Those crazy Turks rose up in rebellion against both the imperialists and the Sultan. In the end, after four more years of war and amazing heroism, sacrifice and determination, they were triumphant on the battlefield. Now in Ankara, the new Anatolian capital, an astonishing political and social rebirth was taking place. A new Turkish identity was being forged.

The end of the Great War was the end of the Ottomans; it was the beginning of a new dawn for a modern Turkish nation. In Paris, Lloyd George, the fiery philhellenic prime minister conspired with the Cretan Venizelos to land Greek troops in Izmir early in September 1919 to enforce an unequal treaty on the Ottoman government. In Cyprus the Greek Church took the lead, once again, celebrating as if Christ had finally arisen, marching at the head of a Greek Orthodox army to reclaim Byzantium. The Greek Cypriots joined the *Megalo Idea*, the sacred ideal of Greater Greece. Pro-ENOSIS demonstrators shouted "Death to the Ottomans", "Long live Greece", "We want ENOSIS." The British colonial rulers looked the other way; the Cypriot Muslims, Ottomans and Turks alike, shared a common and collective disgrace and humiliation; they ran for cover. Even Munir, the committed Anglophone, stayed home for days partly in mourning but falsely believing as well that hiding would somehow reduce the shame he felt on account of the Ottoman's defeat and surrender.

Then Mustafa Kemal, the victor of Gallipoli, landed in the little Black Sea port, Samsun on 19th May 1919, just ten days after the Greek troops landed and ran amok in Izmir, terrorizing and massacring the local inhabitants, and a new war began. The peace of Paris set Asia Minor on fire. This was a war of liberation, of national independence, a war not only against imperialists, but equally a war against the morally bankrupt Ottomans. Just as he had neglected and shamelessly betrayed the generation of Uzun Ali in Cyprus, the Ottoman Sultan cared not for the Turkish heartland in Asia Minor. For the Ottomans, Rumeli, the Balkans, had been their prized home, now lost. The Anatolian hinterland was the Ottomans' neglected hinterland. But out of this long forgotten hinterland, Mustafa Kemal created an army of peasants and demoralized soldiers, lucky enough to come back to their villages, trading defeat on the front for the misery at home. Kemal gave all these desperate folk hope. He raised a people's army of resistance, in defense of a homeland the Ottomans never acknowledged.

By the summer of 1922, the Kemalist Turkey was victorious. It was the greatest moment in Turkish history and personally as a historian I feel a sense of glory that is truly magnificent every time I think how this wonderful victory was achieved, against all odds when all seemed lost, when the simple folk of Anatolia sacrificed everything for freedom. It makes my blood boil with pride, and I rededicate myself, time and again, as a Turk, proud and hardworking, happy to be part of Turkish nation, someone from the island of Cyprus.

A parallel Turkish rebirth in Cyprus was now afoot. The Greek-Turkish world was once again in turmoil, but now the Turkish faces were smiling, Greeks were in mourning. The shoe was on the other foot. Earlier the Greeks had reason to celebrate, when the Greek armies landed in Izmir to launch a new Hellenic empire. Now, it was the turn of the Turks to cheer and rejoice. Mustafa Kemal had defeated the invading Greeks. They were humiliated, all their dreams of New

## UZUN ALI, SHAME AND SALVATION

Byzantium shattered. The British colonial rulers, once again, looked the other way. The Turks, came out in their thousands, congregating in public spaces and in homes, mad with patriotism wrapped in Turkish flags, singing national songs, shouting "We are ready to die for Turkey", "Death to the Enemy", "Long live the Turkish Army," and "Peace at Home, Peace Abroad."

Sure there were contradictions in these slogans, but at least for now, no one noticed them. The new age of modernity had begun. It brought its own set of contradictions. Mustafa Kemal, the victorious Gazi to be known as Ataturk, father of all Turks, was about to launch a brand new program of social and economic modernization. Everybody was expected to fall in and march to the new tune of the new nation.

\*\*\*

Meanwhile, the underworld in Asmaalti and the Grand Turkish Bath area of Nicosia was busy. The news that, in the midst of all chaos, an English lady, all by herself, had checked in at Buyuk Han spread around the Nicosia gangs like a lightning. In those days, there was an underground market for fair English maidens with a well-regulated price: one night for a good sized *chiflik*, but by the time of Mary's visit, the number of Agas and Pashas able to afford such exorbitant prices had declined considerably. Mary, for her part, had absolutely no knowledge of such barter terms of trade in the Nicosia underworld.

That, of course, did not prevent rumors spreading very quickly. In fact, as the news of Mary's presence in the Han started circulating, the news became embellished and magnified at every round. By the time Blind Ahmet, the leader of the gang operating in and around Asmaalti, heard about it, the English lady was elevated to the status of wealthy nobility wearing expensive jewels of great beauty and value.

That is when Ayfer appeared on the scene, now a well trained member of Blind Ahmet's gang, a rising member of his collection team. The last month Ayfer's collection performance had been exemplary and the Chief was well disposed toward the youth.

It was now almost the end of October and that meant planning and preparation for the next round of collection of dues from shopkeepers in the Bazaar. Blind Ahmet was busy estimating the total take, which, to his mind, was a payment for the protection his bandits provided to merchants. He was not very happy with the British; now busy trying to implement their new law and order system, upsetting the customary method. It was so much better all around during the Ottoman days when the extortion money was so orderly divided between the *zaptiehs* and the bandits and no one noticed the difference.

Then, a few days later, it was the big event that Blind Ahmet has planned.

"Ayfer, my boy" said Blind Ahmet. "I have job for you."

In the group it was a privilege to be singled out like this in front of everyone. Young Ayfer was being promoted. There was a good reason for it. Just the day before, he was in the group that brought in the largest collection and the No.2 in charge of the group, called Mistik, had put in a good word to the boss on Ayfer's behalf. "That youth, he is going to be a fine member of the team," he reported. "How so?" inquired the boss. "Because I saw him in action yesterday, how he went from shop to shop, collecting every penny coming to us, and doing it so quickly. He was far away the best in the group." So, that very night, right after dinner when the entire gang was together, Blind Ahmet, called the boy to him. "Come and sit next to me," he ordered. "I hear you are coming along fine" he said, and added: " Mistik told me how efficient you were with the collection." Ayfer was pleased and said: "Yes sir, I do my best." Pleased Blind Ahmet, looked at the boy, and said in a friendly tone: "Keep it up and you will do just fine. In the meantime, let me know if you need anything." Said the boss of the gang.

Almost instinctively, beaming with unaccustomed confidence, Ayfer said: "Sir, may I ask one question?" "Go ahead, my boy" he said. "Why are you called 'Blind' when you are not?" There were giggles all around, but within seconds all was quite, and the boss looked puzzled. He broke the silence that seemed to last a long minute.

"Well, my son, it is like this. Many years ago, I was in a fight. I almost lost my eye. I was hurt badly, but I recovered, it was Allah's will. I was right and the scoundrel, who was then the boss, was wrong. He called me names I did not deserve. So we fought it out, to the bitter end. He deserved what he got. Everyone agreed, and so I became the boss. My eye was covered in bandages for months, though. That is when they started calling me Blind Ahmet."

That was all the night before. Right now, the boss was singling out Ayfer for a special assignment. "Come here" ordered Blind Ahmet. Ayfer immediately ran and stood in front of the boss.

"Yes sir" he said, knowing that he was being promoted in Blind Ahmet's unique way. He was about to be given a big job.

Ayfer knew it, and he was very pleased. He welcomed the chance to demonstrate both his loyalty to his chief and, at the same, to prove his skill. He was only fourteen, but full of confidence that he would go far in the underworld, maybe one day succeed Blind Ahmet himself.

"Now, Listen well, this is a delicate job" began the chief." There is a wealthy English lady staying in Buyuk Han. Her room is upstairs. She is away for the whole day." He had good intelligence from his network of informants that included the innkeeper.

"The door to her room will not be locked. You just push it open gently and get in there."

He paused for a moment. Then he got very serious, walked close to Ayfer, with stern eyes penetrating the teenager's frightened face.

"You have to be very, very careful. Search the room, collect all the jewels and disappear, fast, no games, no delays. You understand."

"Yes sir" said the frightened boy. "I understand. I will do the job and come straight here with the jewels."

"Do exactly as I say. Do not go anywhere else. And don't waste any time. I want a fast and clean job, get it?" He wanted to make sure Ayfer was given clear instructions.

"Yes sir" he said again. "Leave it to me. You will not be disappointed." And Ayfer was gone.

But it was a disappointing performance. It was not all Ayfer's fault. That is the way events unfolded, beyond his control. Mary had come back from Milltown earlier than the innkeeper had expected. She was with uncle Munir, but they both looked angry and unfriendly. Uncle hardly looked at the innkeeper. Perplexed, he watched them go upstairs, heard some English words that he did not understand but which sounded like two people arguing about something. Then, suddenly uncle turned back and came down the stairs and angrily stormed away.

Then within half an hour the English woman was downstairs again. She came towards the innkeeper and said:

"I go walking." He just stood there, unsure of what was happening.

And out she went, not sure where to go. It was mid-afternoon and she had to make plans. Things had gone badly with Munir; they had had fights before, but not like the one today. It looked as if her adventure to come to Cyprus was turning into a fiasco. Munir's family wealth had evaporated long ago and, worst of all, Munir was acting strangely. She had to cut her own losses. Tomorrow she had to make up her mind and plan her trip back to London; it was going to be an ordeal. Her funds were fast depleting.

Outside the Han, she turned right toward the bazaar and started walking toward what looked like an old medieval Cathedral, but with two tall, thin minarets. It was a massive medieval building, with beautiful arches and corridors, and huge courtyard with fountains in the middle. "It must have been some kind of church a long time ago," she reasoned as she got closer and realized the impressive gothic building was now a mosque. Then, as she was about to return and walk back to the inn, she realized that maybe she would need some extra cash for her return journey. "Just in case" she thought, "it might be handy to have a little extra."

She noticed a pawnshop, next to the big mosque with two minarets, and she walked in. There stood a big, fat fellow with a red fez on his head, a big moustache, baggy pants and black long coat. He was smoking a pipe in front of a desk in the poorly lit shop that looked more like a storeroom full of junk and bric-a-brac.

As soon as Mary walked in he got up, put on a big smile and said: "Welcome lady. Have antiques. Very cheap" in his broken English, but Mary understood.

"I want to sell this." She put on the counter a bracelet she was wearing; it was her only piece of jewelry, she had bought it for a couple of pounds in a second hand antique shop in London, partly for a rainy day, but mainly she liked her name printed on it. There it was a large "MARY" on the 18 carat gold bracelet.

Now it came in handy. The pawnbroker took it into his thick hands, examined it with his looking glass and said:" Ten pounds." Mary was pleased. Her investment had paid off. She took the money and returned to Buyuk Han, her spirits a little bit better now.

While Mary was walking and shopping, Ayfer had no trouble at all getting inside Mary's room, as planned, without a hitch. It was still quite bright, around 5 o'clock in the afternoon. No one was around and he looked for jewels and all he could see on the chair, next to the bed, was a beautiful chained silver watch, just like the one in Konak the one he had stolen from the old Kaimakam. He placed it in his pocket in a flash. He was looking everywhere, but it was weird. The room was practically bare with no furniture, and definitely no sign of jewellery. There was a suitcase; he turned it inside out; all it contained was some female garments. But no jewels anywhere. "This must be a mistake," he thought.

Ayfer was losing his cool. "What the hell?" He cursed. "Where are the jewels?" He asked. Why was he sent on a wild goose chase?

Ayfer was confused and beginning to think of leaving, empty-handed. Blind Ahmet might be angry, but if there were no jewels, what was he supposed to do?

Then the door opened. In walked Mary. The two strangers came face to face. Ayfer was frightened. This was totally unexpected. He was told no one would be in the room. He instinctively went for the small dagger, secretly buried in around his wait inside his baggy pants.

Mary screamed and attempted to kick and push Ayfer. It was a foolish, unthinking move, purely an innocent response in self-defense. But Ayfer, already confused, was too frightened to keep cool.

He felt himself under siege, under an attack he never expected. He took out his dagger and in the next instant buried it in Mary's chest. It was a beastly response, as if he was in the jungle. He was acting like a frightened animal. She immediately fell on the floor. Ayfer, forgot the dagger and ran out of the room and down the stairs in seconds, exiting from the rear door unnoticed. The innkeeper, noticing the commotion upstairs, rushed to Mary's room, but it was too late. Mary was dead and lying on the ground in a pool of her blood.

The innkeeper had heard Mary's screams. He exclaimed: "Allah, what has happened here?" Ayfer had already made a clean escape.

In the next minute, the innkeeper made up his mind to walk to the police station and report the murder. On the way to the police station, he decided to say nothing about a murder. It might land him in trouble. So, he made his mind simply to report the death of an English lady. "Let the police carry out its investigation and reach its own conclusion." He decided.

When the innkeeper was gone, another surprise visitor came to Buyuk Han. Seeing no one around, he went straight upstairs to Mary's room. It was uncle Munir, who came to collect Mary and take her with him. He was already feeling remorse for his inhospitable behavior earlier.

He was too late. He came, just hours after their fight, calm now, indeed hoping to make peace with Mary. He had realized suddenly that she truly loved him. That is the reason she had come all this way.

They had had fights before in London and the lovemaking that followed these scenes were some of the most memorable that Munir recalled. He was now calm, sure of his love for Mary, and full of anticipation as he walked upstairs to Mary's room.

But, alas, there was Mary, stabbed to death, lying in blood on the floor.

"My Allah" he yelled. "What has happened?" He covered his hands over his head. He fell on the floor, touching and caressing Mary's lifeless body.

Then he noticed the shining dagger on the floor next to Mary's body. He leaned forward and curiously picked it up to examine it.

Before he could take another breath, the innkeeper and a police officer jumped over him. Uncle was no contest for the ex-wrestling champion. He did not resist.

They took him to the police station and placed him under arrest. He seemed oblivious to it all, as if he were buried in agony and shame.

At the station, his younger brother was off-duty, busy with his wedding. There was nothing he could have done anyway. He was on special leave for his wedding the next day. My uncle admitted to having had a fight with Mary all afternoon. It was verified and witnessed by the sly innkeeper. But, "I did not kill her," he declared. And the police report was so written. Pending further information, uncle was put in jail on a probable charge for manslaughter.

# XVI

The next day, 29th October 1923, was the wedding day. It should have been the happiest day in my parents' lives. That unfortunately is not the way it all turned out.

My father knew mother only as a stunningly beautiful girl, the unblemished perfection herself. He knew nothing about her temper, the legacy of the murder and trauma at her birth. She could explode like a volcano, something father had never seen. He was to find out this split personality, the unknown side of his wife, right after their marriage, in the nuptial bed, after all the guests had gone and her expectations did not quite match his capacity to deliver.

Father was still in shock of the arrest on a charge of manslaughter of his elder brother the night before for the murder of poor Mary. The poor girl had come all this way from London, running after him, only to face death in Buyuk Han, only on her second day. It was all too much. He would have postponed the wedding, but mother would hear none of it, no one could spoil the day she had been waiting for so long. She got her way, and the pattern in these power struggles was set forever. Mother always got what she wanted. Father, second fiddle growing up in Konak, relapsed into the same status in marriage.

The wedding night that was supposed to mark their new happiness, turned into a nightmare. The wedding took place, as planned, on an especially auspicious day, on 29 October 1923, exactly at the moment when the brand new Republic of Turkey was announced in Ankara ending the age of backwardness under the Ottoman Sultanate. The wedding ceremony took place in Samanbahce, on a much more modest scale, but one that nevertheless gave satisfaction to a great number of neighbors and friends. Ozkan had invited several of his police colleagues; he had no blood relatives to invite, his only brother now being held in prison. Aygul, too, had virtually no other relative other than her stepmother, Pembe Hanim. No matter, though, for now she was on top of the world. For Hatice Hanim, the matchmaker, this event was a triumph. "Such a perfect match" she would boast to all present willing to hear her. "They are so young and beautiful. They will have children who will be the envy of the entire world." She was confident. Virtually no next of kin were present for the occasion, except for Pembe and Neslihan, the two surrogate mothers. They were placed in the place of honor, on the right and left of Ozkan and Aygul, as the good folk of Samanbahce stared at the handsome bride and groom sitting for hours on end on the wedding platform looking stiff and serious.

Despite all appearances of modernity, in those days, husbands-to-be did not see their bride at close range until after the *Imam* officially concluded the wedding ceremony. But first there had to be lots of feasting, to entertain the neighbors. Father borrowed the princely sum of three pounds, virtually his entire monthly pay, in order to finance the feast. The neighbors made pilav, dolma, they roasted chicken and potatoes, and lots of salads and yogurt dishes were prepared. There were trays full of *kleftico* kebab, roasted in the earth oven and, of course, several neighbors cooked bread and sweets for the occasion. No one complained of lack of food.

All the while music played in the background. There was a band of drummers, a violinist and *zurna*-player, a flute-like pipe instrument, playing popular songs and airs, occasionally stimulating the lookers on to join in singing a particularly popular tune. There was even dancing, men dancing with men in the yard outside, while women, cooped up inside in one of rooms in Hatice Hanim's house, danced with no head cover and no *hijap*, safely away from men's eyes to spoil their fun.

Lunch was finally completed by about 4pm and then the ladies all teamed up to collect and wash the dishes. They ferried all the dirty plates, knifes and forks into the kitchen where water was boiling in big cauldrons for the washing. Men were seated outside, sipping coffee and trading news and making political judgments on the day's significance.

"Mustafa Kemal Pasa" said one, "He is the greatest warrior. He single handedly orchestrated the defeat of the entire Greek army."

"Not just the Greeks, but the British and the French" added some one else.

"You have seen nothing yet," predicted another. "I heard him talk the other day, saying that his real war is about to start. He wants to make Turkey a modern country."

"What does 'modern' mean?" said the first speaker. Suddenly, there was silence. Then, someone from further ahead, volunteered an opinion.

"It is dressing like the British," he said. "Having cars like them," he continued. "Why should only the British have all the nice clothes and ride in cars and trains?"

Others looked on puzzled, most convinced nevertheless that the speaker had a point, others not quite sure.

The speaker continued: "I traveled on the train just the other day, all the way from Nicosia to Famagusta, in less than two hours. It was so fast. It gave me a new, modern feeling." The traditional journey on a horse-driven cart would take two days and much longer by camel caravan, the preferred route of traders, assuming no bandits were encountered en route!

My father was already modern. He had not only an English-design police uniform; he had copied his trousers and dress shirt from his police superiors and he liked looking modern even when he was off duty. That is how he had impressed his wife-to-be on that day, several years ago, wearing his new pants and shirt, all in the European style. And today, his wedding dress was all modern and European. He was even wearing a tie.

The remarkable thing about merrymakers' idea of modernity was their sincerity coupled with superficiality. It reminded me so much of Grandfather Halil's misunderstanding of freedom back in 1908. Now, fifteen years later, these guests gathered at my parents' wedding were discussing progress and modernity. They all admired and wanted its benefits, material symbols of modern science and technology. They were willing to change their dress and other external symbols adapted from Europe. But, no one present saw through to the deeper, fundamental pre-requisites of modernity. It was as if there was an invisible wall between external world and inner mindsets, the soul itself. No one seemed to realize that human relationships must be redefined; indeed human nature itself must be reordered by individual behavior before a society could call itself modern.

Then, suddenly there was commotion at the front door. Men got up from their chairs and gathered blocking the entrance. Father rushed to see what was going on. He had difficulty breaking through the multitude.

It was uncle Munir and Superintendent Smart. They were smiling.

Father was flabbergasted. The two visitors were the last he expected to see at his wedding. His brother was under arrest for murder. And the big Boss of the Police himself, Mr. Smart, standing right there. What on earth were they up to?

Confused, father could think of nothing else. So he stood to attention to show his respects for his superior. The *impromptu* drill took Joe, for his part, aback and feeling awkward in this motley crowd, he yelled, "Stand at ease!" and waited helplessly for things to calm down.

Then my uncle rushed toward his brother, embraced him kissing him on both cheeks, and shouted: "I am free. It was all a mistake." He said. Father looked on in amazement.

Then the Superintendent Smart began to say something, but no one could follow the English. No one understood a word.

"What happened? How come you are free?" asked father.

"It was a big mistake," he said. "You remember Nilufer from the Konak?"

"Yes I do. She was rather nice to me," said father.

"Well, she came to the police with her son and confessed it all. Ayfer was the murderer." Father was trying to absorb it all. He was too confused and excited. Then uncle said, almost casually:

"We have a meeting tomorrow at 10 am in my office with the old maid Nilufer. She wants to see us. Can you be there?"

Father nodded, unconditionally and obediently.

With that, uncle and Smart were gone, just as suddenly as they had appeared.

All night fathers' mind was on other things rather than rising to the occasion on his nuptial performance. In reality, his mind kept on returning to the rape scene in the rose garden years ago. He was scared of the meeting tomorrow with Nilufer. The more he thought

231

about it, the more nervous he became. My dear mother, not knowing any of this, felt rejected. Father's failure was unfathomable. But no matter, father could not help it. Consummating their marriage had to wait. But the failure to rise to the occasion on what should have been his happiest moment marked for ever father's status as second fiddle and transformed mother from a tormented youth into a tormented wife. She decided there and then. Her romantic dream suddenly turned into an illusion, her marriage looked like a boat that had been shipwrecked even before leaving the harbor.

# XVII

The story behind Joe and Uncle Munir's sudden appearance at my parents' wedding was not all-pure chance. Intense and emotional human action was behind what happened next, human action from a totally unexpected way in the Armenian quarter.

The murder case had been big news in town, and everyone had heard about it. Only one person, Nilufer now the Madame of one of the brothels in the red-light district, acted on the news and her actions were influenced by the murderer, the young Ayfer her unwanted son from the rose garden rape fourteen years ago. When Nilufer heard about her son's apparent crime, she cried her heart out. "My dear son, what have you done? What made you do it?" Then, within minutes, she calmed down, thought about it all, and finally decided to act. She made up her mind: The murder in Buyuk Han was the final straw in a ruined life that stretched all the way to the great violence committed against her years ago in Grandpa Konak's and Nilufer finally was about to have her day in court. Her tears in the rose garden, her torment had to stop.

After the murder, Ayfer was terrified and had nowhere to turn. He had disobeyed Blind Ahmet's instructions. He had used the knife and killed an innocent person. It was all a big mistake; he did not really intend to do his victim any harm. But the awful deed was done. The youth would be severely punished, but, for now, he was confused and did not know where to turn. He did not deserve punishment but he needed some motherly affection. "My mother will understand. I did not mean to kill her," he reasoned to himself, running desperately away from Buyuk Han.

Suddenly he was in the Armenian quarter. He found himself in front of the brothel where her mother was the Madam. He decided to call in on his mother. He had not seen her for some time.

He knocked on the front door, and some young woman answered. It was past midnight and only the most trusted customers were allowed to enter at this late hour.

"I want my mother," he said, haltingly. The woman at the door did not notice the blood on his clothing, but she did observe that the youth was nervous, acting in a strange manner, fear written all over his face.

"Who is your mother?" She inquired.

"Nilufer" He said. And the woman became more serious. "Wait here" she said and disappeared. Within a couple of minutes, Nilufer appeared, took a look and immediately recognized her son. She opened the door:

"Come in quickly" she said, trying hard to remain cool and calm. Her son was in trouble big trouble. Of that there was no doubt. But, what Nilufer heard was a silent voice inside her, telling her that her son was more a victim than a killer. Her motherly instinct to protect and preserve her child took over. She began to reflect, gathering all her moral and physical powers to concentrate and plan.

First, she must get the facts. Then she would decide what needed to be done. She was convinced she had options. Her rapist was a big shot free in town, enjoying the life of a rich and successful lawyer.

"What happened?" She said. "You are in big trouble, aren't you?" She asked her son.

He was terrified. His face showed it. He was completely helpless. Her mother was her last chance.

Ayfer looked uncertain, frightened, but he realized he must tell his mother the truth. He remained silent, holding back his tears with difficulty.

His mother spoke again.

"Look, I do not want trouble. If you need help, you have to tell me what happened." She said with authority, and waited. This time, he put his hand in his side pocket and pulled out Uzun Ali's antique watch, placed on the side table next to her mother.

"This is for you," he said, pretending to give her mother a gift, a token to win her sympathy. Nilufer, recognized the watch immediately, and did not show any sign of appreciation. She was resolved to get to the bottom of what happened. She persisted.

"Where did you get this? You know what it is, don't you? You had stolen it from Uzun Ali many years ago when we lived in the Konak at Milltown."

Ayfer nodded his head, in shame and fear.

"You must tell me", Nilufer insisted. Both stood still, silent for almost a minute. It looked an eternity.

Finally, he told her the terrible details of the murder he had committed.

"I killed an English woman in Buyuk Han tonight. But it was a mistake. I did not mean to kill her. I was sent there by Blind Ahmet to steal her jewels, and she was not supposed to be there."

He started crying, sobbing as if to prove his innocence. In his child's mind, it was as if there might be room for a miracle to bring back to life the dead body that used to be Mary.

The mother sat there in silence. At one point she almost started crying herself, but at the crucial moment, held back.

Ayfer's tragedy was the product of a tragic life, her life. She felt sick. She felt sorry for herself: "My Allah" she appealed for divine help and guidance, mixed with guilt, "What have I done to deserve this? Where did I sin? I was a victim, raped, ignored and kicked out."

Then she collected herself. She took control of her emotions.

Of course, it was not her fault. All along, Nilufer had been an innocent victim, right from the moment of her rape in the rose garden at Konak by uncle Munir's selfish act, or may be even earlier when she was sold by her helpless parents in Circassia, they themselves victims of the Russian-Ottoman War which had displaced and made refugees of so many desperate Muslims in Caucasia. If only fate had dealt her a different deck of cards, or if she had lived in a different age, maybe her tears would disappear and there would be no pain, life then would be worth living.

Then she decided to take control of the situation. Self doubt and pity disappeared. There was one thing to be done. "In moments of crises" an unseen voice inside her soul told her, "you must take charge. With a clear head, decide what needs to be done." That was it. Nilufer, the victim of the rape in the rose garden of long ago, decided

## UZUN ALI, SHAME AND SALVATION

to act. That was the path to revenge and redemption.

She put the silver watch in a safe box in her room. A new day had begun. On the 29th October 1923, holding Ayfer by hand, Nilufer walked the short distance to the police station, while unknown to her, Ozkan and Aygul's wedding was taking place in the nearby neighborhood. She knocked at the big metal front door of the police station. There was no reply. It was too early. The officer on duty was sleeping. At last Nilufer's banging woke him up, only to yell at her: "Come back tomorrow." But Nilufer would not go away; she insisted: "I have information on who killed the English lady in Buyuk Han," she said, and then all of a sudden, the officer was interested. He opened the door and let mother and son in.

Within ten minutes he called in the rest of the investigating team, and then it was decided that the gravity of the situation demanded the presence of the Superintendent himself, and within the hour Superintendent Smart was witnessing an incredible confession by Ayfer and, before too long, Munir was freed. He never came in contact with Nilufer who remained in the interrogation room. The interrogation lasted several hours, then they fetched uncle Munir, and finally, in the late afternoon, uncle was a free man.

None was happier at the turn of events than Joe, who had been a friend of Munir the Anglophile, until the dreadful Mary murder.

"I never believed it" he confided to uncle Munir. "But you know the law. It must be followed."

It was not too late to catch the tail end of father's wedding. Joe Smart, much relieved for uncle Munir, now a free man, wanted to go with him to the wedding. But, Nilufer in the other room was not yet finished. She wanted a private word with the police chief. The Superintendent went back to see Nilufer: "I would like to meet both sons of Uzun Ali in person to heal an old wound. Will you please arrange it for tomorrow morning?" She said. Joe agreed; it was a fair exchange.

It was, therefore, arranged that Nilufer and my uncle and father would meet next morning at ten in uncle Munir's office. "What the heck! It is for old time's sake, right? What can I lose?" reflected uncle, the memory of the rape in the rose garden long forgotten.

It was to be a turning point, a truly landmark in our family history. The meeting with Nilufer became the defining moment of uncle's life. It proved to be nothing less than his resurrection, rebirth of a new Uncle Munir. Everything else in our family flowed out of this meeting.

# XVIII

Next morning, instead of celebrating his honeymoon on his first day of marriage, father went straight to the meeting with Nilufer and his just-released elder brother. At the meeting Nilufer, the former maid at the Konak, currently the madam of a brothel in the Armenian quarter, quickly moved to occupy the high moral ground.

Nilufer had rehearsed it all before. This was her day of settling old scores. She walked to father carrying a box with her and presented Uzun Ali's silver watch to him. She had just learnt of his marriage.

"This is for you," she said as uncle watched it in astonishment. The last time he had seen it was just three days ago when Neslihan Hanim made a present of it to Mary.

"Take it as a wedding gift from me and my son Ayfer" Nilufer said. "I think you are the best person to have it," she said turning her eyes scornfully toward uncle Munir. "Take it and keep it in memory of your father Uzun Ali. Despite his faults, he was a good man, the only fatherly figure Ayfer ever knew in his life." And looking at father, she said: "You were the only friend he ever had – for a short time." Then she looked straight at uncle Munir who remained motionless, emotionless, sensing the punishment Nilufer was about to heap on him.

My father was in shock as well. He was too shaken to even say thank you. No one minded. But an inner voice spoke to him: "Your father's wish is fulfilled. He wanted you to have his watch"

After a moment of silence, Nilufer resumed:

"Now Ozkan, you may leave us alone" she said. "I have something personal to say to your elder brother." Father got up and went into the next room. When he was gone, she turned to uncle Munir:

"Remember the last time we meet?" She asked. Munir replied: "Yes, it was after my father's funeral at the Konak."

"Yes" she said, "you threw me out. Without a hesitation; first you raped me years ago, then you turned me into what I am today. I told you we shall meet again, and here we are."

Uncle was devastated, but said nothing because there was nothing to say. Nilufer continued:

"There is more. I want to tell you a secret I have kept for all these years; something for your own ears." Uncle Munir listened intently aware that the young girl that had been his object of conquest in the rose garden of long ago, now a prostitute, was the moral judge of the moment, sitting in the driver's seat and uncle Munir, the big shot in town, was on the receiving end, about to hear his sentence.

"When you violated me in the rose garden that summer, you took hostage of my body, but not my soul." She took a deep breath, as uncle Munir feeling shame come over him. "Now you have caused the death of another innocent woman. I understand the English woman traveled all the way from London seeking your love." She had done her homework well: "When you meet your Creator you will have lots to answer for because the person who did the killing was your own son."

Munir was stupefied. He could find no words to say.

He just stood there, as if frozen, his mind blank. He had no idea of a son his selfish act in the rose garden had produced. Now it was an event that caused him utter shame. But he could not muster the courage to apologize to the prostitute in front of him. His mind was one confused mess, not knowing whether to feel sorry for Mary or Nilufer.

Slowly, quietly Nilufer got up, walked to the door, opened it and went away. Her head was straight as she walked away toward the Armenian quarter.

Uncle Munir, devastated, sat there in his office, motionless his eyes fixed on the table. He was lost in his thoughts for what he heard from Nilufer was devastating. In one selfish act years ago in the rose garden he had created the monster that now had taken the life of the woman who loved him.

Then, he got up and went to the next room to rejoin his brother. Father sat there unaware of the moral crisis of the elder brother. Uncle Munir's feeling of shame from his violation of an innocent maid was a giant leap along the wrong path that finally led to the murder in Buyuk Han of yet another innocent life. Both cases of female destruction, one in the rose garden in the Konak, the other in London, had the same result: two unwanted sons. The first one, the killer Ayfer, was now waiting a sentence for solitary confinement in a penitentiary and then lifelong imprisonment when he would be old enough to be tried. The other, in some orphanage in Dublin, was still reclaimable.

In the next few days, uncle Munir lived in moral hell. Finally, he took some drastic decisions. First, he reflected on his illegitimate son Ayfer. He tried to visit him in prison, but Ayfer refused to see him. The rejection hurt him to his bones. He then closed his law practice in Nicosia temporarily, and decided to go to Ireland via London in search of a son he had never seen.

The bachelor lawyer was now resolved to do Good. All of a sudden he felt a great deal of moral weight on his shoulders. First toward his dead father, Uzun Ali, who silently kept funding his extra curricular activities in Istanbul and London, while he was sinking fast financially and physically. He also felt a huge debt to his half brother, Ozkan. Never once did he complain of unfair gain from their Grandpa's estate.

Uncle Munir was a man disgraced. He was a lost soul in the wilderness, now desperately in need of rebirth. At that moment he rediscovered Mary anew: she suddenly became his resurrection. She represented love lost, pure and good, cutting across race, religion and color. She had given so much of herself to him in London, unconditionally and totally, she had endured so much coming to Cyprus seeking his love, and all he showed in return was selfishness and abandonment. Now, at last, maybe he could set right a small part of the wrong he had done to Mary.

In Dublin, some two months later, Uncle Munir, now reborn with a clear new mission in life, finally located his lost son in the Catholic convent where Mary left the child. At that point, bureaucratic obstacles were raised in his way in all directions. Who was he? What was his citizenship? Did he have proof that he was the father of the child?

But, once determined to do right, Uncle Munir was not to be stopped so easily.

His Anglo friend back in Nicosia, Joe Smart heading the list as always, came to the rescue. Papers were drawn up, documents furnished and bureaucrats finally relented.

Father and son traveled back to Cyprus and a new chapter, a new leaf in the saga of the Uzun Ali dynasty began.

Uncle Munir and his son, aged 7, now named Ozkan Junior, after his brother, arrived in Cyprus on New Year's Day 1924 and was immediately enrolled in the English School, primary division, grade one. By then, father's marriage, now duly consummated, was off to a rocky start.

In the meantime, Ayfer, uncle Munir's first son, the unwanted child, born out of the rape in the rose garden, preferred a life in jail, to spend the best part of his years behind bars. His life had been hell. I felt sorry for him; who would not? Poor fellow never had a chance. Now facing a murder charge, he was put in a high-security reform institution and kept there until the legal age of eighteen when then the British justice system would kick in. He was found guilty for the first-degree murder of Mary, the unfortunate ex-girl friend of uncle Munir, who explained to the court the full details of his student days in London but nothing was asked from him about the rape in the rose garden and nothing was ventured.

Ayfer's identity remained a secret buried in Uzun Ali's Konak. Uncle Munir, carrying a heavy guilt over Ayfer, left the secret undisturbed. The youth was given thirty years for murdering the lover of the father he had never known. For thirty years, he was out of sight, but by no means finished. His fate was linked with ours, in fact, part of our family. I was yet unborn, but Ayfer was already part of me. We were destined to meet again, many years later.

# THE END

# BOOK III

## DISCOVERY

An Old Konak

Dear Reader, I must now let you in on a secret. The author of the family story recounted so far in the first two books is my sister, Sevgi, three years my junior, now a history professor, a social historian at Ankara University. She made the discovery about our family origin and this inspired her to write it all. What you have read so far in Books I and II is her writing, with English translation and some editing on my part, Tekin Uzun Ali, the first grandchild of the old Kaimakam of Milltown.

How this discovery was made and how Sevgi wrote the study is now what I want to tell you in detail. Once started, I continued with the rest of the story, but Sevgi's contribution here as well is huge. So, in reality, who actually is the real author of this work is difficult to say. Suffice to declare that it is a joint product. And, in truth, that is the way it ought to be. After all, it is the story of our collective memory, our family origin and the identity that we all share and carry.

***

I would like to start with a word about mother Aygul, for she had the greatest influence on me. She was some one special, a giving and yet an extremely fragile woman. You could win her heart instantly with a friendly smile and a kind word. There was no limit to her generosity in return for friendship and kindness. But you could also break her heart with a single misspoken word. She yearned for the affection of others all her life, the love and acceptance of an orphan girl who never experienced enough of her own mother's tender love. She sought affection in others, indiscriminately, from relatives, neighbors, and even strangers. She had always a desperate need for social approval. The company of others, to be included and to be cherished was the ultimate gift for her. Loneliness was the severest punishment. To be wanted and sought out was her greatest reward. Then, she would give you everything she possessed: her time, her friendship, and her total loyalty.

All this made mother an exceedingly vulnerable person. A tiny gesture of reproach would break her heart and soul. A word in anger would cause her no end of torment. She would burst into tears and work herself into a rage. The worst moment was when something really upset her; in those situations all gentleness and kindness in her would disappear and she would turn into a wild beast of the jungle,

243

wanting to destroy everything around her. It was incredible, how in the extreme moments, mother was totally uncontrollable. In these moods, she would recognize no limits, and acknowledged none as her master or mentor: husband, friend or neighbor would mean absolutely nothing. She always bemoaned not really having a 'real' father.

And, then, like the ocean subsiding after a storm, she would calm down towards some magical mean and resume her reasonably ordinary life. Her friendly smile would return to a cordial face and all would be milk and honey. The bitter past would be forgotten. She wanted everyone around to feel just like her, calm and sociable.

We children, growing up had our worries and challenges to know the source of mother's personal torment. Gradually and without question, we all knew of her dual nature: her needfulness and her weakness, father taking the lead in this direction, but we were all constantly aware of her helpless fragility. All of us accepted the huge swings as part and parcel of her nature. None of us children, remarkably, knew the depth of what torment she experienced in her soul, as an abandoned baby and an orphaned child, facing life without her own mother's affection.

Let me now begin at the beginning, my birth.

# I

A son that is I, named Tekin, was finally born on 4th April 1926, to Ozkan and Aygul. It was a day of celebration by parents and neighbors. My parents' shaky marriage was saved at last. It became obvious years later that my birth saved more than a marriage. It also ensured continuation of the Uzun Ali dynasty. Of course, the significance of that fact was to emerge later, many years later.

In 1926, when I was born, what mattered was that Aygul and Ozkan became parents and started a new beginning. But the event signaled more than the arrival of a son. My generation, our family moved into the modern world; the event heralded a fresh start, a new beginning. The Ottoman era was over. Suddenly, like a new day, we were now Turks, proud and confident thanks to the recent victory on the battlefield under the great leader Mustafa Kemal Ataturk. Ankara became the new capital of the Turkish nation, it was a brand new city that grew out of the desert. Ankara was the symbol of the modern world; its mission was western civilization.

In Turkey, modernization came top down. In British Cyprus, it all happened voluntarily. No more Ottoman. Overnight, everyone became Turks. A new identity was created. The British called us Turkish-Cypriot, but the hyphenated identity was foreign. We were simply Turks who happened to be living in the island of Cyprus. Everyone was proud to be part of the new nation building unfolding in Ataturk's Republic.

I was made in my mother's image, in reverse mode, so to speak. Her life symbolized injustice and sacrifice. It was as if my mission was redemption, to rectify the great injustice done to her. Fate cast me as a modern-day Socrates seeking justice; not the narrow personal passion of redeeming mother's revolt against injustice in her father's Ottoman world, but on a more universal scale, attempting always to correct unfairness all around. I made this discovery, of course, years later. But even in childhood, I grew up as a serious minded, reflective boy, a complete opposite to the casual nature of my father. In contrast to the aloofness of father Ozkan, mother heaped on me all the love and affection a child could want. She was the perfect mother; she became my nurturer, protector, mentor and guide.

Publicly my birth was auspicious for another reason. On that day in Ankara, the Turkish Grand National Assembly passed the Modern Civil Code launching the official age of modernity for Turks. About the same time, Ozkan Junior, Munir's son, my cousin was completing grade two in the primary division of the English School at the top of his class. Mary, who had sacrificed her life in Cyprus for a love that never flowered, would have been proud in her unpretentious grave in Ireland.

We the two cousins, Ozkan Junior and I were special. We were modern children, the vanguard generation. We symbolized a new generation destined to redeem the earlier generations for their sins. The Ottoman era ended with our Grandparents, now dead and buried in immorality; our own parents, the intervening generation was a lost generation growing up in war and conflict, unsure of itself, buried in doubt, bitterness and hatred. The modern children were different; we were starting afresh with a clean sheet in a brand new book. Our generation was confident Turks, proud and sure that the future belonged to us.

For the modern children the West represented the ideal. The western model was a target chosen and shaped by Kemalism. Everything western was now re-invented and became Turkish in Ankara, the new Turkish national center and presented as our identity. Western fashion became the norm, not just in dress, but also in ideas and institutions, in schools and in the minds of ordinary folk. School children were drilled in Latin in place of the Ottoman script. In dress, men discarded the *fez* and adopted the European hat; women suddenly wore no more the Ottoman *hijab* and the veil. Being Ottoman was

## DISCOVERY

tantamount to primitive and backward, and how you dressed symbolized whether you were progressive or traditional. Now the Ottoman *millet* system was gone as nationalism became the new religion of the modern age, and living space was Turkish, Greek, Armenian or Jew. The entire face of the Middle East was changing and Cyprus was no different.

\*\*\*

Cousin Ozkan Jr. and I were modern children, confident and eager to learn the secrets of modern science and knowledge. But, of course, we had our own differences. He was blonde like his mother Mary; I was dark like his father. Eight years my senior, he shared his father's pragmatic and down to earth nature, and was, above all success-oriented. I liked modernity even when I did not understood what it meant; he was more skeptical. We also differed on matters of social justice. He concentrated on bettering himself, while I chose to perfect the rest. Maybe it was our chemistry: after all he was at best only half Turkish, the other half being Irish. Growing up in Cyprus, Ozkan Jr. looked every bit English, blonde and handsome in his English School uniform, wearing a tie, and clean shirt and pants. Outwardly, for friends and neighbors, both of us looked the perfect model of the new image of how modern Turks were expected to be. His Irish identity was concealed.

All this wind of modernity in Cyprus was a matter of paradox, blowing in from an unexpected direction. It did not come with the British rulers, who now made the island their colony, and acquired undisputed authority. It came rather from Ankara, symbolizing the brand new identity of Turkish-ness. The unimportant outpost in central Anatolia, Angora of the Ottoman past, now became the hotbed of a huge modernization project led, in a grand top-down operation, by the victorious Gazi Mustafa Kemal. First the Turkish Republic was created; the decayed and decadent Sultanate was gone, buried in history. The Caliphate too was abolished. Then European dress became mandatory, the European hat replaced the red *fez*. Swiss, Italian, French laws replaced the archaic and incomprehensible Ottoman legal code. All this blew in like a storm coming from the Toros Mountains across the waters of the blue Mediterranean in Asia Minor bringing the clouds and rain that nourished Cyprus.

## UZUN ALI, SHAME AND SALVATION

The British colonial administration in Cyprus at first resisted Kemalism. Outwitted at Gallipoli, the British were suspicious of Mustafa Kemal and his ambitions. They discouraged nationalism among the Turks of Cyprus, shipping thousands of families to the mainland in a misguided attempt to appease the Greeks. Then, they adopted a more indifferent attitude. But when it came to Islam, the British colonial administration drew a line in the sand in Cyprus.

"We do not touch religion" was the silent British colonial rule.

This rule was applied in British India, Malaya, and Africa and in every part of the vast Empire shown on maps in red, where Muslims lived. So it was in the British colony of Cyprus. Polygamy remained on the books; the *hodjas* and *mullahs* continued wearing their traditional religious garments, preaching old ways, marching out of tune with the rest of Turkish Cypriots.

The British remained in full control of the Muslim foundation, *Evkaf*, the biggest landowner in the land, atop an accumulation of bequests and trusts of generations of devout Muslims who believed they were performing charity. The rents and income of *Evkaf* were meant for Muslim education, hospitals and social services in the memory of the deceased. The British silently and craftily diverted these funds for purposes of the colonial administration and not a few Anglophones, including Uncle Munir, saw nothing wrong with this practice. Like Uncle Munir, a few even got rich in the process. The Greek Cypriots acquired much *Evkaf* land fraudulently.

The British then applied another double standard in colonial Cyprus: *Divide and rule*. Muslims and the Christian *millets* in Cyprus never had much in common in Ottoman times; each community lived in a different world. In fact the Church, ever since 1821 when Greece was born, made sure every one of its congregation spoke Greek, not just the market version but *Kathareousa*, pure ancient form now forced on the new generation of students in the newly built Greek *Gymnasia* all over the island, built in deliberate classical model to symbolize the Parthenon. Church attendance, too, was compulsory, failure to show up punishable by excommunication and denial of entry into heaven. There was no exception and the poor peasants lived in fear of eternal burning in hell. Villagers, ignorant and educated, followed their priests like docile sheep. Most important of all, there was easy credit available through the village priest for land purchase from the Ottoman Turks, at whatever the asking price might be. "Buy it, no matter what the price is, it is always a bargain. Buy it, keep it and forget it." That was the Church policy. And, one more thing: "Never sell land to the Ottomans."

Now, Muslims and Greek Orthodox in Cyprus became Turkish Cypriots and Greek Cypriots. Everyone liked it, most of all the local politicians who joined the boards and the advisory councils the British created, representing their respective communities with passion and patriotism. Ethnic duality empowered the British. Whatever the Greek Cypriots proposed, the Turkish Cypriots opposed or vice versa, and the British got their way. Of course, the British sympathies were inherently on the side of the Christian Greek Cypriots, but when it came to protecting British interests, then sympathy was replaced by expediency. British interest trumped all else.

One of the places where the British interest was defined and protected was the Nicosia Club. It had tennis courts, game rooms and a large open park, right next to the dry river bed that split Nicosia along ethnic lines from Kosklu Ciftlik the wealthy part of the town where Uncle Munir now lived. The center of political activity in the Club was, naturally, the bar. Amidst the free-flowing Scotch whisky for the men and gin and tonic for the ladies – the Club was open to ladies, but only on certain days to ensure a certain air of decorum – weighty matters of public affairs of the day were aired, discussed and determined. The colonial councils, on which sat those ethnic Greeks and Turks could always be manipulated for rubber stamped executive decisions.

"Administering Cyprus is a peach" summed up the initial views of governors like Ronald Storrs recently brought in from Palestine. Storrs was a Philhellene. At the start of his career, he had sought the help of the Grand Vezir Kamil Pasha, himself from Cyprus, for employment in the Sultan's government, but no luck. He then joined the colonial service thanks to the Old School Boys network including Lawrence of Arabia. Finally he became the Governor of Cyprus. Some of his underlings concurred with the boss, adding an essential comparative dimension from personal experience: "Hear, hear. This place is not like Palestine: Those ungovernable Jews and Arabs. They will fight for ever."

Uncle Munir quickly became a leading figure greasing the wheels of the colonial administration. He became a social climber and rose fast. His English law training made him a natural for the task. An Anglophile, with a son who was half British, Munir was the natural instrument of the British divide and rule policy. He joined the English Club of Nicosia, and became one of the political elite and a regular at the bar. Now, like every other member of the elite, Munir owned a car: a British made Ford, model T, in respectful distance behind the colonial masters who, naturally, preferred Bentleys and Rolls Royce's.

Life was easy then. British elite, a leisure class replaced the Ottoman nobility adopting and surpassing the luxury of the life of the Konak in Milltown back in pre-1878. The Ottomans, who had assigned Cyprus to the British, were gone and the British were now the undisputed masters of the island. Ronald Storrs was intent to remove the last vestiges of the Ottoman trappings on the island, and his sentiments were more for the Greeks than the new Turks of Kemalism.

# II

My birth put new life into the marriage of my parents. Years later I learnt that I was the third and successful pregnancy for mother, the first two ending in miscarriages. Mother Aygul had been a nervous wreck right from her wedding night, and even after my birth she was a woman tormented constantly. Her miscarriages did not help matters either. When finally I arrived, both mother and father were more relieved than happy. The couple was beginning to reach the painful conclusion that Aygul's chemistry was unfit for motherhood.

I was born in the Gemikonak hospital, actually the hospital belonging to the Anglo-American mining corporation, now by far the largest employer in the Lefke region, indeed one of the biggest on the island. That was the reason for Ozkan and Aygul's relocation to Gemikonak in the second year of their marriage. With a growing town and expanding mining business, law and order became a critical issue and so a new police station was established, and Kazim, now an inspector, was dispatched as chief of the station, along with father Ozkan and two other police officers. Soon other officers joined the detachment as the population of the mining town kept on growing.

It was a cost-saving move for Ozkan and Aygul. The Anglo-American mining company gave them free housing in the new town Xero, in one of the new standard housing sections, plus free hospital and medical care. Despite excellent care provided by American doctors working for the mining company, Aygul was not successful with her two pregnancies. The miscarriages lead to serious gossip around the neighborhood. None yet knew of the tormented past of Aygul's.

"My girl, you have to be careful about what you're eating" said one elderly lady, noticing that Aygul was an avid reader, spending a great deal of time reading romantic novels in Turkish original or translation of Western classics.

"Don't worry auntie" Aygul would reply. "I am perfectly fine. I just had a big bowl of *pilav*." She would say and continue with her reading.

"You need to rest more," advised another well-wisher in the neighborhood. "My husband is a chemist in the mine, maybe I will ask him to get you some pills" The lady had no clear understanding of the difference between a chemist and a pharmacist. What mattered was the chance to showoff.

But mother's mysterious affliction persisted. She lost weight and became irritable. Ozkan took her to the mining company hospital for a check up. The doctors at the hospital were puzzled; their tests were unhelpful. Aygul's blood and urine tests were all perfectly OK.

My parents lived in a modest two-bedroom tenement in a low-cost housing scheme built for miners and their families. The couple had adequate income, thanks to father's steady salary, so making ends meet was not a serious problem. But, still mother's health was a mystery. Neighbors gossiped:

"Poor Aygul, she is such a lovely girl. But I do not know what seems to be the problem?

Do you know if her husband loves her enough?" All kinds of speculations and theories floated around.

In fact, mother's sickness was psychological. She carried the scars of a violent early childhood, growing up without the affection and love of a natural mother, a condition not easily discovered or diagnosed. Fortunately Pembe Hanim, her wet nurse in Pineview, had come to Aygul's rescue. She was the perfect surrogate mother in every respect, her love and care for Aygul, from the first day of her delivery to her care by the police, right down to her marriage in Samanbahce 15 years later, Pembe Hanim had been an example of perfection. Aygul looked at her and adored her as the mother she had never seen. But, yet then and now in Xero, nothing seemed to cure her sickness. Father, desperately and privately in love with his wife, was inadequate. Shy and withdrawn by his own childhood in the Konak in Pineview, he was inept in matters of courtship and tender loving care. Most of all, he was entrapped in his own male world, working hard to make ends meet. His time at home was limited and insufficient for the complex and constant needs of his wife.

Mother's problem was specific and had a name: Halil, her father. He became her nemesis, tormentor; her target for revenge; constant defaming and dishonoring him was her obsession. At home with husband Ozkan, and in the neighborhood with her gossiping friends, day and night, whenever Aygul could find a listening ear, it was the same refrain:

"My low-down father, that womanizer, he killed my dear mother. She loved me so dearly, but he took her away from me."

Incredibly, she remembered every detail as if she were not a week old, but a full grown observer of the tragic end in the house on Tanzimat Street back in 1908 right after her birth.

"They drove her to madness. My mother would not kill a fly. The cruelty and inhumanity of that man called my father is what drove my dear mother insane." She would go on. The more she cursed at Halil, the more passionate she became. Grandmother Emine was elevated to moral heights and became an angel betrayed. Her sacrifice was the noblest act of motherly devotion.

Aygul would declare:" May he burn in Hell." And then others would nod and go along with Grandfather's condemnation.

"Aygul don't upset yourself, you are so young and pretty. It is such a shame."

And then the condemnation would resume with someone judging: "Halil was a rotten and worthless man, but you must live your own life." That would start Aygul on another round of cursing and badmouthing.

Then one day, mother had shocking news. Grandfather Halil was out of jail in the summer of 1928. And, to make things worse, he immediately restarted where he had left off. He married a young, blonde, named Sevda, signifying love.

The way it happened was pure womanizing Halil. Three months before his release, he had a surprise visitor, a school teacher named Sevda, a modern, one of the few educated woman of adequate means at the time, a woman of tremendous self-confidence, whose concept of modernity resided in a personalized understanding of gender equality:

"Why cannot a woman take the initiative and propose?" she wondered aloud to herself. She also remembered several years ago about a jealous Muslim woman who had killed her husband's young lover. More out of curiosity than anything else, in April, she decided to visit Halil in jail. Posing as a relative, she gained access to Halil who was pleased to have a visitor; it broke the boredom and loneliness. For her part, Sevda, the schoolteacher who never lacked initiative came into possession of two vital pieces of intelligence. One was the fact that Halil still had good looks, and the other was even more vital, namely that he would soon be a free and eligible man.

A widower in her early thirties, the schoolteacher took matters in her own hand, and through some useful intermediaries, arranged her own marriage. Sevda put her plan into action and visited Halil again and again. As soon as Halil was out of jail, they married and she moved in to the same Tanzimat house that poor Emine had lived her short married life with Halil.

Mother was unstoppable in her rage; she exploded like a volcano. It wasn't the fact that her father had remarried that seemed to upset mother Aygul; it was rather the fact that Sevda was now using her dear mother's *dowry*, possessions, including her wardrobe and bed linen belonging to her mother. Her father never thought of giving them to Aygul and she never forgave him for that.

"That bitch has stolen my mother's *dowry* which should belong to me," Aygul would scream. "She has no shame; she is a whore."

Poor father was at the limit of his endurance, helplessly watching his wife get worse steadily. In mother's eyes father had his own limitations; he was inadequate and vulnerable. He had failed to spark the love that might have filled up the vast ocean of emptiness in mother's psychological world. Ever since the failure on their nuptial night to consummate successfully their marriage, deep inside her psyche mother retained doubts about father's virility. Her own father was an over-sexed bastard, she would admit secretly to herself, but Ozkan was unmotivated. More than that, she wondered if her husband was strong enough, and had in him the necessary courage to meet all challenges. And, the young couple had a constant stream of challenges, one after the other. One day, Aygul would be sick and need medical care, often Ozkan not being available to help. The next day, the glass window would need fixing but father was nowhere to do it. He was always on duty away from home for days on end. And, then the miscarriages, it was as if it was all fathers' fault.

"I sent for you but you were not there" she would declare, amidst sobs and tears. Or, she would accuse him being soft and naïve in dealing with others: "You let others get the better of you. You are so weak." She would start, and always make unfavorable comparisons with his elder brother:

'Look at how well your brother is doing. He is a rich lawyer, with a fancy house, a car and all the comforts of modern living."

If father tried to argue back, mentioning Munir's education or his English connections, inevitably all the argumentation would backfire:

"Aygul, be fair. I was never good at school. I could not become a big, professional man like him. I am grateful that Munir got me this job as a policeman. Aren't you glad about it?" How could I otherwise marry you?" His reasoning with her had no more than a feeble impact. In a day or two, the cycles of bitterness and arguments would be repeated.

Mother's depression changed when I was born, at least temporarily. My birth was the right medicine delivered at the most appropriate time. It pulled father and mother away from the edge of the precipe. The doomed marriage was back on tracks. Aygul and Ozkan finally became husband and wife, a family. Happiness entered the household. The following three years were, like pleasant wine, full of good body and bouquet. But not for long!

\*\*\*

Then, almost unexpectedly, there was a new addition to our family. My sister arrived. This event changed my own life forever.

It was in spring 1928, a rare period of peace prevailed in Xero, where the Anglo- American Mining Company was now in full production, copper mining was booming and a short moment of comfortable living dominated the little town. Incredibly, my parents enjoyed interludes of romance and affection; and mother was pregnant for a second and last time. This time everything was normal with pregnancy, except that during birthing in January 1929, Aygul lost too much blood, and her tubes had to be tied making her infertile for the rest of her life.

The baby was a healthy, chubby daughter, with a lovely blond complexion, a skin and color as smooth as silk. Mother picked her name as Sevgi, meaning love. She choose the name reflecting her hope and dream that her daughter would be lovely and intelligent, go to college and become the intellectual, modern woman fit for the new world. Naming her meant defining her daughter's mission in life. Sevgi now became the designated Aygul that mother never had the chance to fulfill herself.

Sevgi's arrival had another huge impact. It marked the start of a lifelong loving bond between brother and sister. I was to become her mentor and guardian in every sense of the word. Right from the beginning a special bond developed between us. Before Sevgi's birth, I was a lonely boy, shy and unsure of himself and my place in the world. After her arrival, I became a big brother, unafraid of decisions, big or small and taking risks. Of course, it did not happen overnight. But gradually and surely, my little sister defined my role, set me on my course, as if on a secret and long mission. Three years then, I did not realize any of this at the time, but my subsequent discovery of self-confidence was born with Sevgi. When mother was away visiting or otherwise busy, I took care of Sevgi and literally nursed her growth into a vibrant child with a keen intellectual interest. Shortly after I learnt to read myself, I would read to my baby sister from my school books, sometimes from nursery rhymes which mother had purchased for us, and sing her songs I had learnt at school, while the baby Sevgi stared at me with eager eyes full of charm and appreciation.

We grew up with Xero, in those standard housing units that had mushroomed along the riverbed before you reached Gemikonak, the old Ottoman port town. Gemikonak had been all-Ottoman; Xero was now virtually all-Greek. The new row houses that the Anglo-American company built along the river stretched all the way up the mountain toward Lefke, the major all-Turkish hill-town on the way to Karadag where the copper and iron mining was located. Xero attracted miners from all over the island. High wages did it; they worked like a magnet, attracting peasants from villages, laborers from towns, everyone came to work for the Anglo-American mining company. Xero grew literally with us children. New houses were being built all around the neighborhood. But it was a strange settlement, with no roots. Even before starting school, I felt alienated in the new mining settlement; everyday there were new faces and new comers. Soon, the mining company ran out of labor in Cyprus, there were boatloads of new migrants coming in from Greece on those big boats that came into the little harbor to load and take away the ore. My earliest observation was a strange feeling, all this strange language around me, everyone speaking Greek that I could not understand. It made me feel out of place. What actually was happening was that the company was shipping in boatloads of refugees from Greece, now over-flooded with hungry and destitute masses arriving daily from Anatolia. They came in their thousands, desperate men and women, looking for work in the mining industry and the Anglo-American company was there ready to employ them at low wages and make huge profits.

My anxiety and fear of these mysterious events outside was aggravated further at home. I was then a solitary child, father always away on duty, and my mother was either depressed or moody. More often than not, she was spending a lot of time with her neighbor friends, chatting or arguing with others. There were rare moments of tenderness from mother, but there never was enough of tender loving care, not until Sevgi's arrival. There was one compensation: love of books which mother grafted to me early, even before schooling. When old enough to notice, mother transmitted the love of books to me first by her own example. She loved reading, especially romantic novels. But she also would get magazines and newspapers whenever she came in possession of cash. I loved not just the stories in these books, but also their lovely pictures about glorious places far away. It opened new horizons, and this is how I learnt that the world is a big and beautiful place, beyond the ocean and mountains around Xero.

Father in those days was aloof and kept his distance. I did not feel father's influence until I started primary school. Up till then father was distant and tied up policing, most of the time away patrolling and struggling to bring colonial law and order to the rugged region now being transformed into a mining center. But once I started school, suddenly father became interested in my studies. Surprisingly, he had high standards, expecting nothing less than perfect scores from me. Fortunately, I did not disappoint him, but that did not draw us closer. Strangely enough, once he discovered that I was a bright kid, father left me to my own devices, stopped helping with homework or encouraging me with studies. There was one exception: My report card. He wanted nothing less than A's and would taunt and punish me for anything less.

After Sevgi's birth, life was easy and comfortable in the mining town; it was the calm before the storm. The Anglo-American mining company's stock was flying high and everyone, including miners and policemen in Xero benefited from profits. There was lots of copper and iron in the mountains around Lefke and thousands of workers, Turks and Greeks, worked deep underground to bring the ore up, transport it by train to the port and load it on to the boats destined for Europe via Greece. Huge amount of poisonous residue was piled in new mountains next to the town releasing a foul smell, but then no one worried about the environment; they were glad to have the jobs.

Then economic ruin set in; the Wall Street Crash and the world economy went into a tailspin. Metal and commodity prices plummeted. The effects were felt right away in little Xero. Copper prices hit rock bottom, wages were cut and miners were thrown out of work. Everyone blamed the British. Communism began to spread among the miners, coming secretly from Bolshevik Russia via Greece where recently boatloads of cheap workers were imported. *Gymnasia*, those centers of Hellenic nationalism, became hotbed of radical ideas. Two diametrically opposed ideologies competed amongst Greek Cypriot students: Communism and the creation of "new man" for the age of socialism, and the Hellenic *Megalo Idea* of *ENOSIS*. Fanatic priests, once again, preached from the pulpit the dawn of a utopia of Greater Greece, embracing all the land of Byzantium including Cyprus, while men, women and children starved in the Greek mainland. The Church had two enemies, the British and the Ottoman Turks, and fanned the flames of nationalist fanaticism leading a crusade for salvation, to crush and burn in Hell any one who would block the way to *ENOSIS*. Rebellion was in the air, and the British got the rap for bad times.

In the meantime, father started working overtime to supplement his salary, staying at the police station on weekends and at nights in order to support his growing family. Mother entered the Depression Years an unhappy wife, once again. My little baby sister and I were too young to realize what these terrible economic developments meant, except that we experienced the hardships and the deprivations just the same, like all the miners around us.

# III

When I was six and about to start school, mother was constantly depressed and nothing seemed to help. She was miserable and gloomy. She escaped into books and became an avid reader of romantic stories to dream and get transported into other worlds where lovely girls grew up to become princesses, nourished on perpetual love of mothers', always available to love and care, living in beautiful homes under the warm and loving protection of fathers who were like princes charming, totally dedicated to their wives and daughters. Yet, these escapes into fictional worlds of books and stories did not satisfy her. She longed for real relationships, with real people and in real life.

    I started school in Xero, attending the primary school of Teacher Haji Hasan, a kind and humane person in step with the new, modern learning. Ours was a one-room school with about a dozen boys and the same number of girls. Teacher Haji Hasan was the first person, after mother, to spark my interest in books and learning. At school I learnt counting numbers, spelling, first the alphabet, then words and sentences and finally reading. I enjoyed most reading about kings and queens. At home, I would read stories, sometimes feeling sad about princesses and sometimes laughing at stupid monarchs and funny jesters. But it was all a great amazement and wonder to me to learn about far away places and people. Mother always stimulated my interest, showing me wonderful pictures in the magazines and books she was reading.

Our school was a mile away, a long distance for my young legs, in Gemikonak. All the pupils came from Gemikonak. It meant that I was deprived of school friends amidst the mining families in Xero where everyone talked Greek. So my life outside the school was solitary. Except that my little sister Sevgi slowly but surely began to fill the void. She made all the difference in the world. She was a perfect baby, sleeping, eating and smiling at me. I babysat a lot, when mother was away; played with her much like a pet; every day I would take her on walks in the dark blue carriage with huge suspensions, looking proud and, when older, we started play games together.

At about this time, a remarkable transformation occurred in mother. She became a social animal. Mother started cultivating friendships and soon Ayse, living next door became her intimate confidant. Ayse, herself had a dubious childhood, rumored to be the result of a love affair of a Muslim father and a Greek Cypriot mother somewhere in a mixed village near Larnaca. But gossip then was a universal pastime all over the island. Truth and fiction mattered little. The friendship endeared the two neighbors, some element in mother's own psyche hitting a delicate cord of sympathy and shared grief. Ayse brought in Mesude, the chemist's wife nearby who brought in others and the group quickly multiplied.

Ayse's status at that point was a matter of envy; wife of Inspector Kazim, that status gave her some sort of compensation for her dubious childhood. She was almost the same age as my mother. At first, things between the neighbors were cool and restrained. That was neither Ayse's fault, nor mother's. The inspector, who had an air of superiority about him, did not encourage his wife to become too friendly with the wives of his subordinates. It was an exercise in vanity, but then with lots of free time and not much else to do around, the neighborhood developed its own social networks.

It started with daily morning coffee, one time at mother's home, the next at Ayse's and, occasionally the chemist's wife and other neighbors joined in. Soon, there was a circle of young wives club of sorts. Gossiping, big time thus became a pastime, at first quite harmless and exhilarating. The wives would trade information about their husbands, kids and extended families. My mother impressed everyone telling and sharing with them the books and stories she had been

# DISCOVERY

reading. Gradually, gossiping took on a more serious matter and the focus of the group shifted to juicier topics such as who did what with whom.

"Did you hear" one of the women would say, "that young woman down the road had a young man come into the house when her husband was absent at work." Such visits might be perfectly innocent, but it broke the etiquette; sometimes it led to family fights and occasionally domestic breakdowns.

On other occasions the gossip would be about open scandal when characters would be assassinated, specific individuals named and opinions and judgements delivered with passion fit for politicians. "That woman Fatma, two houses down, I am sure, has a lover. Every day, the same man comes visiting her when her husband and children are away."

Some in the group would take sides in favor of Fatma. "No, I know her well. It is her brother from Lefke," she would say. Only to be countered by some one else: "You have been told stories. Fatma has no brother in Lefke; it is her lover, I tell you."

Then, mother got into the act and spoke her mind about her hated father. She was full of venom and bitterness. She went on passionately condemning her father Halil:

"That devil man married again." She began. Everyone in the group joined in. It was amazing how much they seemed to know about Halil and his new wife Sevda. Either they had good intelligence and contacts in Nicosia, or they manufactured news for fun. In the rounds of gossip, truth or lies made little difference.

Mother went on: "I heard that they had a honeymoon in Limassol." It was shortly after the news of Halil's marriage with Sevda, the schoolteacher, and young enough to be Grandfather's daughter.

The chemist's wife Mesude added her bit of gossip: "Apparently, the wife has lots of money. Her father used to be the biggest landowner in his village and that is why Halil married her."

No one asked what the source of this intelligence was. It did not seem to matter. It got mother enraged and she burst into a fury without end:

"May Allah burn both of them in Hell." She went on with her swearing and condemnation, and, of course, it made her depression worse. It hurt mother far more than her father or his new wife away in Nicosia.

261

Then, something happened right there in Xero that caused mother to forget about her father, at least temporarily. She got into a fight herself with the chemist's wife, Mesude. It was over a trivial matter, something about an innocent remark by Mesude about Ayse's habit of drinking her Turkish coffee sweet.

"Ayse, why are you putting so much sugar in your coffee?" She asked and tried to show off. "My husband says sugar has chemicals that are bad for you."

That did it. Mother, loyal to the end, came to Ayse's defense. "Mesude, don't be rude. Leave poor Ayse alone." She declared rather abruptly.

"Aygul, mind your own business" she retorted. "I am only trying to help Ayse" she insisted.

Mother got angry and possessive. "Ayse does not need your help. Leave her alone I said."

And the fight over Ayse became the biggest event in the little neighborhood of Xero. It grew and became larger, as news of the disagreement spread around, and new recruits joined into one camp or the other. It was like political parties of the future making mountains out of molehills. The event manifested the bitterness that was buried inside mother; it burst open like a dyke that under the constant accumulation of rainwater finally could hold no more.

The matter was finally resolved when the chemist family moved out. Of course the storm in the teapot drew mother and Ayse closer. Their mutual loyalty blossomed and the two became lifelong soul sisters, one of the most enduring and satisfying friendships in mother's life. In due time, Inspector Kazim got a promotion and the family moved to the police headquarters in Nicosia. Mother, for several years, was without her dear friend. Fate, however, was to reunite the two again, and they stayed inseparable friends till the end.

# IV

Father's brother and my uncle, the lawyer Munir in Nicosia, was doing exceedingly well under the colonial rule. After Grandfather Uzun Ali's death, shortly after his return from London, his legal practice in the capital took off, his wealth multiplying with no end in sight. As always it was thanks to his British connections. His fluency in English was his greatest asset and he quickly built a specialty on land deals. Whereas his father, in the earlier age managed to make ends meet by selling off land, uncle Munir's secret was his ability to fix papers, to arrange deals, and collect big commissions in the process. The British were land hungry and there were willing sellers. If private land was not enough, the British helped themselves to *Evkaf* endowments and trust lands. No one seemed to care, not even the local Muslim clergy.

Trade expansion was the chosen path of the British. Their current project was yet another upgrading of the port of Famagusta, a natural deep-sea harbor. Huge profits could be realized if ships could load and unload right at the dock. So, a huge public works operation was launched, and the affable Munir got the procurement contract to supply workers and donkeys and other necessary instruments and material needed for port construction.

Meanwhile, the Muftu Hafiz Ziyai Efendi had different plans. An old man from the *Tanzimat* generation of Ottoman reform, some years before he and his network of traders in the bazaar started a Muslim

Saving Chest of Nicosia. The idea was a modest Muslim credit union: to raise some funds for self-help, circulating short-term lending amongst member traders who otherwise might face liquidity problems.

"Each one of us will contribute a pound," said the Muftu to his friends. "Then when one of us needs it, he will get a line of credit."

"How will the loan be repaid?" Asked the other merchant worried about potential loss.

"No interest. Our religion does not permit interest," declared the Mufti in accordance with the Muslim law on usury. "The borrower will repay the principal, and part of his profit."

Making profit was fine. It was in accordance with the law of Allah and the Prophet. But, most important of all, the idea was in keeping with the mood of modernity that swept through the community at the time. Even the most conservative and religious elements were desirous of jumping on the modernity bandwagon and pushing ahead with the times.

The banking idea was a practical and highly successful project. Pretty soon the Chest expanded and when Munir had returned from his legal studies in London, it was already emerging into a bank. Then the colonial administration stepped in worried about its monopoly over banking in the island.

"We cannot have too many banks" the bureaucrats and administrators declared. "We must control money and banking." The Greek Cypriot businessmen were also moving aggressively into banking ventures. So the British colonial administration exerted control by licensing all businesses, and tried to consolidate all banks under one roof and direct British control.

The gambit backfired. The Chest, now expanded into a Muslim Saving Bank, was duly registered but remained outside colonial control. When Kemalism transformed Ottomans into Turks, the institutions followed suit as well. The Chest was transformed into the Turkish Bank, one of the first institutions in the land with a Turkish identity. It continued to grow and expand but stayed strictly as a traders' credit institution, financing a limited import-export business independent of Greek Cypriot banking.

Uncle Munir took a lead part in the transformation. He was a community notable already, socializing at the Brotherhood Club, the former Young Turk association, behind the *Evkaf* offices, where he had a large following. He was, in fact, a leading Anglophile and many shared his views of accommodation with the British masters of the island. It paid good dividends for him and the community, as in the case of the banking venture. Thanks to his lucrative contracts, he had rapidly expanding inflow of cash. He needed a safe place to put his money and earn profit, or interest with a different name. The name mattered little for Munir, so long as it was profitable.

It was the day after the sale of a huge tract of land to Nicosia Club, right across the river from Kosklu Ciftlik. The colonial super class was bored sitting and sipping whisky in the bar all the time.

"We need some recreation," declared the Secretary. "Too much booze and not enough recreation…"

"Quite right" agreed his friend, who happened to be a Scot. "What this place needs is a golf course."

"Capital idea" yelled the next chap sitting at the other end of the counter. He had recently joined the colonial administration from Kuala Lumpur, Malaya, where he had been a founding member of the Royal Selangor Golf Club. "We had such great fun in KL. Golf tournaments every weekend, lots of hot curry and scotch on the 19th hole."

Thus, an idea was born, but not before another fellow declared: "Wherever we British go, we take two things with us: Good administration, and golf. That is the rule." Those present cheered on.

So, at the next General Meeting of the Nicosia Club, a motion was duly presented and approved, unanimously to acquire the prime land along the river and build a golf course.

"How do we acquire the land?" That subsequently became the question. "You know," declared the Secretary, "a golf course requires lots of land."

"We do not need a big 18 hole course," said the practical minded Scot. "A nine hole course would do. A modest 50 donum piece of land would be sufficient for that." He said.

Then Munir came into the picture. He had the reputation amongst his British friends as a deal maker. Mind you he was not cheap, but for a fee, there was no land deal beyond the capacity of the fat little Ottoman. He had been extremely helpful in procuring men and materials in the big reconstruction project in the Famagusta port, now the center of the expanding colonial import-export trade. Soon the park next to the Club was selected and everyone was happy in the Nicosia Club. Winter was approaching and a season of golf would be ideal, keeping body and mind sound. "Capital, capital" agreed all.

Then, the project got stuck in Muslim law. "Damn" yelled the Secretary at the news. "We cannot get the land."

"How so?" asked the Scot.

"It is some infernal local custom. Apparently, the land we thought we had is trust land."

"What does that mean?" asked the practical minded Scot.

"Well! As I understand it, the land is meant for charity. The rent is supposed to provide revenue for hospitals and schools and such. The land is administered by the religious office, *Evkaf*." The Secretary looked somber and agitated.

Then, the Scot asked: "Who runs Evkaf?"

"We do, of course." He was reading the mind of the Scot. "But we simply cannot walk in and take it over. It would look bad."

"Yes, of course. It has to be done with class." Then he added: "Let's talk to that chap Munir. He is always helpful and he can fix up anything."

In the days following, Munir for a hefty fee from the British, arranged papers which showed that, as an act of charity, the office of *Evkaf*, had transferred, for social purposes, a big land grant to Nicosia Club. Thus, the golf course was built and the colonial upper class finally had their opportunity for regular recreation.

# V

In reality, Uncle Munir had become a new man. The golf course episode was several years ago, an episode out of his selfish existence when what mattered was he alone, no one else. Now, almost a decade later, he was a man transformed, dedicated to ethical living. His transformation was all Mary's doing.

I must go back and explain dear reader; how Uncle's ethical living came about. Remarkably, it is all thanks to the females in uncle Munir's life.

\*\*\*

Mary's murder in Buyuk Han on the night before my parents' wedding ended not only the unfortunate Irish girl's life; in a metaphorical sense, it also killed old Munir. The last time Munir of old was seen was on the night of 27th October 1923, the same date when poor pathetic Mary had checked in at the Buyuk Han.

Earlier that night Munir was at the Nicosia club at his best behavior as the ladies man, enjoying the company of English females. He had no idea that it would be his last because he had no knowledge of Mary's arrival.

Munir's latest conquest was an 18-year-old blond nicknamed Lizzy. She was so like Mary that Munir had known in London. Lizzy was very attractive and she would have no trouble going steady and possibly ending in marriage with one of the many eligible English men in the Club, but sex is what united her with Munir.

Elizabeth Knowles was the youngest daughter of Mr. John Knowles, a senior surveyor in the Lands Department. Blond with deep blue eyes and red-hot lips, five foot ten inches tall, she was as lovely to look at, as she was passionate in bed.

Her parents were not happy about her relationship with Munir. "Why he is full 6 inches shorter than you are" her mother would scold her, while his father, the snob in the Club, would taunt her, "Lizzy, don't be silly, that chap is nowhere your class" he would declare.

But in bed the short and dark-skinned Munir was supreme compared to anyone her parents might prefer. And that is what Lizzy liked the most, regardless what her snobbish parents thought about it.

"I am 18 and I can jolly well make up my own mind," she would say.

Her parents were heartbroken every time Munir would show up at the bar at the Club and towards midnight their beautiful Lizzy would slip away in his car, ending up at his house in Kosklu Ciftlik on the other side of the river that separated the Nicosia Club from where the Turkish elite of Nicosia lived.

The night was a particularly bitter one for Lizzy. There was a special awards dinner at which the annual golf prizes were presented, her father winning one of the monthly medals. Lizzy had spent the entire night on the floor dancing with all kinds of young and not so young men. But towards midnight, she gravitated towards Munir, like some addict ready for the next fix.

"Lizzy come and sit with us" demanded her mother, the matriarch, when she noticed her daughter was trying to catch Munir's attention as he sat at the bar drinking with his buddies. All night Munir has avoided her while she danced her heart out on the floor. It was a well-rehearsed pattern. Munir's indifference was part of a bitter, sometimes open hostility at the Club; it was part of their foreplay, ending always with hot sex afterwards.

"Mother" she scolded her, "leave me alone. I can take care of myself." Her father looked on astonished at the anger in Lizzy's voice.

Then Munir turned and looked at Lizzy. "And how is my girl tonight?" he asked.

"Munir lets go away from here. I am going to suffocate," she pleaded. That too was part of their well-rehearsed plot.

# DISCOVERY

The two lovers made a not so private exit from the Club. It was to be uncle Munir's last philandering.

Mrs. Knowles then turned to her husband and said: "John, I can't take it anymore. You've got to ask for a transfer out of this infernal place."

"Yes dear" said the husband dutifully.

Within the next month the Knowles, parents and daughter were gone. Everyone cooperated, especially his boss in the bureaucracy, except for Lizzy. She, too, went back to England, but not with her parents.

Uncle Munir was left alone, again... but not for long.

***

The next day Mary made a brief appearance in Nicosia. Her death also killed old Munir. The new Munir was a man reborn. Uncle Munir's ethical transformation from a selfish into a caring father and a man of compassion was immediate, right after the eventful and emotional meeting in his office with Nilufer the day after his brother's wedding.

His evolution as a community leader occurred more slowly. Slowly but surely, uncle Munir emerged as a top voice of the Turkish cause in the island. The Anglophile now discovered his Uzun Ali heritage.

It all happened thanks to his son then lost somewhere in Dublin. When Uncle salvaged and brought back his son Ozkan Jr. to Nicosia, he set up an educational trust to finance his son's education at the English School as well as his further education to follow. In this he followed his father's footsteps. Ozkan Jr. became a border at the School and Uncle would regularly visit him to monitor his studies and demonstrate his affection. Father and son would go walking in the forest around the School and slowly a closer bond developed between the two. Within a year, the initial estrangement was replaced by a genuine warm affection between father and son. These visits became important emotional ties in Ozkan Jr's life, giving the boy a new sense of confidence, stimulating him in his studies while also giving him a sense of belonging. He began to taste Turkish Cypriot culture and started to befriend other Turkish students at the School. Every time Munir would drive up the hill entering the grounds of the English School, situated right opposite the Governor's Palace, his school mates would gather around Ozkan Jr., admiring his father's shinning automobile and the experience would boost Ozkan Jr's ego sky high. These visits also gave Ozkan Jr. a moral uplift because by now his father was becoming an important figure in the Turkish Cypriot community.

The new Munir became a community leader by accident. The young selfish rapist of Nilufer now became a social reformer, leading the fight against polygamy and women's rights. He felt he owed it to Mary's self sacrifice, although of course his desire to free himself from the shame of Nilufer's rape was also a factor.

Munir was now a key member of the social club, Brotherhood Club behind the Evkaf Office in the centre of Nicosia. It brought together all the leading members of Turkish Cypriot society, businessmen and doctors and lawyers whose numbers were increasing every passing year as more and more graduates came from Turkey and England. The transformation in uncle Munir was so slow that other club members hardly noticed it.

The campaign to abolish polygamy and modernize the family law started almost accidentally when, one morning in the Club when uncle Munir was drinking Turkish coffee with friends in the garden under the shade of the orange and mandarin trees.

"Munir Bey" commented a member "with all your English friends, why don't you do something about this social disgrace of ours?" said a schoolteacher, famed for his zeal for Kemalist reforms then in full swing in Turkey. "The great Gazi is marching onwards and forwards in our motherland, and we are sitting here doing nothing." He lifted his eyes from the newspaper he had been reading, and said: "Look at this article. It is a disgrace. Men here can still marry up to four women, while in Turkey it is no longer legal."

Others sitting nearby, joined in with expressions of approval. In the weeks and months following uncle Munir found himself leading a campaign of social reform.

But it was an uphill battle. In the Nicosia Club, where the Knowles affair had damaged Munir's reputation, his influence was on decline. When he checked the mood of the colonial bureaucrats on the subject, he met stiff resistance.

"I wouldn't touch it with a ten foot pole" declared some one from the Colonial Secretary's Office when Munir remarked sitting at the Bar one night sipping whisky that polygamy was outdated.

"It is unfair on women and children," said Munir. But he got nowhere.

"We cannot touch the religious laws" was the opinion of the senior official present, "it is too sensitive" he said.

Gradually Uncle Munir distanced himself from the Nicosia Club, and devoted more time to social and political reforms of the Turkish Cypriot community. It took years to get results because of British resistance. In fact, the British government at the time, and its colonial extension in Cyprus at the time was having their troubles with Kemalist Turkey over the Mosul affair. The British knew the oil wealth of the province populated by Turkmen and Kurds, and there was no way London would hand it over to the Kemalist power in Ankara. Likewise it was out of question to honor Kemal in Ankara by emulating his social reforms here in colonial Cyprus. So, the British leaned toward the Greek Cypriots and encouraged the mass emigration of Turkish Cypriots, at least those with nationalist sentiments, to leave the island and relocate to the Turkish homeland.

# VI

The man in the center of the new anti-Kemalist policy on the island was Storrs.

In 1926 Sir Ronald Storrs became the Governor of Cyprus and the British implemented a new policy toward the Turkish Cypriots. Until 1923, they believed that eventually the British would return the island back to Turkey in accordance with the original rental arrangement. The peace deal at Lausanne put a sudden end to those dreams. Storrs took pride in his role in defeating the Ottoman Turks in Palestine and in his Oxford days had been a brilliant student of ancient Greek. He saw Cyprus as a modern day manifestation of the Hellenic ideal type; the Greek Cypriots, for the new Governor, became Adonis and Aphrodite reborn.

It made great sense, he reflected, to implement a program of mass emigration of Turkish Cypriots to Anatolia. "Let them go join Kemal and his modernizing crusade."

Many families sold out and moved to Kemalist Turkey. But many soon came back, dejected and unhappy. Life in Anatolia was not at all what they had expected. With refugees streaming in from Greece, and the new regime cash-strapped, there were shortages of housing and jobs. Thousands of Turkish Cypriots who opted for Turkish citizenship and went to Kemalist Turkey learnt the bitter truth that nationalism is one thing, the reality of poverty, war and destruction is quite another.

## DISCOVERY

The British were at the time having a lot of difficulty with the new Kemalist masters in Ankara, especially over the Mosul affair and Iraq. Turkmen largely peopled the region along with tribal Kurds, and it was declared part of the Turkish national territory. But it had rich oil reserves, and there was no way the British would let go of Mosul. Besides, here in Cyprus, the Greeks were agitated and an uprising seemed in the works. It was rumored that a rebellion for *ENOSIS* was brewing to wrest the island from British rule and unite it with Greece.

Uncle Munir, once again, was the man of the hour, but this time round he acted with humility, helping not just the British, but Turks as well. He extended a helping hand for those families who wanted to become Turkish citizens. It took a lot of his time; organizing exit passes, shipping reservations, resettlement papers, and numerous other documentations. One thing, which both the British and Ottoman/Turkish bureaucracies had in common, was an obsession with paperwork. But the job was finally done and thousands of Turkish Cypriot families, close to a third of the entire population, left for Anatolia. Uncle Munir collected no money from the departing Turks.

The changing demographics in Cyprus pleased Storrs. He had helped greatly in ridding the Holy Land of the Turks and one of his proud moments in colonial service was the day watching, next to Lawrence his dear friend, later to become the famed Lawrence of Arabia, his boss General Allanby, on a white horse, triumphantly leading the victorious British troops into Jerusalem. Now Storrs' facilitating the Turkish exodus from Cyprus was merely the latest phase of his empire-building career.

With some of the money he had made from the British in arranging papers for emigration, Munir this time got a brand new car, this time a late model Ford. All around people were worried about falling markets, prices dropping through the floor, farmers going bankrupt and workers losing their jobs, Munir was doing just fine. This time, however, Uncle Munir was involved in several charitable organizations, donating funds for orphanages and spending as much time in Turkish clubs as in the Nicosia Club.

\*\*\*

It was a hot August day in 1931 Ozkan Jr. now 13, and soon to start secondary level at the English School; he needed a break. So Uncle

Munir decided to put a little bit of excitement in his and his son's life. He made a decision that was to have a decisive impact on my life as well as in my cousin's. Indeed, it changed the course of our family history.

"Let's go visit your uncle," he said. He had not seen Ozkan in Xero for several years." I hear they have little boy and you can play with him, maybe we go swimming."

"I would like that" said Ozkan Jr. "Thank you, father."

So, father and son drove out to Xero, traveling west of Nicosia through the rich, citrus orchards of Morphou, and quaint little villages, all green and beautiful like Gaziveren. After two hours, they finally reached the tiny house in which we lived. The visit was a huge success. The brothers hugged and kissed. But the turning point was the fact that I adored Ozkan Jr right from the first moment. I was then six, a big lad for my age, and I immediately warmed up to my elder cousin. He was smart, blonde and very polished. He looked every bit confident, intelligent and smart. Most of all, he was friendly and gave me the impression that he liked me. We hit it off right away. I felt wonderful to have at last a friend to talk to and play with. The next thing I knew, I was proudly introducing him to my sister Sevgi, now almost three years old: "Come and see my little baby sister" I said displaying a touching affection between brother and sister. He sensed it and responded with affection. An equally warm relationship then started to develop between all three of us. Even before the adults finished their greetings, the two of us, with Sevgi following behind, run off, exploring the riverbed and watching Greek kids in the neighborhood playing soccer in the field behind their school.

In the evening the party went to Lame Yorgo's fish restaurant. Elena and Yorgo were now quite old, but still together working in the same old restaurant. The place was little changed from long ago, in the earlier days when Grandfather Halil had had a one-night stand with Lame Yorgo's wife while the police posse was chasing the bandit chief Midas. When the party returned home after dinner, Aygul had to rearrange the rooms and to provide sleeping space for everyone. Sevgi and I moved in with my parents, and Munir slept in the other bedroom with Ozkan Jr.

The next morning was a beautiful, sunny day. After breakfast, mother suggested that we the children should go for a walk in the neighborhood. My favorite was the riverbed behind our house, full of

# DISCOVERY

reeds and stones along a small creek running in the middle. Beyond the river on the other side overlooking the sea the mining company had factories for cleaning and smelting the ore. On the mountainside toward Lefke, there were tennis courts. Only expatriate staff were allowed to use the courts. In the cool morning, there were some players, hitting balls and shouting and yelling in fun, incomprehensible to me, although Ozkan Jr's English was good enough to listen to the conversation on the courts.

Then, suddenly, as we were crossing the riverbed, we came across a small Greek boy holding a tennis ball. My cousin asked the boy where he got it, but he just stood there, motionless saying nothing. Ozkan Jr. got the ball and we started walking toward the courts. He said: "Let's take it to the players. I am sure it's theirs." We started walking toward the tennis court, Sevgi following behind.

Then all hell broke loose. Suddenly two large and over-powering American or British adults surrounded us. They came screaming at us.

"What are you doing here?" asked one angrily. We were stunned, and remained silent. "This is private. Get out," ordered one of the angry tennis players.

Ozkan Jr. replied: "We brought your ball, sir" expecting a thank you. Instead, he got a tongue-lashing.

"Give me that ball. Where did you get it?" said the tennis player. "You must have stolen it."

Ozkan Jr. was amazed. "No, sir" he replied. "We picked it from a little boy." But the angry fellow would hear none of it. He grabbed the ball and was gone shouting angrily.

"You thief, you stole my ball." And the players were gone, leaving us children bewildered by this unexpected outburst of the foreigner who made us unwelcome in our land. We thought no more of it. But it was by no means the end of it.

A couple of hours later when we returned home, punishment waited. The tennis players went and complained to the police, reporting it as theft. Father was angry. Both of us were in serious trouble, we had violated colonial justice. We tried to explain what had actually happened, but to no avail. We both got a tongue-lashing anyhow.

What hurt the most was the unfairness of the American or British players. It was my first practical lesson on the fickleness of western justice.

# VII

Meanwhile, Governor Storrs policy of appeasing the Greek Cypriots began to bear its bitter fruit. Encouraged by his sympathetic leanings, the priesthood of the Greek Orthodox Church launched a campaign for ENOSIS, uniting Cyprus to Greece. It led to violence, open rebellion.

The Rebellion started on 18 October 1931. The fanatic Milonas, the head priest at Phancromeni Cathedral, next to the Gymnasium in the center of the Greek quarter of old Nicosia inside the moat, could hold his passion no more. God must have spoken to him that political action, not theology, is what the greatest need of the moment was. He incited the riot amongst his congregation. The youth and the unemployed all combined in a popular wave of Hellenic fervor, flying Greek flags and shouting "Long live Greece", "ENOSIS Now", "Death to the English", and they made their way through Metaxas Square, marching toward the Governor's Residence. In no time, it was put on fire and burnt to the ground. Rioters in Limassol joined in and burned down the house of the District Commissioner. Then, the peasants in Greek villages, devastated by economic depression and crushed by agricultural debt, joined in as the rebellion became island-wide.

At the comfortable Nicosia Club, the British super class was in shock.

"What is going on? The island is burning," said the Secretary.

"We have to bring in the troops," suggested some one from behind the bar.

# DISCOVERY

"No chance. We have none, to speak of. Only a local contingent of *zaptiehs*, and we cannot rely on those Muslim police."

Then, a voice from among the drinkers said: "Declare a curfew and impose martial law." All eyes turned and looked at the speaker. It was a drunk. Silence followed for a moment.

"Right" said the Secretary. "That is it. That is exactly what should be done."

Later on that day, martial law was declared and a twenty-four hour curfew imposed. Surprisingly, against all odds, it held. So with no troops on the island the British rulers of Cyprus were caught off guard, but somehow they had managed to save the day.

"British luck" said some Irish member, recalling his days in India where with no more than a few hundred officers the British had managed to establish their rule over the entire Indian sub-continent.

In the days following the rebellion subsided and the British colonial administration rule assumed direct control of the government. No more advisory councils, no more democratic experiments involving the Turkish and Greek Cypriots in rule making. Henceforth, till the end of British rule in 1960, the Governor in executive council administered the island. The ENOSIS campaign did not die, it became part of the Church politics and the priests and teachers took the lead to educate and prepare the ground for the next round of the violent struggle.

*\*\*\**

In 1933 I was seven and it was a big day when, in September, I was transferred out of Teacher Haji Hasan's one-room school in Gemikonak and entered the much bigger middle school in Lefke, where I was put in *Muallim (*teacher) Mustafa's class. I felt on top of the world, belonging to such a large and modern school with so many students and teachers. I felt proud, eager to learn. We were engaged in the new Kemalist modernization project, trying to master the basics of arithmetic, geography and civics and physical education. There was much rote learning and the class would chant in unison after the teacher:

"A healthy mind requires a healthy body."
"I am a Turk, Islam is my religion."
"A Turk is industrious, confident and creative."
"One Turk is equivalent to the entire human race."

But what impressed me the most at the time was the motto we leant by heart: "What a privilege is to be able to call yourself a Turk."

It gave the young generation a definition, an identity, a place in the wide world. From then on, it seemed to me that education and learning were the means to conquer the world, to put all wrongs right. Knowledge became my master and guide. It was the Uzun Ali spirit in me!

This discovery made me happy. Each year, I learnt amazing new things. The first years were plain sailing. But I encountered academic problems, though not at school. At home I was having trouble with homework. I was very good with numbers learning addition and multiplication tables with ease. I also loved reading those wonderful stories about fairies and princesses from Hans Andersen fables. My problem was dictation. We were given lists of modern words. Using Arabic was now déclassé and the class had to learn modern words. Gradually, however, the Latin alphabet and words started making sense. Meaning of words, however, presented problems. *Millet* now became *ulus*, *istiklal*, was *egemenlik*. Some words were now taboo, mostly Islamic words, like *Ummet* (Brotherhood of Muslims) or *Halife* (Caliph), were no-no. Turkish nation was now *secular*, a word I never could easily comprehend and teachers could not satisfactorily explain. Everyday we had to repeat big words, that were little understood, individually and in class as a group, that the Turkish nation was now contemporary (another one of those difficult words), and everyone had to march in tune with modern civilization (the most difficult word of all). One key word, which I definitely understood, was modern: What it meant to me was that knowledge was like some magic wand, found in books that enabled one to understand how things worked. It made me inquisitive stimulated me toward a lifelong love of books and learning.

As a result, I was normally the top performer in class. I became a favorite with teachers who gave me small rewards of pencils, *lokum* and short story books. I loved the storybooks the best. When in grade 3 and 4, I acquired the love of reading. That was something I shared with mother, who herself was an avid reader. Our mutual love of books and readings brought us closer and soon she became my confidant and greatest teacher.

Sevgi, now approaching school age, was an informal partner in this self-education, even before her schooling began. In fact, I became

# DISCOVERY

my little sister's tutor at home, summarizing and recounting to her what I was acquiring myself. Sevgi learnt the alphabet even before formal schooling, and her love of books, especially history, was the product of the natural bond between brother and sister reinforced by mother's love of reading.

In those days teachers held a particularly high esteem in community. They were leaders in modernizing the minds of the new generation. Mustafa Nazim, simply known as Muallim Mustafa, was the 4th grade teacher in the Lefke public school. Muallim Mustafa, after a test in class in which, again I had outperformed the entire class, and scored the perfect score of 10, he smiled and said:

"Come here, my boy," I looked at Muallim Mustafa. "I want to say something to you."

He had a strange smile on his face.

I looked at him with excitement mixed with surprise.

"You will go far. You have a wonderful mind. Remember, learning is a great thing, opening new and unknown worlds. Don't let any one stop you."

I was moved by these words. They represented one of the most precious gifts ever given to me. At the time I did not, of course, fully comprehend their meaning, but I was delighted with Muallim Mustafa's words of encouragement. That night when I came home I repeated the message to my parents. It was a rare occasion to remember. I became the center of attention in the family; it was a night of pride in the Ozkan family in Xero. My news from Muallim Mustafa was a bright spot on what had been for my father a particularly difficult and disappointing day at work. He came home announcing that trouble was just round the corner.

Inspector Kazim warned his fellow policemen that a general strike of miners was imminent. The past few years had been difficult. Wages were low and, worst of all, mining was on a declining trend as a result of global depression. "The miners" he announced, "could walk out any day." He was worried: "The workers want higher wages and safe working conditions. In my heart, I agree with them, but officially my hands are tied. The worst part of it is that this time there will be violence because the workers are serious and the Anglo-American mining corporation is equally determined to resist worker demands." Inspector Kazim was justified.

For now, however, father was happy for my success.

# VIII

The big strike in Lefke and Karadag occurred in 1936. Eight Turkish and Greek Cypriot miners lost their lives when an unsafe underground tunnel crushed them. Fear spread around the 2000-strong miners and their families in Xero, Lefke and Karadag. More deaths were expected because the shafts were unsafe. The British American mining company, not yet recovered from the global economic depression, claimed it had no resources to pay attention to the health and safety or welfare of the miners, let alone afford higher wages.

"We have to confront them," decided the managing director. "After all, there are plenty of other workers around who would be happy to work for the company."

It was true. The company policy was simple. When there is a labor shortage, ship in new supplies from Greece. With high unemployment and difficult times there, and empty boats coming to load copper and iron ore at Xero, and difficult economic times, this was not a good time to care about a few ignorant miners dying underground!

Well, their families cared. In fact, they were furious. So were a few labor leaders. Unions all of a sudden mushroomed, demanding safer working conditions and higher wages. In fact the labor movement was in reasonably good shape, with Turks and Greeks in solidarity. The labor movement then was primitive. The Greek laboring classes were divided, some inspired by Bolsheviks of Moscow and others orches-

# DISCOVERY

trated by the Ethnarch, the head of the Greek Orthodox Church who jealously hang on to his Ottoman office as headman of the Greek Cypriot community. But for the mining company, there was one danger that was the communist plot, more imagined than real.

The police were called in and Ozkan found himself embroiled in strike breaking. The strike action quickly became to be seen as a revolt against colonial authority organized by a bunch of ragtag rebels in the guise of miners. The company bussed in truckloads of scabs because there were no labor laws protecting the rights of workers. The plant manager simply wanted to get rid of workers, "throw out the commies" he demanded.

As the climax evolved, the workers were gathered in front of the mine entrance in Karadag to force suspension of any mining activities. Ringleaders were armed with sticks and iron bars. A violent confrontation looked certain.

"No one goes in," shouted an angry worker, as others started shouting, waving their sticks and irons. "Scabs... Rotten thieves go back," yelled the noisy crowd, putting their lives on the line. In those days workers had no rights, no collective bargaining, and no right to strike. Technically, the miners were in violation of the colonial laws, which sided with foreign capital.

Inspector Kazim played safe and order his men, including father, to keep a safe distance between the strikers. "This is no time for heroics," he said to himself. The workers, looking fierce and furious, were at boiling point, ready to take the law in their hands. At any moment they could attack the police with their tools and sticks.

"Why are we here?" wondered father. Then, suddenly he made the connection. "We are doing the dirty work for the Anglo-American company." That, in truth, was an amazing discovery for one with as limited schooling as father.

The stalemate continued. At the end of the shift, father went back to the police station in Lefke as everyone eagerly awaited developments.

Later on that night when he returned home, father was a man with a purpose. The strike confrontation had given him an education like no other. Suddenly he could see cause-and-effect with incredible clarity.

In a rare moment of self-assertion chatting at length with his wife on the strike, father reached an important decision: "Aygul" he said, "it is time for us to move to Nicosia. We must go to the capital where there are better schools for Tekin. Here we are all like the poor workers in the mine; there is no justice in it."

That night mother learnt, from father's account, a new type of injustice, an economic one governing relations between poor workers and an uncaring mining company. What she could not comprehend was the global forces operating behind the strike: Here in little Xero, the Anglo-American mining company and its pathetic miners were simply an insignificant cog in the global network of foreign capital and a system that at the time was pushing everyone and everything down toward poverty and chaos.

Two highly volatile days passed with no change in the battle lines between workers and the company. On the third day the company acted and recruited replacement workers. As night fell, taking advantage of darkness, the company brought in truckloads of scabs. They came in trucks covered with tarpaulin so no one could see what the company was up to. The trucks managed to enter the mine and the scabs were taken down the elevator into the mine underground. But there they were stuck, because the next day, when the strikers were again blocking the entrance, the company realized the human scum down below had become hostages, and a human tragedy would inevitably result unless the strike was settled quickly.

So, reluctantly the company gave in. "We got ourselves into a jam," said the managing director, with obvious bitterness. The workers won a victory and a giant step was taken forward. The labor movement received a big boost in organization and influence.

The day the strike was called off and workers had claimed a victory, father came home a determined man. He immediately put into effect the plan for the family move to Nicosia. It was father's decisive moment.

"We are no different than those poor miners" he said to mother "The company is using us just the same way they use those wretched workers." Mother was astonished. She had never seen father in such a determined mood. She had not heard him talk that way before.

She was herself puzzled. "What do you mean?" She asked.

"I do not exactly know" he began. "Aygul, I must tell you a weird feeling I experienced watching those workers go down the shaft, unsure whether they would ever return." He looked serious and sad.

Mother, in some shock still trying to understand her husband, looked at father. "But Ozkan" she said, "I have come to like it here. We have a good life. I have friends," she said. "Why change it?"

It took father a couple of minutes to respond. He took on a somber look and then explained:

"You know, Aygul, I watched those workers, their expressions of determination on their dirty faces. They had the looks of men pushed to the limit. I felt a funny sense of affinity with those poor workers" he replied. "I said to myself, 'if we stay here in Xero, we will be just like them, what will happen to our children? Become miners?"

Mother looked on in silence. She looked like she got the message.

Then father said: "It is time to go so that our children can escape this miserable atmosphere. We must educate them."

It was a rare occasion when father had taken the initiative and mother followed him. Her resistance melted away when she suddenly realized: "I will rejoin Ayse Hanim," Inspector Kazim's wife who was already in Nicosia. Dear Ayse always sided with her in her arguments with other ladies in the neighborhood. She missed her, and it would be fun to be with her dear friend once again.

Our family had spent twelve years in total in Xero and there, amidst ups and downs, my parents had had two children, me and Sevgi, a boy and a girl. Now it was time to open a new chapter in the saga of the Uzun Ali family, to launch a new beginning. From this simple decision emerged new horizons of learning and adventure that would end in far away places like Toronto, London and Ankara, spreading the modern grandchildren of the old Kaimakam to far-flung corners of the world. The world was changing fast, it was becoming a global village and education was the gateway to this modern village. The Uzun Ali clan was determined to take its place in the modern global village, then in its infancy.

So father, mother, my sister Sevgi and I, all relocated to Kuruchesme in the heart of old Nicosia, a low-rent district. That is what was affordable with the limited family budget. One advantage was that it was a short walking distance of the police headquarters. An equally important advantage for mother was the proximity of our rented accommodation to her friend Ayse Hanim. Mother and her dear friend became, once again, soul sisters.

In Xero, years went by and the metal markets recovered. When the madness of the Second World War started within a few years, the Anglo-American mining company started to make huge profits.

As for the workers, they returned to work, making a few more shillings, but like men condemned, they remained chained to the production of ore for the war machines that soon started to roar, bringing untold misery and holocaust to other innocent lives.

# IX

Our new life in Nicosia began badly. We almost lost Sevgi. My sister and I by now had developed a strong bond, playing and reading together, sometimes partners in childish crime, occasionally getting into mischief together like going to the park nearby and playing till late and getting into trouble with mother. But on this particular occasion, I could not save her from near death.

The snakebite occurred in the old rose garden of the Konak in Milltown, now in a state of advanced neglect and ruin. Maybe it was some strange divine revenge on our family.

It happened during a rare family reunion. Uncle Munir and my cousin came visiting us, shortly after our relocation to Nicosia and a day trip was arranged to the old Konak in Milltown. It was a sunny, hot day in August, just before school holidays ended. The party drove out in uncle Munir's car to Milltown for old time's sake. All came except Ozkan Jr. who was getting ready for his upcoming trip to London for university. He had won admission to the London School of Economics and stayed behind to write some letters. As his departure for London drew closer, Ozkan Jr. became more nervous and somewhat mystical. Everyone noticed he was frequently visiting Buyuk Han for unexplained reason. Father Munir felt it had to do with Mary, but the topic was too emotional for father and son and they never talked about the matter. Ozkan Jr. kept any private secret close to his heart. He was always asking questions and trying to learn what little she knew about his mother from mother Aygul. What he was able to collect was not much; he yearned for more.

It was father's idea to visit the Konak. He had a strange attachment to the old mansion and Milltown. Konak was a ruin now, yet on the drive out it pulled the two half-brothers, now closer to each other ever more than they had ever been. They talked, discussed and dismissed as unrealistic, ideas about restoring the place. "What for? Who will live in it?" reasoned the pragmatic Munir.

"I don't exactly know," replied father feeling more attached to the old place.

"We are all townspeople. Our children are studying to become professionals. No one will come to live in Milltown," said Uncle Munir. It was true.

Reluctantly father agreed and the restoration idea was postponed to some future date.

At Milltown we first had a picnic under the olives next to the weir. Then we stopped to visit the Konak. The adults were walking through the old rooms and stables, exchanging memories. Sevgi and I went to the garden searching to pick figs, now ripe and succulent. We were walking thorough the old rose garden, the secret site of Nilufer's rape almost 30 years ago, about which of course we knew nothing. Where beautiful roses once flourished now grew thorns. Tall dry grass and brush were everywhere. My sister was walking behind me. She screamed and I turned and looked, noticing just in time the deadly viper, *koufi* that accidentally Sevgi stepped on. The lethargic viper was slowly winding away into the brush as my sister fell on the ground in agony.

Snakebites were rare events, but *koufi* was famed for its deadly poisonous bite in Cyprus, resulting in a few deaths yearly. Sevgi was saved from a certain death by quick action on my part. I picked her up and carried her to the Konak where the adults were. Within minutes, I was sitting next to my sister in the back seat of uncle Munir's car, with a pained look at her little facing, as if she was asking: "Am I going to die?" "Don't you worry, little baby" I comforted her; "you will be fine. Just relax," I said to her as the car speeded to the new hospital in Nicosia. At last, the British had built a general hospital in the capital. So within half hour, the doctors administered the anti-venom antidote and Sevgi was saved. The accident drew brother and sister even closer.

# DISCOVERY

Back in Nicosia, life resumed its quiet tempo. Within weeks, I started the final year of elementary school in the Haydar Pasa School, then at the peak of its fame, not far from the Kuruchesme quarter where we had moved. That year was to be the last year of schooling for me on Turkish modernization. Afterwards, my education was to be all English, in a new language, in a new culture. But Haydar Pasa was to leave a lasting impression in my memory, capping my early education as a modern child molded by the grand Turkish modernization project.

In Fall1938 two major events occurred. Mustafa Kemal crowned Ataturk father of all Turks, died in Istanbul on 10th November in the palace of the Sultans and the entire Turkish nation went into mourning. Grown-ups, men, women, old and young, the entire nation wept in the streets. The outpouring of grief was unbelievable. Emotions run high and time seemed to stop, no one wanted to acknowledge the sad reality of the passing of the great man. They did the next best thing and stopped clocks at 9.05 the moment of Ataturk's death. The clock of modernization literally stopped ticking; henceforth Turks, ordinary citizens and politicians, became followers of the Great Man, leaders merely imitators.

The new motto was now: "We will march in your footsteps." Ismet Inonu became the National Chief and one party dictatorship in Turkey began in earnest.

On the day Ataturk died, I had been a student in the English School exactly one month. Of course, the school administration took no notice of the event, but secretly I organized a minute of silence amongst the Turkish students in our class. It was a symbolic act of solidarity with the Turkish world. Otherwise, life went on, as it should. My cousin Ozkan Jr. went to England to study politics and economics at the London School of Economics in Aldwych on the Strand.

Before his departure Ozkan Jr. did one emotional pilgrimage to Buyuk Han to honor the mother whom, like Aunt Aygul, he had never seen. He had heard about her from others, not from his father who kept these things very much close to his own heart. He knew about Mary's short and tragic visit many years ago, searching out, but never finding the love she had come to the island to find. In the meantime, especially in his final years at the English School, Ozkan Jr. had developed a great liking for the English Greats. He loved Dickens' *Great Expectations*, very much identifying with Pip rising to fame and fortune thanks to his mysterious benefactor. But he loved most of all, Hardy's *Tess of the d'Urbervilles*, which, to him, paralleled his own mother's sacrifice for love that never was fulfilled. On this last emotional visit to Buyuk Han, he cried alone in silence and whispered to himself, inspired by Hardy, "What bitterness is buried here, what great injustice!" No mortal heard.

Then it was an emotional farewell visit to his father. It was a proud moment for Uncle Munir. Honoring the memory of Mary had transformed the man, and now his redeemed son symbolized his own salvation. Uncle Munir felt a great sense of satisfaction when Ozkan Jr. walked in to his office, as arranged, for a farewell lunch at the Nicosia Club joining father and son.

They drove through Kosklu Ciftlik, down across the riverbed and into the parking lot at the Club. The next day, the two would drive again, this time to Larnaca for embarkation on the British passenger ship to take Ozkan Jr. back to Britain. Munir's mind sailed, momentarily, back to 1923 when he was on a desperate moral mission to reclaim his son in the Dublin convent. Now the lost son was about to enter the adult world on his own. His son represented all that was morally good in the new Munir that uncle represented, and he felt a rare sense of personal achievement with what he had done.

"I have some arrangements to complete at the bank" he began as they were finishing their lunch before driving to Larnaca for embarkation. Ozkan Jr. looked at this father with interest. "I have set up an education trust for you" he said, adding after a moment's pause, "and for your cousin Tekin" he added, knowing the close relations between the two cousins. "In time, when he goes to University, the trust will finance his studies as well." It was a secret, typical of the kind of man uncle had become, a private act of charity I would discover several years later.

Uncle Munir then gave his son some specific instructions. "When you are in London, go the bank's branch and introduce yourself. They will be expecting you. They will pay you a monthly allowance, sufficient for your needs." He did not mention any figure and Ozkan Jr. did not ask. In respectful silence he knew it was a generous amount.

Then his father added one more piece of information, revealing the generous and family person that the new Munir had become. It was a late acknowledgement of his moral debt toward his brother Ozkan.

"I have provided similarly for your niece Sevgi. She is still young, but very bright and promising. I expect she will go to University in time, and I know my brother will not be able to provide for it." He was quite right.

"Thank you Sir" is all that Ozkan Jr. said, but that was all that was proper for the occasion.

His father's mind was on moral accounting. He just wanted his son to know in barest minimum, the ethical person his father had become. The youth who had violated the maiden Nilufer in the rose garden in Konak back in 1908, the year of "freedom" when another ancestor, his sister-in law Aygul's womanizing father's misdeeds had brought so much tragedy to so many innocent lives, was now settling scores, thanks to his wealth, to facilitate the rebirth of a new generation of modern children, reconstructed afresh, ready to face the brave new world. Ozkan Jr. and his cousin and niece were the vanguard generation of the Uzun Ali family about to go international.

***

Ozkan Jr. in London fell in love. His first love was his political studies. The LSE then was the most famous center of academic socialism. The Webbs were alive and well, teaching theories of new worker rights and industrial democracy. He loved the lectures of the fiery Harold Laski and the younger Atlee, who later on defeated Winston Churchill, the war hero, and became the Labor Prime Minister.

That is how Ozkan Jr. was introduced to the idea of social justice, something brand new for him. He knew something about justice, a purely legal idea, from his lawyer dad in Nicosia, but justice as distributive, normative concept describing how wealth in society was shared, why different economic classes got more than others, these questions were fresh, original ideas for him. And he fell in love with it all. He started reading *Das Capital,* but soon gave it up. It was boring to read, and too deterministic. Everything seemed to happen in a precise, but intricate order, according to some inner force guiding it all. To his young mind and inquiring mind, Ozkan Jr wanted more, more real life challenges and less theories of the new man in the inevitable age of communism.

Then practical politics of war took over and dominated everything, including Ozkan Jr and his life style. As London was bombed and food shortages and hardships ensued, his studies became erratic.

There was too much destruction and pain around to keep his mind focused on books and papers. But he persisted, reading and spending more time than ever in libraries. He moved to a flat in Bloomsbury, and started going to the British Museum frequently reading the classics including Plato's *Republic* and Aristotle's *Politics*. His favorites were the realist political philosophers. Then, as Hitler's bombs fell all around, Ozkan Jr read about Machiavelli's *Prince* and got his first lessons of political realism, of the true meaning of power in a real Hobbesian world when life was really lonely, nasty, brutish and short.

Life was actually getting nastier and lonelier for Ozkan Jr. First he got homesick, but there was no way of visiting his father back in Nicosia. Then he missed the smell and taste of fresh oranges, mandarins and all kinds of fruit so plentiful in Cyprus. Here in London, these were luxuries. Londoners dug in as Hitler rained bombs on them day after day. Life somehow continued amidst ruin and rubble. There were lots of girls at the LSE, beautiful and charming, some very academic and serious, but almost all ready for some fun especially on Friday evenings and on weekends. Ozkan Jr. began to enjoy the pub life.

Then, he met Jill accidentally. It happened in a crowded pub on the Strand.

"Excuse me" he apologized for almost falling on her as he was dodging his way in the crowd.

"That is OK, no worry" she replied with a friendly smile. The first thing he noticed about Jill was her lovely and friendly face. The chance encounter was to be a defining moment for both.

Jill, blonde and slim, long flat hair and blue eyes, was exactly my cousin's type. By now, his friends had dropped "Jr" after his name, for convenience really, almost without anyone noticing the change, in London he became simply Ozkan. No one minded, and least of all my father back in Nicosia who took pride in his intellectual accomplishments.

Ozkan looked at her and she was equally interested in him. The chemistry was appropriate and the timing seemed right. Soon they were standing next to each other around a tiny space in a corner of the bar around a stool, amidst smoke and noise.

"What are you studying?" He asked. She said: "Sociology. How about you?"

"Politics and economics" replied Ozkan. "Oh, heavy stuff, eh?" she said.

Then they talked about the latest war news and drank more beer. Then Ozkan changed the subject back to their studies:

"Do you like sociology? What kind of sociology are you doing?" He was curious

"I love it," said Jill. "It teaches me what I need to know about Wales, why there is so much poverty and social inequality," she said. Ozkan was surprised at her passion. Compared to his own passion with his political and economic studies to become a professional, it sounded like Jill was studying sociology for a personal mission in life. So he asked:

"What do you want to become when you graduate?"

Jill said: "I want to become a teacher" which again surprised Ozkan. He expected to hear a much higher ambition, something higher on the social ladder, like a lawyer or accountant, but he was nevertheless impressed with her modesty. Jill instinctively knew the social limits of the class system in England. Jill was from Wales and her modesty sprung from a rather lowly family background; becoming a school teacher was itself a big advancement compared to her father, who was a coal miner, and her mother who worked as a shop assistant in some grocery shop, barely making ends meet. Jill herself was on a local government scholarship, which she had won for her exceptional academic achievement at the local grammar school. It was awarded in readiness for a big surge in requirements for schoolteachers after the war.

Ozkan and Jill became friends and war time London became more interesting. But more than friendship was involved. It was Jill who facilitated Ozkan's transformation in London into a Turkish Cypriot patriot. During the many years of growing up in Cyprus he had acquired not more than a thin veneer of Turkish culture and had retained his own ideals and values. Now, he was about to get an education, here in London thanks to Jill. The student of sociology was a secret Welsh nationalist who was keenly interested in social justice for coal miners and had made home rule for Wales a personal cause. She became interested in Ozkan's connection to colonial Cyprus and his half Turkish identity. At first, it was more exotic; the transformation evolved gradually, turning into bittersweet anti-colonial flavor, as their relationship grew more serious.

"How very interesting" she replied as soon as Ozkan explained that he was half Turkish Cypriot. "You don't look it at all," she said, mirroring an innocent ignorance of such exotic places and people as Cyprus and Turkey. Then almost immediately, she apologized:

"I am sorry, I am stereotyping, something I should learn to resist," she admitted demonstrating her modest inclination and the influence of her sociology classes.

It was Jill, the secret Welsh nationalist, who turned Ozkan's eyes toward the Turkish Cypriot national cause. She would ask questions that Ozkan had never imagined growing up in Nicosia. "What were Turkish Cypriots like? What aspirations did they have? What did they think of British rule?" The Welsh girl, with her great enthusiasm and curiosity, reminded Ozkan Jr of the memory of his own mother Mary.

At first my cousin was embarrassed with Jill's questions because he was hard put to give her satisfactory answers. In Cyprus, at the English School, he was only taught English literature and British monarchy. He had no knowledge of Turkish subjects. Then he found a solution: Me, his young cousin, back in Cyprus, became part of his life in England He started writing to me, seeking information to satisfy Jill's curiosity about colonialism in Cyprus and its impact on the Turks there. Thus, the two of us, Ozkan Jr. and I, became erratic correspondents under the wartime conditions. British colonial rule, in a mysterious way, pulled his Welsh girl friend and Ozkan Jr. closer. Love between them developed slowly, platonic initially and then more romantic. Their love affair blossomed out of the mutual bedrock of social justice, a blending of their respective political and sociological studies.

I knew nothing of this love affair at the time, of course. But, strange as it may sound, I had a great deal to do with it. My letters from Nicosia, full of the fiery Dr. Kucuk and other nationalist leaders, served a romantic purpose in far-away London: They cemented the relationship between Jill and Ozkan Jr.

# X

When I started English School, my life was changed forever, but the change came less from teachers than my own mother Aygul. I had no trouble with academics; I was a scholarship student all the way, excelling in math, physics and chemistry. I learnt quickly, I made new friends and played soccer, scoring goals and in time became the most loved center forward on the School team as well in my Newham House. The students were then divided into four houses, each with its own colors: Beaconsfield was yellow, Wolseley red, Newham blue and Kitchener green. The names did not mean much then, what mattered was winning. That was my first introduction to competitiveness.

Then suddenly I started getting letters from cousin Ozkan Jr. in London. These letters opened a new horizon for me, introduced me into subjects I did not know. I became interested in political issues. Jill, the sociology girl friend indirectly sparked a growing interest in me, in the social and political conditions of Turkish Cypriots. Cousin Ozkan Jr. was asking all sorts of questions that opened my eyes to my little world around: How the Turkish Cypriots earned their living? How important was farming and mining? What were their political ambitions?

That is how I developed an interest in the newspaper *Ates (Fire)* published by Kemal Deniz at the time. It provided the information that I was able to pass on to my cousin in London, learning in the process myself about farmers' organizations, labor unions, struggling workers and the awakening of political awareness of the Turkish Cypriots. *Halkin Sesi (People's Voice),* another newspaper started by the popular Dr. Kucuk became the main source for my political education. On 23 April 1944 almost single-handedly Kucuk established a national party uniting Turks of Cyprus against ENOSIS and demanding that, if Britain abandoned Cyprus, the island should be returned back to its previous owner Turkey. In the pages of *Halkin Sesi,* Dr. Kucuk, spoke for the national party. He became a progressive voice fighting for social issues such as modern family law and for modernizing the school system on the Turkish model. Most of all, he defended Turkish Cypriots against the British colonialism that appeared willing to cede the island to Greece in line with the ENOSIS demands of Greek Cypriot fanatics.

I was then in mid-teens and a period of war. But the war had not yet affected life greatly. Turkish Cypriot politics became my passion. Kemal Deniz and his rural development ideas impressed me the most. In 1942 I wrote to my cousin: "I read this article which stressed the importance of village organizations to empower farmers". On another occasion, I wrote: "The workers in Cyprus are divided and split on ethnic lines, AKEL and PEO, the Greek Cypriot trade unions do not want to cooperate with the Turkish Cypriot workers because they want ENOSIS although they are fighting over strategy amongst themselves. Turkish workers are now struggling to establish their own unions." Later on, I gravitated toward the nationalism of Dr. Fazil Kucuk, the fiery anti-British orator, the Swiss-trained physician who looked to Modern Turkey for guidance and inspiration, much to the horror of the British colonial rulers.

I enjoyed the letters I received in reply from Ozkan Jr. They were full of fresh ideas about Laski and Hobhouse the great teachers he was exposed to at LSE. My cousin's girl friend Jill was the catalyst as three of us followed Kucuk's ideas and strategies. Jill would ask the most interesting questions which in turn excited us on to learn more. Though distance separated us three, it was fascinating to learn that the tiny Turkish Cypriot leader was actually implementing grassroots democracy in line with the social justice theories of Laski and Hobhouse at LSE.

Meanwhile, at the English School they kept teaching us about English Kings and Queens and world geography. It was all useful stuff, shattering my belief that Cyprus was the center of the entire world. Overall, our teachers were rather undistinguished, except for the

# DISCOVERY

music teacher, an Armenian named Schomelian. Music was his passion and he drilled classical music into hard heads in the huge auditorium, which was his classroom as if it were army barracks and us students were cadets in his charge, learning the basics of marching in tune. Schomelian's favorite pieces were the oriental airs, Mozart's *Abduction from Seraglio* and *The Turkish March*. His instrument was the violin and he would go on forever, his eyes closed as if he was dreaming with his music, playing List and Verdi, Mozart and Beethoven, while the class listened, some enchanted but most simply bored and unappreciative. That, of course, did not matter.

I belonged to the small appreciative group. Schomelian's music nurtured a close relationship between my teacher and I. One day, in the 5$^{th}$ form and one year away from graduation, Schomelian must have judged that I was old enough to know, he asked me to stay behind after class.

"I would like to invite you to come to visit me in my home. Would you come?" I was surprised. No teacher had ever asked me for a private visit like that. I felt shy, and then replied:

"I will ask my mother," I said.

By this time, my mother was my chief mentor, showing far more interest in my school life and my studies than father who, as always, was living in his own, separate world. So long as we were fed adequately and healthy, he was satisfied, whereas mother showed a keen interest in my books as well as my friends. I always depended on her for guidance.

"OK please let me know. There is something special I wish to talk about." Schomelian said.

Mother viewed the invitation with favor. "Your teacher will reward you for good work" she said.

The next day, with mother's approval, I accepted Schomelian's invitation and later on in the afternoon the same day I went to his indistinct house in the Armenian quarter next to Arabahmet Mosque.

"Welcome" he said and showed me to a chair in his spacious living room. It was a beautifully decorated room with family heirloom and photos, antique chairs and prayer rugs on the floor. I was duly impressed.

Schomelian then offered me a cup of tea and some biscuits. He seemed alone in the house. I sat in my chair, feeling uneasy and unsure of what to expect.

As we were drinking tea and eating biscuits, Schomelian said briskly and in a cold tone as if admonishing me:
"You know, your Grandparents did horrible things to my people in Turkey." I froze. I did not understand what my music teacher was talking about.

"I am sorry sir," I said. "My Grandparents were never in Turkey."

"No, that is not it" he replied, recovering. "I do not mean your own Grandparents, but your people, Turks in Anatolia."

I am sure I must have looked totally shocked. After a moment, Schomelian went on.

He talked about forced marches and starvation of thousands of Armenian families walking through deserts to Syria and Lebanon. He went on for what looked like a long hour, maybe even longer. I just sat there, listened patiently in silence. It was starting to get late.

I knew nothing about what Schomelian was talking about. All I knew about the Armenians was that they lived in a quarter of the town, around the Arabahmet Mosque, that they spoke Turkish, which should mean that they were a friendly people, but beyond that all I could think was that they were just like any other people. There were rich Armenians like Ouzunians and a lot of poor ones making and selling *lahmacun*, the popular pastry pizza. That was about all I could remember at the time.

When finally the music teacher finished, he got up to go. He looked sad, almost ready to cry. His eyes were questioning me as if to ask: "Do you understand my pain?"

All I said was: "Is that why you play music with so much passion, your eyes closed, Sir?"

Schomelian replied: "Yes, my dear boy." He stood still and then added: "You are very bright boy, Tekin. I know you will someday become a successful man, maybe even a teacher yourself, and that is why I have asked you to come today."

Then, he went on: "I want you to promise me to remember one thing, will you?" He asked and waited for a reply.

After a pause: "Yes I will," I said.

Then Schomelian continued:

"Turks and Armenians used to be friends. That is why Armenians even today speak Turkish," he said. I nodded my head in approval. "Terrible things have happened in the past, a great injustice... many years ago." He stopped, took a deep breath. He looked as though he was about to cry, but somehow he controlled his emotions.

A full minute later, he resumed, but he had the look of a man who was about to reach a major conclusion:

"But in future they will be friends again, I know. Will you remember me and my words today?"

I stood still, motionless. Almost a minute of silence passed. Then, I promised and then got up to leave.

He walked me to the door where we stood, teacher and student, ready to part. But as I was about to exit, and began saying good-bye, I noticed a young man, maybe in his early teens, coming downstairs.

"This is my son, Armen," said Schomelian.

I smiled and acknowledged, while the young son looked with at me with surprising hostility. He did not shake hands, nor said a word of greeting. He looked angry and unfriendly. He just walked out on to the street and I thought no more about Armen. Schomelian and I stood there. The boy was troubled, and it would take years, far away in Ottawa, Canada, to find out why.

I went home to mother and reported my conversation with Schomelian and my chance encounter with his strange son.

Mother had just returned from her mother's grave. She was extremely fragile on days of her visits to Grandmothers' grave in the cemetery. Her heart was filled with her mother's grief, the mothers' love she had been denied, and healing that never took place. Aygul only heard a story that at her birth the midwife who had delivered her was Meryem, or Mariam, an old Armenian woman. But she knew nothing about Meryem's kindness in befriending and comforting grandma Emine in her moment of greatest need.

"I do not know much about the poor Armenians" she began. She was visibly in agony with her own torment.

"But I do know about pain and loss. Life, like my poor mother's, can sometimes be cruel. Nothing but suffering…" She took a deep breath and went on:

"We are all Allah's creation. Everyone is a human being, feeling joy and pain. In the Great War there was great suffering and injustice; many innocent lives were lost. I came into this world at the hands of an Armenian woman, my auntie Pembe Hanim used to tell me. When you are an adult and know more, I am sure you will understand your music teacher better." She stopped as I listened, my curiosity aroused by mother's remarks.

Next day, I went to the library searching for books on Armenians. There were none.

Time passed. I was in my final year. I had already begun to think about following cousin Ozkan in London for university studies. In fact, I had written to him on the subject. But I wanted to discuss it with mother. Our conversation took place on a day after her visit to grandma Emine's grave. Earlier on that same day, I had received a letter from cousin Ozkan Jr. in London. He was full of news of hard times in London, of suffering and devastation by German bombings, but at the same time he had good news about his own political studies. "Tekin, please I want you to know that you'd be welcome to come and stay with me," he said, adding that he was about to graduate and start working, but keeping secret his intention to marry Jill. I mentioned this to mother.

She said: "I am not surprised. I expected something like this. You, too, will go like your cousin to study to become somebody." She added for emphasis: "That is what you should do."

I appreciated that, but waited for her to continue. I felt like she had more to say.

After a brief moment, she went on: "Son, I want to share with you a family secret."

"Your cousin and I share something very dear to my heart." She said:

"What is it, mother?" I asked excitedly.

"We both lost our mothers prematurely. He and I, we never experienced mothers' love."

I looked at mother, astonished. She was having trouble controlling her emotions.

It was almost eternity before she resumed: "The two of us, cherish our mothers in secret, privately because neither of us have experienced the true love of mothers. We were not given the chance…" She was breathless. Like fish coming up for fresh air, she took a deep breath. Mother struggled to stay calm and control her tears. I was shaken, a witness to some tragic event of long ago.

She kept on: "Mary came to Cyprus all the way from London, right after the First World War when traveling was very difficult. She was looking for a man's love, your uncle's. Then something dreadful happened and she was murdered in Buyuk Han. Ozkan Jr. is like me, deprived of the love of a mother we never saw. " She stopped and then said added one more thing:

# DISCOVERY

"Remember your teacher Schomelian because in his own private way, I think maybe he is like me and Ozkan in London, we are all looking and searching for redemption, release from past sins we carry. We are travelers in a dark tunnel, but I do not know whether light exists at its end."

I got up, hugged her, and we both cried together, in silence. In that moment, I felt closest to mother, I understood her vulnerability and her deep, abiding love for me.

# XI

In March 1942 my mother finally got her revenge on her hated father. Grandfather Halil and his last wife, Sevda now almost fifteen years married, but still childless, both suddenly died from food poisoning. It happened in the middle of the War, when things were going particularly badly for the British and the Monty's Desert Rats were being chased in the deserts of Libya by Hitler's armies. England needed help desperately from Turkey, now solidly under the rule of the timid, or cautious Ismet Inonu. It was right after the big meeting in Nicosia between Foreign Minister Anthony Eden and his Turkish counterpart Sukru Saracoglu.

The town was decked in flags, Turkish and Union Jacks everywhere. Uncle Munir and his English friends were all smiles and properly attired for the big occasion. Turkish Cypriots were in a celebration mood hoping, and some praying, for an Anglo-Turkish alliance. On the day of the meeting between the two Ministers, the people were especially excited, shouting "Long live Turkey, Long live England" and school children waved their paper flags and pictures of the new King as Turkish war planes flew low over in the sky.

But it was not to be. Ismet Inonu, never one to take any risk, however small, refused the British request for Turkish help. Failure of the talks was bad news for uncle Munir who expected an alliance and friendship between Ankara and London. It never happened.

# DISCOVERY

Then, at that same moment, a worse turn of events was unfolding nearby in Grandfather Halil's house on Tanzimat Street.

That morning father arrived for work early in the morning for crowd control duty during the Foreign Ministers meeting. The celebration was over and everybody went home or to work and normal life returned to the town. Father did not see his father-in-law in the crowd and he thought it odd, because a patriot like Halil would surely be there, waving the Turkish flag and shouting patriotic slogans. Later on he and his fellow officers went back to the police headquarters and thought no more about Halil's absence. His father-in-law, now in his mid-fifties but still enjoying a reputation as a jolly fellow, famed for his sexual exploits, was the subject of occasional gossip.

"Ozkan, how is your old man?" said some one casually.

"The old playboy is probably celebrating," suggested the next, before father could reply that he did not know.

Two more hours passed, and father's duty was over. He decided to walk the short distance to Grandfather's house on Tanzimat Street. He had not seen his father-in-law for a long time, mainly out of deference to Aygul's resentment of him, lately turned into hate for her father's injustice at taking on yet another wife.

Father was back at the headquarters within half hour with the bad news. He was truly alarmed and in shock.

"Both Halil and his wife are dead, lying in bed." He reported to the duty Sergeant as his friends gathered around the Sergeant to catch the news of Grandfather Halil.

"What happened? Tell us what you saw and found," ordered the Sergeant. Father had little information to report.

"I do not exactly know, sir" he began. He explained quickly that he had to break the front door to get in after his repeated knocks produced no response. Neighbors came and said they knew nothing, saw nothing unusual all night before and till that moment. "No one came, no one entered, everything looked normal" said a neighbor.

Then the bodies were sent for autopsy. Later on, the awful result was announced: death by food poisoning by a heavy doze of arsenic. It looked premeditated murder, but there was absolutely no evidence of a plot or motive. Pending new evidence that might come up later, the case was shelved. For now, there was nothing much to be done in the police station.

## UZUN ALI, SHAME AND SALVATION

Poor father, he went home to Aygul in Kuruchesme and conveyed the shocking news. Mother broke into a hysterical outburst at the news of her father's death. It was a strange mixture of grief and vindication, something father was hard put to comprehend. He just stood by and watched the weird response of his wife.

"Oh my Allah" she would say one moment, "what a terrible thing to do. What have I done to deserve this misery?" She made it sound as if it was her own fault.

And, then in the next moment, she would cry: "The bastard is gone, may he burn in Hell." Clearly mother was in an emotional mess.

Father just stood there and watched in shock as his wife alternated between pain and remorse mixed with revenge. It went on for days. Officially, the family was in mourning. But it was without any feeling. The neighbors came and expressed condolences, and like mother, we all went through the motions of acknowledging Grandfather's death.

Mother's days of self-inflicted torment continued. One morning she would cry hysterically as if her father had been the dearest soul in her life; the next she would utter voice of revenge for her long-lost mother, speaking in a voice from her dear mother's grave that the tormentor was finally gone, that justice was finally done. Mother's last act on the matter of her father's sudden death was to make sure his grave was at the further possible location in the public graveyard in Nicosia.

Actually the old womanizer was the victim of an Ottoman-Byzantine type of jealousy and revenge, a planned conspiracy carried out secretly and effectively. Sevda was as jealous as Halil's first wife, but far smarter. When Halil continued his fun-loving, plundering ways in the red-light district with new and younger prostitutes, at first she decided to contain the sex hunger of her irrepressible husband at home. She experimented with perfume and sexy nightgowns, but nothing seemed to work. Halil's desire for variety was incurable. For his part, Halil behaved indifferently toward Sevda; he never rejected her. Sevda thought, quite naively, that she could then ration her sexual availability to Halil, but that made things worse. Sweet talk, too, got her nowhere.

So, in the end, when at last she could bear no more neighbors' demeaning gossip, she concluded that Halil was a lost case. Rather than share him with prostitutes, it was better to bring to a sudden end

# DISCOVERY

both their lives. She administered arsenic in their dinner, their last supper, which was followed by furious sex, one last time before slow but sure death.

***

Grandfather Halil was one of the last Ottomans of the old school in Nicosia. His womanizing ways had brought death and destruction to several innocent female lives, my grandma Emine and the unfortunate Maronite girl Elana. It brought a lifetime of misery to my dear mother Aygul, scaring her forever for the torture and injustice he inflicted on the hapless Emine whose love he never neither acknowledged nor appreciated. His male world contained no room for female respect; he had no understanding of fidelity. The old hedonist sought love outside, in cheap places, because, as an Ottoman to his final days he confused love with sex, and mistook fidelity for female weakness. For Grandfather women belonged in the harem and he knew not how to deal with a modern woman like Sevda, nor one brought up in the classic mould as a submissive Ottoman homemaker.

Like other Ottomans of his generation, Grandfather Halil did not understand the modern world, and he died in decadence, a victim of his own folly. His sins, their sins scarred others who deserved tender love but instead were burdened with shame and disgrace.

***

My sister Sevgi, meanwhile, was doing well in the secondary school, developing a keen interest in Ottoman history. The person behind Sevgi's attraction to history was a Turkish teacher from Ankara, Zeynep Burdurlu, a dedicated early feminist from Kemalist Turkey whose mission in life seemed to be to discover bright young women for university education so women might be as educated as men and contribute to modern nation-building in the footsteps of Mustafa Kemal Ataturk. Zeynep, originally from the town of Burdur in western Anatolia, was a recent graduate of the Faculty of Languages and Social Sciences at Ankara University and was seconded for a year's assignment in Cyprus.

It must have been towards the end of 1943. On a cold, wintry day, Sevgi came to me for help with an assignment she was working on the history of the transfer of Cyprus from the Ottomans to the British.

"Dear brother" she began, "I am puzzled. I do not understand why the Sultan allowed it?" I looked at her, surprise and sadness written all over her youthful face.

"What is it Sevgi? What do you not understand?" I asked.

"If the British wanted to help the Sultan against the Russians, how did giving Cyprus help anyone? The island is so far away from the Russian border." I must say Sevgi's logic was impeccable and I was, for a moment, perplexed myself.

"You are absolutely right," I admitted. "It is a good question. All I can say is you must check it out. Go to the library and read on it all you can."

"I already have" she said, "with guidance from Zeynep Hoca, my teacher."

"Well, what did you find?" I asked.

"Not much" she said. "Apparently, the island was transferred in a secret convention and it was kept under wraps. Resistance was expected from the Ottoman subjects on the island against the deal and so the Sultan's advisors decided to say as little on the matter as possible."

I must say I was impressed. Sevgi was already on the way to becoming a future academic historian, a keen, inquiring mind, willing to turn every stone for answers to embarrassing or difficult questions.

She went on: "I also talked to mother about it, and then I went to father." As my interest in the subject increased, she continued: "What I learnt from her is that there is a family connection to this whole sordid affair."

Now, my interest was really aroused. "How can it be? What kind of family connection" I inquired.

My younger sister, displaying a great deal of excitement about my own curiosity in her assignment, went on:

"I learnt a great deal from father. Our Grandfather Uzun Ali was the Kaimakam of Milltown at the time. Father has only faint memories, but he recalled that Grandfather had lost his job and fortune when the British became masters of the island. Uzun Ali was demoralized and died a broken man. Father recalls that his father was angry at the Sultan and felt betrayed."

I listened with amazement. Then I collected my thoughts and said to Sevgi:

# DISCOVERY

"Dear sister, what you have done and what you are learning is important. Keep it up. Pursue your inquiry. I am sure you will discover something no one knows about our past, our family roots."

I did not know at the time, but later on, many years later in Ankara, Sevgi confided in me that my words had the impact of a revolution upon her, stimulating her love of Ottoman social history in general, kindling a lifelong project in discovering our family heritage buried in Ottoman history.

\*\*\*

In London, later on the same year, cousin Ozkan Jr. graduated from LSE with high honors. Uncle Munir very much wanted to go to London for the graduation ceremony, but wartime conditions prevented a reunion between father and son. Actually there were also pressing social and political action that required uncle Munir's presence in Nicosia. He had now become a close associate of Dr. Fazil Kucuk, the nationalist leader now editing *Halkin Sesi,* the newspaper financed by the Ankara government as a voice of Kemalism in Cyprus. Kucuk declared war, a publicity war, on the colonial masters of Cyprus for the pitiful lack of progress and modernization of the Turkish Cypriot community. At long last, after two decades of struggle, uncle Munir realized his aim of ending polygamy when the British gave in and passed a modern family law.

By then, the politics in Cyprus was changing fast. The end of the War brought peace and reconstruction in Europe, but it opened a period of violence and bloodshed in Cyprus.

# XII

While cousin Ozkan Jr was learning his Machiavelli in wartime London, two Greek Cypriots were busily plotting Machiavellian conspiracies. Their actions led to bloodshed and death in Cyprus, on much larger scale than Halil's womanizing misdeeds. Now the conspiring Greeks took the center stage: coups and campaigns of violence and death followed.

The War had ended and the British were victorious. But England was in ruins. People were exhausted and wanted a new beginning. Peace and reconstruction were orders of the day and politicians were busy planning, taking advantage of generous US aid to put devastated economies back on their feet. Churchill was gone; Attlee's Labor was at the helm.

Schemers and revolutionaries, however, were just as busy. Makarios and Grivas behaved like spoiled children, declaring war on the mighty British Empire. It was sheer arrogance. The two master schemers could not have been more dissimilar, one a man of the cloth, a prince of the Greek Orthodox Church, soon to be crowned Archbishop and Ethnarch in Cyprus. The other a Colonel in the Greek Army, schooled on fascism fighting the communists in the Greek civil war, a hero to some; each outdid the other in their passion for ENOSIS, uniting Cyprus to the center of Hellenism.

Their dreams and passions drove each in separate ways to start with. While Grivas created his secret network of terror to be launched against the unsuspecting British colonial masters in Cyprus, Makarios, as soon as he was given the mantle of Mylonas, the hero of 1931, organized a Church plebiscite getting an almost unanimous support from the congregation, to legitimize his demand for ENOSIS against an unwilling Britain. The British had stolen Cyprus from the Ottomans back in 1878. So why can't the Greeks steal it now from the British?

In the early fifties, with the scars of the European War behind, and Germany already showing signs of a miraculous economic rebirth, EOKA, the Greek Cypriot terror organization, was busy, secretly preparing guerrilla warfare to kick the British out in favor of ENOSIS. Underground networks in Athens and all over the island were in full gear, raising funds, procuring arms for the coming war, and shipping in secretly boatloads of guns and ammunition. Hundreds of volunteers were in training, learning how to make and throw Molotovs and operate machine guns and bazookas, and lay surprise ambush attacks on British soldiers. Killing in the process was a necessity; not just British soldiers and colonial administrators; they were the obvious enemy targets. But even more significant was the reign of terror to be launched against those public enemies within the ranks, the Greek Cypriot peasants and the business tycoons who got filthy rich during the war selling at outrageous prices to the imperialists!

Grivas had learnt his lessons well in the Greek Civil War, when Greek killed Greek, ruthlessly and unashamedly. It was to be repeated in Cyprus, a decade later in order to force everyone to obey Grivas and support his violent campaign for ENOSIS now.

Grivas, with support from Makarios and fascists in Greece, had set up an underground terror group, EOKA, recruiting school children to fight the British army. Violence suddenly exploded on April 1, the Fool's Day in 1955, while Makarios was launching his diplomatic action plan for ENOSIS internationally. He went in all directions, courting with Communism, with capitalism and with others in between. He went to Bandung, in the newly independent Indonesia in his impressive black robes, dining with Chou en Lai, Nehru and host Sukarno, fresh from his own nationalist victory against the Dutch; here in the beautiful, cool Indonesian highlands, Makarios observed first hand how a federal state originally could be transformed into a unitary state by strong leadership.

## UZUN ALI, SHAME AND SALVATION

"First get the British out. You can have the unitary state you want after."

That is precisely what Sukarno had done against the Dutch. Sukarno had achieved a unitary state in Indonesia in two steps. Initially he had to agree to a United Indonesian Federation merely to kick the Dutch out. Once this was accomplished there was nothing to prevent him from staging a coup, abolishing the Federation and declaring a unitary Indonesia, his dream from his youth.

Makarios learnt well because when, finally the time came for the British to hand over power not just to Greek Cypriots, but also the Turkish Cypriots as well, he signed the independence agreement, only to disown it a couple of years later, employing Sukarno's easy trick. Actually, neither Makarios nor Grivas ever considered in their devious minds that they might have to share power with the Turkish Cypriots.

***

Unaware of all these Byzantine games, right after the War, in 1946 my own life underwent a momentous change. I went to London to live with cousin Ozkan Jr, now married happily to Jill. I was admitted into the engineering program at University College, London.

In Cyprus, after graduation from English School, I had worked for a couple of years to save for university education and finally I arrived at the Victoria Station in August to Ozkan's warm welcome and a brand new chapter began in the life of the Uzun Ali family. Like the rest of Europe, London was in ruins from years of war and conflict. Germany was divided and in ruins, but life in London was only slightly better. The Allied victory did not improve living conditions overnight. Food was in short supply and everywhere there were signs of destruction, destitution and hard times.

***

Cousin Ozkan, now 26, had married Jill shortly after graduation, four years ago while the war against Hitler was raging. All Europe was in flames and the wedding was a low-key affair. Shortly afterwards, Ozkan joined the Royal Air Force which was being reorganized and provided with new Canadian built single engine mosquitoes to take revenge for the devastation of London that Hitler had caused. Ozkan

## DISCOVERY

was sent off to an air base in Sussex where he was assisting in fueling and equipping mosquitoes on their nightly bombing raids over Germany. He was hearing terrible news from the pilots, how cities like Dresden were bombed out, factories and all, with innocent people dying like animals. Churchill got his revenge against Hitler who, not to be outdone, had carried terrible atrocities against the Jews of Germany. All Europe was in madness as Man's Inhumanity against Man raged in full force.

After the War, the people in London and all over Europe were sick and tired of war. Churchill had been a hero, no doubt, but now that the fighting was at last finished and the slaughtering stopped, everywhere there was a wish for peace. Ozkan and Jill became schoolteachers. Teaching was not Ozkan's preferred choice, but jobs were hard to find and it was even more difficult for a non-native like Ozkan. He wanted to go into private business and get rich. For the time being, however, that was no more than a pipedream.

My arrival in London coincided with these changes. Of course, my reception was nothing but warm and hospitable. I was following in my cousin's footstep, eager to proceed to university education. It was an emotional reunion at the Victoria Rail Station between the two cousins. Jill was at home expecting their second child, and looking after their three- year old son Erol, a name that was both English and Turkish and therefore held particular significance. Just six months earlier, they had moved out of their rented flat in Bloomsbury into a nice three bedroom bungalow they had bought in Golders' Green in a Jewish neighborhood peopled by émigrés lucky enough to have escaped Hitler's ovens.

That night we did not sleep; but talked, going over childhood memories and family news. Although I was exhausted from the journey, cousin Ozkan was eager for news of family in Cyprus, his father, uncle and my mother Aygul, and life in general during and after the war.

"How is my dad?" He began right after dinner and as soon Jill left the two of us alone and went to put Erol to bed.

"He is well" I replied. "Actually he is doing quite well. His practice is flourishing as always, but lately in addition he is now very active in public life" I said and summarized his political activity especially his work for the elimination of polygamy and the passage of modern family law.

"How are your parents and sister?" asked Ozkan.

"My parents are fine. Sevgi is doing really well at school, very keen on history. She wants to study Turkish history at a Turkish university in Ankara. She is keen to learn how the British snatched Cyprus from the Sultan."

Then somewhat uneasily I passed on to the less happy news. I talked about mother Aygul.

"My mother seems much better now that her father is no longer alive" I said haltingly. I was unsure of the impact of my words on the touchy subject of mothers on my cousin.

"Oh! What happened?" asked Ozkan concerned. "I did not know that Aunt Aygul had problems with her father," He said truthfully.

"Yes, major problems, related to her childhood" I began, summarizing what I had heard from mother herself. "Mother grew up as an abandoned child. It was all a strange relationship, apparently having to do with his womanizing in the old days, and how Grandfather Halil had terrorized grandma Emine, whom I never saw. Come to think of it, my mother never saw her either. In fact, as I understand it, that was the essence of my mother's problem: she was denied her mother's love and affection. That, I am afraid, scarred mother for life."

Then cousin Ozkan became visibly uncomfortable. He stood silent for a rather long interlude. Then he made a confession.

"I can relate to that," he said from the depth of his heart. Both of us sat in silence. Minutes passed. I looked at my cousin, lost in his thoughts. Sadness was written all over my cousin's face. My words had opened a deep wound in his psyche, bringing to him memories of growing up in the convent in Dublin, lonely and abandoned until rescued by a father seeking his own redemption.

Then he began:

"It reminds me of my own rejection in those early days in the convent in Dublin" he said haltingly, and stopped. The two of us sat in silence for what looked like a long time, and both wanting to change topics, recalling happier childhood memories. But we remained silent for want of words. In truth, I was now curious.

Suddenly, he looked at me and smiled, and said: "Remember Tekin, that time in Xero, when dad and I came visiting you. You were no more than five at the time and we went near some tennis court." He looked at me waiting for confirmation.

"Yes, of course," I said, "I remember the day well."

# DISCOVERY

"I never understood the anger of the tennis player. We did the right thing, but still got into trouble," said Ozkan Jr.

Then I spoke my mind. "It was my first lesson about justice," I said. "In my heart we had done the right thing, returning the ball to its rightful owner, but the fellow judged us guilty. Funny thing, I have often asked myself: What is Justice? Whatever it is, you can feel it clearly in your head, but it means nothing if others believe differently."

Ozkan replied: "You know, in London I have often thought about the same thing. Often people here make up their minds too fast; I do not know whether it is prejudice or lack of information. I feel an invisible distance that separates me from the English."

After a moment, he continued: "Justice is an elusive thing," he said, his mind gravitating on his own mother and her murder in Buyuk Han. He obviously had thought on this emotional subject many times, and had reached his own practical conclusion: "I think we have to overcome our insecurities and make the best of the opportunities that come our way; we cannot live in the past. We owe it to our parents to do better than they did" he said bravely.

Ozkan's understanding of justice was shaped by his mother Mary's sacrifice. He had visited her grave in Dublin as soon as he was in London, but it was for him Buyuk Han in Nicosia that represented Mary's sacrifice. It was the one secret buried in his heart that he dared not share even with me. I could sense that he desperately wanted to share his innermost thoughts with me. But some invisible force held him back.

"Have you been to the Buyuk Han?" is all he could bring himself to ask about the place that Ozkan Jr. had made his own secret temple. I felt his pain as I replied in sadness:

"Well, yes I see it every time I go the bazaar. It is, am afraid, very much in ruin now. It ceased to be an inn many years ago." Silence ensued and then Ozkan said:

"Tekin it is lovely having you here" and we got up and hugged in an emotional union, which was amazingly comforting.

No more was said that night. The two cousins went to bed, heavy in heart on the unresolved question of justice, but glad to be reunited.

# XIII

It was several days after my emotional reunion with Ozkan Jr. I was having lunch in the college refectory, enjoying a rare treat in those days, a piece of roast chicken. The place was crowded, and another fellow came and sat at the table opposite, unannounced and with no word of greeting. I took no notice, for I was lost in my own world thinking privately while enjoying my chicken. I did not even realize that I was holding a drumstick in my hand, biting off a chunk of the well-done meat on the bone.

Suddenly the man opposite spoke in an unfriendly tone: "Tell me, young man" he said, "what do they feed dogs in your country?"

I was shocked by this unexpected rudeness. His words embarrassed me and I stopped eating. I looked in his eyes. His face was pink and pale; he looked sickly. Without thinking, my eyes focused on the fish-and-chips in front of him, as words came out of my mouth:

"Fish and chips!" The words had a devastating impact. The pink and pale fellow opposite now had a red face.

The fellow was stupefied. I got up and left, my lunch unfinished. Privately, I felt vindicated, but almost instantly I felt sorry for the fellow.

\*\*\*

## DISCOVERY

I thought about this incident all afternoon. I felt miserable and came home early and started reading Cronin on social justice. I was transported to a world of Harley Street doctors getting rich plying fake medicine and prescriptions on affluent middle and upper middle class patients with more money than brains. These doctors, it seemed to me, would do anything for money, take the law in their own hands and even play God with hapless patients. It was amazing how little professional ethics they seemed to possess. They were not Cronin's heroes; like him, I identified with the country physicians, generous and dedicated to saving the lives of poor miners in Wales or simple peasants in rural communities in Yorkshire or Scotland. The inequalities of the English class system appalled me, with the nobility at the top, and City tycoons and Harley Street doctors desperately trying to join them in their pursuit of decadence. The remarkable thing, the paradox of it all, was that ordinary fellows, like the one with fish-and-chips, wished to emulate the decadent nobility, the robber barons and the Harley Street doctors, who, in their expensive and exclusive clubs in Mayfair and Piccadilly gambled away and played with loose women, not much different than Uzun Ali's Harem in Milltown long ago. It was all so depressing, and lonely.

My first two years of engineering studies in London passed uneventfully, interspaced with visits to Ozkan Jr. I adjusted to the hardships of the immediate post-War, staying focused on my studies.

*** 

Then I met Elizabeth Mann of Lyme Regis, Dorset. She was also studying at University College and we met after a chemistry class in which I was stimulated to ask a question. The lecturer was impressed with my question. So apparently was Elizabeth as well.

"Excuse me" she came and talked to me after class. I looked at the pretty young girl, smiling and looking at me with obvious interest. She obviously lacked no self-confidence, what she lacked was knowledge of Chemistry. "I am Elizabeth Mann" she introduced herself, adding "and a student having lots of problems with Chemistry. Can you please help a damsel in distress?" Elizabeth decided that I was to be her private tutor in Chemistry. She was used to getting what she wanted.

I looked at the pretty face. She projected calm beauty and confidence. She had long, blonde hair and lovely blue eyes. She was smartly and expensively dressed, obviously a young woman from a wealthy family.

I must say I was taken aback by her abruptness, but her smile and looks conveyed a charming attraction. We walked into a coffee shop nearby. Over coffee I agreed to meet her twice a week and help her in Chemistry.

My life changed in the following weeks. Our relationship grew, going beyond Chemistry, meeting on weekends, going to movies and plays. I liked her company, her warm and friendly personality. She suggested that I call her Lizzy. I sense that beyond my native intelligence she found me exotic and mysterious. In any event, we became friends. Within a month, at Spring break, I was on the train to Dorset for a long weekend visit with Lizzy and the Manns, a farming family with a large estate near the Dorset-Devon boundary. It was Thomas Hardy country and that was an added attraction for me. We agreed we would visit the cottage where the author lived and wrote.

The visit began promisingly, but ended in disaster. It rained almost the entire weekend and we did visit the Hardy sites that I so much wanted. Then I discovered that Elizabeth's handicap was not limited to Chemistry. At home, she was not the confident girl she had been in London. Instead, the poor girl was completely under her mother's domination. She could not make up her mind on anything unless mother proposed or suggested it.

The Manns were hospitable and kind. Mrs. Mann, a kind former nurse who was straight out of Jane Austen, dominated the family. Her mission in life was finding a suitable husband for Elizabeth, their sole offspring. Mrs. Mann was rather embarrassed of her own lowly social origins and wanted to climb up the social ladder. She was duly impressed with my intellectual achievements, having been lectured on these by Lizzy, but what counted the most with Mrs. Mann was that I was the grandson of local nobility, the Kaimakam Uzun Ali of Milltown

"Oh, Lizzy dear, you must go visiting Lady Osborne and introduce Tekin" she would instruct her, assuming that was exactly my wish. Then, later on before dinner, she would order her much older husband: "Dear Tom, be a dear, go down to the cellar and bring two bottles of burgundy; it will go so well with the roast lamb." Tom dutifully did what he was assigned on this occasion and on all others.

Mrs. Mann enthusiasm and her desire to control all around knew

## DISCOVERY

no bounds nor did she tolerate any excuses. If and when I expressed a desire to sit and enjoy a moment of quiet near the fireplace, Mrs. Mann would come practically yelling: "Dear Boy, there you are. You must be bored, sitting there all alone. Where is Lizzy? Eli—za –beth" she would yell, "come here right now and entertain your guest" Everyone had to fall in to sustain peace.

On the last evening at the Mann farm, I was especially uncomfortable. Mrs. Mann, always in control, pulled me aside, after a huge dinner, and bluntly asked: "Well! Young man, what do you think of Elizabeth? She is a lovely girl isn't she? I am sure some eligible man will soon snatch her up. I would act fast, if I were you."

I was stupefied and could find no words to say. I just stood there, looking foolish and embarrassed.

On the train back to London, at the end of an unhappy weekend, I realized that Elizabeth was a lovely girl, but not my type. We stopped meeting. I concentrated on my studies with finals approaching fast.

*\*\*\**

Then I met my ideal girl. She was Eleanor Kirk of Windsor, Ontario, Canada. It was one month before my graduation, in June 1948. I was still undecided what to do, whether to return to Cyprus or stay in England and try to get an engineering job. I had no idea then, but clearly I stood at a turning point in my life. My meeting with Eleanor was one of those mysterious events that mere mortals may not fully comprehend. I am not a superstitious person, but I have often wondered since our chance meeting in London, whether some unseen or divine force had pulled Eleanor and I together. At that time I was 22 and she was 16 with her family, her father a young professor of sociology spending a sabbatical in the London School of Economics. She was finishing high school and the family lived in Highgate in North London, not far from the statue of Karl Marx.

It was a Saturday in May; I was feeling homesick and exhausted with studying, so I decided to dine at my favorite Armenian restaurant on D'Arby Street, Soho. I was sitting alone in a table in the poorly lit specious restaurant. It was mid-afternoon and the place was virtually empty, with just one family dining. The Kirk family was enjoying their *kebabs* and *dolmas* at the next table. I first noticed Eleanor from her excitement over whatever she was having and enjoying so much.

Then I noticed her beauty. She had stunning blue eyes, blonde and smooth skin, long and smooth hair that came down practically to her shoulders. She was vibrant and vocal, enjoying the Turkish food prepared by expert Armenian cook with obvious relish.

"Mom, try this, you'll love it" making her try the pastry. Or, she would say "Oh! This is wonderful, have some dad. I do not know what it is, but it tastes delicious."

I just stood there, watching and admiring silently the joy coming from the next table. It was captivating witnessing so much delight at the strangers' table with my own favorite dishes. I just could not restrain myself.

"It is *yalanci dolma,* liars' dolma," I volunteered from my table. Eleanor was the first to respond: "Why is it called liars' *dolma*?" she wanted to know with genuine curiosity.

"Because it contains no meat." The Kirks were impressed and I was then subjected to more questions. Then I introduced myself.

Soon I was engaged in a dialogue. It was friendly and appreciative. The Kirks showered me with questions about this plate and that. The Armenian waiter was sidelined, and he did not mind as some new customers walked in. Within minutes I was invited to join the Kirks at their table and immediately I became their cultural interpreter. I could not decide who was more interested in me, the sociologist father, the mother who had seemed to adore everything Turkish, or Eleanor who loved anything exotic, which, at that point, is what I must have represented for her.

By the end of dinner, I began to feel something warm and special with Eleanor. It was her looks, the way she would fix her penetrating eyes on me, looking straight at me. She projected a genuine interest in whatever I was saying. I then noticed her blue eyes and her well-rounded red lips. Gradually, the table talk was transformed into a private two-some conversation. I soon learnt about the Kirks, what they were doing in London and, most of all, I sensed that Eleanor found me attractive.

It was my final month before my graduation. The Kirk's return to Windsor, Canada was about the same time. Our romance blossomed during those four weeks.

I saw Eleanor several times, taking her to the theater and out to dinner. It was platonic as we both shared a strong sense of social justice, of doing the right thing, standing up for the small guy. It came

# DISCOVERY

from her father, John Kirk, who had a special interest, as a professional sociologist, in the rights of minorities. At the LSE he was writing a thesis on self-government amongst the Canadian native population, and the Kirks, without exception, took an interest in my origin as a Turkish Cypriot. The Kirks, but especially Eleanor, had a keen interest in other cultures and peoples. We spent long hours talking about history, music but most of all, about the great social issues of the day, independence for African nations, the newly created United Nations and, of course, the rise of the Labor Party in England.

Eleanor changed my life. Before the month was gone, I decided to apply for a job with Ford Automobile Company in Windsor and within weeks, as soon as I got my degree in mechanical engineering, first class, I began preparations to travel with Eleanor and the Kirks on the liner to Canada.

*\*\*\**

In the midst of my preparations for departure for Canada, a reply arrived from my sister Sevgi in Ankara. I had written to her, as well as to mother in Cyprus, briefly explaining my decision to go to Canada. Sevgi's letter was full of enthusiasm and heart-warming news, which I would like to share with you, dear reader.

"Dear Elder Brother,

I hope this letter finds you well and in good spirits. I am fine in Ankara, completing my first year at the Faculty of Sciences and Arts of the Ankara University. Thanks to my teacher Zeynep Hanim, I came here almost a year ago as a scholarship student and the past year has been just wonderful. I visit her occasionally as she now lives and works here in the capital. In fact, she has become principal of a Lycee in Samanpazari, a quarter not far from university.

Our faculty is in a brand new building, huge and impressive, overlooking the Youth Park in the center of the city. Ankara is a modern town, with clean and wide boulevards and parks. I have many wonderful friends and we often go walking in the Park, which is full of trees and ponds. About five kilometers away from the downtown, there is the massive Mausoleum on a hill. It is Ataturk's tomb that dominates Ankara's skyline.

I love my studies and books. I am majoring in Ottoman history, this year concentrating on the period of expansion and conquest. Next year we will study the period of decline from 17th century on. I am now busy learning to read and write Ottoman. It is so extremely complex with so many letters and sounds. Also, there are so many rules for formal writing, which is how the Court proceedings and formal documents are written. Within the year, I expect to be able to decipher these documents, which we are required to utilize in our essays.

It is too early for me to even think about post-graduate work, but as you know, our uncle Munir, years ago, provided a generous education fund for you and me as well as pension fund for mother Aygul. Ankara is amazingly cheap and food is plentiful, but still money is needed to cover my books and other daily expenses. I am so grateful to our uncle for giving me this opportunity. Without his help, I would not be here.

How is cousin Ozkan? Please give him my best wishes. I learnt about your plans to go to Canada to work for the famous Ford Company. It must be exciting. Please do write and give me your news. Staying in touch with you is so important to me.

With loving affection, your sister Sevgi."

I wrote back to my sister immediately. I decided to write her a short and frank letter, explaining my situation as clearly as possible, especially my decision to go to Canada rather than return home in Cyprus.

"Dear Sister Sevgi,

Your letter was wonderful and it cheered me up no end. Here in London, it rains most of the time, not like sunny Cyprus. As well, life is difficult with food rations and economic hardship widespread. People have suffered greatly during the war, but now with demobilization, finding jobs is not easy. That is one reason why I am glad to be going to Canada to work for Ford Company in Windsor.

I must tell you the main reason for my going to Canada is Eleanor Kirk, a beautiful Canadian girl I met quite by chance here in London. Her father is a sociologist spending a year at the London School of Economics, the same place that cousin Ozkan studied. I thought of returning to Cyprus, but as a qualified Engineer, I feel I must gain international experience. And, from what I gather, Canada is a vast country with huge opportunities for qualified persons like me. Of course, Eleanor is the main reason and I do hope you and mother in Cyprus will not object to what my heart compels me to do.

Please stay in touch and write to me about your studies and life in Ankara. You seem to be very happy, pursuing the academic interests dear to your own heart. I am very glad about this and wish you all the best in your studies in Ottoman history. Perhaps you will discover important findings about our family, from documents written in the old Ottoman script."

I also wrote another letter to mother, but I was sure she would understand as she always did when it came to deciding about my future.

In the afternoon I visited cousin Ozkan and Jill and we said our good-byes. "We shall meet again, soon I hope." I said, but unsure when. I shared with them Sevgi's news and we agreed to stay in touch by mail.

That night, for the last time in London, I met Eleanor in our usual spot at Piccadilly and we went to dinner and show. It was a fitting good-bye to wartime London that had been my home for the last four years.

# XIV

Moving from London to a new life in Canada was relatively easy; adjusting to Windsor in the southern tip of Ontario was much harder. Unlike its English prototype, Windsor, Ontario was a lunch-bucket town, a blue-collar cultural hinterland, under the shadow of the American car-metropolis Detroit across the river.

The Kirks lived in Walkerville, an Edwardian suburb of Windsor which itself was unique as the southernmost location in Canada, actually located below the USA. It was the underbelly of the center of the American car industry, with its large Black community. The University at which Mr. Kirk taught sociology was several miles distant from Walkerville, next to the Ambassador Bridge over Detroit River that was the international border between the two countries.

Windsorites suffered from a double inferiority complex: their town was dwarfed by the bigger, metropolitan US city on the American side, and with no cultural life of their own, they felt like an orphan, poor and unattractive compared to the vibrant American city to the North over the river. Detroit is where the rich people lived, made rich by the auto industry. Detroit's skyscrapers were an awesome sight, while Windsor had ugly railway sidings and derelict riverfront. It was a widespread custom for the rich Americans from Detroit to come over to poor Windsor, park their car under the bridge near the University and admire the pretty Detroit skyscrapers especially in moonlit nights. That photographic view concealed all the violence and crime and ugly underworld in the Black neighborhoods and crime-infested downtown.

Walkerville was different, a charming town within a city. It had class. People lived in mansions, not houses. All this wealth, however, was the result of some illegal trade, strangely American in character and origin. Walkerville, the outwardly impressive town was a place built on whiskey running. This was the illegal liquor trade during the 1920s, directly as a result of the prohibition days, when puritanical politicians imposed a ban on the manufacturing and selling of whiskey. As a result, the Italian mafia, led by such notorious figures such as Al Capone, controlled an illegal whiskey trade across the Canadian border. Whiskey flowed one way, huge amounts of money flowed the other way into Walkerville. All those lovely Edwardian houses and mansions in Walkerville were financed from whiskey running across the Detroit River.

"There are still valuable treasures of whisky lying in that river" was a favorite joke circulating in the town. Whiskey and Canadian rye smelt heavily in the air of Walkerville when I arrived there shortly after the war. In Windsor, around the University, the air smelt of pollution with poisonous gases blowing from the power stations on the American shore of Detroit River. On both sides, the riverfront was in a terrible state, full of warehouses and dirty railroad machinery. It was ugly but in the lunch-box town, no one seemed to mind.

The air was foul. Clouds of heavy smoke bellowed out of the huge power plant chimneys and the winds carried them over Windsor and Walkersville. "How can people breathe this foul air?" I asked the Kirks as soon as we arrived. "Oh! You get used to it" was the answer, which satisfied no one. Later on I found out that it killed lots of people. In those days, environmental quality was not yet a public concern.

My first impression of the Ford Motor Company was not much better. The workers were provincial, accepting their status or station in life as working class. Each group belonged to a specific ethnic community. The French Canadians lived in the poorer district in east end; the large Italian immigrant community lived next to the French Canadians; the English, clearly the dominant group, lived around the University, and in South Windsor. Italians were interspaced between the French and English, and they soon developed their own ethnic institutions, from Churches to restaurants. Everyone called Windsor a

## UZUN ALI, SHAME AND SALVATION

"lunch bucket" town, because it was a blue-collar town, every one taking to work a box of spam sandwiches, sometimes upgraded to chicken or turkey, and all worked in a pattern of well defined shifts, like armies of ants, performing set tasks dictated by the machines. There were machines for every operation: pressing, cutting, shaping and installing. Machines regulated workers; it was called automation!

In Windsor then, there was no room for thinking. Routine and conformity dominated life. Sunday was a day of Church and rest. While churchgoers attended service, most slept till midday, and then spent most of the afternoon in the numerous pubs and bars, drinking beer.

Routine and conformity were not things to my liking. I detested boredom. Wartime London was difficult, but it had culture. Windsor was the boondocks. I disliked the place right from the start. There was only one exception: my girlfriend Eleanor. She made it all worthwhile. She was in her last year of high school; a good student and both her parents wished her to go to University. Had it not been for me being there, Eleanor would have studied English at her hometown university. But no sooner than I arrived in Windsor, than Eleanor decided to quit Windsor. Actually it was me, I must admit. Within three month I decided to quit Windsor, submitted my resignation from Ford, while Eleanor made plans to enter the University of Toronto. I was overqualified for the big motor company in Windsor. I had no trouble finding a job in Toronto, and ended up with Ontario Hydro.

\*\*\*

Yet, another chapter in my life started. This time I was not alone. With dear Eleanor we started afresh in the capital of Ontario in November 1948. It was after the war, and signs of demobilization were evident everywhere, soldiers returning home, many with war brides. Downtown Toronto was still a traditional, conservative town, locally known, as Hogtown for its unappealing appearance. It was nevertheless the business hub of the province and very much a competitor for Montreal as the pre-eminent city of Canada. It was before the influx of non-British "ethnics." Toronto then was boringly British, mostly Irish, Scot and English, each community strictly organized as a distinct religious congregation. "Like the Ottoman *millets* or like *mahalles*" I thought. All observed Sundays as the Lord's Day of rest and mandatory Church going. "Toronto the good" was the image everyone joked

# DISCOVERY

and accepted, especially in the pubs that were as numerous as churches. The other thing all Torontonians shared was their love of their ice hockey team, *Maple Leafs*; they were passionate about their National Hockey stars, another source of competition with Montreal whose pride were the hockey team, *Canadiens*.

As luck would have it, we arrived in Toronto at the right time: The city was about to take off, economic boom was about to start, but right then it was still traditional and rigid. Soon, however, all this was about to change as the peacetime reconstruction was gathering momentum. Residential construction was everywhere, and expressways, and a new airport just North of the city in Downsview was in the works. Demand for electricity was hitting the roof and power lines and new grids were going up in all direction. Engineers, all kinds, were in great demand and my career was about to be launched in earnest. I felt I was part of the economic boom all around me. I felt a special person, someone really in demand as a professional.

Eleanor adored her father even in her studies. She wanted to become a sociologist, following in his footsteps. Her interest was SUICIDE. While she specialized in what drives people to commit suicide, I concentrated on my engineering career. We lived unmarried and separate for two years, she in residence in the University College, while I rented a flat on New Brunswick Avenue, near Spadina and Bloor, not far from her residence. In those days Spadina was a Jewish town, peopled by lucky immigrants who had somehow escaped Hitler's ovens and ended up in Toronto, bringing with them their skills and industry, and turning Spadina into a thriving center of knitting and textile capital. Everyone got rich quickly. Then, a few years later, came the Hungarians, escaping Communist terror unleashed on innocent people who dared to demand liberty. Khrushchev, the dictator in Moscow, replied with tanks and bombs and thousands perished in the streets of Budapest. The lucky ones escaped to Spadina, becoming our neighbors. Exotic new central European restaurants and vegetable markets sprung suddenly in the neighborhood. It was amazing how people who had suffered so much oppression so recently could have so much energy and be so cheerful. Everyone loved being Canadian. It was well before multiculturalism.

Eleanor and I loved ethnic food, blintzes, wienerschitzel and goulash; we would often walk from Bloor and Devonshire all the way to New Brunswick Avenue and enjoy the vibrant European atmosphere

## UZUN ALI, SHAME AND SALVATION

of the area, watching young people play soccer in parks, which seemed to be everywhere. Soccer was a new passion for the new residents. Older generations knew only ice hockey in winter and Canadian football in summer. What impressed me most was the way in which waves of new immigrants were harmonized, blending so smoothly in commerce and culture. The Jews and Hungarians mixed so well with the resident Irish and English and all seemed to enjoy variety in food, sport and languages of all sorts. No one seemed insulted by it all. It was so different than the life in London where each ethnic group seemed to live in a separate ethnic neighborhood, and the English, atop the social pyramid kept aloof with traditional snobbishness.

Toronto was a clean, modern city. There was civic pride everywhere. Its modernity, soon to be multiplied and magnified several times over with the 401 expressways in the North, and a post-modern towering City Hall downtown, was perfectly in tune with my own modern mindset educated in colonial Cyprus. Now, I, raised as a modern child, was witnessing, living and contributing to a modern city come into life. What I failed to find in Windsor, I experienced in Toronto: arts, culture, theaters and a vibrant urban life. Torontonians were friendly and welcoming diversity. Everyone minded his or her own business. In Cyprus religion and culture divided people. In Toronto, cultural differences, like Hungarian goulash, were celebrated as an essential spice of life. Of course, Quebec separatism was unfolding quietly all the time; Quebec then was years away from its Quiet Revolution, throwing off the oppressive influence of the Church.

On weekends, Eleanor liked visiting her Aunt and Uncle Littles in upscale and fashionable Rosedale, not far from the bohemian village of Yorkville. We loved to visit this section, enjoying jazz at *Penny Farthing, Bohemian Cafe* and a great variety of music in dozens of other coffee shops where poets and aspiring authors with long hair and shabby clothes exchanged ideas and ideologies. The Littles were well established independently wealthy, James Little the fifth and youngest son of an English family whose wealth and fortune was acquired from timber during the war. Aunt Hilda was an interior designer. So much money, but the couple had no children. So Eleanor filled an emotional gap. Almost immediately I developed a close friendship with Jim and Hilda. They seemed to love everything I represented: looks, my exotic Turkish background and my engineering skills. We talked and discussed endlessly about rapid urban development of Toronto. Their easy, comfortable and friendly disposition matched perfectly his emotional need for family they did not have. The Littles had a passion for the great Canadian outdoors and clean air outside the crowded city. It suited my own temperament exactly, my love of trees and forests that I could trace back to the Five Fingers Mountains in Cyprus. In Toronto, especially in Yorkville and Rosedale, I felt at home and at last my opinion of Canada slowly started to recover from the pollution of Windsor that even the false Edwardian architecture of Walkersville could not erase. Rosedale was far more authentic and clean.

\*\*\*

Uncle Little's family had a retreat, a palatial summer cottage in Haliburton on Lake Kashamawigamock, an unpronounceable Indian name, but a stunningly pristine natural wonderland. Eleanor and I were invited to go there with the Littles and so we had our first weekend holiday in Haliburton.

"Uncle Jim and Aunt Hilda invited us to their cottage in Haliburton for the weekend" announced Eleanor one Thursday evening. "Would you like to go?"

"How very nice of them. Do you know the place?" I asked, out of curiosity.

"Yes, I have actually been there. It is a lovely place on a beautiful lake, surrounded by forests and lots of lakes in the area." Replied Eleanor and I was excited at the chance of driving into the outdoors and see a little bit of Canada outside Toronto.

"We will go on Friday and return Sunday night" said Eleanor. "We need to take warm clothes because on the lake it gets quite chilly at nights."

Then I thought of the disastrous journey to Devonshire with Jill, while a student in London. But there was no comparison, not because the landscapes were unattractive; in fact, the English countryside was just as green and beautiful as the rugged Canadian pine forest and the blue lakes that seemed to be everywhere. What made the difference between England and Canada were the people, more precisely the lack of a class system. The Littles were perfect Canadian hosts, egalitarian and welcoming. I was accepted as part of family exactly as

I was, without any preconditions or entry requirements.

"This is our family retreat," announced Jim as we completed the four-hour drive from Toronto through gorgeous country, passing Lake Simcoe and traveling through miles and miles of pine forest, numerous little towns, and countless lakes. "Canada is a huge lake interspaced by some pieces of land," I thought to myself. We stopped for dinner at a wayside restaurant not far from our destination. Finally we arrived at the cottage at 10pm, all exhausted. We went to bed and slept soundly.

The next morning, a sunny and bright Saturday we had a glorious breakfast in the dining room overlooking the blue waters of the lake with the pine-covered hills in the background. Afterwards we went for a walk around the lake, through the forest and up and down the valleys and creeks. It was wonderful and exhilarating. We had a light lunch at a coffee shop in the town. Then in the afternoon we walked back home and everyone helped prepare what turned out to be sumptuous roast beef dinner, complete with mash potatoes, gravy and Yorkshire pudding.

At dinner table, Jim asked me about my surname: "What is Uzun Ali? Does it have a meaning?"

"Yes, of course, it means Long Ali" I replied. Jim had the look of curiosity all over his face. He waited for more, and I went on.

"It belonged to my Grandfather, on my father's side. He was an Ottoman Kaimakam, a sort of District Officer in his region."

And then, for the next hour, I recounted our family history, the *Selamlik* and the *Harem* at the Konak how Grandpa Uzun Ali had gambled away the estate, after the British took over Cyprus, and how he died a broken man, but how his two sons, especially my uncle Munir, the British trained lawyer had managed to recover the family fortune.

"What about your mother's family" asked Aunt Hilda? "What were they like?" she asked.

"Ah!" I began. "That is a different story, at least according to my mother." I stopped, unsure how much detail my hosts wanted to hear.

"Please go on" said aunt Hilda as Jim nodded his head. "We would love to hear as much as you wish to tell us."

I summarized the best way I could.

"My Grandfather Halil on my mother's side was a womanizer. He cheated on my Grandmother, he arranged some sort of abduction and

## DISCOVERY

attempted polygamy and did all kinds of terrible things. In the end, the pain and suffering drove my Grandmother mad and I understand she was involved in some kind of murder. I do not know all the details because my mother was always complaining about her father's infidelity and his mistreatment of her own dear, beloved mother who died when my mother was only a few days old."

I was exhausted, more emotionally than physically, looking sad.

"I am sorry," said Hilda, "I did not mean to open old sores." But, the talk had a strange, warm effect pushing me closer to Uncle Jim and Aunt Hilda. Dear Eleanor sat through the whole story with great interest and curiosity.

We then retired for the night.

The next day, a Sunday was once again sunny and bright. The Littles took Eleanor and me on a boat ride on Lake Kashamawigamock, which was somewhat long and narrow, with virgin pine and spruce forest all around. The Little cottage, actually it was a huge country mansion, dominated the surroundings; there were hardly any cottages around yet.

I reached two important decisions on that Sunday. One was an investment; I decided to use a portion of my salary at Hydro Ontario to buy some lakefront property close to the Little estate. It was after our visit to the Scottish landowner who owned all the farmland in the area and selling lakefront property at an incredibly low price of $50 a foot. The low price, but primarily the natural beauty of the area, delighted me and I started thinking.

"I love this place" I confessed at lunch to the delight of Uncle Jim and Aunt Hilda, "I would like to purchase one of the lots on the lakefront near you." Uncle Jim encouraged me. "I am sure lake frontage will keep on appreciating" he said, "There is no more land."

It was true. It subsequently became one of the best investments I ever made.

My second decision was even more momentous, but I postponed its execution till the next day. Monday evening, I invited Eleanor to dinner at our favorite Hungarian restaurant on Spadina and Bloor, "let's go to dinner," I said. "I have something important to say to you."

"What?" she asked impatiently. "I am not saying till coffee time, after dinner" I did not wish to tell her that I wanted to propose, but I sensed she guessed it.

Later on that evening at the end of our Hungarian goulash, Eleanor accepted to be my wife, to unite our lives, in a celebration of love bridging two souls from so different cultures, accidentally meeting in London and now embarking on a new life in Toronto. Outside the restaurant I purchased a single red rose, a symbol of my love, and we exchanged kisses as we walked along Bloor Street. I felt warm and sweet inside as we walked, talked and started making plans. I had never been so happy in my life. Canada, Toronto was my new home. I reflected on my family heritage: "I wonder what my Grandpa would have thought about his name spreading to Canada? If he ever thought that education could bring continents and cultures closer?"

The next day I wrote letter to mother in Nicosia, sister Sevgi in Ankara and cousin Ozkan in London announcing my decision to marry Eleanor, the wedding to be determined later after Eleanor's graduation. I promised that we would travel to Cyprus as soon as possible for a family reunion.

Time flew by. Toronto was by now a boomtown, and we benefited from it. I was busy in my engineering work at Ontario Hydro and Eleanor focused on her studies at the university. In Spring1951 she graduated with her BA in sociology and got a teaching job with the North York School Board. We got married in October 1951 and a joyful event it was. The Littles hosted a big wedding reception for us. The Kirks came from Windsor and I was only sad that none of my family could be present. Shortly after, we moved from our downtown flat into a new three-bedroom bungalow we had purchased in Willowdale, a highly fashionable and newly developed region of Toronto. Then, our daughter Susan was born on Christmas Eve 1952 and life was as peachy as it could be. Or, so it seemed to me in Toronto the good and prosperous.

Cyprus, however, was heading toward big trouble. And, that meant a new cycle of bitterness and unhappiness for our family.

# XV

In Cyprus a new round of violence erupted on April Fool's Day 1955. The violence campaign had been in planning for a long time. The chief of EOKA was a Colonel Grivas, a hero of the Greek Civil War, a fascist from Cyprus who swore to achieve ENOSIS during his life, snatching Cyprus from the British and attaching it to Greece almost a thousand miles away.

Soon, a few hundred Grivas guerrillas, hidden in well-guarded mountain hideouts, had managed to pin down tens of thousands of British troops. These rug-tag patriots, mostly students till yesterday, were fanatics ready to die for Hellenism. They had sworn to take revenge on the British who stood in the way of the age-old dream for ENOSIS. They scorned the British soldiers, who in reality were led by second grade politicians and military officers. In London these politicians had realized that the British Empire was dying. The military officers, a motley group priding themselves about their exploits against the natives in the dying days of the Empire in Burma and India, were now assembled in Cyprus as British pulled forces for economic reasons from east of Suez. But as a last show of gunboat diplomacy, the British, along with the French and Israelis, bombed Nasser's army on the Suez, using Cyprus as a staging station.

The Americans were alarmed. They got the UN to step in and stop the British at Suez. The Great Game now was truly finished. In the new

Middle East, Americans took over as masters.

The British lost not only in Suez. They were also losing in the rugged mountains of Troodos and the Five Fingers Mountains in Cyprus against the well entrenched and heavily armed men of Grivas. These guerrillas were everywhere; they would sneak into villages, killing and terrorizing peasants into forced submission to the sacred cause of ENOSIS, and increasingly, the secret armies of Yorgacis, Makarios's Home Minister, the top man in charge of national security, together with Papadopoulos and Sampson, would venture into cities killing innocent British wives and children while on shopping expeditions and laying ambush on soldiers all around the island. They seemed unstoppable.

"We are fighting a noble and sacred cause against imperialists."

"British get out of Cyprus; ENOSIS NOW."

"Traitors beware: Death to the British and Traitors"

These were the messages delivered to the rank and file in leaflets secretly distributed through *Gymnasia*, the churches and in posters as shootings and bombings targeting military and civilian assets escalated. At first the fight was between the elusive Grivas, the mythical *Digenis*, and his British pursuers. Like the scarlet pimpernel, they searched him here, they searched him there, but he was nowhere to be found. The British tried everything; they changed generals, exiled Makarios, imposed curfews, they even brought in publicity experts. Lawrence Durrell of the *Alexandria Quartet* fame came and resided in the beautiful mountain retreat village of Bella Pais, just outside Kyrenia, drinking Cypriot wine with his many men friends, and wrote about the futility of it all in *Bitter Lemons*.

The war soon engulfed our family. My father, Ozkan the policeman, got dragged into it, paying for it dearly. He became a small pawn in a big game. The big game was the old British divide and rule, all over again. The British army decided to recruit more and more Turkish Cypriot special police auxiliaries, and substitute them for the *Tommies*. The predictable happened. It became a civil war. EOKA gunmen targeted Turkish Cypriot policemen. In January EOKA gunmen in Paphos gunned down Sergeant Abdullah Ali Riza and on April 23 another policeman, Nihat Bash, was killed in Nicosia. The Turkish Cypriot fighters from VOLKAN retaliated. EOKA responded with greater violence. The Greek Cypriots set up checkpoints on highways, killing innocent Turkish Cypriot peasants, kidnapping women and children, as the reign of terror engulfed the entire population all over the island.

***

Even Toronto newspapers were reporting on violence in Cyprus, ridiculing Makarios in his black Church robes, with British blood on his hands, daring to challenge the mighty British army! My sister Sevgi had by now become my main source of information on the terrible reign of terror that had descended on our beautiful island. A letter arrived from her shortly our move to Toronto.

"Dear Brother Tekin,

I am well in Ankara and I hope you are settling down in your new life in Canada. My only sadness on this score is that you are so far away and I understand Canada is a really cold place. I hope you are keeping well and warm. Please give my best wishes to Eleanor and her family.

My studies are progressing well and I expect to complete my doctoral thesis within a year. I am now working as an assistant in the department. I expect that soon I shall to get a promotion once I complete my degree.

In Cyprus things are bad. The Greek Cypriots have launched a war against the British. EOKA gunmen are killing not only British soldiers, ambushing convoys and bombing military installations, they are also killing civilians. The British have arrested some Greek students, and will soon be hanging someone called Karaolis who murdered a British woman and a baby. The Greek gunmen are also waging war on Turkish Cypriots whom they accuse of collaborating with the British. I am very worried about father because the Greeks are especially targeting the police. Mother is worried to death, but nothing can be done. The situation is not good at all. We just have to wait and see what comes next.

Please write and give me your news. Your loving sister, Sevgi"

## UZUN ALI, SHAME AND SALVATION

I wrote back and gave Sevgi my news and, with some unease, briefed her of the comfortable life in Toronto that Eleanor and I were enjoying. The contrast with the reign of terror prevailing in Cyprus made me very restless, feeling especially sorry for father and mother there, but there was nothing to be done. Unexpectedly, our family was rushing towards tragedy and an unplanned reunion in Nicosia.

\*\*\*

It was a particularly hot August day in 1955, several months after the start of EOKA violence on the island. It was a rare occasion as father Ozkan was at home alone and suddenly there was a knock at the front door. Some unexpected visitors, wearing dark glasses and looking menacing, stood in front of him. Mother was out visiting neighbors. Three men walked into the parlor and introduced themselves.

"We are from the organization," said their leader. Father took a good look at him, and recognized Alpay and behind him Mehmet Ali from VOLKAN. He knew them casually from the sport club where he would go on his time off playing cards and exchanging news with friends while sipping Turkish coffee.

"We are here to request your help in an important assignment," spoke Mehmet Ali, looking very serious. Others looked on.

Father had heard rumors about a secret society to defend Turkish Cypriots. The leader of the group continued: "We need some cover. We have cells in villages; we have men, volunteers, ready to fight EOKA." My father listened intently, as Mehmet Ali continued with the plan.

"We need to supply our fighters with guns and ammunition. That is where you come in."

Father asked: "What do you want me to do?" He realized he had no chance but cooperate.

Mehmet Ali said: "We will come back tomorrow night. We have plans for Milltown. For now say nothing to nobody." They were gone.

That is how father Ozkan, the police officer, became a secret member of VOLKAN to counter EOKA attacks on Turkish Cypriots. He provided the cover and facilitated delivery of arms to cells in villages and towns from secret supply centers in Nicosia. These cells included doctors' clinics, homes of ordinary citizens, schools and barns in villages. It was war and everyone was expected to contribute and do his

## DISCOVERY

or her duty. At home, mother Aygul was not happy, but father's logic was persuasive: "There is no choice. We are fighting a war. Everyone is in it Kazim, my boss, included. No one can say No. It is life or death." He had a sad and distasteful look on his face, unhappy and helpless.

The next night, they came and the old Konak in Milltown, long abandoned and in ruin, took on a new life.

"There is a storeroom in the back of the Konak in Milltown," the leader began. Father listened; "We need to store some material in it. It needs fixing up first, but don't worry, we will take care of it."

The next day, father went to see his elder brother, Munir. They had not seen each other for quite some time. He was rather surprised at the weight loss he observed in Munir. In fact, unknown to Ozkan, his elder brother had lately been having some health problems. He had been complaining of problems urinating, and the doctor had put Munir on a strict no-salt diet.

"Brother Munir" he began, "you have lost weight. Are you OK?" asked Ozkan.

"Oh yes. Everything's fine" replied Munir, not wanting to reveal his declining health and his prostate cancer. So, father came to the point of his visit.

"Brother Munir" Ozkan said taking on a serious look, "I have decided to do some small renovation at the Konak in Milltown." Munir, who ignored his health and concentrated on his latest deals finding housing for the ever-increasing military families arriving in Cyprus daily, was totally surprised.

"But the place is in ruin. And we are in the middle of an emergency, don't you know? You are a policeman and know better. Is it worth it? " Of course, Munir was right to be skeptical. This was no time for investment.

"I know" father said. Investment was not what he was after, but he could not disclose his plans "If you don't mind, I'll go ahead and fix up the barn, and then see what to do next."

Uncle Munir was surprised but said to father: "OK, if you wish, but I still think it is not such a good idea."

That is how Konak became a secret depot in the inter-communal fight between VOLKAN, EOKA and the British army. It was a bitter, ugly war. No one won, but father Ozkan lost his life.

***

## UZUN ALI, SHAME AND SALVATION

The end came suddenly and quickly. Father's party was ambushed and he was shot dead on a dark and stormy night in the middle of January 1956. It was so unseasonably cold; there was snow on the slopes of the Five Fingers Mountains. Father's group was secretly hauling a cache of weapons, sten guns and bazookas, when they were ambushed in Miamilia, a Greek-Cypriot town on the way to Milltown. Their police jeep, looking official and bedecked with colonial military emblems, was an easy target for the EOKA gunmen. Their ambush plan was carefully set. A few days before they had been tipped that the party would be traveling in an apparent police jeep, through the Greek Cypriot territory, taking guns and ammunition to Milltown for future use in defense of the town against an expected Greek attack.

At the turn beyond the railway trucks, past the ceramics factory just outside Miamilia, there was a stand of pine trees, where the road made a sharp left turn. That is where the EOKA men laid their ambush, under the cover of trees. There were six of them, three on each side of the tarmac around the bend. The police jeep appeared as expected at the ambush spot, around 8pm when it was dark. There were three in the jeep, the driver, father seating next to the driver, and one other in the back. It slowed down to negotiate the turn. At that point the shooting started. Bullets rained on the unsuspecting party. My father, who was sitting in the front seat next to the driver, was hit on his head, and died instantly. The fellow at the back was injured, but luckily the driver was unhurt and he was able speed away, carrying the dead body of our father.

While his English superiors were surprised what on earth Ozkan was doing in the jeep, father became a hero and was heralded as a true patriot in the Turkish Cypriot press. There was a national funeral and eulogies were delivered and the multitude carried slogans, which said it all:

"Cyprus is Turkish; it will remain forever Turkish."

"This Land is Sacred, nourished with the Blood of our Heroes."

Father's sudden death drew mother and uncle Munir closer. It started when he came to pay his respects to her on his half-brother's premature death. Sevgi, who had flown in from Ankara, welcomed him. She looked very pretty, but clearly shaken by the unexpected loss of father, but looking very smart in her black gown. "Welcome uncle" she said as she showed him into the living room where mother, in

## DISCOVERY

black mourning attire, was hosting visitors and relatives who came to pay their respects.

Uncle Munir, after the usual, ritualistic remarks, said: "He died a hero, may he rest in peace. I know our father would be proud."

Uzun Ali, long in his grave now, would have been proud. Father Ozkan, as his name implied, had symbolized for him the modern age he did not understand. The old Ottoman Kaimakam wanted his children to succeed in the modern world. But one thing Grandpa Uzun Ali or no one else could prevent nor predict was that with modernity came ethnic conflict and all sorts of new risks and dangers. His sons and grandsons took these risks, learnt to adjust and manage them, and became modern children able to achieve success in a manner Uzun Ali never could have imagined.

***

I rushed from Toronto; flying at the earliest opportunity to London and from there together with Ozkan Jr. flew to Nicosia a week later. Sevgi from Ankara was already with mother, but in those days travel was still time-consuming. We all missed father's funeral because in the Muslim tradition, the dead must be buried within 24 hours. Our reunion in Nicosia consoled mother and that was the most important duty we shared. We all talked and remembered father with due respect and decorum befitting Muslim tradition. There were the obligatory three days of *mevlit*, the chanting in the memory of the deceased, attended by all friends, relatives and neighbors.

It was very difficult for mother. She had the greatest difficulty accepting his death and she kept on confiding to us her fears and worries about the secret mission that father had assumed that had cost him his life. Publicly his sacrifice had made father a hero, but privately this did not lessen our loss. It was unbearable to us. Mother would weep privately because, unlike her early years of their marriage, she had come to depend on father as a reliable and honest life partner. We mourned with her, cried together and reminisced day and night. We stayed with her one more week, and then we began the long journey back, again by way of London. When in London, I decided to prolong my stay with cousin Ozkan Jr, just to be with him and to visit my teachers and friends.

In Nicosia, after father's death, an important new development occurred. Uncle Munir started to visit mother Aygul regularly. On his next visit after the funeral, he made a confession to her. "I am surprised Allah has called my younger brother first." Aygul looked at him, a bit surprised and wondered what he wanted to say:" I am ten years older than Ozkan, and lately I have been feeling my age." He was in his mid-sixties, still overweight and privately he noticed lately that he was having difficulty urinating. It was an indication of prostate cancer, but he took no action to have it checked and, untreated it grew worse.

"Only Allah knows how many more years I have in this life." He said and she waited for him to continue. "I have decided to make preparations for my death and write my will," he announced.

Mother looked at uncle Munir with surprise. It was the first time ever that he was taking her into his confidence. Lately she had been worried on financial security because father had died without providing adequately for her old age. He had a pension from his police service, but it was hardly enough.

"I will leave most of my wealth naturally to my son in London" he declared, "but I also want to provide for your old age as well, acknowledging the moral debt I owed to Ozkan" he said. "Now my son has graduated from University in London and married and both he and his English wife are teachers, they are now having children. They are comfortable but I want to help them."

The first time he felt this kind of generosity, he had acted in symbolic terms, naming his newfound son in Dublin in Ozkan's honor. That way vicariously at least, he felt he could add weight to his brother's effort to ensure survival of the Uzun Ali family. Afterwards, back in 1942 when Ozkan Jr. was sent away to London for a university education, the new Munir had generously and privately set up an education trust for the Uzun Ali grandchildren, not just for Ozkan Jr. but for me and my sister Sevgi as well. Now Munir, the wealthy bachelor, wanted to demonstrate his obligation to Ozkan by providing financial security for his wife in her old age as well. "I want to give, for in giving lies the rewards of redemption" he would say to himself quietly and privately.

As he got up to take his leave, uncle Munir hesitated and then stopped and looked at mother Aygul. She wanted to convey her appreciation of the gift for her children, but he spoke first:

"There is one more thing I would like to tell you Aygul," He said. "It concerns a secret of the Konak at Milltown just before Mary was

## DISCOVERY

murdered in Buyuk Han." Mother looked at uncle Munir with renewed interest; she knew he was about to share an important family secret with her. She stood in silence, and after a moment, he went on:

"Mary was murdered by my own illegitimate son, Ayfer, whom I never knew. He was born to an *odalik* Nilufer, my mother's maid in the Konak. I raped her in the rose garden when I was young and foolish. After the rape, I went away and knew nothing about Ayfer. I wiped him off my mind. But he lived and I discovered Ayfer from Nilufer years later, when it was too late, the day you married Ozkan, the day after the murder."

He stopped. He stood there in silence. Mother Aygul was in shock, her face blank. Minutes passed. Uncle then concluded:

"I have never told this to any one. It has been my torment and redemption, all in one. In my later years, my terrible act of selfishness in the rose garden became the inner force to redeem my other son, born out of Mary and left behind in London and Dublin, who now carries your husband's and my brother's name. The education trust I set up was a moral cleansing. It was the only debt I could repay to my dear Mary, the only woman I loved, but who, unknowingly and foolishly, I had sent to her grave in Buyuk Han."

He then left mother, still in shock and speechless, and went out.

\*\*\*

Father's sudden death was only the beginning of bad news for our family. Once the angel of death enters a home, it seemed that other victims followed in quick order. First the old lady Neslihan died in the Konak; she had led a full life, always in the background befitting an Ottoman lady knowing her place behind her husband and in the harem. Not many wept for Neslihan; her death did not arouse much excitement because, poor woman had no relatives or other family in Cyprus.

Not quite a month had passed when uncle Munir became victim to cancer, a condition he discovered late and chose to keep secret. The mortal disease had spread to his liver and the end came quickly. His had been a tempestuous life, self made in a material sense, but one that owed a huge moral debt to the old Kaimakam of Milltown, his father who shared Munir's prediction that the future now belonged to the British. Uzun Ali had died a broken man, an Ottoman minor official

337

secretly blaming the British for his downfall. His favorite son, Munir, should have been happier, so carefully molded by his father for the age of the British. But he had messed up too many lives, Ottoman and British. He, too, had passed away a broken man in his heart although in a material sense he had everything that both father and son could have wanted.

Out of Munir's sins and thanks to his generosity, symbolized by his educational trust set up during the war many years before his death, the next generation of Uzun Ali clan, scattered in far-flung places from Cyprus, lived in a modern world in a manner our Grandpa could never have imagined. I am sure the old Kaimakam of Milltown would have been proud of Ozkan Jr, Sevgi and I, what each one of us had accomplished in the modern world while maintaining our roots in Cyprus.

When uncle Munir died I was still in London with Ozkan Jr. Sevgi sent a telegram to us from Ankara, advising against returning back to Nicosia. She would herself go back to be with mother. It was Ozkan Jr's call. He quickly decided against going, not sharing his reasons with me. He simply agreed with Sevgi. I had no choice but to respect his decision. I must admit, however, I felt that my cousin had done some deep soul searching privately, alone.

In London, we mourned in private, the two cousins, joined by Jill and children. It was hardest on my cousin. He just went silent, grieving in private. For days he stayed alone, lost in deep thought and Jill and I shared his agony. How I wished I could get into my cousin's head to feel and experience his grief, and understand what sad thoughts were passing through his mind, how deep his loss must have been. I did feel a strange thought that he was mourning not just his father's death, but at the same time he was remembering Mary, the lost love that could have unleashed so much happiness but for the rape in the rose garden that had resulted in Ayfer.

"How similar to my own mother's torment" I reflected.

This reflection opened an old sore for me. I could not help draw in my mind a parallel between my cousin's private mourning in my company in London and mother Aygul's predicament, thousands of miles away in Nicosia, both thinking not only of uncle Munir, but also poor Mary and her sacrifice in Buyuk Han for him. "They had not died in vain," a voice kept on saying to me inside my mind and, with all my heart, I wanted to believe it. Yet, I felt this strangest feeling in my

# DISCOVERY

confused mind that reminded me of the similarity between Mary and mother Aygul: Both women lived and yearned for love, a man and a mother, yet neither experienced it, love was beyond their grasp and each ended a victim of injustice. The one solace was that others, in particular we the children, carried the torch of redemption for the sins of our elders.

*\*\*\**

In Ankara my sister Sevgi was doing us all proud. She had left Cyprus in the summer of 1949, aged 20. Thanks to uncle's endowment, she had enrolled in the Faculty of Sciences and Arts of the University of Ankara, specializing, on the advice of her teachers, in Ottoman history, painstakingly learning the Ottoman script to be able to translate old documents, writing her doctoral thesis on the politics of the transfer of Cyprus from Ottoman to British rule. Ten years later, she was a Turkish citizen, by way of her marriage. Her husband, Aydin Bozkurt, was originally from Cyprus, his family immigrating to Turkey in 1925.

Sevgi and Aydin, her husband to be, had first met at a mutual friend's house in Istanbul during a holiday in the summer of 1955. Then nothing further developed between them until after father's unexpected death in January of the following year. When romance finally blossomed between Sevgi and Aydin, again it was linked to Cyprus.

When father's death had, unexpectedly brought us together briefly in Nicosia, I was able to learn from my sister Sevgi about her new life as an academic in Ankara. She was a rising young scholar, rapidly becoming an authority on Ottoman rule in Cyprus and how the island was suddenly given over to the British in a secret convention in 1878. Her passion now was social life in the Ottoman period. She was busy traveling to towns and cities, in search of letters, family papers, *firmans* and other court documents all in Ottoman script in which she had by now become fully proficient.

"You know, brother Tekin" she said to me quietly when we shared a brief private moment together during father's funeral ceremonies, "I intend to come back to Cyprus, as soon as possible, and conduct a search for documents. I would like to spend time digging at the Konak where Grandpa lived his years. I am quite sure there are some yet undiscovered documents there that will hold great importance about

339

our family history. That is what I would like to do. As an academic I have developed the skills of a social historian and have become very good at digging all sorts of fascinating old documents in family attics and odd places. I am sure our family secrets lie hidden in the Konak. " She said.

I was both impressed and amazed at Sevgi's clear thinking and her determination.

"That would be wonderful," I said encouraging her. Before we could say a word more on the subject, we were interrupted and we were both obliged to resume our duties toward the funeral guests and visitors who kept coming in a stream to express their condolences. The police force came in official capacity, friends and neighbors, relatives and strangers all joined in a grand remembrance of father, celebrating his heroic and premature death.

We never had a chance to talk again. And we did not meet for five long years.

# XVI

In London, my cousin and I, both entered a period of depression. The loss of fathers, so soon and sudden, one after the other, had at first a numbing shock on both cousin Ozkan Jr. and I and then, suddenly, the shock turned into a depression, lasting for days. At first, I started crying in private for my father. I could sense my cousin was doing the same for his.

Then, tears and sadness turned into a self-appraisal, a reflection on my relationship with father Ozkan. In truth, I had to accept that there had been an invisible barrier between us. He was unlike mother Aygul, never interested in books; but I always cherished dad's decision in Xero to move the family to Nicosia so I could pursue higher studies. Father was a good-hearted man, never ambitious or daring; he knew his limitations and always stayed within those limits. But when he recognized my intellectual potential, he became supportive; he would spare no effort for his son. Ozkan, the modest policeman, from the start of his life in the old Konak he never lacked moral courage, a value his elder brother only rediscovered later in life. My father wanted his son to succeed; to reach the very top of the heights his intelligence could take him. That was the true Uzun Ali spirit in him; he may not have known how to display it, but he never lacked it. I was eternally grateful to him for that.

When buried in my doubts and still mourning, I wanted to

comfort my cousin, for he had the same emotional needs and doubts. Sometimes we just sat there, our tears flowing down our cheeks in silence, the two cousins communicating without exchanging a word, yet each of us feeling, sharing and reading other's mind. In these periods of mutual sadness, Jill was so comforting, gentle and understanding, consoling with her kind words, but most of all leaving us alone in our private, silent vigil. Somehow togetherness lightened my sorrow, our loss. Yet, the pain of it all persisted. Days followed in aimless struggle within us. Gradually the agony of private mourning for father and uncle worsened my doubts about myself. "Was I meant to be an engineer? Perhaps I was in the wrong career path." Engineering was an interesting field, and I was happy in Toronto, happily married with Eleanor. But, my vulnerability made me wonder if I should be happier with a career in humanities or non-engineering pursuits.

The private mourning lasted almost a week. Then we started going out, walking in the park. We went to our old meeting places in Golders Green and Hampstead Heath.

That is when we unlocked the dark passage to our inner selves.

It was a rainy, gloomy day. We were in our old coffee shop near the underground station facing the Heath. Then the fog in our minds suddenly lifted. These sad events of the recent past led us to a major discovery for both of us: Our parents' generation was over; the torch had now passed to us, the mantle of Grandpa Uzun Ali was resting on our own shoulders. Thousands of miles away from Nicosia on a kind of voluntary exile, we had not yet fully understood the paradox of our circumstances. Here in distant London we were guided by some mysterious spirit of the Konak at Milltown, the two of us were like two shipwrecked souls on a lonely island. We were the new generation entrusted to carry the line of Uzun Ali; the future of the family lay in our hands. That future was now *Us* and was no longer centered in Milltown and the small island of Cyprus. Our future was international, our field of opportunity the global marketplace. Uzun Ali was now truly an international family. The discovery was like the sun rising on a clear morning, a bright new start full of promise and confidence.

It was a defining moment, a landmark in our lives. At that moment both of us acquired a brand new identity. At last, Ozkan Jr. discarded his uncle's image and became truly himself. It was what our fathers had intended. For me, looking back, I felt liberated, a Canadian

Turk with roots in Cyprus. Now I was a new person with a new confidence, a new purpose in life that did not exist before. The transition happened in a mysterious way as the two of us shared with each other their deepest sentiments.

It was cousin Ozkan who first spoke, as we sat in the coffee shop facing the Heath.

"You know Tekin," he said, now quite comfortable in middle age, "we now grieve the passing of our fathers. The common grief is the glue that binds us. But I feel there are deeper bonds between us."

I listened intently. He went on.

His words had an electrifying effect on me for I had been thinking the same. "Amazing you say that" I replied. "I was thinking exactly the same thing. Here we are two cousins, in London as strangers, but I believe some mysterious spirit unites us. Is there a message in our loss?" Then almost instinctively, I went on: "How close were you to your father Ozkan?" I asked boldly.

"To be honest, we were not that close." He replied. He took a deep breath as if he was gathering his strength to say something momentous. I waited eagerly. Then he started:

"I always felt there was a secret, some invisible torment of past storms that my father never wanted to share with me. I wish I had known my mother. I do not know what exactly happened between my father and mother on that fateful day when she was murdered in Buyuk Han. I am sure it left scars that she took with her to her grave. All I know is that Mary was a poor Irish girl who met my father in London and they had a love affair. I came to this world out of that love, an unwanted child, left in the care of nuns in the orphanage in Dublin. Now, here I am back in London, in the shadow of uncle Munir's disgrace, his late discovery of a son left behind. I am now an identity in transit from an unknown origin to a double-hyphenated Turkish-Cypriot-British."

"No" I protested strongly. My emphatic response surprised Ozkan. I was so loud, people at the next table looked strangely toward us. Ozkan looked at me with shock and eagerness, all combined in a strange look on his face.

Words came out of my mouth at random. I had no time to think or organize my thoughts.

"You miss out one important dimension." I started to lecture my cousin.

343

"Your father's redemption is your beginning, but your identity is non-negotiable. You are Uzun Ali, you will always be. You have Turkish-Cypriot roots, strong and clear. Those roots are real and deep, no more and no less than mine. That is what binds you and me together, forever. You and I are Uzun Ali's grandchildren, in true Ottoman tradition of an exotic mixture. Our roots are buried in the Konak at Milltown. Nothing can alter that. Like you, I do not know all the mysteries of the past. How the British took over Cyprus from the Ottomans? What were the personal and family scars in the transition? We bear them, know it or not."

I stopped and looked at him. "Tekin" he said, "I think you are right."

He waited and then added: "It is now up to us, you and me. We hold the future in our hand. The future is international. Our roots lie buried in a small island, but our destiny is the whole world."

He smiled, serenely, with confidence and there was brightness in his eyes that I had not noticed before. It was like sun rising afresh in the distant horizon on a new morning.

We finished our coffee. It never tasted better. We got up, our meeting at an end, stood and looked at each other in silence. No more words were needed; we communicated deeply, emotionally. Outside it was raining harder, another wet, typical London afternoon.

Then, I realized there was one more thing to be said.

"You know, something else Ozkan," I said just before parting: "Your father fulfilled our Grandpa's dream. Yes, he did something foolish when he was young and unthinking; for all his faults, he also had his moral principles. In his own way, I believe, he tried to compensate for his sins through you and me. Your father's education was the old Kaimakam's legacy, of eternal value. It is our treasure. Your father has expanded this family treasure. You must be proud of your father, my uncle." He looked at me with certain approval and appreciation.

I concluded: "I am grateful to Uncle Munir because without his help, his endowment, I would not be what I am today. Our generation, you and I, are the Uzun Ali line, we shall take our place in the big wide world, which is what makes us Grandpa's special and worthy successors."

"Yes" said Ozkan, "My father was a good man. I believe he loved my mother, in his own way, initially in his student days in London,

# DISCOVERY

and then more maturely after he had lost her. Just like Cyprus and the Ottoman Turks; their loss of Cyprus signaled an end of their Ottoman world. But not *our end... We go on.*"

These words were uttered emotionally, deeply felt. Now we, the cousins, were more united than ever before. We stood there, on the pavement in the rain, looking at one another. We took an oath, a secret covenant, cousin to cousin. Some day, only God knows when, we would go back to the Konak in Milltown and maybe, just maybe, some good angel would guide us to secrets yet undiscovered.

The next day I flew to Toronto. It had been six weeks' absence from Eleanor and Susan and my job. A new beginning was waiting me in Toronto.

\*\*\*

In the summer of 1956, Sevgi met Aydin one more time, again in Istanbul. She had at last completed her doctoral dissertation and was taking a well-earned holiday with friends before starting her academic career as a young assistant professor of history. Aydin, for his part, was an aspiring accounting postgraduate.

This time relations between Sevgi and Aydin took a more serious turn. For starters she was fascinated to learn that he was also from Cyprus, and this discovery brought the two closer. They agreed to meet the next day at Taksim Square in Central Istanbul. It led to unexpected and unpleasant events.

They were walking through the main shopping district along Istiklal Caddesi, the independence boulevard, at the Galatasaray Lycee end, overlooking Beyoglu. Suddenly they found themselves surrounded by rioters, entering the boulevard from all the surrounding alleys, screaming and shouting and breaking into stores, mostly Greek owned, unprovoked but seemingly well planned. More and more crowds poured in, wave after wave of youth and mobs. The police were nowhere to be seen. Shops were being broken into and looted. Anger and terror spread all over the neighborhood. Aydin and Sevgi managed to seek refuge in a restaurant. They watched the torrent of violence in shock and awe. The motley crowd was waving Turkish flags, chanting slogans, "death to the Greeks", "Cyprus is Turkish" while hooligans with sticks broke shop windows and set fires in a reign of uncontrolled violence. Then the crowd burst into the restaurant. In horror Sevgi and Aydin run for cover, escaping for safety through back alleys as far away from the scene of riot as possible.

The violence on Istiklal Caddesi, in a mysterious fashion, cemented the love between Sevgi and Aydin. When they both returned to Ankara to pursue their academic pursuits, they stayed in touch. They were a perfect couple. Sevgi, young, bright and beautiful, matched Aydin's requirements for a professional, intellectual, modern Turkish wife. There was no question that families on both sides would be delighted with their decision to marry. Union between two intellectuals was very much in line with the Turkish custom and national sentiment prevailing in the island.

They were supposed to get married in the spring of 1957 and I was making plans to be there, along with mother Aygul from Cyprus. But the unexpected deaths of father and uncle Munir delayed the wedding. They were finally married in October 1957 with only mother Aygul attending from our family. I was tied up with a big airport project in Missisuaga, just north of Toronto. The project contained a major Hydro Ontario works program for which I was directly responsible. There was, in short, no possibility of my getting away. All I was able to do was to telegram our best wishes from Toronto. Similar congratulations came from London, from Ozkan and Jill.

Now our family reunion in Cyprus had become more necessary and urgent. Sevgi's marriage prompted us all to resolve to meet in a grand family reunion in Nicosia, soonest possible, at a date yet undetermined.

# XVII

When uncle Munir suddenly died, he left all of his estate to Ozkan, except for the education trust he had arranged for me and my sister Sevgi and a generous pension for mother Aygul in her old age. After the lawyers cleared the will, Ozkan was amazed to learn that he had been left with a princely sum of almost half a million pounds. Now, at last, he could realize his ambition of going into private business and get rich.

The huge windfall changed Ozkan's life forever. It began when an official letter arrived from uncle Munir's London Bank addressed to his son. It was six weeks after our emotional vigil and discovery in London that the mantle of our Grandfathers had now passed to our generation. Little did we know that this new responsibility came with a huge financial package and that our international family was now to play a new role in the world of finance with new commercial horizons opening before our very eyes.

When he read it, Ozkan could not believe his eyes. "The estimated current market value of holdings left to you by the late Mr. Munir Uzun Ali is 495,000 pounds sterling" it said. Then Ozkan noticed further down in the letter a bit of professional advice. "It is respectfully suggested that you call to arrange a visit to our Bank, at your most convenient time for expert advice on how best to utilize this significant amount. Our Senior Investment Officer will be glad to assist you in accordance with your fathers' instructions…"

Ozkan took the advice and called the Bank to make an appointment with the Senior Investment Officer one week hence. Then he went to the public library and started reading about Malayan rubber stocks. His interest in rubber trading was aroused first by Somerset Maugham. His short stories about planters and tycoons in Singapore, Malaya and the Far East had impressed him. He enjoyed the stories and fancied himself as one of the speculators who would become rich overnight just by a few clever stock dealings.

"I am interested in buying some stocks" he said when the Senior Investment Officer asked Ozkan if he had any options for the utilization of the large estate left for him by his dad.

"Stocks can be speculative" the Senior Investment Officer began, "but then if you make the right decision; they can make you rich sometimes very quickly." He said.

"I do not want penny stocks. I want blue chip," said Ozkan, proudly displaying the knowledge of the stock market deals he had been reading about in the days earlier. "And I hear Malayan rubber stocks are good buys."

The banker was impressed. He had read some expert opinion that the Korean War had pushed commodities, in particular strategic ones like rubber, sky high, and with a war looming over the Suez at the time, rubber prices were expected to increase anytime, returning multiple earnings within a relatively short period of time.

So, after a few hours of discussion, Ozkan ended investing 200,000 pounds of Uncle Munir's estate in the stock of the Malayan rubber giant Sime Darby Company. The balance was placed, as the Senior Investment Officer recommended, in UK government bonds fetching a steady 3% per annum, or almost 10,000 pounds income annually.

***

In the following months, Ozkan became an entrepreneur, specializing in building materials. He figured it out correctly that in the postwar period, construction was going to be the growth sector. It was the right decision, signifying his business foresight and laying the foundation for his corporate success.

Within six months of the purchase of the Sime Darby stock, Ozkan doubled his investment. As expected the war over Suez boosted rubber prices. He put the windfall gains in building materials. In turn, they multiplied in value and by the late-fifties; Ozkan was now a wealthy Turkish Cypriot in London.

# XVIII

Meanwhile, in Cyprus and in Turkey terrible things were happening. Violence and conflict tore apart lives and people. Families like ours paid dearly for the folly of Greek fanatics. The EOKA campaign of terror in Cyprus erupted into a three-way civil war engulfing the Greek, Turkish Cypriots and the British army in a bloody conflict. The Turkish Cypriot cause was now a national cause in Turkey, stage-managed in Ankara by the increasingly dictatorial Menderes government and his charismatic foreign minister Fatin Rustu Zorlu. The result was a terrible riot in Istanbul in 1956. My sister Sevgi was accidentally in the middle of this horrible event, finding romance amidst terror.

Sevgi, now Mrs. Bozkurt, resumed her correspondence with me shortly after my new life in Canada. The last time we had exchanged letters was shortly after our father's and uncle Munir's sudden death. For several years past, every summer Sevgi and Aydin used to spend a month or two in Nicosia, something that the extended family enjoyed as much as she did herself. These visits were not purely personal; they provided her with opportunity to carry out research into the Ottoman history of the island. At last she decided to focus entirely on how the British acquired Cyprus in 1878. She discussed the idea with mother. "I am not a historian, dear" she replied, "but I like what you are saying. Maybe you should write to Tekin in Canada for an opinion." After a moment, mother's intellectual potential kicked in and she added, "After all Canada has been a British territory I hear. Write and ask Tekin how the British took control of Canada?" And then she added" "Your cousin Ozkan, in London, too, might have some useful ideas as well on the subject. I'd write to him too."

These letters led to a comparative study and in 1956 Sevgi finally produced a doctoral Thesis entitled *British Colonialism and Ottoman Rule Compared: How Britain Acquired the Island of Cyprus?* Sevgi, using original and secret documents, was able to demonstrate that corruption was at the root of the deal. The sad fact was that some of the top officials of the Sultan had been privately bribed, or more correctly, bought by the cunning British officials acting on strict orders of the Prime Minister Disraeli.

Afterwards, Sevgi concentrated on her specialty, social history. In the next several years, she produced some pioneering studies of the late Ottoman nobility, including Prime Minister Kamil Pasha of Cyprus and other notables, based on original archival documentation. She used land titles, wills and private letters of all kinds, visiting different parts of Turkey. Then, her interest shifted to Cyprus, specifically our own family. Especially after the death of father and uncle, Sevgi concentrated on Uzun Ali, her own Grandfather, the old *Kaimakam* of Milltown. That is how my sister Sevgi decided, with her love of family archives, to bring back to life her own Grandfather and discover our lost identity.

***

It was the summer of 1958, and the EOKA terror was raging full swing in Cyprus. There were more than 25,000 British troops on the island locked in a futile fight against Grivas and his guerrillas in the mountains. The mailman delivered the following letter from my sister Sevgi from Nicosia. She and Aydin were, as usual, spending their holiday on the island.

"Dear Brother Tekin,

This letter may come as a surprise to you as it has been years since we saw each other. We are all well. Mother is well too and sends her love.

## UZUN ALI, SHAME AND SALVATION

Life in Cyprus is now very dangerous; EOKA under Grivas is killing British soldiers, their wives and children, but also more and more Turkish Cypriots. It is ugly and becoming an inter-communal fighting. It is very dangerous to travel and so we are staying in Nicosia, seeing a lot of mother but not much of Aydin's family in Limassol.

Lately I have been working on a paper on our Grandpa. As you know he used to be a *Kaimakam* at the time the British took over Cyprus. I am tentatively calling the paper: *The effect of Colonial Rule on local administration in early British Cyprus: The transition from Kaimakam to the District Officer.* I want to use our Grandfather Uzun Ali for a personal narrative of the replacement of the Ottoman Kaimakam system with the British system of District Officer

I need some help from you in connection with this work. I know, as an engineer, you may not have much to say on the subject, but anything you can tell me about Grandpa will be a great help. I am also writing to cousin Ozkan in London because I understand from mother that his dad, Uncle Munir had been Grandpa's favorite son. Our Grandfather, as you may know, had his own Ottoman ways and he was a secretive man in many respects, but maybe Uncle Munir passed on some useful information to his son.

Please give my best wishes to Eleanor your dear wife and kiss Susan for me. Hoping to hear from you soon,

Your loving sister,
Sevgi."

Her letter made me very happy. I was so excited about her plans. At last Uzun Ali was to be resurrected through the pen and power of Sevgi. I mailed her the following letter from Toronto.

# DISCOVERY

"My Dear Sister Sevgi,

I was delighted with your letter. It is amazing that finally someone, especially you in the family, will look into our family history and give it a small space it deserves in academic work.

I never knew our Grandfather. He died well before I was born, as you know. But father used to talk about him all the time, usually with a pinch of salt. Apparently, the old Ottoman Kaimakam had his favorites, Munir, our uncle, was the apple of his eyes, his heir to the throne. He spent the family fortune, that part of it he did not gamble away, on educating Munir who was an Anglophile. My sense is that the old man never adjusted to the British takeover of the island. In fact, I once heard father say that Uzun Ali believed the British stole the island, cheated the Sultan's ministers to get it.

You must write to cousin Ozkan in London. He is a central figure in the story. Uncle Munir finally did become a lawyer in London but he had a love affair with an Irish girl called Mary. She came out looking for Munir and was murdered in Buyuk Han. Cousin Ozkan was born in London shortly after Uncle Munir returned to Cyprus, so when he found out about his son from Mary, uncle Munir went and brought him and raised him in memory of Mary. He named his son, Ozkan, after our father, for some moral debt that our mother knows about. Cousin Ozkan knows about the tragic love affair between his parents, we talked about it when I was last in London. I have a strong feeling he is yearning to discover some family secrets. Whatever you dig out will make him happy.

I am really excited about your work. Stay well, keep up the good work and do let me know your progress.

Your loving brother,
Tekin."

From London cousin Ozkan wrote to Sevgi as well.

## UZUN ALI, SHAME AND SALVATION

"Dear Cousin Sevgi,

Your letter about our Grandfather Uzun Ali was a real treat. It made my day. I am so glad you are digging into our family history. There are lots of questions unanswered in my own mind and I would love it if your research can enlighten us. Here is what I know.

Father was very close to Grandfather who died a broken man. After the British takeover, Uzun Ali's life and power were in effect finished. He became a dysfunctional landlord, trying to lead a life of an Ottoman autocrat, keeping a *harem* full of servants, living beyond his means. I understand he was quite a gambler. My father took years to complete his education, and that cost a pretty penny, I am sure. But Grandpa kept the money coming to pay for father's education in London. It was wartime and it was not easy.

In London father had a love affair with my mother, Mary, a poor girl from Dublin. Just as the war ended, father completed his studies and returned to Cyprus, but not before I was conceived. Mary did her best to raise me, but in the end she had to place me in an orphanage in Dublin and traveled to Cyprus, looking for dad's love, but some mysterious murder took place in Buyuk Han. I lost my dear mother. The place is for me a *Mecca* that contains mother's secret and I desperately want to dig and discover the truth of her killing. Maybe one day I will discover something more about her, some link to her.

There are many holes in what I know. I hope your research will lead to important discovery and lighten my burden. Keep on and stay in touch.

Say hallo to Aunt Aygul and best wishes in your studies.

Your loving cousin,
Ozkan"

## DISCOVERY

Letters continued to be exchanged between Ankara, Toronto, London and Nicosia. Plans were made and expectations set for the Grand Reunion. Finally, in the summer of 1961, the Uzun Ali's three grandchildren converged from different points in the world in Nicosia.

# XIX

In Nicosia mother Aygul was finally serene. She had passed her menopausal phase by the time the new generation of us, the global children, had crowded her modest home in Kuruchesme. It had been a difficult menopause, with vomiting and one moment feeling cold, the next hot all over. But now it was all behind her and at long last, she felt a big weight was lifted from her shoulders. For the first time in her life, Aygul felt at ease with herself, she experienced an inner peace, tranquility that had always eluded her. Ayse Hanim, her dear friend and neighbor from Xero days became her closest companion, once again. The two enjoyed each other's company, visiting one another and recalling joint memories of brief joy in the mining town.

Mother was the first to notice the change in her psychological condition. The change occurred gradually. In fact it took years for her to calm down, to face her past and come to terms with her tormented life. But once she attained serenity, the acceptance was quick. Her neighbors noticed the change in mother as well. What they said or did seemed too trivial to upset her. Gossip or taunting excited Aygul no more. She became more detached, more philosophical, accepting people as they were rather than as she wished them to be. Even her father's image, the nemesis she had fought all her life, started to change. All of a sudden, initially even without her noticing the change, doubts started to emerge in her own mind about her father.

# DISCOVERY

"I wonder if I might have misunderstood him." She reflected in her private thoughts about her father, in one of these moments. An inner voice, urged her on in this self-doubt: "Is it at all possible that he was a victim of his time?" She wondered, adding "Just as my own life and my own children. Look at them spread all over the world, for reasons beyond my wish or control."

Then, Ayse Hanim, her confidant from their all too brief happy days in Xero started calling on Aygul more frequently and this renewed friendship itself had a moderating influence.

"Ayse Hanim" said mother at one of these meetings, "you remember the times when we used to fight and argue all the time in Xero?"

Ayse laughed and replied: ""How can I forget them Aygul? Those were the happiest days of my life." mother concurred. "Yes indeed, they were." She said.

"But you know what" continued mother. "There is something, a sort of personal secret I want to share with you now." Her friend looked at mother with heightened interest. She continued:

"Maybe it is nothing or maybe it is my mood," she began, "but I feel there is a big change in me. I think I am beginning to see things differently." Ayse got curious. These were words she was not accustomed to hearing from Aygul. Instead of a bitter and angry woman, the person in front of her was a voice of reason, speaking the language of peace and reconciliation.

"Even about my father, the scoundrel he was, I sometimes think he might have been a lost soul, someone who behaved abominably in a complicated period when all seemed lost and crumbling." Ayse looked at her friend, not quite sure where she was going.

Aygul, her closest friend with a tormented past, was now suddenly assuming the role of a philosopher and a moralist. It was a role that Ayse was unsure about.

"Life is a gift of Allah, our Creator, but it is also a gamble" mother pronounced. "We are dealt a hand of cards and we are obliged to play, choosing to put down this card or that card, always with incomplete information because we do not know the cards of the other players." Poor Ayse, she was astounded, and gazed at mother.

After a pause, mother carried on: "Maybe my father was a victim; a prisoner with limited opportunities. He was a proud Ottoman, patriot at heart, but he was obliged to work for the British."

Ayse was perplexed, still uncertain about all this moralistic platitudes. She simply asked a question:

"Aygul, you have changed," she said. "Tell me, why do you think like this all of a sudden?"

"Well," said mother, "it is because of my daughter Sevgi."

"How did Sevgi change you?"

"In her last letter from Ankara Sevgi said something that got me thinking. You know she is now a historian, a professor." She added with pride. Ayse nodded and Aygul continued.

"Sevgi is studying how the Ottoman Sultan handed Cyprus to the British. She said that it was done in secret and all the subjects of the Sultan in the island were sold out."

Ayse Hanim was amazed and she was fully attentive. Mother continued:

"What Sevgi said suddenly opened my eyes. I began to see things in a different light. I first understood my father-in-law, Uzun Ali better. He was a Kaimakam, an important man. After the British came, he lost his status and identity and gambled away the family fortune. Ozkan never said a word in anger about his father." She stopped to catch her breath and continued while her guest listened intently.

"Then through Uzun Ali's life I started to think about my own father. I have always adored my mother and that made me see her as the innocent victim. Then, all of a sudden my father appeared as a victim as well; a victim of his time." She took a breath and after a moment, as Ayse waited, Aygul said: "My father was like Uzun Ali, victims all, as helpless as my poor mother."

Ayse sat there in front of Aygul, astonished at what she was hearing. In all her life, all these years since their days in Xero, she had never once witnessed, nor did she contemplate the day when she might hear a word of understanding, let alone forgiveness from Aygul's lips when it came to her father.

"Well Aygul," she said, "I am glad to hear you say these things. It must be a great weight off your mind. I am glad for you." They smiled at each other.

After Ayse had gone, and mother sat alone in contemplation, she said to herself ever so quietly: "Happiness is beyond liberation. It is a stage that follows forgiveness. It is a calm sea after the storm. I forgive my father for all his sins because in forgiveness lies the path to redemption."

The mere thought of redemption filled her heart with warmth and contentment. She was now thinking about salvation.

In the days, weeks and months following mother became more accepting of differences and faults in others. The torment in her was gone, replaced by inner peace. At long last, she was attaining the tranquility in life that she had been searching all these years. It was inside her, all that time, except she did not have the capacity to discover it.

# XX

When Ayfer was finally released from jail in 1956, he was a reformed man in a totally strange world. No one came to meet him when he walked out of prison a free man. Nilufer had died many years ago and he knew no one else. The poor Circassian maid passed unnoticed. No one mourned her.

It was a period of EOKA reign of terror. It was gangsterism of a kind that Ayfer knew nothing about.

Before leaving prison, Ayfer had resolved that in his middle age he would go straight. Now, he was reborn and determined to spend his remaining years as a new man. He had some cash, thanks to the generosity of the British penal system, which paid inmates, even convicted murderers like Ayfer, a few shillings a month for good behavior. With free food and lodgings in jail, Ayfer had saved it all.

So, now he had more than 100 pounds in his pocket, a handsome amount in those days. With the money he set himself as a pawnbroker, purchasing a store in the center of town, near the Grand Bazaar next to the Great Mosque now named the Selimiye Mosque. He also rented rooms nearby. He resumed a normal routine, waking up every morning to the muezzin's chant at dawn calling the faithful to prayers, spending his days in his store, and returning to his lodgings and a hearty self-cooked meal in the evening, before retiring to bed for a deep slumber.

# DISCOVERY

Ayfer's shop had a special, memorable history. It was the same store Mary visited during her last few hours, on that tragic day at the end of October 1923. Ayfer knew nothing about such historical side effects of the murder he had committed. The murder was for him an act of crime he had now repaid, and Buyuk Han was a place of shame, a sad piece of history, best forgotten. Now as a small businessman Ayfer was a new man who concentrated on making a success of remaining life, though he could not help note the irony of his situation: He was in the same Bazaar, on the other side so to speak, where long ago he had served in Blind Ahmet's gang as a young criminal, terrorizing businessmen like himself.

Ayfer, the transformed businessman, now decided that the pawnshop needed a face-lift. When he bought it, it was more like a dark and dirty warehouse, unappealing to potential customers. That is why he was able to get it at such a bargain price. Then, he sorted out the contents, classifying the glassware, the china and the wooden artifacts, neatly rearranging things in sections so customers can see what was available. When he completed all the tidying and renovations, he took a look at his creation. "Not bad at all" he said to himself. Truly his shop was now like an antique shop, and he was pleased with his minor reform.

What he did not know was that one day, here in this shop, he would come face to face with his half brother, the son of the woman he had murdered in Buyuk Han back in 1923, the son with whom he shared the same father.

# XXI

Uzun Ali's grandchildren, *de facto* exiles, finally assembled in Cyprus in May 1961 and their reunion was the fulfillment of covenants and pledges made years ago.

It was a large, international party. Ozkan and Jill came from London, Eleanor and I from Toronto and Sevgi and Aydin from Ankara. The children stayed home with Grandparents.

It was a large group to host for Aygul, so we stayed in the Saray Hotel, the new 8 storey hotel built in the old Konak Square from funds supplied by the departing British as indemnity for mismanagement of the *Evkaf* trust properties.

We arrived at a time of great optimism. The arrival of the Uzun Ali clan followed in the wake of a political miracle, a rebirth one never imagined. The Greeks and Turks, not a little nudged by the Americans through NATO headquarters in Brussels, suddenly reached a deal on Cyprus in Zurich and London. The agreement forced the British to go along, relinquish most of the island for a political resurrection. Independence was in the air and Turkish Cypriots and Greek Cypriots, enemies till yesterday, were obliged to enter into an arranged marriage, one that was too fragile to last a long time.

But for now, in 1961, we, the exiled Uzun Alis, were happy to be there, like private detectives, on a mission to solve their long forgotten family mysteries centered on Uzun Ali of Milltown. And we had

# DISCOVERY

one week to accomplish our mission.

Sevgi and Aydin met us at the airport. They had arrived a week earlier from Ankara and had already completed their mandatory family visits in Limassol and had made the necessary bookings for us all in Nicosia. Mother Aygul, now approaching her mid-fifties, came to welcome us as well. She was in such an emotional state; she could not hold her tears, seeing us all together. Everyone hugged and kissed, while other passengers and custom officials looked on, smiling and understanding our emotional reunion. Then, our party drove to the hotel, and by the time we checked in and were shown to our rooms, it was evening. After a cordial dinner, exhaustion from the long flights took hold of us all, and so we retired earlier than usual. We did not wake up till past mid-morning the next day.

After breakfast, we collected mother, and all drove to the Konak at Milltown and spend the whole day walking and wandering around the old place. Ozkan and Jill remained outside, surveying the grounds that once used to be the orchard and the rose garden, long ago abandoned and now indistinguishable from the thorns and brush that covered the entire backyard. Sevgi and Aydin checked the barns and the storerooms, while I led Eleanor to rooms upstairs where the *harem* and *selamlik* used to be. The best part was still the large living room in Neslihan's *harem* where she had received Mary and uncle Munir and had made a wonderful gesture of giving Grandpa's silver watch to Mary, hours before her murder in Buyuk Han. The walls were now full of holes, the plaster falling, but the floor was solid and the Ottoman settees still remained intact, though covered in dust and dirt. The shutters on windows were broken, and birds flew in and out of their nests in the roof.

The place had a sad, eerie atmosphere. My heart sank; the ruin was worse than I had imagined. We returned to the hotel and got ready for dinner. The mood was less than cheerful. Everyone agreed the Konak was a total ruin.

"We must conclude that it has seen better days," said Ozkan. It was a deliberate understatement. It looked pointless spending days there on a wild-goose chase.

Only Sevgi thought differently: "I would like to spend a little more time there" she declared, "looking for old documents. I am sure there are old documents hidden somewhere."

"I would like to see Pineview," said Eleanor. And Jill added: "Yes, it will be lovely to go see the places where Halil and Elana used to meet and plan their elopement."

So, the following two days were spent sightseeing in Pineview, Kormacit and the beautiful area in between on the foothills of the Five Fingers Mountains. The second day, we honored mother Aygul's wish to visit Pembe Hanim, her surrogate mother.

"She must be over 80?" I asked. "Yes, she is getting old. That is why I want to pay her a visit," said mother.

So we drove through the Five Fingers Mountains, going through the same pass that Halil and Elana, so many years ago, had traveled on their famous elopement, and where the bandit Midas had ambushed the English tourist party and made away with Lady Ramsbottom's royal jewels. Down below, toward the blue Mediterranean, the same fields and meadows stretched, where young and dashing Halil had made innocent love to Elana unconcerned about taboos and customs of the day.

We knew nothing of this romantic history at the time. We were travelers on our own journey, but all three traveled together as if pulled by the strong winds of these mountains on which the demi-gods in clouds above looked down and smiled at mortals, disclosing none of the secrets they had witnessed through time immemorial.

It was a visit just in time, old Pembe, delighted to see her adopted daughter Aygul, was now at the end of her long life. What a life it had been! Mother and Pembe sat together, oblivious to us strangers around them, as their minds and memories drifted back, years ago, to long-gone times of happiness and grief. They embraced and kissed, Aygul now in a forgiving mood at last for her father's torment. Pembe talked of her own sons and daughters, of the new generation of grandchildren; and her mind drifted far away from her strange and distant relatives assembled in Pineview, momentarily and for reasons to complex to comprehend. They left with the sadness that her death was not far.

***

It was the last day before departure. Ozkan wanted to go, one last time, to Buyuk Han to pay homage to Mary. "I'll come with you," said Jill, "I would like to do some shopping in the Grand Bazaar."

"If you don't mind," said Sevgi, "I would like to go back one last time to Konak to look for old documents."

I then thought of an idea. "We can have a picnic at the spring in Milltown. It is a beautiful spot under the grand old maples. And, then you can go to the Konak, which is not very far" I said to everyone's approval.

"And, for our last dinner, lets all meet for a grand feast at mothers'. We will cater and have a big farewell dinner together." That was the unanimous decision and so our party was split into two, Ozkan and Jill went to Buyuk Han and the Grand Bazaar nearby, while the rest of us went to Milltown.

Ozkan and Jill spent the whole morning at Buyuk Han. They walked in the deserted courtyard, went upstairs and wept in the abandoned, empty room where Mary had slept and died, staying there alone for a long time. "Mother, oh dear mother" he prayed in silence, Jill standing besides him, "I wish I could read your heart. I only know about your sacrifice, your quest for love. Why was it denied to you? Especially when father so loved you? That is my own torment. Rest in peace and please forgive my father for whatever his sin. He spent his entire life redeeming himself. I am the living proof of his redemption. And I promise you one thing: I will always cherish and honor your sacrifice. I will try to be a worthy son."

Then they came out of the Han, and with Jill in his arm, he walked toward the Selimiye Mosque, next to the Grand Bazaar. He wanted to purchase something, some little memento to take back. So he wondered, quite accidentally, into an antique store, next to the mosque. It was the same old pawnshop that his mother had visited long ago. But now the shop was spruced up and looked inviting. And, the shop owner was extremely friendly. He was a skinny man, in mid 50's, smiling and welcoming. There was a weird strangeness in the air.

There stood the two half brothers, Ayfer and Ozkan, face-to-face, for the first and last time, but as total strangers. The encounter lasted but a few minutes, till the transaction was completed. None knew the other. The two had come from places far away, one recently out of jail in a world that time had passed by; the other from London, rich and alien.

"Welcome" said the shop owner. "Come in, come in. I have many nice things. Good price." He said in broken English.

The half brother said nothing, with curiosity written all over his face, he just smiled and walked in, unsure of what he was looking for, searching aimlessly.

Then, he saw it.

There in front of a table, amidst the bric-a-brac, in a box of old stuff, was a discarded old bracelet, covered in dust. In the box one item caught Ozkan's attention; the bracelet had some writing on it. He cleaned the dirt and there was the word MARY. He felt like his mother was there with him at that moment. He stood frozen, almost motionless, staring at the bracelet. Jill stood by him, sensing the deep meaning of the moment.

Some inner voice said to Ozkan: "This is your mother's" and he believed it. With conviction and certainty... It was like solving a mathematical problem, QED.

He bought it and went out of the shop. The transaction between two half brothers was consummated.

Ozkan, at last, had found the treasure he had been searching. At long last he had something of mother's, something he could touch, feel and cherish. He felt reborn, resurrected from the dead; he had never felt closer to his mother.

Mysteriously without each knowing the other, the two half brothers, brought together by fate to transact a business, had their chance meeting, like travelers at the some invisible crossroad, but then immediately each kept on traveling in separate paths going in different directions. They were never to meet again, nor know each other's identity.

\*\*\*

The rest of the party went ahead with a huge picnic in a beautiful spot under the maples near the main spring in Milltown. After a sumptuous lunch, Sevgi took leave while I and the rest of the party stayed on till sundown enjoying the serene quiet of the place as the afternoon breeze from the Five Fingers Mountains gently swayed the leafs of the tall maple trees and the water in the canal murmured rhythmically down the stream. It reminded me of pleasant childhood memories. Then, without noticing I fell asleep in a wonderful and cool nap that one could only enjoy in such places in the island of love.

Sevgi had her own plans. She went to the Konak to dig for old documents, realizing at last her long-planned ambition. She knew where to look. She went straight into the attic, right above the old

# DISCOVERY

*Selamlik*, where Grandpa Uzun Ali had held court and where he conducted his business as the provincial governor of the district.

There, in a chest, she hit upon an amazing discovery. Her timing was itself incredible, coming just hours after Ozkan's own huge discovery in the antique shop earlier that day. These discoveries, all in the same day, were fantastic, revealing long-lost truths about our roots and identities lost and found.

Excitedly Sevgi opened the chest. It contained some papers and notes, but amidst all of it, there was one sealed envelope. It was written in Ottoman script and Sevgi looked at the bottom and read it, thankful that she had spent all those years learning the difficult Ottoman grammar:

"This is the life story and testament of Uzun Ali the *Kaimakam* of Milltown; written in 1918" She read the manuscript in full, barely controlling her excitement:

"I have decided to put down a few thoughts on paper after I had a surprise visit yesterday by Halil Osman, a former policeman and now in jail serving a long prison sentence for the death of his young wife. He felt great remorse for the wrong he did to his wife and daughter and he came asking for my permission to arrange marriage between his daughter and Ozkan, my younger son. The marriage of our children, he felt, was to be his redemption, his release from the sins he had committed. He assured me that Ozkan was keen to marry in his daughter. He had the proof by a matchmaker and he asked for my blessings to proceed. I said to him, I would not block my son's happiness; if that was what Allah willed, so be it.

Then he told me his story. What Halil told me influenced me greatly; it made me understand myself better. That is why I write these few lines for my children and grandchildren.

He and I shared the same loss when the British came and took over Cyprus, completely as a surprise. My life was ruined overnight. Suddenly, I was no longer Kaimakam. I lost everything, but most of all my dignity. Material ruin followed; my wealth trickled away like water in the sands of the desert. I gambled seeking pleasure, hoping against hope that the bad dream of British occupation was temporary; that somehow the good old days would return.

The wars came, one after the other, the Balkan War, Italian War and then finally the Great War. The British got stronger and I went into debt to educate Munir, but more to finance my addiction. My

367

escape from the ugly reality was like a drug. My gambling habit consumed me.

Then, Halil, the scoundrel appeared in front of me. He told me his life story. What a wonderful life he had growing up in his village in Pineview, up in the western slopes of our Five Fingers Mountains. Anyway, his father was rich and with money in his pocket and his good looks, women came to him, throwing themselves at him. The British encouraged him in his excesses, first by joining him in his womanizing escapades in the Armenian whorehouses, then rewarding him with a job. Halil was unhappy and unfulfilled at home and brought a Maronite girl, intending to make him his second wife, but his first wife was too jealous and would have none of it. His British bosses accepted polygamy and watched from a distance as his life and family were ruined. Halil's folly was that he broke all the rules: Ottoman decency, British justice, and above all, Allah's law of fidelity. But then our generation did not know by whose rules to conduct ourselves. We were like lost sheep. Our world suddenly crumbled all around us. I pitied Halil for his abduction and infidelity, but then on second reflection, I said to my self: "The scoundrel lived an exciting life."

I now realize one thing: The British took away my dignity; they covered up poor Halil's indignity. The British are smart and clever; they rule the world. Our generation failed to understand this, forces beyond our borders. Our leaders in the seat of power in Istanbul were ignorant of world affairs, and they were selfish, interested in filling their pockets. As a result, we were all disgraced, sold out by our own Padisah.

I now see clearly a parallel between Halil and myself. We are both victims in strange world we did not understand. Halil became a hedonist, I a gambler. In the end we both lost. The world now is British and neither Halil nor I, the last Ottomans, have a place in it.

I know I will die soon. I now want to tell you a little about my father so that you know something about your family roots. My father Tahsin was a *tahsildar*, a tax farmer, a man of property and wealth. You see until some years before I was born, tax collection was a highly lucrative business. For centuries, the tax revenues used to be collected by the Archbishop from the peasants. When the Greeks revolted against our Padisah, the Church was no longer reliable and so the government appointed *tahsildars* who would buy portions of tax collection in open auctions, paying large sums of money up front and

## DISCOVERY

then collecting the *vergi,* the tax, from villagers. It was a good life for our family, except in times of drought and locusts. That is how I became involved in the locust campaign. We worked hard but in the end the dreaded locust was eliminated.

Now, I must look ahead, to the future. Ignorance is our common enemy; education is the way forward. I am proud of Munir's education. This is my one lasting legacy. I trust the legacy will enrich my line. I feel great remorse for having done so little for my younger son Ozkan; his elder brother was luckier. Maybe he will find happiness in his marriage. My one wish is that Munir will take care of my grandchildren.

I ask my sons to forgive me for my sins, but also to be proud of the name of Uzun Ali so that my grandchildren may stand tall, prosper and find happiness in the modern world

Uzun Ali,
*Kaimakam* of Milltown."

***

When Sevgi brought us the great news, we were overjoyed. We made her read the letter several times. It was a stunning discovery for us all. Uncle Munir, unknowingly, has redeemed his father's wish. It was a miracle.

First we unanimously agreed that the testament should remain in Sevgi's possession. It would be framed and hang in the place of honor in the Bozkurt family in Ankara.

Then we experienced rejoicing with Sevgi's discovery of our roots and destiny as the Uzun Ali clan.

"Sevgi" I said, "please make brilliant copies of Grandpa's testament, one for each, and send it to us, so we can frame it and place it in the place of honor in our homes. You keep the original in your possession. " All cheered their approval.

Dinner that night was a joyous and emotional farewell. It lasted till wee hours of the morning as the Uzun Ali clan gathered around in a last supper with mother Aygul.

Ozkan finally at rest with the reality of Mary, having at last found a precious belonging of his mother, opened the conversation on Grandpa's testament.

Turning to Sevgi, he said: "What you have discovered Sevgi, is nothing short of magnificent. It makes me proud to be Uzun Ali's grandson, proud of my father. But I want to hear what you all think about it."

Sevgi responded: "Our Grandfather at the Konak in Milltown was a lost soul, but with a good heart. He tried to adjust to the British takeover of Cyprus, but he never accepted it. In his heart he was always a patriot like Namik Kemal, a disappointed Ottoman who yearned for the progress of his nation, but he died before seeing it in his life."

I then joined in with a question for Sevgi: "What was Grandpa's message, my dear historian?"

Sevgi, the academic rose to the challenge, saying: "My point is this: Had Grandpa Uzun Ali lived, he would have embraced Kemalism, secularism and modernism. His legacy was transmitted to us through Uncle Munir. He would die a happy and proud Turk were he to see our eventual success. Uzun Ali's conviction was that the Turks of Cyprus were sold to the British in Istanbul in some underhanded way, secretly while some middlemen at the top of the Ottoman bureaucracy got rich; they will be redeemed via education and knowledge in due course… in Ankara and elsewhere."

"Well put!" I said. "However, there is another point to add, a point of eternal value" I added.

"Our Grandfather is showing us the way to redemption. He was a lost soul, no doubt, but a victim of his times. He wanted to do the best for his family and children. But external forces beyond his control interfered. His example lies in pointing out to the Turks of Cyprus the significance of international forces. You must conquer these forces, or else they will blow you away. The Turks of the island must realize they are part and parcel of a big Turkish nation. Only as part of this great nation can they overcome international challenges. Closed within the island is the path of isolation and ultimately ruin. Thinking only in local terms is like our Grandpa losing his hope, and turning to gambling. He lost a fortune in gambling, but the fortune was lost anyhow abroad, in far away Istanbul. Grandfather Halil was no different; his freedom was an illusion, concocted once again by hotheads with half-baked ideas in Istanbul. Halil was an Ottoman adrift in a world coming apart. In the end, just before his death Uzun Ali discovered an eternal truth." I stopped to catch my breath, and then continued.

"To liberate one's soul from past sins, you must broaden your horizons. We, the new generation who understand the international scene, must take charge, to help those of our brothers and sisters in Cyprus to achieve success. For that we need to forgive our forefathers for their sins and transgressions. We must seek modern knowledge and join forces, those inside and outside the island, to do better. That is what Grandpa tried to tell us in his letter. Knowledge is the path to success in the new world. This is the spirit of the Konak: wherever we live, the love of the island unites us. We the grandchildren, living in different parts of the world, knowing the modern ways, are all Uzun Ali's, but the bond that unites us all is spirit of the Konak."

"I can relate to that," said Ozkan. "I feel I am myself a living proof of what Tekin is talking about. After my mother was killed in Buyuk Han, my father rescued me from the convent to redeem himself. He also had the spirit of generosity to invest in all of us. Now it is up to me: I must honor both as a member of the Uzun Ali family in upholding the spirit of the Konak. We with Turkish blood living abroad must link up with those brothers and sisters living on the island. That is the path to success."

Then silence followed. It was silence of union, or harmony, of being one. I felt a deep sense of fulfillment: Sevgi, Ozkan and I had at last discovered the unifying spirit, buried in the Konak that held us together.

***

After breakfast the next day, the party got ready to go to the airport. But another emotional event awaited me. Mother Aygul pulled me aside and said:

"Son, this is for you" handing me an old jewelry box. It was Uzun Ali's silver wristwatch. It was a touching gift. I looked at it with gratitude, admiring this thing of wonderful beauty that had witnessed so much of our family history; now it was to be my prize possession.

I hugged my mother, kissed her hand in the old traditional way, but said nothing because on that occasion, only feelings mattered and both mother and son knew exactly what each had in mind: My thoughts wondered off to father Ozkan Sr., the quiet way of a husband accepting Uzun Ali's gambling ways, and the father whose decision to depart from the little world of Xero so I could seek education in the global world was the defining moment of the son's entry into the modern age.

Then, the three grandchildren hugged and kissed each other. Reciprocal invitations were exchanged and promises made for future reunions.

Finally it was Aygul turn for a good-bye reckoning: "May Allah protect you always, wherever you are" she began. "I feel lonely at times, with both my children in far away places. But, as I get older I am closer to my Creator. I believe He is showing me the way to inner peace. I am now thinking about my father in a different way; he does not torment me any more." It was an unusually spiritual farewell for her. We hugged and kissed her on both cheeks.

Then, Aygul said: "My friend Ayse is coming for a visit. We always have so much to talk about old times. I so enjoy our chats…" Her mind was already drifting away from us.

We wondered at first who Ayse was. Then we remembered Aygul's confidant from the Xero days, Aygul's happiest. It was a happy ending.

\*\*\*

The rendezvous in Cyprus had paid off. The grandchildren had discovered something else of eternal value about Uzun Ali's family. Like thousands of Turkish Cypriots in England, Australia and elsewhere, now the Uzun Ali family was a global family with Canadian, English and Turkish branches.

# XXII

Ozkan returned to London on a lucky streak. The god of the market place smiled on him.

The entrepreneur was like Midas: Ozkan could do no wrong; whatever he touched seemed to turn into gold.

He soon became one of the wealthiest Turkish Cypriots in town. From an ordinary construction materials seller, Ozkan grew rapidly, vertically and horizontally. From construction, he started buying houses and real estate, and then expanded into furniture and white appliances and so on. Jill was a fantastic support. The husband and wife became a business dynamo. And the cash flow grew exponentially.

The ace in the pack turned out to be the Sime Darby stock that Ozkan had purchased back in 1956 when his father had left him half a million pounds. Now that Malaya had become an independent country, enjoying an economic growth, the stock kept on rising, going through the roof. Ozkan became a multi-millionaire.

Fame followed him, not from his wealth but generosity. As his financial empire grew, Ozkan gave freely in support of the Turkish people in Cyprus.

"I have no choice" he would say, "whatever I have, it is all owed. None of it is mine. It is Uzun Ali wealth. I am holding it in trust."

Jill, his wife, went along with it all. The Welsh nationalist in her heart and her avid interest in the Cyprus problem made the couple a crusading family. They donated money and much of their time in London to publicize and support the Turkish cause in Cyprus. Jill started magazines and sponsored books to educate the ill-informed English about modern Turkey and what being a Turk in Cyprus meant. Husband and wife, and now their children growing up, were no less passionate about the rights of Turks in Cyprus than Turkish Cypriots in the island. To prove his commitment, Ozkan started investing in a variety of projects specializing in tourism in Kyrenia and in Nicosia taking an active part in the restoration of Buyuk Han in memory of his mother.

Ozkan exemplified the new breed of Turkish Cypriot entrepreneurs. He was a success on the world stage. He started purchasing companies and creating new ones. A risk-taker, just like his gambling Grandfather, the old Kaimakam of Milltown, Ozkan had a shrewd sense of timing, knowing when to buy and when to sell.

Uzun Ali's wish was at last fulfilled. The modern children, thanks to education and knowledge, had taken their place in the globalized world. Ozkan in London, Tekin in Toronto, and Sevgi in Ankara, were the successful modern generation. The world seemed too small for them.

# THE END

# BOOK IV

## HYPOCRITES AND ANGELS

Five Fingers Mountain Peak

# I

Our family has been shaped by history. We are all children of, not just our parents, but as well of the times we lived through. Our historical experience, good or bad, bitter or sweet is what shapes us into what we are. I make no moral judgment on what has happened; I just observe, read and record it as best as I can. The past is gone, beyond our reach or influence. Now is what counts and future is what we can shape, if we learn from the past. We are like leaves floating on a huge ocean swept here and there by storms all around. Generation after generation, our family has undergone great transformations, not so much due to the force of its personalities, but rather because of the times in which we had to live.

The generation of my Grandparents witnessed the death and destruction of a great Empire, the Ottomans. In Cyprus, after the Ottomans the British came and everyone tried to cope with things British. Alas, the British hold in Cyprus was casual and temporary. My own parents' identified more with the ideals of the Kemalist revolution in Modern Turkey than the colonial rule. New threats and conflicts appeared on the horizon as increasingly it appeared as if the British rule of Cyprus was merely a prelude, an excuse for handing the island to Greece. That would mean not just yet another identity transformation. It would have meant our end. When cultures collide, there is no middle ground. Either you perish or you pack up and go, as the Greeks and Turks did after the First World War. Giving up one's identity and religion is simply not an option, anymore than cutting a tree's roots is preserving it.

***

When, in 1960, the miracle of independence occurred in Cyprus, I was in Toronto and my sister Sevgi was a young academic in Ankara. Ozkan was in London, a successful businessman. Mother Aygul was living alone, but serene in old age in Nicosia. We were already a scattered family with tentacles in all part of the shrinking world.

The Cyprus independence was an event that surprised me and raised in my mind all kinds of difficult questions. I was as astonished as anyone else that suddenly violence was to be replaced by an age of milk and honey: The age-old Turkish-Greek enmity gave way to an apparent show of friendship and cooperation. Cyprus was a brand new partnership state to be governed jointly by Turks and Greeks. It was unbelievable that the British were leaving, although as part of the independence deal they retained large parts of the island as sovereign military bases. My mind was full of difficult questions and worries about the future: "Why did Makarios, the sworn enemy of the Turks, suddenly agree to share power with the Turks? What happened to his dream of ENOSIS?" Could he be trusted? "Why did the Turks, who until yesterday were rioting and demanding that 'Cyprus is Turkish' and the island should be returned back to Turkey, now agree to half a loaf?"

Frankly, looking back after many years, my fears and concerns were justified. Independence in Cyprus was doomed. It did not last even three years. The Turks and Greeks of the island made a mess of things. Again, our family, like others, ended up paying the price. Our generation was already scattered all over the world, but now, as a result of renewed violence and inter-ethnic fighting, our family became a global family. This is the story of how it all happened, written by a Canadian who wishes to remain anonymous.

***

In the summer of 1968 two Cypriot politicians, Rauf Denktas and Glafcos Clerides met in Beirut to discuss the Cyprus problem. The recent fighting in the Turkish village of Kofunye on the highway to Limassol in which the Grivas forces massacred a large number of

Turkish Cypriots had shifted the moral balance, once again, in favor of the Turks of Cyprus. This was the second time the world was outraged by Greek massacres in Cyprus, the earlier case being the Christmas 1963 onslaught on the Turks of Cyprus when Europe was minding its own business and the USA looked the other way.

The massacre at Kofunye marked the end of the Republic, which had given Tekin and Ozkan so much optimism back in 1961. As it turned out, this Republic was doomed from the start. It was the most unnatural thing imaginable, with no more chance of success than Halil's marriage to Emine. The British had replaced the Ottomans in Cyprus, but misrule did not end on the island. In Ottoman times, the two ethnic communities had lived peacefully, in worlds apart; now under the British they were at each other's throat in the forced marriage brought about by the British called the Republic of Cyprus.

The Greek tragedy in Cyprus followed quickly and predictably because just as Halil's parents had conspired to bring about a forced marriage in Pineview, so the handmaidens of the Republic had been the British and the Americans who had conspired with the Greek and Turkish military to force the Republic down the throats of Turkish and Greek Cypriots who had never had anything in common. The basic problem was that the Turks and Greeks of Cyprus did not know each other. Historically they lived in worlds apart. They had no shared experience except the island itself. Even the Maronites of Kormacit had had more contact with the Turkish Cypriots of Pineview, though poor Elana knew almost nothing of the Ottoman world when she willingly entered Halil's harem on the Tanzimat Street.

The British were now gone. Actually, they left only in part, retaining two large bases in the south of the island guarding the Suez and the Middle East oil fields. Having secured their defense interests on the island, the British were in reality quite happy to be unburdened of Cyprus. Now, the Greeks and Turks could fight it amongst themselves.

The Greeks now turned their fire on the Turks of the island. Greek Cypriot fanatics planned extermination plans while Makarios prepared the ground with cunning diplomacy. He gave the Turks an ultimatum at the end of 1963: either accept an inferior status, with minority rights in a Greek-controlled Cyprus, or face violent destruction. The Turks of Cyprus resisted and Makarios encouraged the fanatics to attack them, the prince of the church once again opted for blood and violence.

The Makarios plan seemed to work; he got his first reward at the UN. In March 1964, the UN Security Council recognized the Makarios regime as the legitimate government of the island and the entire world looked on. Turkish Cypriots created a citizen army of resistance. Peasants suddenly became soldiers; families bonded together to share food and help one another. Gradually they discovered a moral strength they never thought they had. The world press had been full of bloody pictures of the dying Turkish Cypriot women and children when Greek Cypriot EOKA fighters, victorious against the British, launched a general attack in Christmas 1963 in a well-organized plan to destroy the Republic and make Cyprus Greek. The Turkish Cypriots suddenly became refugees in their homeland, imprisoned in villages and cut off from the outside world. But they survived.

Now in 1967, they acted by declaring unilaterally a separate Administration in the North of the island. UDI was then in vague, the latest case being Ian Smith in Rhodesia. Grivas took matters in his hands and launched an all-out attack on the Turkish inhabitants of Kufunye, lately greatly reinforced by refugees streaming in from surrounding villages. But the Turks were outnumbered in every respect and suffered large number of casualties. It would have been a full-scale massacre had not Turkey threatened to send in its troops. In the end, Grivas was stopped, forced to leave the island, and the diplomats met in Beirut to try to settle the differences between the two ethnic groups in Cyprus.

The Greeks in the South were, as always, split down the middle between two extreme camps. On the one hand, the Grivas extremists wanted ENOSIS now and they were ready to die for it, even though the British were gone. A tool of the colonels who recently took power in Greece, Grivas believe he could destroy the Turkish Cypriots quickly, and he set to prove his point in Kofunye. Grivas was distrustful of the wily Archbishop Makarios, who suddenly seemed to abandon his Enosist ideal in favor of grandstanding on the world stage, much to the disappointment of the American and NATO conspirators who had designed the unnatural Republic.

***

The Beirut meeting got nowhere. Others, equally futile in Paris, Vienna, Geneva, New York and other genteel places, followed it. The

## HYPOCRITES AND ANGELS

Cyprus Problem was now in the hands of international diplomats. The diplomats wrote minutes, drafted resolutions, agreed to meet yet again, but got nowhere. The wiser ones amongst these diplomats recognized that they were trying to square the circle. The Turks and Greeks in Cyprus never lived as one nation, so what was the point of forcing them to become one now?

"We do not take sides," declared the UN diplomats when obliged to speak. "The UN is strictly neutral; the Secretary General is merely performing a good-offices mission." No one bothered to ask what exactly a "good-offices mission" was?

As if further proof was needed, the diplomats insisted. "The UN position is explicit: We maintain the principle of non-intervention in internal matters of member states."

The UN process on the Cyprus conflict did not produce peace. Hypocrites took the center stage in a motley dance of diplomats going in circles in a mission impossible.

Canada had a big hand in the diplomatic games over Cyprus. Lester B. Pearson, the energetic Canadian chief diplomat at the UN at the time, almost single-handedly engineered the creation of the UN Peace Force for Cyprus and the Canadian troops, the Van Doos from Quebec, were dispatched to the island early in 1964 even before the UN had adopted the necessary resolution. The UN soldiers came to the island for six months initially as that was the time thought necessary to solve the Cyprus problem.

The first thing the UN soldiers did in Cyprus was to draw a green line separating the Greek and Turkish Cypriots. The line at that time was limited to Nicosia. The separation became more or less permanent, and the UN troops remained in the island ever since, the six-month duration becoming a sort of UN rubber-stamping procedure.

In July 1974 the Greeks resorted to violence yet again. An all-Greek civil war was fought in Cyprus for immediate ENOSIS. Makarios was toppled, but in the end saved by the British. The Greek Junta in Athens installed a puppet Sampson in place of Makarios with orders to declare Union with Greece by *fait accompli*, repeating what had been done successfully in Crete in 1912. Then the Turkish Army landed to prevent ENOSIS and rescue the Turkish Cypriots from ethnic cleansing by the Greek soldiers.

As luck would have it, Tekin and his Canadian family were present in Nicosia and observed first hand the 1974 civil war that led to the

Turkish military intervention. This chance presence occurred thanks to a rather unique round of UN assignments in Africa that had taken Tekin and Eleanor away from Canada. Here is how it all happened.

# II

Canada, 10,000 miles from Cyprus, was the last place on earth to get embroiled in the Cyprus Problem, but the British and the American diplomacy sometimes work in mysterious ways. Tekin, a professional Turk from Cyprus and now a new Canadian, did not expect his adopted country to become a player in his original homeland's messy politics.

In the mid- 1960s Canadian economy was booming and the country was changing fast. It was the best of times. Pierre Elliot Trudeau became the Prime Minister. Trudeaumania followed the Centennial celebrations; it created one long party atmosphere and all Canadians joined in. Trudeau was the creation of Prime Minister Lester B. Pearson, who, when in charge of Canadian foreign policy, had single-handedly invented UN peacekeeping for Cyprus and sent off Canadian troops to stop the Greek Cypriots massacring Turkish Cypriots at the end of 1963.

Pearson passed his mantle to Pierre Elliot Trudeau, who took the reins of power in Ottawa and became the Philosopher King. Though from Quebec, Trudeau was a staunch federalist. An autocrat at heart, he had one thing in common with Grandfather Halil. They both had female problems. But Trudeau had a big advantage over Grandfather. He could solve his domestic problems with his much younger hippie wife, Maggie, with political deftness in parliament. Then, when like

Cyprus, Canada faced division and ethnic conflict in 1972 he suddenly imposed martial law in Canada to fight separatism in Quebec.

Soon, Trudeau invented the multiculturalism policy, a sort of Canadian version of the Ottoman *millet* system. It was meant to embrace all new comers from Africa, the Caribbean, Hong Kong, India and all four corners of the world. Canada was a now a land of song and music, of boundless opportunity. "Unity amongst diversity" became the new slogan.

Like the Ottoman experiment with Liberty in 1908, Trudeau's good intentions produced Armenian terror in Canada, terror directed against innocent Turkish diplomats. Years later, Tekin was to be dragged into this inferno with surprising roots in Cyprus from his student days with his Armenian teacher Schomelian.

***

Tekin's engineering career at the Hydro Ontario was, like Canada itself, skyrocketing on an exponential rising trend. Prosperity was everywhere and it looked like the good times would last forever. Immigrants poured in and economic boom continued. New expressways were built; towns and industries mushroomed in all areas. Demand for electricity meant expansion in Hydro Ontario and Tekin was the right man at the right place. He was constantly in demand, preparing blueprints for new power stations, grid lines and projecting demand for electricity.

But at home Eleanor began to get restless, yearning for overseas adventure. Their daughter Susan, now in her teens, was in a boarding school, and Eleanor felt a bit lonely. In any event, she was ready for some adventure and excitement. She belonged to a Wednesday coffee club with a few friends from her university days, and she had come into some useful information about overseas assignments with CUSO (Canadian University Service Overseas), a Canadian version of the US Peace Corps. Under the scheme Canadian professionals would be sent overseas for a term of two years doing development work in Africa or Asia.

That is what Eleanor wanted to do; exotic lands and adventure appealed to her and she reasoned that if you did not go out and discover the world while still relatively young, you would never be able to do it. She was especially interested in Africa, with all its exotic flora and fauna, natural reserves and wild life. Africa from afar looked enticing and exciting.

"Darling, why don't you look into some of these overseas assignments?" She would ask Tekin. "It would be so much fun. I'd love to see the wild animals in Africa."

Tekin was quite happy at Hydro Ontario. In fact he had just been offered an appointment as District Manager responsible for the entire Northern Ontario region, where a great potential existed for power generation for the expanding industry. The new job would have required relocation to Sudbury, a bleak outback town, which Eleanor was secretly hoping to avoid.

When the family was discussing the merits and demerits of relocation to Sudbury, Tekin came home with great news for Eleanor.

"Darling" he said, "I have some exciting news for you. If you are still interested in overseas assignment," he did not quite finish his sentence. Eleanor jumped with joy, and said; "Yes, yes, of course I am interested."

"Yes," he said, "I have an offer. But, I am afraid you may turn it down when you hear about it."

"No. I won't. Tell me" she demanded. He went on with less than full enthusiasm:

"It is an assignment in Liberia, where vocational schools are being built and they need teachers to train future electricians." He said.

She had a sinking look on her face. Liberia was not exactly the exotic African picture she had in her mind. In fact, she could not even place it on the map.

"Where is Liberia?" She asked gloomily. Geography was her least favorite subject at university. But, in all honesty, she had not heard of a country called Liberia.

"It is on the west coast of Africa. A small country, I am told rather primitive, a hardship country." Tekin was less than enthusiastic about the assignment. In fact, he would have turned down, except that he first wanted to share it with Eleanor.

Then they took out the maps and books, and studied the location of Liberia and discovered that its capital was Monrovia, named after some early US president who had started a project in Africa to resettle freed American slaves back in early 19$^{th}$ century. They looked at each other, each waiting for the other to make the first choice. Meanwhile, Eleanor was thinking to herself: "Either Sudbury or Liberia" and it did not take her a long time to opt for Monrovia, Liberia.

## UZUN ALI, SHAME AND SALVATION

\*\*\*

The assignment was with an UN agency called International Food Organization (IFO) and Tekin would join a team of engineers to work as teachers in a vocational school near the capital city of Monrovia. It was a 2-year assignment, which meant that Tekin would have to get an unpaid leave of absence from Hydro Ontario. No problem was expected on that score. He was, however, sorry to miss his promotion to District Manager in Northern Ontario.

Within a month, Tekin and Eleanor were off to Liberia. Susan was happy in the boarding school with her own friends. The trip started badly and got steadily worse. First, they had some distressing family news. Dear old Aygul was taken ill and Tekin had to cancel plans to proceed to Monrovia and go first to Cyprus to visit Aygul and family. Greek Cypriots were then in total control of the island. Fortunately, by the time the Canadian party had arrived Aygul was very much on the mend. It was pneumonia but, thankfully, it was detected early enough, and as soon as Sevgi arrived from Ankara, Aygul got all the rest and care she needed.

Tekin and family were not so lucky. Their problem started at the airport in Nicosia when they checked in for their onward flight to Rome and then on to Monrovia. The Greek Cypriot official at the airport would not permit the Uzun Ali family to board the plane to Rome.

"Mr. Uzun Ali" he said very seriously, "I am afraid you cannot board the plane."

Tekin was dumbfounded. He asked calmly: "What seems to be the problem?"

The Greek Cypriot official said: "You have an unpaid tax bill."

"What sort of unpaid bill?" asked Tekin.

"I do not know. All I know is that you are on my black list and you cannot go until the debt is paid off." He said.

Then Eleanor stepped in. "We are with the UN. We are off to an important assignment and we have to be in Rome tomorrow."

The official looked at her and behaved as if he had heard nothing. He said nothing.

Then Tekin asked the officer: "What do you suggest I should do?"

"Well!" he said, giving the impression of a crook in official uniform, he pronounced. "I would go to the Department of Inland Revenue tomorrow morning and settle the debt to the government."

That is what Tekin did, but it took him 3 days to find out what was owed and arrange to have it paid. It was some outstanding debt from a land deal from his uncle Munir. When he protested he had nothing to do with it, he was asked point blank: "Do you want to go to Rome?" So, finally when Tekin paid up for his uncle, accepting the blackmail as a kind of hefty exit tax, the family was allowed to travel to Monrovia via Rome. "Some Greek Cypriot justice" he thought.

The blackmailing in Cyprus was a precursor of what was to follow. Far worse awaited Tekin and his family in Liberia. It started the very next day after their arrival in Monrovia.

"The Minister would like to see you right away, sir" said the secretary as soon as Tekin reported for work. Initially, and secretly, he was pleasantly surprised that the top man would show an interest in Tekin's assignment.

"Mr. Uzun Ali" began the Minister of Education. "I have a house to rent and I suggest you take your wife to see it right away. The rent is $2000 a month." It was an astonishing amount in a country where the average salary for a government official was $100 a month.

Tekin was astounded and all he could do was an inadequate response:

"Sir, with all due respect, I cannot afford that kind of rent."

The Minister went on: "Don't worry about it," he said smiling broadly. He figured Tekin must be a novice in this line of work. Or else, he was extremely naïve, too unfamiliar with how the international aid system worked in Monrovia.

Tekin was silent and unconvinced. The Minister spoke again, this time in a carefully soft and persuasive tone. He offered his standard offer, an offer that Tekin's predecessors apparently had no trouble in accepting.

"IFO will pay the rent, they always do. You pay me half of it, and keep the other half." Tekin was shocked. He had never been exposed to corruption before. He looked nervous and unsure of his ground.

The Minister got up, came close to Tekin and said, paternalistically: "Don't worry, it is normal business here. That is how the aid system works." Still Tekin remained non-committal. After a long pause, he thought of something to say:

"Well, sir, I will talk to my wife. Maybe we can go, see the house." He said lamely. The Minister had no choice but to go along.

The next morning they saw the house, and in the afternoon he informed the Minister of his decision.

"I am sorry sir, but the house is too big for us" He said as he had agreed with Eleanor.

The Minister was obviously unimpressed. Tekin walked out of his office.

That was the last time he was to see the Liberian Minister of Education.

Then, in the following days and weeks, things got worse, much worse. It was due to what Tekin began to observe about the food aid program. The food was supposed to be distributed freely to feed the school children. But the manager of the program, a certain Dutch fellow called Van der Zam, was selling the food on the market and dividing the revenue, 70:30, with the Minister of Education, the Minister getting the larger share.

Tekin found about this scheme by accident. One day, some students came to complain. "Sir," they said, "we are hungry. How can we learn and work with empty stomachs? Why do we get so little food?"

Tekin asked a naïve question: "I do not understand it. IFO delivers lots of food aid. What happens to it?" The students explained the corruption scheme.

"Can you write this down?" He asked and the students did it.

Then Tekin took the letter of complaint to the Chief of UN Mission in Monrovia. With written evidence, the UN bureaucracy had no choice but to act. There was an official inquiry and within the next month, Tekin's assignment was terminated.

A telegram arrived from Rome: "Due to technical reasons, your assignment in Liberia is terminated and you are transferred, effective next month, to Entebbe, Uganda. Kindly make travel arrangements to come first to Rome for briefing and then to report to work in Entebbe in four weeks to conduct an agricultural survey of the food potential of the country." The chief of IFO, Rome, signed it.

Thus the Liberian assignment of the Uzun Ali family came to an abrupt end. Eleanor hardly got a chance for an exotic experience in West Africa. The family traveled to Rome and then via Cyprus to visit Aygul and family, then on to Idi Amin's Uganda.

The stopover in Cyprus was intended to be an interlude. It was, in fact, more: There was dictatorship unfolding there, a precursor of the military dictatorship in Uganda the Canadian family would encounter. Unknown to them, the military dictator then in control of Athens was planning to extend his rule to Cyprus.

# III

Tekin and his family arrived in Cyprus the summer of 1972 in the midst of a bitter power struggle, Greek versus Greek that was as immoral as the corruption they had seen in Liberia. The Greek Junta in Athens was locked in a deadly war with Makarios, the master of Cyprus at the time, who now flatly refused to go for ENOSIS so long as Athens was under military dictatorship. The Junta had its army in Cyprus, and Makarios had his own.

It was curious to put it mildly why Makarios was making his U turn on ENOSIS. There were all sorts of theories. The Americans thought he was courting Communist Russia, hobnobbing with the leaders of the Non-Aligned Movement at the UN. Others claimed he was enjoying the world stage and did not want to become second fiddle to Athens.

The wily priest, the former passionate voice of ENOSIS, now was singing a new tune; he did not want to make heroes out of the fascists, now dictators in Athens. Whatever his motives, Makarios was locked in a deadly fight with the Junta.

The Athens Junta had lots of money to buy men and arms. One of the men Athens did buy in the end was Nicos Sampson, a former EOKA killer and now the owner of a fanatical newspaper, *Makhi* (Battle). It left no doubt that the conspiracy Athens was planning was illegal, violent and immoral. But then, as Tekin had observed in

Monrovia, immorality had no bounds, not even in the UN.

Grivas then was back in Cyprus, secretly sent there by the Junta to start the conspiracy against Makarios. He had been kicked out of the island, in disgrace, for the Kofunye massacre of 1967. But now he had come to the island, though no one was sure why he came. He did not come to kill Turks, but it seemed, to go to war against Makarios. He set up a new underground organization, EOKA B, recruited men and shipped in arms, while the Junta also built up its regular military force on this island. Actually Grivas came back to die; he died within the year, but by then Cyprus had become a dangerous place.

Against this background, the Turkish and Greek Cypriot politicians went through the revolving doors of UN diplomacy, having endless talks aimed at solving the perennial Cyprus problem. Actually, a very modest plan for settlement was in the making. It provided no more than local government for the Turkish Cypriots who were now reduced to a pitiful state of an abandoned and persecuted people, pushed into enclaves on the island that the UN Secretary General had declared "a veritable siege." But Makarios would hear none of limited local government for the Turks of Cyprus.

"The constitution does not provide for local government" he declared and threw out the deal. No one bothered to ask the master of Cyprus then how much respect he himself had for the constitution.

***

When Tekin and his family arrived in Uganda; a month later the coup began. This was Idi Amin's economic war against the innocent Ugandan Asians. They were the traders and businessmen, descendents of Indian coolies brought over by the British imperialists almost a century ago to build the colonial railways that transported coffee, sugar and other commodities from the African interior to the factories of Europe. While the profits enriched the colonialists, the hardworking Asians rose to control the wholesale and retail businesses in Uganda, and the African majority lived in abject poverty.

Just as the Greek Junta in Athens, the military mind of Idi Amin had a simple solution.

"God spoke to me last night" he announced to the Nation. Tekin thought of Makarios in Cyprus, another leader with a private line of communication to God. "Why do political leaders always think they are guided by the Almighty?" he asked Eleanor. "They are hypocrites causing so much death and destruction to their people playing God" she said.

Idi Amin declared: "The Ugandan Asians must go." The Nation cheered and loved it.

"They are guilty. These Asians came over from India; they milked the cow they did not feed." The Africans cheered on and celebrated late into the night. They cheered Idi Amin on. He gave them more. He declared an Economic War on the hapless Ugandan Asians. The world community, the UN, looked on while a hardworking people vanished. It was the UN impotency in Cyprus all over again.

"I give the Asians 90 days, no more. They must go. Everyone must leave Uganda, every one of the Asians, young and old, sick or dying. No exceptions; they must sell off and move out." Idi Amin declared amidst cheers; the African masses went wild with joy. A new day, a new age of prosperity for Africans was promised. All believed it.

Except, it seemed, Tekin. Poor fellow, he came home and said to Eleanor.

"It looks bad. I fear soon we will have to go...again"

"But why, I am just beginning to like it here." It was true.

Uganda then was a lovely country. High in the central African plateau, with lakes and game parks, rich in wild life, Uganda was very much like Switzerland. Especially the southwest, the district of Kigesi, near the Rwandan border, had an exotic music that Eleanor came to adore.

"Finally, I have seen something exotic" she said.

"I do not like the politics of Idi Amin" began Tekin. "This expulsion of Asians will destroy the country. How can you expel all your professional and traders and expect life to remain normal?" He asked.

"I am here to conduct an rural survey for electricity supply. It is now impossible," He said.

The morality of the situation was clear. In good faith Tekin could not stay idle, draw a big UN salary and do nothing. Mind you that is exactly many other international aid personnel were exactly doing in Kampala and Entebbe, but Tekin was troubled by the immorality of it all.

Tekin's had personal motives as well. He did not wish to put his family in harms' way. With the Ugandan Asians gone, he reckoned, the retail and whole business would be ruined and food shortages would emerge. Already there were signs that security was worsening as soldiers and police started looting the houses of the departing Asians. Susan, Eleanor and him could be stopped on the road and kidnapped. Worse things could follow and no one at the UN could lift a finger.

Eleanor agreed. The next day Tekin drafted a cable for his superiors in Rome. It read:

"Request urgent transfer out of Uganda as the rural survey is now not feasible due to expulsion of Ugandan Asians. Expect chaos, so please advice soonest."

The bureaucrats in Rome were by now getting fed up with Tekin and his frequent problems. They wondered what to do with him. Wherever he was sent, trouble seemed to follow. Then someone in the personnel department found the solution and a reply was sent to Tekin in Entebbe. It read:

"Your contract is due to expire in two months time. With no immediate alternate positions available, suggest you take leave prior to end of contract. Kindly make travel arrangements for departure from Uganda at your convenience."

Tekin performed one last special assignment for the UN in Entebbe before leaving Uganda. Like all UN personnel, he was drafted to act as an observer at the airport "to make sure everything went off smoothly" said the UN Mission Chief. It was on the night of the 90th day, the last day for Ugandan Asians to exit their homeland. On that final day, hundreds of flights took up to 10,000 desperate people to other destinations, all around the globe, to start a new beginning.

The Entebbe airport that night was under the full control of the soldiers of Idi Amin. The soldiers had one objective: to get rich. Passports were checked and documents controlled, but it was money that the military was after. So, they worked a system of rotation. Groups of soldiers would take turn at the exit gates, asking the poor, desperate Ugandan Asians one question:

"Do you have any Ugandan shillings?"

Almost always the answer was the same: "Yes."

So, the poor people had to suffer one last indignity before boarding the plane; they had to surrender their last cash to the greedy soldiers of Idi Amin.

Tekin, who was reminded of the day of his blackmail in Nicosia airport en route to Liberia, shared the humiliation that the poor departing Ugandan Asians felt. His sense of fair play was being violated in a cruel and systematic way. He decided to do something about it. He walked to the major whose pockets were now full of money he had collected from the Ugandan Asians.

He asked the major: "Why are you taking their money?"

The major was taken aback. But he recovered fast, saying:

"Because" he said, "it is illegal to take Ugandan currency out of the country."

Tekin then asked: "Should you not give them receipt for their money?" He made sure the major saw his blue UN band signifying his official status.

The major got angry. "Go away" he said angrily.

Tekin went straight to the Chief of Mission not far from the scene to report the incident and ask for guidance.

The Chief said: "Observe and Report."

# IV

Their last night was spent at the Entebbe Hotel in which the Uzun Ali family was treated to a sex orgy of a different type. The Hotel, situated on the shores of Lake Victoria next to the airport, was the favorite of the aircrews and, on account of the large exodus of the Ugandan Asians; it was full of young British and Scandinavian hostesses, and a smaller number of male crewmembers. Actually Tekin had been hard put to get rooms for the night.

"We are solidly booked," said the reservation clerk when he first inquired. It was true; the hotel was full of airline crews, young and beautiful hostesses, and pilots in uniform and stewards and air personnel of all kinds.

"I am with the UN" he replied and that made the difference.

"Oh I see," said the clerk. "Just a minute please. The UN has a block reservation. How many nights will you stay with us Mr. Uzun Ali?"

"Just one please" he replied. "We are departing tomorrow."

"OK, sir. We will give you room 24. It is a lovely room, overlooking the pool, with two double beds."

"That would be fine," said Tekin, unsuspecting what awaited them in rooms 23 and 25. These adjoining rooms, like the rest of the rooms on the floor, were crowded with airline personnel.

It seemed the young air hostesses and crewmembers were interested in two things: sun during the day and sex during the night. All day long, in the hot and bright African sun, the hostesses, in seductive and scanty bikinis were lying on chez-lounges around the hotel pool while most of the males slept upstairs in the bedrooms. The low-action part of the day was the morning breakfast time was extremely quiet. The tempo at Hotel Entebbe would pick up, the hostesses would assemble for sun tanning around the pool sometime at noon and by late afternoon the men from upstairs would join them, and then by dinner time the entire place was a bee-hive of activity.

Tekin and Eleanor were the odd twosome in the entire Hotel.

"What is going on here?" asked Eleanor. Nowhere in Africa had they seen so many beautiful blond and white people in one place wearing the latest Paris bikinis and beachwear fashions. It was as strange as watching a Tarzan movie with no Africans in it at all.

"I am not sure, but I have an idea," replied Tekin, "I think these young people are sex-crazy. They are making the best of their interlude here in between flights, taking out plane-loads of Ugandan Asians."

In the next hour or two another strange event took place. What looked like an almost entirely whites-only gathering of young people gradually became multi-national and multi-racial. Actually it was only black and white affair, the brown Asians having all finally departed.

The fact was that there were not enough white males in relation to females at the Hotel. And, what Tekin and Eleanor were witnessing was a well-established pattern, something that had evolved over the preceding three months as flights came in to take out the Ugandan Asians. The easy and free sex at night had attracted a steady stream of young Africans to the Entebbe Hotel, obviously the cream of the local elite.

The dinner was a fairly ordinary, orderly affair. Waiters in black suit and white tie served roast beef dinner and steaks to a full house of young hostesses and stewards, while in the bar next door equally young Africans crowded the place, poorly lit and full of smoke from cigarettes and cigars, and beer and whisky flowed like torrential floods on the dry savannah. In the corner sat Tekin, Eleanor and Susan, dazzled by the crowd and the huge roar of chatter and laughter. No doubt, the Hotel Entebbe was a scene of great joy and gaiety, far removed from the human tragedy that Tekin had observed at the airport just hours before. If someone had come from Mars for a snapshot observation at the Hotel, it would be impossible to note that the country was in the midst of a human crisis.

The real fun did not begin until after 11pm. Tekin and Eleanor, went for a short walk in the garden around the pool right after their dinner, and then walked up to room no. 24 to get ready for bed. It had been an exhausting 24 hours, first with the special duty at the airport, then packing and all kinds of final preparations for departure, and the Uzun Ali family planned an early night and a good sleep in readiness for their long flight to Nicosia via Beirut.

They were in for a surprise. Indeed, it turned out to be the most action-filled night in their entire Ugandan stay.

By 11.30 pm, the noise and music from next room woke them up. First it was Eleanor, the light sleeper in the family who was woken up.

"Tekin, wake up" she said. Tekin opened his eyes he immediately asked: "What is that noise?" He turned on the light.

"That is what I'd like to know?" said Eleanor. "It is so loud." And within an instant, she yelled: "My God, it is so foul. What is going on?"

"I'd better call the reception" Said Tekin. It was clear that a wild party was going on next door. European women, African men were uttering all sorts of strange words, interspaced with sexual and foul language.

The clerk at the reception was very polite and promised to look into the matter.

Eleanor and Tekin waited, nothing happened. There was plenty booze and the orgy seemed to get more heated and the erotic screams and yells louder. Soon wild screams and yells were coming from both rooms on either side. No doubt it was a group affair and it got juicier by the minute. The voices, initially joking and taunting, began to take on porno character.

"Oh yeah baby! Fuck me baby," yelled one delirious female.

"Come on, blondie, suck my black dick" demanded a man in a deep African voice.

Tekin and Eleanor looked at each other in total shock. "My God" Eleanor said, "it looks like an orgy is going on."

"I better go down and talk to the reception clerk" but then he changed his mind. "I do not know that it will do any good," he said.

He phoned the reception again. It was a different person who answered and he knew nothing of Tekin's earlier call.

But this person was more honest. "I am sorry sir," he said. "The noise is something we cannot control."

"Why not?" asked Tekin.

"They are so many. The airline companies have reserved the entire hotel and we simply cannot kick all the guests out."

Tekin tried one more option. "Can you move us to another, more quite room?"

"I am so sorry," replied the clerk. "The hotel is full, solid."

"You mean it is like this all over?" he asked rather naively.

"Yes sir" replied the clerk with equal naiveté.

So, the Uzun Ali family's last night in Uganda was spent, without sleep but with a demonstration lesson in the intricacies of international travel during the exodus of the Ugandan Asians.

It was Eleanor who wisely remarked: "Don't be too angry with the hostesses Tekin, they will probably be serving us tomorrow."

# V

When they left Uganda, Idi Amin's economic war against the Ugandan Asians was changing course and focus: Now that the Asian Ugandans were gone, it was now becoming inter-African tribal conflict and more bloody. Economic chaos had now turned into food shortages. Lawlessness and revenge killings were everywhere, as Obote's tribes, Ankole and Langi, started fighting Amin's own Nilo-Hamitic tribes near the Sudanese border and life in the Uganda capital Kampala as well as in Entebbe and everywhere in the country descended into hell. The issue at hand was who exactly should get whatever the Asian Ugandans had left behind. The conflict grew more bloody every day. Bodies were lying in the jungle and kidnappings on highways were daily occurrences.

The UN and the international community watched on helplessly, just as in Cyprus when the Greeks were massacring Turks. Nothing was done to check Idi Amin and life in Uganda under the dictator went from bad to worse. Soon kidnappings and disappearances of ordinary citizens reached alarming proportions. At the height of general insecurity, Tekin and Eleanor made a safe exit from Idi Amin's hell on 13th July 1974.

"What is the use of the UN if it can do nothing but watch the likes of Idi Amin executing their evil schemes?" wondered Tekin.

# HYPOCRITES AND ANGELS

\*\*\*

When they arrived in Cyprus the next day, little did they know that they were simply exiting one hell and entering another. They felt lucky to escape Idi Amin's killing fields; unsuspectingly, they walked into an all-Greek civil war that erupted just hours after they flew into Nicosia.

Tribalism and arbitrary killings were not African only. They had been going on amongst the Greeks in Cyprus. Makarios, who was collecting millions from the British and Americans while courting with Moscow, was involved in a bitter struggle with the Junta in Athens. That infuriated Grivas and other fascists who wanted ENOSIS with Greece at all costs. The fighting amongst Greeks climaxed on 14th July the arrival date of Tekin and his Canadian family in Nicosia. How many died in this all-Greek blood bath was not known; later on the killings were attributed to Turkish soldiers. For almost one week the killings continued as leftist or pro-Makarios forces battled fascist and pro-Junta forces in the streets of Nicosia and thousands were killed. Then Sampson, the "Killer of Omorphita" as he was notoriously known for one of his bloodiest campaigns on innocent Turkish families, was declared President, a puppet dancing to the tune of the Junta in Athens.

The coup in Nicosia was hatched in Athens. The Junta there began by buying men willing to die for its cause. The Junta believed they could cheat their way to ENOSIS and make themselves a national hero. The recruitment of Sampson was initially secret; it was part of much larger conspiracy, on a bigger scale of immorality and corruption than anything Tekin had witnessed in Africa. Sampson was bought, precisely because he was weak and unfit, just to be a puppet. At the right time of the Junta's choosing, the conspirators would announce ENOSIS, the long cherished dream of Hellenism. It was as simple as Idi Amin's plan for Uganda and the rental scheme of the Liberian Minister.

The Athens Junta did not select Sampson arbitrarily, but carefully and competitively. Other candidates for the purchase were considered. Other potential recruits to be bought before Sampson was chosen including judges of the Supreme Court, but the Junta, acting like Idi Amin, preferred to take the law into its own hands. For four days terror and wanton killing raged in Nicosia as Greeks killed

Greeks and Makarios miraculously escaped seeking refuge from the once-hated British. He turned up at the UN in New York condemning Athens for destroying the Cypriot Republic, the one he had himself killed in Christmas 1963.

For the next four days, Tekin and family watched the all-Greek fighting from the safety of Aygul's house in the Turkish quarter of Nicosia. No one knew how many Greeks were killed by their own in the civil war.

On the 18th of July, they flew out of the warn-torn island.

\*\*\*

At midnight of 18th July 1974, only a few hours after Tekin and family's departure, newscasts all over the world announced that the Turkish army was landing in Cyprus. War broke out between Greeks and Turks all over the island. It had been a long time coming.

Captain Bettie was on duty at the Nicosia International Airport commanding a battalion of Canadian troops in UNFICYP, the UN force in Cyprus. "The Turks will land paratroops to take control of the airport. Imperative that action is taken to keep it under UN control" said the military order. Captain Bettie had only a few hours to mobilize and spread men in the terrain around the airport before dawn when the Turkish paratroops were expected.

Most likely the landings would take place in the large plateau broken by ravines and dry river beds in the rugged and hilly terrain between the airport and Gonyeli, the large Turkish town some three miles distant from the airport which housed a strong Turkish military base too the north, towards the Five Fingers Mountains, lay the large Greek Cypriot town of Dikomo. To the east of the airport lay the Greek part of Nicosia where the Greeks, for the last four days, had been locked in a bloody fight among one another.

The news of Turkish landings immediately halted that fight and Greek soldiers began hasty defensive operations all over the island, including near and around the airport, to fight the Turks. They collected all Turkish Cypriot men, women and children and herded them into schools, jails and open-air football stadiums. Many were shot and killed and in several villages massacres were carried out on innocent peasants.

"Bloody hell" said Captain Bettie when informed of Greek military moves on his eastern front. "We will be interspaced between two armies." That is exactly what happened.

At around 5am, at the crack of dawn, the Turkish paratroops began to land in a large areas extending toward Gonyeli. The Turkish battalion, stationed there, fanned out from the village, with tanks fanning in a wide arc, to provide cover for the paratroops coming down. Then the Greek army moved in a pincer operation, with tanks attempting to encircle the Turkish battalion and cut them off from linking with the paratroops. Captain Bettie and his Canadian van Doos stood in the way. Then, as the sun emerged from the east, Greek planes appeared to counter Turkish jets and immediately a Greek plane was shot down killing several Greek soldiers. The Greek soldiers on the ground panicked and started running off. In the ensuing battle, several Greek tanks were destroyed. The Greek warplanes escaped. Soon, the Turks had full control of the skies and now reinforced by the battalion from Gonyeli, the paratroopers were all around Captain Bettie's Canadians.

"Request permission to open fire, sir" demanded his subordinates. "Hold your fire and withdraw," ordered Bettie. His UN orders were clear and specific: "DO NOT FIRE... Unless in self-defense." But it was becoming virtually impossible to know the exact line separating defense and offense.

"Move back to the perimeter of the runway," ordered Bettie his troops.

The Nicosia International Airport consisted of a single runway, covered by a barbed wire fence containing an area not more than 10 square kilometers. That was the area, which Captain Bettie decided to defend and keep under UN control. It was the only outlet to the outside world and must be held. In desperation Captain Bettie tried to establish contact by cable with the Turkish commander in the area. That was easier said than done. For one thing he was not sure the commander spoke any English and Bettie knew no Turkish himself. In addition, he did not know who the commander might be. In the meantime, the Turkish soldiers pressed forward and were now within a couple of hundred yards from the runway while jets above kept bombing Greek troop movements on the ground. Bombs exploded all around Bettie and his Canadian van Doos.

"Fire your rifles in the air," ordered Captain Bettie at last when the Turkish soldiers were clearly visible, advancing all around in a highly disciplined encircling operation coming in all direction. Then, suddenly, the Turkish advance stopped and all was quite. A virtual cease-fire went into effect.

Some ten miles to the north of the Nicosia International Airport, on the Five Fingers Mountains next to the medieval St. Hilarion Castle dominating the pass through which the Nicosia-Kyrenia highway snaked its way, the Greek soldiers went into an offensive action of their own. The Castle was in the hands of Turkish Cypriot forces, but the well-armed Greek and Greek Cypriot soldiers held all the mountaintops around.

Below, in the plain between the Five Fingers and Gonyeli, the Turks had hastily constructed a runway of their own at Bogaz and all through the day paratroopers landed, fanning out in all directions. These Turkish paratroops were to be reinforced by a small band of Turkish Cypriot fighters coming from the Turkish village of Agirdag next to Bogaz. A large Greek Cypriot column advancing from the east, from the large Greek Cypriot village of Dikomo, five miles from Agirdag overwhelmed them.

The Greek soldiers had the advantage of mountain heights and with the aid of the large Greek Cypriot force moving west from their positions in Dikomo; they seized control of the highway at Bogaz. That effectively prevented the Turkish paratroops from linking up with the Turkish Cypriot forces in St. Hilarion Castle and in Agirdag. The Greek and Greek Cypriots had superiority in numbers as Turkish paratroopers concentrated on the Nicosia International Airport corridor, exposing their northern flank on the slopes around the pass at Bogaz. The Greeks took advantage of these weaknesses and by late afternoon they controlled the area north of Gonyeli. They could then attack the Turks from the rear around the airport still in Bettie's control from the north.

Then, in the evening as the sun began to disappear behind the Five Fingers, the tide turned against the Greeks. The Turkish battalion at Gonyeli, now recalled from action around Captain Bettie's men at the airport, began to move toward Bogaz. Tanks and artillery came to the rescue of the highway at Bogaz. As soon as the Greeks from the heights around Dikomo sighted the advancing Turkish forces from Gonyeli they panicked and started to run back, abandoning their foxholes and defensive positions in command of the highway at the pass. The Turkish troops smashed their way and managed to link up with the Turkish Cypriots on the heights at St. Hilarion. But then, the Greek forces in the mountains stood and fought. A fierce battle ensured, fought in the slopes, amid pine forests and on the difficult, rocky terrain all through the night. Both sides suffered heavy casualties.

By next morning, the Greeks were in retreat on all fronts. At daybreak, the Turkish warplanes were back and bombed Greek positions. By mid-morning, the Bogaz pass was securely in Turkish hands and the Nicosia-Kyrenia highway was opened as troops, which had landed on the coast yesterday linked up with those in control of Bogaz. Turkish Cypriots of Nicosia, unable to touch the blue Mediterranean since 1964, finally had a corridor to the outside world. The Turks of Cyprus finally evened the score and secured a living space on the island.

# VI

Division and ethnic conflict awaited them in Canada as well; but it was all Canadian style... polite and diplomatic, all in the democratic political space.

Within a year of returning home to Toronto, the Parti Quebecois, led by Rene Leveque the separatist leader, won a landslide victory in Quebec and Canada, just like Cyprus it seemed, looked set for a division on tribal lines similar to those in Africa. Canada faced a mortal danger of breaking up. But, Trudeau, the Philosopher King, did not seek the help of the UN. He initiated a series of landmark reforms in Canada intended to weaken separatism in Quebec. A major part of his reform was Multiculturalism policy to replace the age-old dual, Anglo-French character of Canada.

The economy was not doing too well either. There was stagflation, high prices and high unemployment. The unions demanded big wage hikes and Trudeau, now unusually autocratic, brought in price and wage controls.

Tekin and Eleanor first went to visit Susan at her boarding school. She was in her final year and was planning to go to University of Toronto. At home at last Tekin, with Eleanor's support, took a major decision. They had had enough of bureaucracies and meager monthly salaries. Tekin, impressed with his cousin's business success in London, decided to try his luck as a private entrepreneur himself. He asked for a loan from Ozkan who wired the funds immediately and soon Tekin became a landscape engineer moving to King's Town, some ten miles north of their home in North York.

"I want to buy a small farm" he said to Eleanor, "and turn it into a nursery, growing and selling plants and flowers." Land was still reasonably cheap.

At first, she was surprised at Tekin's choice of a new career. "But why landscaping?" she asked.

"Toronto is expanding. Look it is well beyond 401; North York is part of the city. New suburbs are opening up everyday. With new housing, demand for gardens and trees will increase. I believe there is a potential gold mine in landscaping." Eleanor was impressed with her husband's analysis. "Well, dear" she said, "If you believe it, it must be true."

It turned out pretty much as Tekin had predicted. It was unbelievably easy. The cash started flowing into their bank account almost as rapidly as the water that flew in their creek cutting their farm into two. Tekin built a nice pond and divided the farm into two parts, one for flowers and the other for trees and shrubs.

The land purchase was itself a bargain. He bought it from a retiring family for 50,000 Canadian dollars at an average price of one thousand dollars an acre, using half of the loan from Ozkan as a down payment, the other as a bank loan from the Royal Bank of Canada, his own branch in King's Town. He also sold his Halliburton lakefront lot for five times the purchase price and invested the proceeds in his new company. The business almost doubled in value in one year. In fact, in two years the landscaping business became so profitable the entire loan was paid off.

Tekin by then was an employer with a crew of workers. He started with two workers, laborers doing the menial jobs on the farm, planting, harvesting and building hot houses and a million other chores, while he looked after the accounts and Eleanor became the public relations manager answering the endless phone calls, taking orders and arranging deliveries.

They were now on easy street, financially secure and enjoying life. Susan was doing well at her studies and she had lots of friends. Tekin was in constant touch with the Uzun Ali clan all around the world. He corresponded and spoke over the phone with Ozkan in London, now a major international businessperson in his own right, and with his sister Sevgi in Ankara building a solid reputation as a social historian at the University.

The family had time for leisure. Tekin and Eleanor were happy.

# VII

Gradually, almost accidentally, Tekin and Eleanor were drawn into ethnic politics in Canada. It started one evening when Eleanor was reading the local newspaper.

"Tekin look at this," she said as the couple was sitting in their comfortable home north of Toronto. Susan was home for the weekend and she was busy helping her friend with a party of former school friends.

"Local Armenian cultural club of Scarborough wants to change the school history books" Eleanor summarized what she had been reading.

"What is wrong with that?" asked Tekin as she handed him the newspaper.

"Read and you will see," she said. "They want Canada to recognize the Armenian genocide."

Tekin read the story. A group of local politicians representing Armenian-Canadians were taking advantage of the Multiculturalism policy to push through their version of history. The article gave details of similar initiatives in California and Massachusetts, USA.

"This is wrong," declared Tekin as he finished reading the article. "Canada is repeating the mistakes of the Ottoman Empire. We will end up converting schools into battlefields, one ethnic group fighting another." He said.

Then they had a long discussion about Canadian multiculturalism. Eleanor was initially in favor of this policy, as she adored anything about Trudeau.

"I do not understand your reasoning," she said to Tekin. "Canada is not Turkey or the Ottoman Empire. We are a modern country, welcoming everyone from all over the world."

Tekin replied: "Yes I know that. I am myself a new Canadian" he began. "What worries me is ethnic division. Trudeau is fighting Quebec separatism, but at the same time he is encouraging new Canadians to organize themselves in ethnic communities. Multiculturalism hyphenates Canadians. It divides them into ethnic groups, just like the Ottoman *Millets*. Indians now will remain as Indian-Canadians, the Chinese will be treated as Chinese Canadians, and now the Armenians will import nationalist policies into Canada."

"OK" she said, "that is Canada. You get active as well. What is there to stop you?" She looked at him.

"I do not like politics. I came to Canada as an engineer. Not to play politics," said Tekin raising his voice in frustration.

"I am afraid you do not understand Canada" she said and gave a short lecture on the Canadian political system. "It is easy to sit in your armchair and do nothing. If you do not like some policy, then you have to act, you have to do something to change it."

Tekin thought about it for a while and in the end he agreed.

"The paper says there will be a meeting tomorrow night at the local Education Board to approve Armenian proposal for new history curriculum," he said.

"Then, let's go to the meeting" Eleanor said with conviction.

The next evening the couple found themselves in a meeting hall, surrounded by hundreds of Canadian Armenians. They were assembled there to celebrate and cheer the adoption of a new history curriculum drafted by the Armenians.

The meeting opened, sharp at 8pm. The Chair, a white haired educator, calling the meeting to order. He first invited an Armenian-Canadian professor history to address the meeting. After preliminaries, the professor made his point forcefully and emotionally.

"My Grandparents perished during the forced marches from Van to Zor" he declared as the congregation listened with full attention. "One and a half million Armenians perished. We in Canada today are fortunate. We live in a civilized country where there is a new multiculturalism policy, which celebrates our national and cultural heritage. Armenian Canadians now demand justice. They want recognition of the murder of a nation in Eastern Anatolian. Genocide is our heritage, ingrained in our soul. Justice demands that all Canadians accept and recognize our genocide. I congratulate our School Board for the courage it has shown in drafting the new history curriculum which does precisely that."

When the Professor was finished, the Chair asked if anyone else wanted to speak

Without thinking, moved purely by what he had heard, Tekin raised his hand. The Chair said: "Yes, I see someone on the right, wishing to speak. Please come forward. You have ten minutes."

Eleanor looked on in surprise as Tekin got up and walked to the podium. He had not come to make a speech.

"Mr. Chairman" he began. "I am not a politician or a professor. But I am opposed to writing history by executive decisions like this." There was uproar of angry words from the crowd of Armenians.

The Chair was caught off guard. The meeting was in danger of getting out of control. The Chair turned to Tekin and asked:

"Sir, please introduce yourself to the meeting." Tekin did. "I am Tekin Uzun Ali, a business man, of Turkish origin, from Cyprus."

Jeers and insults followed. He did not mind the noise.

"Mr. Chairman" declared Tekin, "I am a Canadian citizen, and a taxpaying business man and I believe in Canada there is freedom of speech. I wish to speak on the motion."

There was silence. The Chair looked at Tekin. "Please proceed Mr. Uzun Ali," he ruled.

Tekin did as instructed. He turned to the Chair and asked:

"Mr. Chairman, do you know where Eastern Anatolia is?" He asked. The Chair looked puzzled. The crowd was now silent.

"This is a very complicated issue," he stated. "There were large numbers of Ottoman Turks, Muslims as well as Armenians killed during the First World War. This was a period of war and conflict. Both sides suffered. Armenians revolted and killed many Turks. No doubt many innocent Armenians died in this conflict. Should we only recognize the losses of the Armenians? That would be unjust." He looked at the crowd which listened in shocked silence.

The Chair looked at Tekin, and asked: "Mr. Uzun Ali what do you suggest we do here?"

Tekin replied as if he were an experienced politician. "Get expert historians to study and report on what actually happened in 1915 in Eastern Anatolia" he said.

The Armenian crowd yelled and jeered. But that is exactly what happened. That night no decision was taken. In the end, the School Board did nothing. The Armenians were disappointed.

An Armenian, called Armen, decided to take justice into his own hands.

# VIII

The Armenian terror campaign was carefully hatched in Montreal. It had long roots stretching all the way back to Cyprus.

Armen Schomelian, the son of Tekin's music teacher in Nicosia, belonged to an Armenian Student Organization located on McGill Street, downtown Montreal. The group was busy with plans to launch an attack on the Turkish Embassy in Ottawa on the upcoming 24th April demonstrations. The group was operating on two fronts: one open, normal student body, a collection of young men and women pursuing university studies in Montreal. The other, an underground front was a secret arm of ASALA, the Armenian global network to avenge the Armenian massacres in the First World War in the dying days of the Ottoman Empire. It was fighting to unite western Armenia in eastern Turkey to the Armenian homeland.

Armen was a leader of the student body formed in the permissive atmosphere of the Canadian multiculturalism policy. "For me my cultural heritage is my lost homeland in Greater Armenia and revenge is what I am after" he believed, and all means, including terror and murder of Turkish diplomats in Canada, justified the plans he had in mind.

He came to Canada about ten years earlier originally from Cyprus, but by way of Beirut and Paris. He was educated in the Melkonian Institute, Nicosia, which is where he was inducted into ASALA;

actually he did not take a great deal of convincing about seeking justice for the Armenian victims in 1915. His teachers were already opening his eyes on this great injustice, and his own father was telling him terrible stories of killings and death marches. The survivors were lucky to have made it to Lebanon and then to Cyprus and elsewhere.

From Melkonian the organization sent Armen for further education and training in Beirut, and then off to Paris where he learnt about tactics, both for underground operations and also for bombing attacks against Turkish diplomats. His final destination was Montreal where in the multi-ethnic metropolis he easily felt at home with the large and prosperous Armenian community. The multiculturalism program which the Canadian government was promoting actively at that time was ideal for the kind of activities Armen was, by now, quite expert in.

The Armenian networks were well organized and worked on two levels, one political the other underground. Professionals, politicians, academics and teachers handled the political action with good English and knowledge of how the Canadian system worked, at the local, provincial, and federal levels of government. That was not Armen's forte; he left it to others, born and raised in Canada, who knew about committees, platforms and political contributions. These activists were proficient in getting funding from the Canadian government in order to prepare reports and papers for the Armenian cause, all thanks to the multicultural policy.

"So long as it cultivates Armenian heritage, there is money for it" would say the funding officer from the Canadian Heritage Department. "Our policy is diversity within unity."

What Armen specialized in was making bombs and launching attacks on unsuspecting diplomats. One of his closest friends was Jean-Pierre, an ardent Quebec separatist; recently back from Cuba where he was exiled for some bombing incident in Montreal in the cause of Quebec independence.

"I am a born separatist and I will die one" was Jean-Pierre's boast.

"If you cannot get your way peacefully, then violence is justified" agreed both Armen and Jean-Pierre.

"The justice of the cause justifies the means." It made perfect sense.

Jean-Pierre was very sympathetic to Armen's idea of armed struggle to avenge wrongs done on the poor Armenian. "We are both peoples who do not have a homeland" he said when Armen explained how the Armenian nationalists fought in Van in 1915 to establish an independent Armenia. Truth mattered little, if at all, for Jean-Pierre. He was a man of action.

Jean-Pierre readily saw a parallel between the defeat of the French on the Plains of Abraham in 1763 and that of the Armenians in Eastern Anatolia in the First World War.

# IX

Armen's other mentor in Canada was Marios Zefiris, known simply as MZ, an accounting clerk from the Greek town in Toronto around Bloor and Danforth. MZ was a Zorba dancer and specialist in fund-raising, or more specifically getting grants from the Canadian government under its multiculturalism policy. MZ was popular with his zesty dancing but his real claim to fame in the Greek Canadian community was due to his ability in getting funding for the annual Greek Fest, a highly popular cultural event. Canadians of many ethnic origins participated celebrating song and dance from Greece and eating lots of kebabs and other Middle Eastern foods. As result of his successful fund-raising initiatives, MZ quickly rose in the local chapter of AHEPA, the powerful Greek lobby in North America to promote Hellenism in the new world. MZ's latest fund-raising was for a Greek Community Center that would also house a Greek Orthodox Church.

"You provide the building, we will provide the priest for the Church" was the message given to MZ and his committee from the national center in Athens and that was enough to launch a major fund-raising campaign amongst the Greek town in Toronto.

"We can get matching funds" said a Greek Canadian politician and MZ began visiting the Department of National Heritage in Ottawa pretty regularly to get one dollar for every dollar collected from Greek traders and businesses for the community center. It was during one of these meetings in the Canadian national capital that he met Armen.

The occasion was the quarterly Multicultural Committee, with representatives of every imaginable ethnic community in Canada, Palestinians and Jews, Indians and Pakistanis, Caribbean and various Afro-Canadians, Russians, Germans, and several Balkan nationalities.

Armen was there on behalf of the Montreal Armenians and what made him take notice of MZ was the presence in the Committee of a Turkish Canadian who was a new comer in Canada and who now wanted to apply for membership on the Multicultural Committee. MZ was opposed to the membership of Turkish Canadians.

"The Turkish government is a military dictatorship that denies the Armenian genocide," he said. It was music to Armen's ears.

During the coffee break Armen went to MZ and introduced himself.

"I am Armen Schomelian" he said, "I was very impressed with your argument against the Turks" he added.

Soon they were friends and they sat at the meeting together and began to develop common strategies and action plans.

"Canada is a wonderful country," said MZ. "There is plenty of cash from the government for promoting our own culture and history. We have to keep out those bloody Turks." That was a sentiment close to Armen's own heart.

Before long, Armen was getting an education on the intricacies of the Canadian funding procedures

"Matching grants is a piece of cake," said MZ. "You raise one dollar from your Armenian shop keepers, and the Canadian government gives you one dollar free. It is that simple" he would say, while Armen looked amazed.

"That is how I am raising all the money we need for our Community Center in Toronto. I go around the restaurants, dry-cleaning stores and mini-markets in Greek town and everyone donates minimum $10. So, in one-month 1000 donations raises $20,000. I expect we will get our Community Center within 5 years at the most." As MZ talked about fund-raising, Armen could not but be impressed with his dedication and commitment.

MZ added: "To supplement our donations, we often organize dinner dances, bingo nights and Saturday morning collection on the street from the Canadian public. It is all for the cause and every penny is a help." And then, after a pause, he went on:

"I know an Italian friend; he raised 5 million dollars for an old folks' home for Canadian Italians on matching grants. It took him 5 years and lots of dinner dances and bingos, but he did it." MZ was passionate about fund-raising in Canada.

MZ and Armen collaborated but they pursued different objectives. Armen was not interested in building community centers. His objective was revenge for the Armenian genocide and if violence was to be used for it, then violence on Canadian soil was justified. His aim was clear and simple: He wanted to bomb the Turkish Embassy in Ottawa, killing and injuring Turkish diplomats.

"I want revenge," he said. "I want to organize demonstrations in front of the Turkish embassy in Ottawa and, if necessary, even bomb the entire building to avenge my people."

"What you do with the Turks here in Canada is your own business," said MZ. "Whatever you decide to do to keep Turks out here in Canada, I am with you. I say you need lots of money, Canada is an expensive place, and everything costs lots of money. I can help you get money from the government" he said.

"OK" said Armen, "I am your student."

MZ continued the lecture: "You need to organize your people, buy the equipment you need. Busing people to Ottawa costs money, pamphlets and placards cost money. Demonstrations need money." MZ was emphatic.

"What is the best way to get money from the Canadian government?" asked Armen.

"Matching grants" said MZ.

And in the days and weeks following Armen and his friends in Montreal were busy planning and strategizing all for the purpose of taking advantage of Canadian multiculturalism funds for their violence against the Turkish Embassy in Ottawa. That is how Armen and his anti-Turkish campaign of violence in Ottawa hijacked the well-intentioned Canadian multiculturalism policy

# X

In Montreal, Quebec City and Ottawa the face of Canada was changing. The Canadian Confederation, now over a century old, was in mortal danger of breaking up. Or so it seemed to top politicians in the federal capital Ottawa.

In 1975 Rene Levesque and his Quebec separatist party became the government in Quebec City. Canada like Cyprus had two major people, and the French, like the Turks of Cyprus, was in the mood for independence. Another politician, also from Quebec, led the federal government in Ottawa, Pierre Elliot Trudeau who was also facing his own private separation from his estranged wife, Margaret. Pierre, Rene and Maggie were all idealists, hippies in their youth, *au courant* with the Flower Kids generation. They had worked in the *Peace Corps* or similar organizations in Africa and Asia and they believed they could change the world by their own idealism.

Rene's passion was an independent Quebec, Pierre's a united and a centralized Canada and Maggie's was free love. The friends gradually but surely fell apart as they approached middle age. Canada paid the price for their follies. In the independence referendum, Canada was saved from breaking up and becoming the first Yugoslavia, by just 50,000 votes.

Pierre's folly, at home and in parliament, was his arrogance. The Philosopher King, dedicated to liberty and democracy fought the separatists in Quebec by suspending Canadians' liberties and freedoms. He fought the unions by imposing wage and price controls, and the otherwise good Catholic husband disowned his wife, very much like Uzun Ali had divorced his first wife in Milltown, by decree of his own.

While Rene schemed for Quebec independence, Pierre's centerpiece in uniting Canada was Multiculturalism. The old Canada of two founding people, Anglos and French, must go. A new Canada of ethnic diversity must be created. It was a laudable policy: "Canada must be united," he declared. "All Canadians must be equal." The face of Canada was changing: Blacks came from the Caribbean, Indians from India, the Chinese from Hong Kong, the Africans from all over Africa.

But Trudeau's multiculturalism had an ugly face. It not only produced ethnic politicians. It also spawned terrorists. Some had deep roots and heritage in the Ottoman Empire. Armenian terrorism had been schooled there in the dying days of the Ottomans.

A day was fixed for the attack on the Turkish Embassy in Ottawa, the federal capital. "After all, the 50th anniversary of the genocide has to be celebrated in a visible manner," said Armen, "it is only fair that we should get active and do something."

As the day for the attack on the Turkish Embassy got closer, others, specialists brought in from Beirut and Paris, joined Armen accompanied by Jean-Pierre. But to make it all look like a peaceful demonstration, just a bit excessive maybe at the edges, busloads of volunteers from Montreal and Toronto were dispatched to Ottawa. Local Armenians from Ottawa would also join the demonstration. The whole group would assemble on Parliament Hill and then march, carrying placards and slogans, all the way through the business district of Rideau Street to the Turkish Embassy on Wurtemburg Ave, just before the bridge on the Ottawa River.

The demonstration had started well enough on Parliament Hill. It was a large crowd, with lots of anti-Turkish slogans. People marched through the busy market section of the town, and the Canadian public looked on curiously as the marchers went by. Then when the group got to the front gate of the Turkish embassy, Armen was pleasantly surprised to find that there were no police to be seen anywhere.

"This is very interesting," he said to Jean-Pierre. "Do you think they did not know?"

"They knew all right," said Jean-Pierre remembering the huge police crowd he had encountered in Montreal during the FLQ days.

"I think they are not taking our demonstration very seriously." He concluded. This encouraged Armen to become bolder. He surged ahead of the demonstrators, climbed over the fence of the Embassy.

The rest happened very quickly.

Armen saw someone at the second storey window, looking outside below to see what was going on. At that moment he threw a Molotov cocktail he was carrying on him right through the window into the Embassy building. It exploded and smoke started coming out. The person in the building was hurt. But Armen did not stop to look around. He jumped over the fence into the bush in the park and was gone in no time flat.

It took a long time for the police to arrive on the scene of bombing because of a typical Canadian jurisdictional problem. It was not clear whether the area came under the jurisdiction of the Ottawa police, or the Ontario Provincial Police, or the Royal Canadian Mounted Police. By the time it was determined that it was not the OPP, and the job was far more complicated involving external relations, and therefore RCMP should handle the bombing in the Canadian capital, Armen and Pierre were well on their way back to Montreal.

\*\*\*

In the meantime, the person at the window was the Turkish Ambassador. The curiosity had the better of him. He looked out to see what was going on and he was surprised at the large and hostile crowd below. Armen's Molotov landed just outside the window, and he was badly hurt, luckily not mortally. Otherwise, little damage was done to the embassy building.

By the time the Canadian security forces arrived, the Armenian crowd was gone. Armen had scored a victory of sorts on Canadian soil.

# XI

In October 1980 Tekin was in Ankara visiting his sister Sevgi, now a full professor of history at the University in the Turkish capital. The occasion was to honor Sevgi's success as an academic: she had just been promoted to the post of Dean of Arts and Sciences at the university. Tekin came with Eleanor, while Susan, now a graduate student at university, stayed home. From Ankara, Tekin, accompanied by Eleanor, planned to visit her mother in Nicosia. The last letter from Cyprus indicated that Aygul health was failing.

Sevgi was not only a successful academic; she was also a happily married woman. She had married another Turkish student, Aydin Bozkurt, the son of a family that had migrated from Cyprus to Turkey in 1920s when the British were eager to transfer Turks out of the island. Aydin was also an academic, an accounting professor at the Ankara University. Sevgi and Aydin had two children and the family regularly visited Cyprus, now effectively divided into a Turkish North and a Greek Cypriot South.

Aydin's family still owned considerable land in Limassol, and had relatives there. These relatives became refugees in 1974, after they were imprisoned by the Greek soldiers and then transferred via Turkey, finally relocating to Bella Pais, the medieval monastery town made famous by Lawrence Durell, situated on the evergreen slopes under the towering Besparmak Mountains overlooking the blue

## HYPOCRITES AND ANGELS

Mediterranean east of Kyrenia. Aydin was a Turkish nationalist, and still felt passionately about Cyprus and had joined the group of student-warriors who staged a daring landing at Erenkoy in 1964/5. On this beachhead he and some hundred student warriors had spent two horrible years, surrounded by Greek soldiers, where he had witnessed the death of some of his closest friends in action. To this day, he carried the scars of this terrible episode, physical and psychological. Nevertheless, he was comparatively mild in his opinion on settling the Cyprus problem, still believing that a partnership state between Turks and Greeks in Cyprus was feasible and desirable.

When Tekin and Eleanor visited them in Ankara, Sevgi and Aydin had two children, a boy and a girl, now in their teens. Sevgi and Tekin had kept in touch by mail since their last rendezvous in Cyprus in the summer of 1961. They had not been at the island together since. It was not a good time to visit. The sixties had been years of humiliation, a period of dispossession and displacement for Turkish Cypriots. More than two thirds were forced to leave their homes and properties behind and seek protection in Turkish enclaves surrounded by Greek soldiers who controlled all roads and movements in the island. In fact, the Greek Cypriots were then masters of the island, and Turkish Cypriots were isolated from the rest of the world, living off handouts from Ankara. The Turkish government looked on helplessly as Makarios's and Grivas's armies kidnapped Turkish Cypriot men, and gangs conducted humiliating body searches on Turkish Cypriot women and children. Every time the Turkish government tried to come to the rescue, the American or the British intervened and all the while the Greek Cypriot nationalists got bolder, preparing the coup of 1974 when finally the Turkish army intervened. The realities on the island were now totally different.

In 1976, Aydin built a house in on the slopes below Bella Pais and the Bozkurt family regularly visited the island, spending their summers there, much to the delight of his extensive family as well as Aygul's, now in her mature years.

But now Turkey was in turmoil. In 1980 the Turks stood at the precipice of a full-scale civil war and national bankruptcy. Then, the Turkish army staged its own coup in Ankara and Tekin's visit was in its aftermath. It was a good time for reflection because the Turkish military intervention in Cyprus had failed to bring peace to the island. Nor did it help Ecevit, the poet Prime Minister who had ordered the army to Cyprus, become the national hero he expected. Instead he got into a hopeless political tug-of-war with his arch-rival Suleyman Demirel and, together, they ruined the economy and pushed the Turkish nation to the brink of a civil war. The generals then moved in September 1980 and Turkey was under military rule when Tekin arrived from Toronto to visit his sister.

Tekin was surprised at the general mood of optimism he encountered in the Turkish capital. He was eager for an explanation and evaluation. He had anxiously been reading in Toronto about the steady descent of Turkey into a virtual civil war, with daily shootings and killings while the Turkish economy collapsed into bankruptcy.

It was Eleanor who first made a surprising observation of the post-coup Ankara. "People seem to be happy," she said to Tekin on the ride from the airport. It was true; it was unlike the military rule they had experienced in Africa. It was like a festival, people smiling and celebrating.

"Why are people so happy with the military takeover?" he asked his sister, as soon as hugs and kisses were exchanged and introductions made and they all sat in the Bozkurt family living room.

"People are glad to have law and order in the streets" began Sevgi. Aydin nodded his approval, as she went on:

"It is a popular coup. There was anarchy in the country as politicians fought with each other in parliament, and private armies on the left and right turned the country into an ideological battleground. It was especially bad on the university campuses," she said.

"Many professors were killed for their views. Students fought students for ideology. And many reporters were killed. It was awful. Something had to be done," added Aydin.

"Isn't this bad for democracy?" asked Tekin.

"What democracy" replied Sevgi. "There was no democracy in the country before the coup. There was general anarchy the streets were not safe. I feared for my life in the classroom. You never knew who might take exception to what I said and come and shoot me. Any crazy student could do it, and no one was able to stop it." She was terrified. Aydin concurred.

As the family sat down for dinner, Tekin was curious to learn more and especially what would happen next in Cyprus. He had been hearing that conditions in the Turkish Cypriot North were not very encouraging: large number of refugees came from the Greek South, and also many settlers came from Anatolia. Life in the North was disorganized, economy in bad shape, and now that Makarios was dead, the Greeks had announced a new policy of non-cooperation with the Turkish side. The chances of a settlement in Cyprus looked remote.

"What happens now? What will happen in Turkey and Cyprus?" He asked.

"I do not expect the military will stay in power for very long" began Sevgi. "That is what they promised. They may stay for a couple of years until a new constitution is written and new elections are conducted. The army is popular and the Turkish generals know their limit. Turkey is not like African or Latin American countries under military rule." She sounded quite optimistic and confident.

"As far as Cyprus is concerned" Sevgi resumed, "the general feeling here is that it is essentially solved. The intervention in 1974 created two states, a partition of the island. Whatever the UN or the international community decides, it cannot change the reality on the ground," said the history professor. Tekin was quite impressed with the confidence her sister was now speaking. She had well rehearsed her words, clearly uttered several times on previous occasions.

"It may take a long time to come, but in the end Turkish Cypriots will have their state in the North of the island, the Greek Cypriots theirs in South." She declared. Aydin reinforced his wife's position from his own experience: "There is no going back. The Turks and Greeks have fought a war in Cyprus, starting in 1964. I was there at the Erenkoy beachhead where a group of students lived through Hell for two years, many of us died in action. It is impossible to forget the sacrifices and suffering that was endured."

It was Eleanor who spoke. "Remember the time when we were blackmailed by Greek Cypriots at the airport back in 1971? It was terrible" she began. "It is best if the Greek Cypriots have their part of the island, and the Turkish Cypriots theirs."

Sevgi was impressed with Eleanor's logic. "That is the most logical statement I have heard on Cyprus," she said. But added: "Will the Greeks ever accept partition?"

Then Tekin joined in: "In time they will. At the moment, they think the UN will help them win back in diplomacy what they lost in war. In the end, they will realize the futility of international solutions for the island's problems. Island's history is the guide and for me Uzun

Ali of Milltown, our Grandfather is the example to follow. He had Greek friends, he played cards with them, but he always respected the cultural divide between their world and his own."

# XII

The next day they received news that Aygul was seriously ill, close to death. "Please try and come as soon as you can," said the telegram and Sevgi, Tekin and Eleanor made plans to fly out to Nicosia. Tekin called Ozkan in London and, despite some financial deal he was negotiating to purchase a Canadian company to add to his expanding multinational business empire, he decided to fly alone the next day.

They were late. The doctors could not save Aygul.

Her liver cancer was too advanced. Aygul passed away before the party stepped on the ground at Nicosia international airport. She was 72. It was a lonely death in the hospital where she was taken, thanks to Sevgi's father in law, whom she phoned from Ankara requesting his help in arranging Aygul's hospitalization. When Sevgi, Tekin and the rest of the party arrived in Nicosia, they got busy with the funeral arrangements.

It was, once again, an emotional get-together in Nicosia. The three grandchildren of Uzun Ali were unexpectedly reunited, this time by Aygul's death. She was buried next to her beloved mother's grave in the Nicosia cemetery in a quiet, family ceremony. Just as in her last years Aygul had found inner peace through forgiveness, so now in her eternal sleep she had returned to her mother, to the love she never experienced through her bittersweet life.

At the funeral, Ozkan ran into Denktas, now a towering leader of his people. He and Ozkan had become friends and they would often meet in London whenever the Turkish Cypriot leader was in London.

"How long are you staying?" he asked.

"I am afraid I have to fly back to London tomorrow, a big project is waiting my return" said Ozkan.

"I'd like to see you," said the leader and they arranged to meet in the afternoon.

***

That night the group gathered for a remembrance vigil in honor of Aygul. They were five, the three grandsons of Uzun Ali, joined by spouses Eleanor and Aydin.

"I saw mother last three months ago in August when we were here for summer holidays" began Sevgi. "We had a long talk about old times" as others listened intently. "The thing that impressed me most was how serene she had become. Gone was the old fiery rebellious woman always tormented by a selfish and uncaring father who had so wronged his wife and child. Now, at last, mother had come to terms with her past and I think she died a reasonably happy person, perhaps sad that both her children were away."

Then Sevgi made a remark almost casually about Turkish Cypriots. "You know the Turks of Cyprus like to have their children around them. It makes them more secure."

Then Tekin picked up the argument and challenged the others: "What a strange family we are? Look at us, none are living in Cyprus, but we all owe our identity, our roots to this place. It defines who we are, but I wonder what the future will bring? Is this our last meeting?"

"I am sure we will come back," said Ozkan without hesitation.

"What makes you so sure?" asked Tekin. Sevgi and Eleanor looked at Ozkan.

Ozkan responded. "I may start building a few big hotels, here," he said referring to his earlier meeting with Denktas. "But that is personal" he added. "I want to speak in general" he said and then expanded.

"Turkish Cypriots are like birds; they have two wings. One represents the islanders, the other the diaspora, those like us living abroad, making a success of their lives" said the businessman. "I know many living in London and my business takes me to other places, like Australia, USA and other countries, where I meet successful businessmen, some big but many who are small. They all love the island and they cannot live away for too long. They must return, like the salmon returning to the ponds where they are born. We are no exception. This time we are here for Aygul's funeral; next time it may be a wedding or a holiday."

Eleanor joined in: "I once read a book which said, 'no one can visit Cyprus without falling in love with it.'"

"Yes I can relate to that," said Tekin and Ozkan nodded his approval. A moment later, Ozkan said

"I want to go back to what you said about a bird with wings." Others looked on.

"Last time I was in the island was almost twenty years ago. People were optimistic about the future. Now I am struck by how much the islanders have changed." He said.

Tekin asked his cousin to explain.

"I do not exactly know," said Ozkan. "I feel a sense of fear and insecurity in the air, the old optimism is gone. But, really I would like to hear Sevgi and Aydin because they come here often."

They looked at Sevgi and then she spoke.

"Ozkan is right" she began. "The people here have changed. The sixties were hard times, everyone lived under siege, deprived of freedom and forgotten by the rest of the world. Then came liberation after 1974, but it was liberation with new difficulties: resettlement, refugees."

Aydin, the student warrior from the Erenkoy campaign, then joined the conversation.

"Now there is a general booty culture," he said. "There are conflicts over redistribution of Greek properties left behind as they moved south. For the first time, Turkish Cypriots experienced social division as some became rich while others did not do well. Their sense of justice got twisted."

The group listened as Aydin went on.

"And then something else happened. As more and more mainland Turks came, the islanders realized they were different. The islanders feel themselves superior: Better educated, less religious and more tolerant maybe. At the same time they feel helpless. "

The mood changed to pessimism. "The old unity of purpose amongst Turkish Cypriots is gone. Look at what happened in Turkey after 1974. Ecevit and Demirel split and fought, just like here in

Cyprus, and the country ended up in civil war; the army intervened to rescue the nation" concluded Aydin.

"Politicians come and go," said Ozkan the businessman. "Look at England suffering from the British Disease. Now Margaret Thatcher has taken over from Edward Heath. The Irish problem continues. A new Europe is being created with England in it. There is no need to be pessimistic. Businessmen, both Turk and Greek, hold the keys of the future here in Cyprus and the world beyond. You have to have confidence to be successful," he said.

Aydin countered: "That may be all fine for big countries with large populations. But here in Cyprus, how many Turkish Cypriots are there? People here are lazy; we need to bring workers from Turkey even to grow vegetables." He was the most authentic islander in the group.

"Maybe what is needed is new blood, new identity. I know so many businessmen in London ready to invest here. We can turn this place into a success story, another Singapore," he said.

Tekin then spoke, drawing on experiences in several countries, rich and poor.

"I agree with Ozkan" he began. Turning to Aydin, he said, "Immigrants build a country, whether Canada, USA or Australia. Expelling them like Idi Amin impoverishes a nation. The Turkish Cypriots have to learn nationhood and it starts with strong families. Family ties are what unite a people, but investment is what builds a nation… Investing in education, in industries, in buildings. That is what counts."

"Like our own Uzun Ali clan" added Sevgi.

"Precisely… The Turks of Cyprus may not be large by world standards but now they are part of 60 million on the mainland. That is why I talk of Turks of Cyprus. The world is now a village, where you live is less important than your sense of belonging. And it is always changing. Years of experience with the UN in several countries have taught me one thing: Identity is never constant, but a constantly evolving thing, through education and knowledge. We all change as we learn new things and new techniques. Practical success is the defining quality in life," said Tekin.

"Exactly my point" said Ozkan. All around looked at him…after a moment he went on.

"A global marketplace is being created, and I want to be part of it. That is where our people belong. You safeguard your own identity with your success. And you change as the world around you changes" he said.

After a pause, and turning to Sevgi and Aydin to make his point, Tekin went on: "The two of you are the best example of what I am talking about. You are both Turks of Cyprus, living in Ankara. You are Turks in Turkey, Ozkan is in London, and I in Toronto. Yesterday we were Ottomans, today we are Turks, Canadians, British and God knows what else. Tomorrow who knows what we shall become? Yet, we are all connected to Cyprus, like wings of a bird, just as you said. We fly and migrate all over the world in search of success. Turks in the homeland are one wing; we, the Turks in the great wide world are the other wing. Our connection is our heritage that binds us; each one of us belongs to the Uzun Ali clan, a family with deep roots in the Konak, now gone but its spirit in the power of education and knowledge lives on."

Eleanor had the last word. She said: "The future belongs to those who cherish their heritage, yet are not afraid of rebirth in a changing world."

# XIII

Up above the clouds, beyond the horizon, just outside the House of Eternal Serenity, it was the dance of the spirits and angels. They assembled from everywhere, all corners of the world, *millets* of diverse people with no church or religion to divide humanity.

Here wisdom alone ruled. From the graveyard in Nicosia, came to the party two spirits, one of Uzun Ali the Kaimakam of Milltown before the British, the other belonging to the hedonist Halil. They were joined by several other spirits, from Africa and Canada and elsewhere, all merrymaking and partying.

"Justice is at last done," said Uzun Ali's spirit. "The British stole the fair island of Cyprus from the Ottomans and destroyed my life. Now the Turks are back," He added with a bittersweet feeling of revenge.

"You are wrong," said another spirit. "The Ottomans first took Cyprus from the Venetians" said the voice. Uzun Ali pondered the remark and countered:

"And who did the Venetians get it from, pray tell?"

The voice said: "I am no historian. What does it matter?"

"I'll tell you," said someone with a gun in his hand, coming out from behind the bushes to join the party: "Once the island belonged to Byzantium. It is where Zenon taught and Aphrodite made love. It is rightfully Hellenic and justice will not be done until ENOSIS is achieved."

## HYPOCRITES AND ANGELS

A bearded cleric appeared, smiled and then disappeared, but only after he declared: "ENOSIS is sweet wine, but sweeter still is Power."

The reference to Power attracted a group of angles in military uniform. It was a strange group who had once been stationed at the NATO headquarters and they looked nervously in all directions as if they were being chased:

"We meant well," the conspirators of the Zurich-London Agreements said, "when we thought of an independent Republic in Cyprus."

"What made you think that a Greek and Turkish Cypriot partnership would work?" asked a skeptical angel.

"Multiculturalism" said a wise voice. "The future belongs to those who share a common vision. Look this place in heaven; it is full of cultural diversity."

Then two Canadian spirits from the North appeared and joined the conversation, giving a Canadian perspective to the debate.

One, no doubt a Pearsonian Liberal, said: "I agree. Unity in diversity is what the world needs. Multiculturalism is the way forward."

Some heads were scratched and some got ready with questions. But then a voice interjected:

"Multiculturalism is an illusion." He was from the Caribbean.

Then the Quebecois spoke:

"I am from Quebec. I am distinct. I came here first," he claimed. Now there was pandemonium.

"What is multicultural?"

"What is distinct about Quebec?"

"Who came first? Who was here first? Who are the first people?"

"Who is Canadian?"

All these questions and no one seemed to have clear answers. Silence fell, and the party mood sank. The earlier cheerfulness was now replaced by gloom and doom.

Then Ottoman spirits came to the foreground.

Uzun Ali said:

"Multiculturalism reminds me of our *millet* system. Every nation then had its own customs and traditions."

Immediately, there was a reaction:

"Nonsense" said Halil's spirit. "I loved all women," he said, "for me Maronite, Greek, Armenian, Muslim, non-Muslim made no difference."

Another spirit joined in supporting Halil: "Love conquers all. Love is all you need."

## UZUN ALI, SHAME AND SALVATION

Then, a female voice, the spirit of Emine joined in: "I suffered so much pain on account of Love. Give me Fidelity" she grieved and again, a mood of despondency set in.

The arguments flew in all directions and the party of the angels seemed to go on endlessly, aimlessly. The group was beginning to feel depressed, stuck in an impasse of its own making.

Then U Thant's spirit appeared, the man who was the UN Secretary General in 1964 who negotiated with Mike Pearson and others but who, most of all, had listened to his good friend the Greek Cypriot delegate Zenon at the UN at the time. He looked very sad:

"Ah! Forgive me" he said, "I am a troubled man, looking for forgiveness. I have heard Cyprus being discussed and on that subject I have a heavy heart" he confided to the group.

"Why? What seems to be your problem?" They asked. "We thought we are the ones needing salvation."

"No, no" said U Thant's spirit. "I now realize the lies I was fed at that time." He admitted and went off, leaving the group to ponder. They looked puzzled and depression took hold.

"Is there no hope? No salvation?" asked a new comer. "I came to Canada from Africa" he said. "All I want is an opportunity to get rich." He must have lived in Uganda.

Others cheered their approval.

Then, finally, the Senior Angel appeared, attracted by all the noise and argument.

"What is going on here?" He asked.

"We are having a party and we seem to be stuck on a land dispute," explained one.

Another added for clarification:

"Whether in Africa, Cyprus, Palestine or Canada, it seems it is all about land. Whose land is it?"

Then the Armenian spirit, Schomelian's perhaps, appeared and said:

"Young people do not understand. I kept on saying to my son, Turks and Armenians were friends and once again, they will be, but he does not listen."

"I know," said the spirit of Aygul, who had been listening patiently by, "forgiveness for past sins is redemption. I wish I had the knowledge to forgive my father earlier."

The young Armenian joined in: "I want my land," he declared as everyone turned to look at the voice.

Then spoke the Senior Angel because even in the Angel's Land there was hierarchy:

"Have no fear, there is lots of land. Canada and Africa are huge, there is enough for everyone, man and beast."

But a Greek Cypriot voice shouted:

"Cyprus is small. It was all mine and I want it back" and all looked in the direction of the voice.

The Senior Angel said: "It is not the size, nor ownership. It is the people."

All argument seemed to stop. A minute of silence passed, and then the Senior Angel spoke again:

"It is greed, if you must know." He said. "If you want it all you risk everything. If you think by lies and cheating you can fool everybody, then at the end of the day, you fool only yourself."

Then another asked: "Why did you make man and woman imperfect like this?"

"Because" he said "Being is never constant; perfection is always evolving." He stopped for a moment to make sure he was understood. Then he continued,

"We endowed man and woman with two gifts: Freedom and Knowledge. We gave them Freedom to love and sin, and Knowledge to find Redemption. The wise seek Redemption to enter the House of Eternal Serenity, where Justice rules."

# THE END

CPSIA information can be obtained at www.ICGtesting.com
Printed in the USA
LVOW131920010512

279898LV00026B/91/P